This book reveals how IFES leaders grappled with the waning of imperialism, postcolonialism and decolonization, with race and civil rights movements, Vatican II and the Lausanne movements, and the challenges of indigenization and contextuality as the Majority World has injected a new energy into a vision of student ministry. *The Priesthood of All Students* perceptively points to new frontiers where there is a shift of emphasis from doctrinal defense to a more socio-missiological focus that engages the whole university and reaches through it to the world. Every leader in IFES and world missions to university will benefit immensely from the rich insights and searching issues that this book brings into the present and heralds for the future.

Terence Halliday, PhD
Emeritus Research Professor,
American Bar Foundation and Honourary Professor,
Australian National University, Australia

Timothée Joset's *Priesthood of All Students* is a welcome scholarly contribution to the missiological significance of student ministry in diverse contexts for the rapid expansion of global Christianity. His in-depth analysis of the internal ethos, theology and formation process, integrating diverse cultural identities and apprehension of the Christian faith, gives insight into why students and graduates of IFES continue to play significant missional roles in all spheres of engagement. It also comes as no surprise for products of such internal process to be entrusted with leadership roles within church and society. Without a doubt, the ongoing vital impact of student ministry in universities as a whole will continue to have implications for the configuration of the global mosaic of Christianity and mission. I commend this book to all students of God's mission in our generation and beyond.

Femi B. Adeleye, PhD
Executive Director,
Institute for Christian Impact, Ghana
Research Fellow,
Akrofi-Christaller Institute for Theology, Mission and Culture, Ghana

This book is a timely contribution as we celebrate seventy-five years of IFES ministry, since its formation in 1947. In *The Day of His Power* (InterVarsity Press,1983), Pete Lowman provided an inspiring and exciting account of the formative decades of the fellowship. Now, Timothée Joset comes up with a fresh, passionate, energetic, yet thoughtful review of the past seventy-five years. He avoids the bias that an ardent militant might have by copiously exploring the literature that advocates for or criticizes the strategic and missiological choices made by IFES in its history.

Beyond the purely descriptive perspective of a historian, he suggests and establishes a coherent missional basis for IFES's engagement in campus ministry. He finds in the concept of the "priesthood of all believers" the adequate thread that leads to understanding the theological, ecclesiological and missiological rationale that underpins IFES's ministry and strategic choices.

This book is a must-read for all leaders within IFES today and those involved in university ministry. For those involved with IFES it serves as a perfect marker in the fellowship's journey: reminding us where we have come from, giving thanks for where we are today, and providing us with confidence for the future. In a nutshell, it strengthens our sense of identity, nurtures our trust in the faithfulness of God and "praises His wondrous deeds to the next generation" (Ps 145).

Michel Kenmogne, PhD
SIL International Executive Director

Based on intense archival research, Joset's ambitious history of IFES is both theological and global. This useful study will stimulate further research into the important contribution of IFES in the making of worldwide, multi-cultural evangelical Christianity. It convincingly demonstrates why the missiological analysis of global networks is essential to understanding world Christianity today. I highly recommend it.

Dana L. Robert, PhD
William Fairfield Warren Distinguished Professor,
Director, Center for Global Christianity and Mission,
Boston University, Massachusetts, USA

Evangelical ministry within universities has been a crucial shaper of the contours of contemporary world Christianity, especially in disproving the false connection too often drawn between conservative theology and indifference to issues of social justice. Timothée Joset's well-documented and theologically informed history of IFES will become a standard source for future researchers.

Brian Stanley, PhD
Professor of World Christianity,
University of Edinburgh, UK

In seventy-five years a remarkable movement of Christian mission to university students has swept across more than 165 countries. How did this come to be? What were the impulses, the struggles and turning points, the sociopolitical contexts, the theologies and callings that shaped the remarkable expansion of IFES to the present? Timothée Joset's learned and deeply researched book traces the incipient power of belief in a priesthood exercised by students that can be personally and institutionally transformative.

The Priesthood of All Students

The Priesthood of All Students

Historical, Theological and Missiological Foundations of a Global University Ministry

Timothée Joset

GLOBAL LIBRARY

© 2023 Timothée Joset

Published 2023 by Langham Global Library
An imprint of Langham Publishing
www.langhampublishing.org

Langham Publishing and its imprints are a ministry of Langham Partnership

Langham Partnership
PO Box 296, Carlisle, Cumbria, CA3 9WZ, UK
www.langham.org

ISBNs:
978-1-83973-832-6 Print
978-1-83973-876-0 ePub
978-1-83973-877-7 PDF

Timothée Joset has asserted his right under the Copyright, Designs and Patents Act, 1988 to be identified as the Author of this work.

All rights reserved. No part of this publication may be reproduced, stored in a retrieval system or transmitted, in any form or by any means, electronic, mechanical, photocopying, recording or otherwise, without the prior written permission of the publisher or the Copyright Licensing Agency.

Requests to reuse content from Langham Publishing are processed through PLSclear. Please visit www.plsclear.com to complete your request.

Unless otherwise stated, Scripture quotations are from the New Revised Standard Version Bible, copyright © 1989 National Council of the Churches of Christ in the United States of America. Used by permission. All rights reserved.

British Library Cataloguing-in-Publication Data
A catalogue record for this book is available from the British Library

ISBN: 978-1-83973-832-6

Cover & Book Design: projectluz.com

Langham Partnership actively supports theological dialogue and an author's right to publish but does not necessarily endorse the views and opinions set forth here or in works referenced within this publication, nor can we guarantee technical and grammatical correctness. Langham Partnership does not accept any responsibility or liability to persons or property as a consequence of the reading, use or interpretation of its published content.

To the many women and men of all five continents whose names never appear in this research but whose often unnoticed yet faithful, prayerful, sacrificial and humble missionary commitment has made the history, theology and missiology of IFES. One day we shall know and rejoice about your world-changing witness.

Contents

List of Abbreviations xiii

Acknowledgments xv

Introduction 1

Part 1: A Selective Overview of the History of IFES

1 Student Work before IFES (1800–1909) 15
2 The Master Narrative of a Separation (1909–1935) 19
3 Meeting for Conferences (1934–1946) 27
4 It All Began in a Changing World (1946–1962) 31
5 Good News for a World of Revolutions? The 1960s 61
6 When the South Comes North: The 1970s 91
7 Growing Partnerships: The 1980s 109
8 A New World Map to Finish a Century: The 1990s 129
9 IFES in a New Millennium 163

Part 2: IFES Activities

10 The Practical Functioning of Student-Led Ministry 169

Part 3: Ecclesiological and Missiological Reflection in IFES

11 A Firm Basis 189
12 IFES Authors Discussing Ecclesiology 219

Part 4: Theological Resources

13 The Priesthood of All Believers 239
14 Dogmatic Reflections: Laypeople in the Church 253
15 Missional Ecclesiology 265
16 A Ministry of Expansion? Roland Allen's Missiology and IFES
   Ministry 291

17 Participation in the *Missio Dei* 301
18 Apostolicity, Theology and Missionary Expansion 317

Part 5: Some Ways Ahead
19 Student Ministry in the Light of the Priesthood of All Believers. . . . 329
20 General Conclusion 355

Appendixes
  Appendix 1: Two Speeches That Changed Evangelicalism 363
  Appendix 2: The IFES Doctrinal Basis 367
  Appendix 3: Bibliology in the Doctrinal Basis 369

  Bibliography 383

List of Abbreviations

AGS	Associate General Secretary
CICCU	Cambridge Inter-Collegiate Christian Union
DB	Doctrinal basis
EPSA	English- and Portuguese-Speaking African region
GBU	Groupes Bibliques Universitaires (French Christian student organization)
GC	General Committee
GS	General Secretary
(I)EC	(International) Executive Committee
IFES	International Fellowship of Evangelical Students
IVCF	InterVarsity Christian Fellowship
IVF	Inter-Varsity Fellowship
NT	New Testament
OICCU	Oxford Inter-Collegiate Christian Union
OT	Old Testament
RCC	Roman Catholic Church
RS	Regional Secretary
SCM	Student Christian Movement
UCCF	Universities and Colleges Christian Fellowship
WA	World Assembly
WCC	World Council of Churches
WSCF	World Student Christian Federation

Acknowledgments

As it is customary to say, I will not be able to properly acknowledge all the people who have supported me in the long project of a doctoral dissertation which became this book. Yet I wish to specifically acknowledge at least the following:

My parents, Josiane and Pierre-André Joset, for their love of history, literature, music and theological reflection, which have paved the way for my academic journey in four countries, as well as for their essential financial support of the PhD adventure which became this book.

Prof. Dennis Ngien, for his initial impetus to endeavour into doctoral studies with his empowering mentoring and support during my theological studies at Tyndale University (Canada); as well as Prof. Ronald Kydd, for his extraordinarily wide church history teaching perspectives.

Prof. Mike Higton, whose initial scepticism towards my project turned into committed, responsive and dedicated support. I always left the regular Skype and then Zoom supervision meetings encouraged and empowered, even if it sometimes meant rewriting or cutting (large) parts of my work.

Prof. Pete Ward, for his insightful comments on the original thesis proposal as well as on earlier drafts of this work.

Prof. Stefan Paas, whose writings I discovered late in my research but whose missiological acumen is deeply illuminating. It is an honour to benefit from your expertise as an external examiner.

Kirsty Thorburn, for her introduction into the inner workings of IFES as I was a young student discovering an international board. For her patient help in supporting my navigation through the IFES history and for granting me access to electronic archives.

Tim Adams, IFES General Secretary, for his friendship and trust in granting me unlimited access to the IFES archives.

Dr. Femi Adeleye and Dr. Augustin Ahoga, for their patience in initiating a young white student into the intricacies of postcolonial Africa and the necessity of broadening my theological understanding.

Dr. Vinoth Ramachandra, for his insightful reading of an earlier draft of this work and for helping me broaden my theological and missiological perspectives.

Dr. Daniel Bourdanné, at the time IFES General Secretary, for his encouragement to venture into this research and to save enough time to complete the work. For the example of his humility in serving IFES.

Lindsay Brown, former IFES General Secretary, for insightful discussions and encouragements in the early phases of this project.

Christian Schneeberger, the first GBEU staff worker who mentored me as I was discovering the world of the university at the same time as taking on the leadership of the local group. The almost sleepless nights we spent discussing theology during camps and trainings have greatly encouraged me to refine and be more charitable in my thinking.

Prof. A. Donald MacLeod, Stacey Woods's biographer, for his unexpected and supportive friendship as I was tentatively developing the research proposal which led to this work.

Tony Lai and Iris Youngsun Eom, who not only welcomed us into a new community in Canada but who mentored my wife and me in ministering to international students in eye-opening ways. The time spent with them was an extraordinary addition to formal theological studies. Many insights gathered during the weekly ISM meetings have flown into this research.

Igors Rautmanis and Dr. Kosta Milkov, two dear mentors who have helped me keep spiritual and mental health during these frantic years of research and ministry.

Célia Jeanneret, Esther Fernández Saá, Leïla Jaccard and Baptiste Bovay, members of the Neuchâtel GBUN group, who either helped me with quotations across languages and/or also took care of Agathe as I was editing this manuscript.

Prof. Hannes Wiher, for his mentoring in developing my missiological acumen, for his support, trust and friendship, for his urging to complete my dissertation within a reasonable time frame, and for his efficient reading and astute commenting on an earlier version of this work.

Rev. Dr. McTair Wall, for his friendship and mentoring into the complexities of the world of francophone missiology.

All those behind the ministry of GBEU Switzerland. Over the five years of this project, their financial support of my ministry has also made this research possible and kept it anchored in the reality of ministry to the university.

Jacqueline and Carmelo Cavaleri, my parents-in-law, whose table always offers rich and savoury meals, which are welcome breaks from writing at my desk.

My sister Anne-Eve Favre and her husband Cédric, whose apartment was an appreciated oasis of calm and rest when we too rarely took time off with them.

Dr. Bonnie Aebi, who patiently and very efficiently proofread the entire manuscript during the last weeks of the final editing of the dissertation from which this book was written.

A number of friends and colleagues in IFES who have read parts of earlier versions of this work and have commented, asked questions and made suggestions about what I could explore.

Many friends and colleagues who have – sometimes hesitantly – regularly asked about the progress being made on this work. I have often declined invitations, delayed answering emails or WhatsApp messages, or shortened time spent together in order to carve out enough hours for academic work. Your encouragements and prayers have meant a lot.

My dearest and unabatedly supportive wife Natacha, without whom neither my initial theological studies nor the painstaking work involved with such a long-term project would have been possible. Concentrating on academic work has often meant weekends were short, holidays few and the apartment not as clean and tidy as it should have been. It is an immeasurable blessing to journey in the Lord with you, for "*Qui trouve une épouse trouve le bonheur: c'est une faveur que l'Eternel lui a accordée*" (Prov 18:22).

And, most evidently, to the One in whom I live and move and have my being. *Soli Deo Gloria.*

Introduction

The International Fellowship of Evangelical Students (IFES) is one of the most ethnically diverse, geographically widespread and interdenominational student ministries. This book explores how its theology has developed throughout its history and suggests a new way to make sense of its work. I propose that the doctrine of the *priesthood of all believers*, combined with a missiological understanding of ecclesiology, offers a firm basis for understanding its work and development.

The idea of a priesthood of all believers suggests *immediacy, mediation* and *participation*. Students, by faith, have an *immediate* connection to Christ and do not need to rely upon the mediation of a priestly order or any other hierarchy. Second, students *mediate* or *represent* Christ to the world, calling those around them to direct fellowship with Christ. Third, students join in Christ's priesthood by virtue of their *participation* in the *whole priestly people of God*: the church.

Historical Background

As modern universities develop in the nineteenth century, groups of like-minded students gather for activities of common interest. In many countries, Christian students assemble for prayer, Bible study, common witness and mutual upbuilding. These groups gather either under clerical supervision, as in the case of "university congregations," or without such oversight, as with "voluntary associations." Some aspire to deeply theological and political engagement with society and the university, while others prioritize personal piety and missionary witness.

As with other voluntary societies consisting of individuals who are also members of local churches – most notably the burgeoning missionary societies – the question of the ecclesiological legitimacy of such gatherings is raised by theologians. On what basis can laypeople gather and engage in church activities? What is their relationship to ecclesiastical hierarchies, and especially what differentiates these groupings from local churches? Are they to be seen as "churches," and if not, what should they be called?

Diverging answers are given to these questions. Opposition, suspicion and, in some cases, excommunication do not stop the emergence of such groups. In many cases, Christian students heavily involved in Christian student societies during their studies become deeply involved members of local churches and recognized leaders of other Christian organizations, soon to be called "parachurch organizations" for lack of a better umbrella term. The most famous of these early organizations is the World Student Christian Federation (WSCF), founded in 1895.

Apart from groupings linked to state or mainline churches, evangelical groups also rise to prominence in the late nineteenth century. Such groups are not isolated from the theological currents of the times. As the university encourages hard thinking and broadening horizons, student groups often find themselves taken into the deep theological debates over which churches divide. Correspondingly, Christian student groups split because of theological or missiological questions.

Founded in 1947 and promoting an ethos of decentralization through local leadership and insistence on student initiative, IFES rapidly grows in the decolonization era. IFES promotes a contextualized approach to evangelical missionary practice in advance of its time, while at the same time insisting on the universal validity of the core tenets of evangelical faith. This ethos allows the organization's survival through the turmoil of the 1960s' call for a "moratorium on missions." Supporting student leadership implies supporting lay theological reflection among its member movements. Numerous IFES workers develop a "missiology from below," figuring out missionary engagement with the realities of vastly diverging university contexts throughout a very diverse world. As the world changes, new questions are raised by students on campuses, and new theological answers need tackling, such as the role of Christians in a world of (Marxist) revolutions, the cultural embeddedness of Christian doctrinal formulations or new challenges to traditional Christian ethical teaching.

Core activities taking place under the IFES umbrella are Bible study, prayer meetings, and witness to fellow students through friendships and public events on campus. Some student leaders develop a habitus of Christian reflection in contexts that train them to contextualize the Christian message in the Majority World in ways not often seen before in evangelical circles. This becomes especially evident at the Lausanne 1974 Congress, where numerous influential speakers have an IFES background. The fellowship had been the context in which they developed their leadership skills and theological acumen and were given a voice they would not necessarily have had in other, more centralized missionary organizations.

It was never possible for national IFES movements to hire enough staff members to constantly oversee the activities of local student groups spread across their respective countries. In many cases, students had been meeting long before any staff member heard of the meetings. This firm belief in the ability of students to lead fellow students in Bible study, prayer and witness was, more importantly, the consequence of a deeply ingrained evangelical tradition of relying on the doctrine of the "priesthood of all believers." This theological idea, highly disputed between the many branches of Christian traditions and rooted in later Lutheranism, reworked in the Free Evangelical Church tradition and especially in Brethren circles – out of which numerous early IFES leaders came – presumes that *any* Christian student can mediate God to his or her fellow students, whether Christians or not, by virtue of his or her *immediate* relationship to God.

The Priesthood of All Believers

I contend that the doctrine of the "priesthood of all believers" has from the outset been essential to IFES's specifically non-clerical approach to student ministry. Even if this theological foundation is only seldom explicitly mentioned in official documents, it provides the implicit rationale for encouraging students to minister to other students long before any of them could have formal theological training or official accreditation by ecclesial authorities. It also explains why most staff only receive theological training "on the way" and only a handful of the senior staff are ordained in their respective traditions. Such a *common-sense* approach to ministry causes clergy members of all corners of the world to challenge the legitimacy of the ministry of IFES and to wonder whether student groups are considering themselves to be local churches on campus. Whereas this was sometimes incidentally the case, the IFES leadership always took great care to develop its ecclesiological thinking to affirm the fact that student groups made of Christian students, and therefore members of the church, were not themselves churches but the *missionary arm of the local church* on campus, reaching a specific population requiring special understanding, and sociologically strategic for both society in general and future church leadership.

I conclude that despite the challenge of potential individualist excesses, the "priesthood of all believers" provides an essential building block on which to establish a ministry flexible enough to take into consideration the high volatility of the world of higher education and the variety of social, geographical, ecclesial and economic contexts in which IFES movements operate. Such agility is necessary for practical reasons, but also for deeply missiological ones: if the Christian message addresses every human being, they must be able to respond in ways appropriate to their culture, thought forms, language and aspirations.

A shared common doctrinal heritage offers a solid and trustworthy orientation, but the "deposit of the faith" must be appropriated by those who receive it. Students are best placed to identify the challenges their fellow students encounter in the world of higher education. It is missiologically crucial to consider the target group on its own terms. If an essential dimension of university education involves training students to examine the world and critically reflect on it, the Christian message must also be open for thoughtful examination. Such "safe spaces" outside of the constraints of ecclesial traditions and loyalties allow for fruitful inter-traditional encounters that foster understanding among Christians and train them to engage with others, *mediating* the gospel in respectful and thoughtful dialogue. Otherwise, a ministry to students runs the risk of allowing only for a faith that could remain sealed off from actual life and studies-related challenges that any student encounters, and hence not be sustainable once the support structures of the local student groups are left behind. For the principles of *immediacy*, *mediation* and *membership* in the church and in God's mission can sustain the lives of Christians far beyond their years at university.

Methodology

The idea that the priesthood of all believers could make sense of the work of IFES was first a personal intuition based on my extensive personal acquaintance with its work. Ultimately, I am claiming not that the priesthood of all believers is *the* way in which IFES's leaders and constituency explain their work, but that it provides a way of gathering together key claims made within IFES and key practices of IFES, and providing them with theological missiological underpinnings that make sense of them.

I wanted to understand why IFES goes about its mission the way it does, and how it legitimates it theologically. Further questions included how laypeople gradually developed theological acumen throughout their involvement in the fellowship – this notably including women – and how this whole enterprise manages to work on a global scale. For preliminary insights into these areas, I read published works of key actors such as the IFES General Secretaries, but also of other senior staff such as René Padilla, Zac Niringiye, Samuel Escobar, Vinoth Ramachandra; and finally of theologians close to IFES such as John Stott, Jim Stamoolis and Chris Wright, among others. None of them articulated the work of IFES in the way I am proposing here. Yet most of them made short allusions to the legitimacy of lay mission, attributing it to the importance of immediate access to God as the necessary premise for Bible study and missionary engagement. Prior to my dissertation work, I discussed my ideas with Lindsay Brown and Chris Wright, and notably both confirmed I was on a promising track. In one of the few oral interviews I was able to conduct – because of both the space limitations of this work and COVID – Escobar confirmed my insights and also pointed me towards further writings by Padilla which essentially made the case for lay ministry along the same lines as this work.[1]

These preliminary conversations framed the way I went about my archival work.[2] I surveyed internal papers – committee minutes, correspondence, discussion and position papers, conference documents. They document the way IFES has understood its own work and reflect at great length on how to present it to the outside world. Not all discussions are recorded in the minutes, for many also take place informally, yet the historian cannot access any of these except through very extensive oral history, which also has the limitation of the memory and interests of any given conversation partner.

I read these archival documents, to which I had been granted unlimited access, looking at them thematically through three main "key concepts": theology (the legitimation of IFES's mission); ecclesiology (the legitimation of the form of IFES's mission); and university (the context of IFES's mission). These concepts were sometimes explicit, sometimes implicit, understandable more in the context of the examined documents, their authors and their aims. I took extensive notes of the main arguments of the documents I read – going from the most formal memorandums and vision papers to the more informal newsletters – and subsequently organized them in a large library of themes and subthemes. In the final stages of writing, I retained only the documents which most articulately discuss the above "key concepts," reluctantly leaving aside a very significant number of other sources – notably correspondence by more local actors – which would make the description more substantial yet not significantly alter the argument I offer here. This research combines insights from the different branches of theology – systematic, biblical, practical – but also of history, offering a combination of comparative thematic analysis

---

1. Samuel Escobar, Interview (Coma-Ruga, Spain, 2018).

2. The IFES archival records for the years 1935–91 are preserved at the Billy Graham Archival Center in Wheaton, Illinois, USA. The archives for the following years were still located at the IFES international service centre in Oxford when I started my archival work in 2016.

with elements of contextualized discourse analysis. Though not following a strict social-scientific approach, like a formal coding methodology it can be understood as a sort of hermeneutical spiralling through layers of normative texts, field experiences and accounts of these experiences. Besides internal documents, I read most IFES published documents – journals, books, newsletters, presentation documents and so on – which were published either directly by IFES or by its member movements.

The historical part 1 is neither a factual history nor a catalogue of the work of prominent figures. It is no "history of the great men" but rather a "theological history of ideas," focusing on how ecclesiological and missiological questions have arisen during IFES's history.[3] Studying an organization spread, at the time of writing, through about 170 countries is a daunting task, and fairly representing the wealth of geographical, theological, socio-economic and cultural diversity exceeds the strengths of a sole author. I have tried as far as possible to give a fair voice to all the IFES regions. However, I realize that much more work will be needed in the future to give justice to the many anonymous yet committed actors who have shaped the fellowship throughout its history. An important area of work that could only be sparsely hinted at throughout this work but would be worth in-depth consideration is the whole field of high school ministry, which is extremely strong in many countries – much more important than university ministry. Similarly, careful study of the fellowship's leadership, structures and financial operations would certainly be worth the time of future researchers interested in the inner workings of an organization of the scale of the United Nations yet operating out of a fraction of the latter's budget.

One of the limitations I was aware of before starting the work is that a ministry like IFES, which works essentially with volunteer human power and a few generally humbly paid staff, does not usually invest great sums of money in writing about its work. Some national movements have published histories of greater or lesser analytical depth – some are quoted in this work. IFES itself has published a few self-reflecting works. However, overall, an extraordinary wealth of wisdom about the ins and outs of university ministry gets lost as each generation of students and staff members moves on to other places of work or ministry.

---

3. Due to lack of space, I was unable to historically contextualize all of the theological developments and discussions reported in this work. For this, the reader is advised to look for broader overviews, such as Brian Stanley, *Christianity in the Twentieth Century: A World History* (Princeton: Princeton University Press, 2018).

Significantly, this is the first full-length book assessing the overall work of IFES from a scholarly perspective. Short articles and an in-depth biography of its first General Secretary have been written, but much remains to be done, especially in uncovering the work of the many committed women who have shaped the life and ministry of IFES.[4] This work aspires to shed some historical, theological and missiological light on an important actor in the world of Christian student organizations. "Students" is used throughout as an umbrella term for the core IFES constituency. It can at times imply high school students and certainly encompasses postgraduate students. Moreover, if this thesis is convincing, it could support a slight reframing of the IFES vision such as to consider it more deliberately as a ministry to the university and not only to those with official student status – professors, non-academic staff and more generally, the whole academic endeavour.

About the Author

IFES has been a congenial part of my own academic journey. I became a student leader in my last year in high school and my first year of university. I have spent countless hours in student group activities of all sorts in Switzerland, Germany and Canada, assuming almost all levels of leadership. I wrote this dissertation while working part-time with the French-speaking Swiss IFES movement, GBEU, as well as regularly travelling to IFES conferences and being involved in student training in IFES groups on three continents. From early on, I read almost anything I could on the identity and vision of our work. In my first year at university, the GBEU General Secretary suggested that my future master's thesis examine the history of my movement. That first thesis – defended in 2012 – was the beginning of a fascinating journey of which this work is the culmination. As the first work was written in a history department, I was frustrated not to devote more energy to theological thinking. Throughout my subsequent theological studies, I realized that the theological world almost ignored everything about student ministry, especially in secular universities, and how its missiological insights might enrich theological thinking, including in ecclesiological matters. Most of my friends and colleagues simply lack time to write and reflect on their ministry.

---

4. A notable attempt at highlighting these powerful influences is Vivienne Stacey, ed., *Mission Ventured: Dynamic Stories across a Challenging World* (Leicester: Inter-Varsity Press, 2001).

Therefore I have launched into the daring endeavour to write an account of IFES which, though that of an insider, aims at being as fairly critical as it can be. Such is the way a Christian historian aims at writing, even if it means, at times, having to report uncomfortable elements: ultimately, all IFES actors, as humans, are redeemed sinners. This is why it was crucial for this work's intellectual honesty, as well as for the sake of IFES's self-knowledge, to let critical voices, whether from inside or outside the fellowship, speak in their own terms. We dare not suppose ourselves immune to righteous criticism, correction, conviction of sinful actions, writings or opinions. As part of the church, IFES needs correction and improvement, as we all do.

IFES readers with long experience might feel that some aspects of the ministry have been neglected; others, that I have stressed some elements too strongly or misinterpreted some actions or writings. Such is the fate of the historian navigating vast amounts of archive materials and the theologian who is forced to limit the themes he or she can focus on. Suppose readers from outside IFES understand its work in most of its dimensions, including those they see most critically. Suppose people with a long experience in IFES recognize key elements and maybe (re)discover aspects of this ministry which they had not before been aware of. In that case, the following account will have contributed to a better mutual understanding in the very complex world of Christian theology and ministry.

The consequence of what precedes is that my own *Sitz im Leben* means that theologically, this book is written from *within* the *evangelical* theological tradition of IFES. Essentially, in what follows and in dialogue with other traditions, I will presume a low sacramentology, an a priori low account of church order, and high confidence in the capacity of believers to make sense of the Bible. I am offering a contribution to an ongoing evangelical discussion and not trying to defend evangelical theology, for many authors have done so elsewhere. Even if I have read and benefited extensively from non-Western authors, my own academic journey is essentially Western, but with the hope of not being too insular nevertheless.

Summary

The first part of this work is a historical survey of how IFES developed from its foundation in 1947 until 2000. The survey focuses primarily on theological reflections and debates. As a selective account, it does not provide a complete narrative account of the rich history of how independent national movements came together, networked, debated theological and missiological issues, and at times fought against each other.

This part will show that in relation to *immediacy*, the work of IFES revolves around a commitment to the authority of the Bible and to the capacity of all believers to discover the plain sense of Scripture for themselves. Questions have emerged in the history of IFES about the relationship between that capacity and the authority of IFES as a body to determine and express what scriptural plain sense is. IFES responded to this challenge by crafting a *doctrinal basis*, serving as an authoritative summary of the theological essentials of the fellowship. This basis arose in a particular historical context and has since played the role of an identity and boundary marker. Hence, questions arise in the history of IFES about the relation between that context of origin and the many other contexts in which IFES operates.

In relation to *mediation*, I will first show how the history of IFES displays different attitudes to the intellectual contexts of student ministry, including especially an embattled defensiveness early on which has continued to shape the movement in many ways. Second, the history of IFES displays a striking and early move towards missiological indigenization, albeit one in which there are persistent tensions between indigenization and central oversight, and all sorts of complexities about the role of (foreign) staff.

In relation to *participation*, I will show how the insistence on the immediacy of each student's access to Scripture, and on the indigenization of the ministry in each national context, has gone together with all kinds of support and encouragement flowing around IFES; but also that there are persistent questions about how far IFES as a whole is able to receive the gifts of intellectual and international indigenization from each of the contexts in which it operates.

Part 2 supplements the historical account by offering a description of the core activities of IFES groups, based on archival evidence. These activities rely on deep theological assumptions linked with my understanding of the "priesthood of all believers." Witness, prayer, Bible reading and fellowship are all activities of local student groups which question and answer issues of *immediacy*, *mediation* and *participation*; so does the complex role of staff members, finding themselves at the intersection of student-led groups and church authorities.

The third part shows that substantial ecclesiological and missiological reflection has taken place within IFES. I argue that the "priesthood of all believers" is best linked with a *missional ecclesiology* which slowly but steadily developed within the fellowship in dialogue with its context and the wider

Christian world. This reflection took time to emerge. The first context in which some of it was outlined was the key theological statement of IFES, its doctrinal basis, which I examine in some detail. It was also articulated in theological and missiological writings penned by people influential in the IFES world as well as increasingly beyond it. The experiences gathered by these authors gradually shaped the way they conceived ecclesiology in a missional way congruent with each believer's calling to *mediate* his or her beliefs to his or her environment.

Part 4 deepens the theological pool of resources by examining first how a missional reading of sample biblical texts can sustain *a missional understanding of the priesthood of all believers and a corresponding ecclesiology* starting with the calling of the people of Israel and continuing in the priestly understanding of the people of God in the church. Initially far from the theological seedbed of IFES, Roman Catholic official texts, as well as the writings of Hans Küng, convincingly map out what I then go on to argue; namely that "parachurch" organizations, once properly understood in the context of a missional ecclesiology, are neither beside nor outside the church but are its very incarnation outside the walls of traditional gathered assemblies. Missiologist Roland Allen, well known for his reflection on the realities of foreign missions, is helpful here in understanding what it means to *mediate* a message in distant lands and to focus on essentials. For ultimately, what all believers do when they share the message of their faith is to join in with the *missio Dei* which, by its incarnational nature, is shaped by the contexts in which the gospel is proclaimed and received. This *participation* in the mission of God shapes the identity of believers who understand themselves as *pilgrims and priests* of the apostolic gospel.

The fifth and last part of this work contains the constructive proposal of a *missiology for the university*, formalizing the way in which the "priesthood of all believers" helps to understand the ministry of IFES and can inspire student ministry more broadly. Students are a *specific public* with *special needs*, and they represent a challenge to ecclesial structures in the same way that university studies challenge their faith – or absence thereof. As students are leaders in training, a robust missiology takes their sociology seriously. It considers their needs to experiment, critically assessing their faith and its connection to the world of the university, which in essence is at the front line of epistemological exploration. This is congenial to how the "priesthood of all believers" is understood and practised: in the same way students have *immediate* access to God, they have close access to knowledge and to people. An intense *multidimensional mediation* takes place as the university *mediates* knowledge to students who, in turn, are called to *mediate* the gospel to the university. Ultimately, this means *participating in* the *missio Dei* and being a blessing to the campus, which in many cases is an ecclesial foreign land. What is at stake is a creative and faithful engagement with contextual realities. The articulation of *apostolicity* as "sentness" is explored in the context of IFES as an organization spanning the two thought worlds of *imperialism* and *postcolonialism*. As the university world is also a globalized world under heavy Western influence, this last part comes full circle with considerations of how a mentality of *pilgrims and priests* can encourage students to be *faithful witnesses* in the fascinating world of academia to which God has called them.

Part 1

A Selective Overview of the History of IFES

Officially founded in 1947, IFES was built upon existing models of ministry to students but separated from other structures for a variety of reasons. In what follows, a brief historical sketch of the significant events, people and orientations of IFES will allow the reader to become more familiar with the background to the theological considerations that follow this historical section. This account is highly selective, concentrating on events, people and discussions which seem most illustrative of the theological and missiological developments within IFES, especially in relation to the thesis of this work.

1

Student Work before IFES (1800–1909)[1]

Precursors of IFES[2] include the Jesus Lane Lot, a group of young students involved in Scripture teaching and literacy work among underprivileged people in Cambridge, founded in 1827; the "Daily Prayer Meeting" (DPM) founded in 1862 by undergraduate students who had experienced daily prayer in their former school; and the Cambridge University Church Missionary Union, formed in 1875, which came to include 10 percent of the local undergraduate constituency, and provided structure for a growing concern of British students for world mission at this time of world colonization. In rapid succession, the Cambridge Inter-Collegiate Christian Union (CICCU, 1877) and the Oxford Inter-Collegiate Christian Union (OICCU, 1879) were founded. They were led by students independently of university chaplains and aimed at gathering students for prayer, Bible study, and mutual encouragement for witness in the university context. Witness mostly took the form of personal discussions

---

1. This is a very cursory account. For good historical overviews, see Tissington Tatlow, *The Story of the Student Christian Movement of Great Britain and Ireland* (London: SCM, 1933); Clarence Shedd, *Two Centuries of Student Christian Movements: Their Origin and Inter-Collegiate Life* (New York: Association Press, 1934); Donald Coggan, *Christ and the Colleges: A History of the Inter-Varsity Fellowship of Evangelical Unions* (London: Inter-Varsity, 1934); Ruth Rouse, *The World's Student Christian Federation: A History of the First Thirty Years* (London: SCM, 1948); Johnson, *Brief History*; Howard, *Student Power*; Douglas Johnson, *Contending for the Faith: A History of the Evangelical Movement in the Universities and Colleges* (Leicester: Inter-Varsity Press, 1979); Oliver R. Barclay, *Whatever Happened to the Jesus Lane Lot?* (Leicester: Inter-Varsity Press, 1977); Lowman, *Day of His Power*; Potter and Wieser, *Seeking and Serving*; Oliver R. Barclay and Robert M. Horn, *From Cambridge to the World: 125 Years of Student Witness* (Leicester: Inter-Varsity Press, 2002); Boyd, *Student Christian Movement*; Shedd, *Two Centuries*.

2. These are mostly English-speaking groups, which does not mean that there were no earlier similar groups in other countries. Their history mostly remains to be written, however.

with fellow students. However, CICCU students soon felt the need for a more public proclamation of their beliefs and called on American evangelist Moody to serve as a speaker for a university-wide mission in 1882, aimed at reviving – or giving birth to – a personal faith among students. Moody agreed to come despite not being a university graduate himself. One student who led noisy resistance to the meeting commented that "if uneducated men will come and teach the Varsity, they deserve to be snubbed."[3] Many students did not welcome this rise of more evangelical piety.

The Christian Unions[4] soon decided that some closer links between them were necessary, and hence the Student Christian Movement (SCM) was founded in the context of the Keswick conferences in 1893. The early SCM was essentially evangelical, "drawing on the Evangelical traditions of the CICCU, on Keswick and on the American revivalism of Moody, Wilder and the Northfield Student Summer School";[5] it was also interdenominational, comprising notably Anglicans, Presbyterians and Free Churchmen; and it was characterized by "missionary zeal."[6]

A towering figure of this period was the American John Mott, who had himself been converted through the teaching and counselling of a British student in a university mission in the United States in 1886.[7] Mott was the chairman of the new Student Volunteer Movement (SVM) founded in 1888 and travelled widely to recruit students for missions – understood at the time as essentially "sending people abroad."[8] Firmly convinced of the importance of recruiting laypeople,[9] he proclaimed that the aim of the SVM was "the

---

3. In Barclay, *Jesus Lane Lot*, 24. The student later personally apologized to Moody.

4. In the rest of this work, the abbreviation "CU" will be used to designate local student groups connected with IFES. In this introduction, we stick to this usage, even if it is somewhat anachronistic.

5. Martin Wellings, *Evangelicals Embattled: Responses of Evangelicals in the Church of England to Ritualism, Darwinism and Theological Liberalism 1890–1930* (Carlisle: Paternoster, 2003), 275.

6. Wellings, *Evangelicals Embattled*, 275.

7. Studd is said to have advised Mott "not to rely on any dogmatic conclusions arrived at by other people, whether doctrinal or otherwise, but pointed him back to the original sources, directing him on the one hand to study his New Testament and, on the other hand, in particular to place his reliance upon a personal relationship with Christ for the guidance of his life." Basil Mathews, *John R. Mott, World Citizen* (New York: Harper, 1934), 47–50.

8. On Mott, see Mathews, *John R. Mott*; Robert C. Mackie, *Layman Extraordinary: John R. Mott, 1865–1955* (London: Hodder and Stoughton, 1965); Charles Howard Hopkins, *John R. Mott, 1865–1955: A Biography* (Grand Rapids: Eerdmans, 1979).

9. John Raleigh Mott, *Liberating the Lay Forces of Christianity* (New York: Macmillan, 1932).

Evangelization of the World in this generation."[10] The SVM committee was "optimistic that if the 10 million Christians in the world would each witness to 100 people within fifteen years, then the entire current population of the earth would hear the gospel by the year 1900."[11] One key theological aspect of this view was the premillennialist hope that Christ's second coming might be hastened if the whole earth was reached.[12] This task was deemed achievable, provided enough personnel could be found. Universities appeared to be one of the most promising grounds for recruitment. As a pivotal figure of the WSCF later recalled,

> this fundamental maxim of WSCF philosophy was not chosen fortuitously by a certain group of leaders. Does it not seem that the thought of Christian students as an ordained instrument for the redemption of the world must be a fragment of the eternal thought of God made manifest in history at His chosen time?[13]

Mott's approach was very influential for the structural understanding of international missionary ministry. As one of his colleagues recalls, Mott thought

> that instead of attempting to organize the Christian students under any one name and according to any one plan of organization, it would be better to encourage the Christian students in each country to develop national Christian student movements of their own, adapted in name, organization and activities to their particular genius and character, and then to link these together in some simple yet effective federation.[14]

Mott aimed at encouraging local initiatives for mission in as many contexts as possible. This prioritizing of ministering to the lost world over ecclesiological divisions and separations was a fundamental characteristic of contemporary

---

10. Dana L. Robert, "The Origin of the Student Volunteer Watchword: 'The Evangelization of the World in This Generation,'" *International Bulletin of Missionary Research* 10, no. 4 (October 1986): 146–49.

11. Robert, "Student Volunteer Watchword," 147.

12. Robert, 147.

13. Rouse, *World's Student Christian Federation*, 308.

14. John Mott, *The World's Student Christian Federation: Origin, Achievements, Forecast; Achievements of the First Quarter-Century of the World's Student Christian Federation and Forecast of Unfinished Tasks* ([London?]: World's Student Christian Federation, 1920), 4.

missional currents, as expressed at the 1910 Edinburgh Congress.[15] It rested not only on pragmatic premises but on the theology of the activist evangelicals:

> for Evangelicals, "the church" was the body of true believers,[16] united by a common experience of grace and devotion to Christ as saviour, wherever they were to be found. Unity consisted in a shared openness to the Bible and its teaching, spiritual friendship and cooperation in common causes, especially mission. This ecclesiology was the basis of the "ecumenism" that characterized the movement. In addition to being transnational, Evangelicalism was transdenominational. This capacity for wider affinities had important organizational consequences. Apart from sympathizing with one another, the men and women of the evangelical diaspora came together in parachurch organizations that became a distinctive feature of the movement.[17]

These movements gathered around a set of core beliefs – notably the authority of the Bible, the virgin birth, the deity of Christ, universal sinfulness and so on – which formed a consensus broad and especially transferable enough for worldwide dispersion. This generated the "capacity to create the cross-denominational organizations that sought to turn aspiration into achievements. Such organizations in turn fostered a sense of belonging to a community committed to social service and, above all, to evangelism and mission."[18]

Some of these organizations later formed IFES. Its movements emerged from these earlier student movements concerned with devotion, mission and (to a lesser extent) Christian social action, in a context of emerging interdenominational evangelical unity in mission, underpinned by agreement in some theological fundamentals; and in the context of an emerging idea of students as key local agents for worldwide mission. Yet these movements were sometimes challenged.

---

15. Jeremy Morris, "Edinburgh 1910–2010: A Retrospective Assessment," *Ecclesiology*, September 2011.

16. The IFES doctrinal basis (clause D) explicitly mentions "all true believers" as forming the church.

17. Geoffrey Treloar, *The Disruption of Evangelicalism: The Age of Torrey, Mott, McPherson and Hammond* (London: Inter-Varsity Press, 2016), 3–4.

18. Treloar, *Disruption of Evangelicalism*, 5.

2

The Master Narrative of a Separation (1909–1935)

All schism within Christian circles must be regretted; but when our most precious possession, the free gospel, is at stake, we dare not compromise on a single point.[1]

It might seem peculiar to give sustained attention to the story of a specific local group, the CICCU, in a historical sketch on IFES. Yet most existing IFES historical accounts mention the events around 1909–1911, which led to a split between the CICCU and the national SCM, as *the* foundational event legitimating the existence of IFES.

The story will be only sketched here.[2] Founded sixteen years before the SCM, CICCU remained for some time one of the SCM's main member groups. However, from the late 1890s onwards, divergences arose between the CICCU leadership and the SCM, leading to a disaffiliation vote from the SCM in 1910.[3] Many actors tried for several years to influence the CICCU in one direction or the other, the last failed attempt at reverting the split taking place in 1919.

---

1. Johnson, *Brief History*, 45. Johnson quotes an early leader of the Norges Kristelige Studentlag, later the Norwegian IFES movement.

2. Concurring and diverging accounts in Cambridge Inter-Collegiate Christian Union, *Old Paths in Perilous Times*, 1st ed. (Cambridge, 1913); Bruce, "Sociological Study"; Barclay and Horn, *Cambridge to the World*; Goodhew, "Rise"; Justin Thacker and Susannah Clark, "A Historical and Theological Exploration of the 1910 Disaffiliation of the Cambridge Inter-Collegiate Christian Union from the Student Christian Movement. Unpublished Conference Paper" (Evangelicalism and Fundamentalism in Britain, Oxford, 2008).

3. Thacker and Clark note that the vote was carried out by only twenty-two students and, furthermore, that "few people outside of the Christian environment in Cambridge considered the events significant." Thacker and Clark, "Historical and Theological Exploration," 1.

Status of the Bible

The question was considered settled, despite agitating the spirits of students and church leaders for many years. The "precise reasons for the disaffiliation remained contested territory."[4]

Status of the Bible

The role and status of the Bible in the life and witness of Christians was intensely debated. Manley,[5] commenting later on the events, asserted:

> It is not so much a question of the "verbal inspiration" or "inerrancy" of the Bible but of the deep conviction that the Bible is the word of God, and therefore true. The IVF [Inter-Varsity Fellowship] goes to the Bible to be taught by it: the typical SCM attitude is to discuss it. This involves two distinct and opposing attitudes to current theories of biblical criticism. In the IVF, we regard these theories as undermining faith.[6]

The reaction to contemporary trends of biblical criticism did not relate only to private devotions and public events: it had broader implications for the cultural involvement of CICCU students and especially for the students' attitude to intellectual challenges. Two main approaches seemed available: either "to engage with the intellectual challenges but that perhaps risked lessening its view of the Bible,"[7] or to "withdraw from the intellectual questions, on the premise that engaging with the debates would be to deny biblical truth and reduce the simplicity of Christ."[8]

This contributed to the growing division between the two factions:

> The SCM was most frequently attacked for arid intellectualism; for neglecting the spiritual life in favour of study. Their bible studies were regarded by the Evangelicals as being studies "about" the Bible rather than "of" it. The SCM members in turn saw the

---

4. Thacker and Clark, 4. CICCU leaders exposed their views of the story in Cambridge Inter-Collegiate Christian Union, *Old Paths* (1st ed.).

5. Former Fellow of Christ College, Cambridge, and chief editor of the influential G. T. Manley, G. C. Robinson and A. M. Stibbs, *New Bible Handbook* (London: Inter-Varsity Press, 1947).

6. "G. T. Manley to J. C. Pollock" (n.d.), J. C. Pollock, Papers on the history of CICCU, Cambridge University Library; quoted in Thacker and Clark, "Historical and Theological Exploration," 9.

7. Thacker and Clark, 5–6.

8. Thacker and Clark, 5–6.

conservative Evangelicals as *untutored readers of ill-understood shibboleths*; sincere but blinkered. . . . By artificially restricting the meaning of "intellectual" and "spiritual" both sides in the controversy made the label they gave themselves a compliment and the label attached to their antagonists, an insult.[9]

Understanding of the Atonement?

The doctrine of the atonement has usually been assumed to be the crux of the matter,[10] and is one of the critical theological markers of the later IFES doctrinal basis.[11] However, this was most probably not the case in 1910,[12] since the first edition of the explanatory pamphlet *Old Paths* – written to explain to younger students why the split had occurred – never mentions a penal view of the atonement. Conversely, the 1932 second edition, with significant expansion, states the matter as follows:

> The basic doctrine for which the C.I.C.C.U. stands is that of the expiatory atonement made on the cross by the Lord Jesus Christ for the sins of the whole world. The blood of Jesus is the whole theme of its preaching, the cross and its application the essence of its teaching.[13]

The question was about the need for atonement more than the theory of atonement,[14] for the latest archival research tends to demonstrate that theories of the atonement did not play a significant role in the 1910 split. In an observation that supports this view, Thacker and Clark comment that in the archived correspondence dating immediately from before and after the

---

9. Bruce, "Sociological Study," 209–10; emphasis added.

10. Barclay, *Jesus Lane Lot*, 82.

11. Most notably by Bruce, "Sociological Study," 219–20; as well as Barclay and Horn, *Cambridge to the World*, 86. The IFES doctrinal basis affirms "redemption from the guilt, penalty, dominion and pollution of sin, solely through the sacrificial death (as our representative and substitute) of the Lord Jesus Christ, the incarnate Son of God." See below, chapter 11.

12. Thacker and Clark, "Historical and Theological Exploration," 7–8.

13. Cambridge Inter-Collegiate Christian Union, *Old Paths in Perilous Times*, ed. Basil F. C. Atkinson, 2nd ed. (London: IVF, 1932). It is of anecdotal interest that the same Atkinson is said by Chapman to have introduced the young John Stott to the idea of "conditional immortality," a doctrine explicitly combated in later revisions of the IVF-UCCF doctrinal basis. See Alister Chapman, "Evangelical or Fundamentalist? The Case of John Stott," in Bebbington and Jones, *Evangelicalism and Fundamentalism*, 204.

14. Cambridge Inter-Collegiate Christian Union, *Old Paths* (1st ed.), 13.

split, neither letters from CICCU members nor from SCM members make any significant mention of the atonement as being a contested cause.[15] So what seems to have happened is that the atonement was later retrospectively thought to have been central in 1910, as a result of the 1932 account of the 1919 reunion meeting later described by the in-house historian Oliver Barclay as "one of the most famous conversations in IFES history."[16] Grubb reported that

> after an hour's conversation which got us nowhere, one direct and vital question was put: "Does the SCM consider the atoning blood of Jesus Christ as the central point of their message?" And the answer given was, "No, not as central, although it is given a place in our teaching." That answer settled the matter, for we explained to them at once that the atoning blood was so much the heart of our message that we could never join with a movement which gave it a lesser place.[17]

The 1919 decision not to join the SCM was not the only approach of the future IVF group members. In 1925, OICCU decided to become the "devotional wing" of the local SCM but broke away again in 1927–8.[18]

A Social Gospel?

A frequent scholarly motif presupposes indifference among early evangelicals to social justice issues, yet this approach has been challenged.[19] Treloar underlines that

> far more substantial than generally supposed, early twentieth-century evangelical social commentary provided impetus to the ongoing application of the gospel to the conditions of contemporary society. . . . Seemingly wherever there was a

---

15. Thacker and Clark, "Historical and Theological Exploration," 9.

16. Oliver R. Barclay, "Guarding the Truth: The Place and Purpose of the Doctrinal Basis. Workshop at Formación 89," *IFES Review* 27 (1989): 30.

17. Coggan, *Christ and the Colleges*, 17; John Pollock, *A Cambridge Movement* (London: John Murray, 1953), 195; also in Barclay, *Jesus Lane Lot*, 82; Thacker and Clark, "Historical and Theological Exploration," 10.

18. See Bruce, "Sociological Study," 228–29; Wellings, *Evangelicals Embattled*, 279.

19. A notably balanced and in-depth treatment can be found in Brian Steensland and Philip Goff, eds., *The New Evangelical Social Engagement* (Oxford: OUP, 2013).

need, Evangelicals of the era developed a ministry or created an institution to alleviate that need's effects and remedy its causes.[20]

Treloar further notes "numerous books analysing contemporary social problems, explaining relevant biblical teaching and advocating various responses"[21] that were written by evangelical theologians, besides the signing of petitions. CICCU members, however, did not consider social involvement to be their task. In fact, *Old Paths in Perilous Times* sets the scene with the strong affirmation that

> while believing that it is always part of Christian duty to try and ameliorate distress, the CICCU cannot be enthusiastic about schemes for bringing about world peace by means of political bodies such as the League of Nations, or social uplift by methods of reform. It holds that in the gospel of Christ alone lies the only hope for the world by regeneration of the individual.[22]

Bruce interprets this as implying a case for "the uselessness of social reform."[23] An alternative way of understanding this reluctance to be diverted from "sole gospel preaching" is proposed by Barclay in his own account of the CICCU story:

> At a time when few nominal Christians knew the gospel, concern with social questions seemed a fatal distraction from the main job in hand, and CICCU leaders thought that they could see that social concern had led the SCM into spiritual ineffectiveness. The CICCU overreacted to the SCM as did Evangelicals generally. The questions to be asked should have been, first, is such concern biblical and second, what sort of priority does it have?[24]

This line of explanation fuses two main threads: the pragmatic need to focus a group's energy, and a strong sense of the priority of the individual's conversion over that of social involvement. The latter would come later in life.[25] That said, Barclay seems aware of the importance of the social involvement component in the story of disaffiliation, for he offers an interesting explanation

---

20. Treloar, *Disruption of Evangelicalism*, 99.
21. Treloar, 93.
22. Cambridge Inter-Collegiate Christian Union, *Old Paths* (2nd ed.), 38.
23. Bruce, "Sociological Study," 220.
24. Barclay, *Jesus Lane Lot*, 119.
25. Barclay, 120.

based on the relevance of social issues to student life. Commenting on CICCU members who later became involved in societal issues, he noted that

> they may not have had that attitude to social questions while they were students, but once free of the need to take a stand over against the SCM it was easier to ask in a more open way what the teachings of the Bible really imply for social questions. . . . The CICCU has increasingly seen social concern as right but needing to be left very largely until one is in the more real world of employment and the wider community where the problems and opportunities are no longer armchair questions. It has never been more than a very small number of members who have felt, while still students, that these questions had high priority.[26]

While the justifying thread in the assertion is unmistakable, it nevertheless points to another potential explanation that has so far been only hinted at in the existing stories and scholarly analyses of the CICCU-SCM debate. Contemporary documents give the impression that the rejection of social involvement rested on essentially theological reasons. Yet the socio-economic origins of students and senior supporters might have played a role hitherto underestimated. Boyd observes that "most university students at the time came from well-to-do families with little experience of how other people lived."[27] Their social location may have obscured darker realities outside the wealthier circles.

Long-Term Consequences

Reflecting the importance of this episode for the later self-understanding of IVF Britain and even later of IFES, Coggan summarizes the deliberately separatist stance of CICCU after 1919:

> From that time onwards, it was perfectly clear to the members of the C.I.C.C.U. that their decision had to be the same as their predecessor before the war. Although they gladly recognized that individual members of the S.C.M. might be true servants of Christ, yet as a movement it had apostatized from the truths upon which it had been founded, and the C.I.C.C.U. must remain absolutely separate, in order to give a clear witness in the University to God's

---

26. Barclay, 120.
27. Boyd, *Student Christian Movement*, 29.

way of salvation through Christ. This decision was also the real foundation of the I.V.F., for it was only a few months later that the realization dawned on us, that if a C.I.C.C.U. was a necessity in Cambridge, a union of the same kind was also a necessity in every University of the world, with the isolated exceptions of those where the S.C.M. still maintained its original witness to the truth of God's Word.[28]

IVF leaders took great care to ensure undesirable speakers would not be allowed to speak at IVF events so that influences outside the agreed lines would not gain traction. The primary device for this was the doctrinal statement, for "the CICCU now realized that a clear and explicit doctrinal statement was needed in a world in which almost all the great doctrines were being doubted or denied by leading theologians and church dignitaries."[29]

This historical boundary marker would significantly shape the British IVF but also the future IFES. Treloar observes that instead of remaining a local accident, the CICCU split was an event with wide-ranging effects: "The disposition to take a separate stand in the name of biblical faithfulness spread as the students of 1910 became leaders at various points around the world."[30] Many times indeed, former CICCU members became the active members of pioneer IFES groups in different countries, especially in the context of the new universities founded in the wake of decolonization. They took the narrative with them.

If during the 1920s CICCU was rather marginal,[31] the decade would provide the basis for later strength and resurgence, culminating in the 1928 foundation of the Inter-Varsity Fellowship. Conferences would prove to be one of the most important tools for connecting student groups, both nationally and internationally.[32] After Grubb restarted the Oxford-Cambridge conferences,[33] they were broadened so that the first official "Inter-Varsity Conference" was

---

28. Coggan, *Christ and the Colleges*, 17.
29. Barclay, *Jesus Lane Lot*, 87.
30. Treloar, *Disruption of Evangelicalism*, 88.
31. Goodhew, "Rise," 65.
32. Rouse notes pointedly about the British IVF that "it uses the S.C.M. methods – conferences, a volunteer missionary movement, travelling secretaries, etc., and by the date of writing has branches in many countries." Rouse, *World's Student Christian Federation*, 293.
33. Bruce, "Sociological Study," 230–31.

convened in 1921 in London.³⁴ The adventure was a combination of strategic thinking and vision. Grubb recalls that the impetus for the foundation of the British IVF came to him in a vision and from the outset was oriented towards worldwide development:

> I cannot remember the exact day, but it was sometime about the middle of that Michaelmas term, 1919, *that one day in my room, God gave me the clear vision of the I.V.F. that was to be. I saw that not only must there be this witness in every University, but that God was going to do it.* Probably the fact of Noel Palmer's catching the vision of starting an O.I.C.C.U. at Oxford and his going to do it, enabled God to open our eyes to the much bigger thing: Anyhow, the immediate outcome was that we saw that the first step towards the realization of the vision would be to have an annual Inter-Varsity Conference, at which we would get as many as we could from other Universities, and enthuse them with the vision of starting a branch in their own Universities.³⁵

A consequence of this world vision was the habit of the British movement to be influential through inviting other students to attend their camps. Even if no such direct mention can be found in the IVF writings, the underlying assumption might have been that of "British Christian thinkers in the 1920s [who] portrayed their nation's empire as uniquely committed to disseminating the distinctively British values of liberty and progress toward democracy."³⁶ Not everything happened in or out of Britain, however: camps and conferences were happening in Canada, Switzerland, Norway, Sweden and other countries.

At this point, IFES did not exist, but some of its foundations – studied here in the example of IVF Britain – were laid in movements defining themselves in part over against liberal theology, or more positively as a defence of biblical authority and of a soteriology focused primarily on individual conversion. That left unresolved questions about the relation of these movements to social issues and contemporary intellectual developments.

---

34. As to the intriguing name, which is still used by numerous movements in the world today, it goes back to a very specific event: "in December, students from Oxford, Cambridge and London met for an 'Inter-Varsity Conference' – so called because the date chosen was that of the 'Inter-Varsity' rugby game between Oxford and Cambridge, and therefore the time (it was thought) when the most Christian Students would be in London." Lowman, *Day of His Power*, 50.

35. As quoted in Coggan, *Christ and the Colleges*, 19; emphasis added.

36. Stanley, *Christianity in the Twentieth Century*, 16.

3

Meeting for Conferences (1934–1946)

In September 1934, the first International Conference of Evangelical Students was held in Oslo, with delegations from Britain, Denmark, Estonia, Finland, Germany, Hungary, Latvia, Norway and Sweden.[1] Keynote speaker Hallesby gave a noted address titled "The Hour of God." He insisted that theological currents had recently pushed student movements towards liberal theology and that the time was ripe to take a firmer stand. Hallesby stressed the traditional character of his message contra the modernist influence:

> We did not wish to start something new, we desired only to work on the old lines on which Christian student work had been run from the beginning. Right from the beginning our programme has been the old, full gospel, preached for revival, conversion, and new life in service for our Lord, at home and abroad in the mission field.[2]

A year later, the second conference, gathered in Sweden, drafted a constitution aimed at structuring the conferences adopted. The first clause stating the objects of the meeting was programmatic of the structural understanding to prevail in the future:

> The objects of the Conference shall be, consistently with the doctrinal basis of the Conference, – (a) to unite and strengthen the

---

1. Lowman, *Day of His Power*, 67.
2. Ole Hallesby, "The Distinctive Message of the Conservative Evangelical Movements: Address Given at the First International Conference of Evangelical Students, Oslo, September 1934," in Johnson, *Brief History*, 180.

> national Evangelical Unions, [and] (b) to seek by all means amongst students in all the countries of the world to stimulate personal faith in the Lord Jesus Christ and to further evangelistic work. (But nothing in this clause or elsewhere in this Constitution contained shall be so construed as to give any power to the Conference or its Committees in any way to control the activities of the national Evangelical Unions, which shall remain autonomous.)[3]

The meeting was a milestone in ensuring durability and fostering collaboration between the countries.[4] Most of the senior actors of the 1935 conference gathered again the next year in Switzerland for an International Conference for the Revival at Universities in Europe. Described by one of its pre-eminent figures and later IFES President Pache as "a little international convention,"[5] it was significant in strengthening student work in continental Europe, but also tightening the number of similar groupings which might later join the common cause: "since we had placed ourselves firmly on the ground of the inspiration of the whole Bible, many personalities, well known in the student world, said they could not join with us."[6]

The same senior leaders were invited to gather again in Budapest in 1937 for one of the last meetings of the pre-war era. The conference was not a great discussion gathering but a "conference" in the traditional sense of the term. A note from the Dutch delegates observes in direct terms that

> this conference surely is overloaded. One has to hurry for [a] meal, take the meal in a hurry, and to hurry again for the meeting. . . . We would appreciate some discussion. For instance, could it be managed that there [could be] one or two meetings in the conference open for discussion? We consider the tendency of the conference to be principally evangelistic; if this be so, we think it the best method of evangelizing to present the Word of God

---

3. "Constitution of the International Conference of Evangelical Students" (9 Sep. 1935), pt. 3, BGC #193.

4. "This sometimes took the form of Christian academics associated with the student movements (e.g. Professor Hallesby or Professor Rendle Short) making speaking tours of other countries; but it also involved the exchange of student teams, most of whom travelled at their own expense." Lowman, *Day of His Power*, 68.

5. Quoted in Paul Gruner, *Menschenwege und Gotteswege im Studentenleben: Persönliche Erinnerungen aus der christlichen Studentenbewegung* (Bern: Buchhandlung der Evangelischen Gesellschaft, 1942), 389. Unless otherwise noted, quotations from non-English sources are translated by the author, sometimes assisted by the online translation service DeepL.

6. Quoted in Gruner, *Menschenwege und Gotteswege*, 389.

and not personal experience. [No matter] how great personal experience may be . . . we are fully convinced that as a method of evangelizing, the delivery of a personal message has to stand far behind the disclosure of the Word of God.[7]

Another participant urged the planning committee of the next conference to "plan so that some consecutive portion of Scripture is left illumined . . . [and] that younger virile and instructed speakers be chosen, considerable use being made of present undergraduates."[8]

These notes were heard and considered in the programme of the last important meeting of the pre-IFES era convened in Cambridge in June 1939. One thousand delegates from thirty-three different countries gathered, including eight hundred students.[9] "Christ Our Freedom" was the programmatic title on the eve of World War II. The main sessions treated topics such as "The All-Embracing Claims of Christ and the World of Thought, The Evangelical World View, Christian Service and Professional Life, The Christian and the Orders of Society, The Challenge of the Open Gates."[10] The aspect of enjoying "fellowship with like-minded people" seems to have marked the participants and the stories they told subsequent leaders, as Chua recounted of the Cambridge Conference many years later: "Since 1934, European evangelical students had profited enormously from these fraternal gatherings. Many had to maintain their evangelical position amidst ridicule from theologically liberal church leaders. They were greatly refreshed by the excellent Bible expositions and their faith was confirmed through fellowship with like-minded student believers."[11]

If the organizers of the Cambridge Conference had envisaged the foundation of a larger movement, the outbreak of World War II put these plans on hold. "Within a year some of those present, entering the armed forces, had fallen in active service for their countries";[12] but this did not prevent students from gathering and national movements from continuing their work as well as they could. The delegates were aware of the world situation:

---

7. To Chairman Rector Hoïg, "Notice by the Dutch Delegates" (1935), BGC Box #193.

8. Godfrey Captain Buxton to Rektor Hoïg (11 Sep. 1937).

9. Barclay, *Jesus Lane Lot*, 107.

10. Douglas Johnson, "Christ Our Freedom: International Conference of Evangelical Students Cambridge; Advertisement Paper" (1939), BGC Box #193.

11. Chua Wee Hian, "With Evangelical Students," in *Martyn Lloyd-Jones: Chosen by God*, ed. Christopher Catherwood (Crowborough: Highland Books, 1988), 111.

12. Johnson, *Brief History*, 68.

There was a general opinion in most circles in Britain that a great European War was inevitable + that only a miracle could prevent War from breaking out in the early Autumn. "It was agreed that in the event of war, contact be maintained with each other as long as possible + all available help given between movements both during + subsequent to hostilities. It was incumbent upon the Executive Committee to feel a very special responsibility to get into contact with each other as soon as communications have been restored between their several countries + to seek to strengthen the surviving friendships + to press forward with the task of Christian co-operation."[13]

Collaboration took the form of interpersonal contacts and correspondence, as well as theological writing. These contacts formed the seedbed for the foundation of IFES.

---

13. "Minutes of Meetings of the Executive Committee of the IFES" (Examination Hall, Cambridge, 27 June 1939), 3, IFES e-archives.

4

It All Began in a Changing World (1946–1962)

Founding a Fellowship

In the immediate aftermath of World War II, the mood was one of energetic reconstruction: "Across the board, Evangelicals sought to cooperate with the energies released by war and reconstruction in order to remake the religious face of the world."[1]

The evangelical leaders of the interwar period were determined to meet again and resume the constituting work of a worldwide fellowship for evangelical students. In March 1946, the Executive Committee appointed at the 1939 conference gathered in Oxford with delegates from twelve countries. Whereas there had been some misgivings before the war regarding doing more than organize conferences, the war had altered minds. Johnson recalls that "those who had been hesitant about the danger of developing a top-heavy international organization – and this was probably in the minds of most of the delegates present – felt that further hesitation would be disobedience to a call of God."[2]

The main task of the 1946 meeting was to prepare a constitution to be approved by the delegates of an official foundational meeting of IFES the following year. Amendments to the draft constitution were summarized by Martyn Lloyd-Jones,[3] who soon took a prominent role in the IFES committee

---

1. Mark Hutchinson and John Wolffe, *A Short History of Global Evangelicalism* (New York: CUP, 2012), 180.

2. Johnson, *Brief History*, 73. Johnson himself attended all of the pre-IFES conferences.

3. Lloyd-Jones (1899–1981), Welsh Calvinist preacher, though not formally theologically trained was very involved in the early days of the British IVF, as chairman (1947–57) and

meetings. In terms of personnel, "it was agreed that it might be some time before a Travelling Secretary of the right kind would be available – but eventually such a worker or workers would become indispensable for adequate co-ordination."[4] Two countries were especially noted in the conference: China, which was asking by telegram for affiliation with the soon-to-be-founded international fellowship, and Germany, which had just lost World War II. The Chinese interest is notable, for it was interpreted as heralding a "new era when Christian students from countries with little or no evangelical heritage could be welcomed as members of this new worldwide Fellowship."[5] The situation of Germany was discussed, and the delegates agreed that "the Church of Christ was the only hope of the world and of this desperate situation in Europe in particular. It was for Christians now to show the healing power of the Gospel."[6] Consequently, Germany remained on the delegates' radar and German delegates were to be invited to conferences as soon as this could be done.

Mail discussions continued about the creation of an organization supporting national student movements. The main concern remained ensuring the strength of missionary vision and motivation among students. The same year, the first American Foreign Mission Conference gathered in Toronto. What would later be known as the "Urbana Conference"[7] was attended by 575 students. IFES-linked circles were being true to the roots of the Student Volunteer Movement. Many were convinced as half of the delegates of the Toronto Conference went abroad as missionaries.[8]

The IFES founding meeting eventually took place in the heat of August 1947 in Boston, Massachusetts.[9] Student workers, pastors and some significant figures attended the committee meeting,[10] thereby showing a broader

---

president (1957–67) of IFES. D. Eryl Davies, "Lloyd-Jones, David Martyn," in *Biographical Dictionary of Evangelicals*, ed. Timothy Larsen (Leicester: Inter-Varsity Press, 2003), 370–74.

4. "Minutes of a Meeting of the General Committee of the IFES" (Library of Regent's Park College, Oxford, 28 Mar. 1946), 7, BGC Box #193.

5. Chua Wee Hian, "Evangelical Students," 113.

6. "Minutes of a Meeting" (28 Mar. 1946), 5.

7. Named after the Urbana-Champaign campus where many of the subsequent conferences would take place.

8. Lowman, *Day of His Power*, 305.

9. Most of the costs for the pre-1947 meetings were covered by IVF Britain, as well as IVCF USA (especially through the funds of a German-American businessman, John Bolten, later to become IFES treasurer).

10. "The Canadian delegation was headed by one of their senior friends, Justice John Reid, of the International Court of Justice at the Hague; the Americans included the president of Rotary International, Herbert Taylor, the chairman of their board; amongst the Australians

sponsorship than only that of church dignitaries or aspiring youth pastors. Notably, however, no student delegates were present. In an anecdotal tone, Lowman renders Stacey Woods's stereotyped memories of the interplay of national and church sensitivities to be navigated during the meeting:

> When it came to planning, there was the careful precise British way of doing things – "It's always been done this way"; there was the brash American assurance that the American way was God's way; there was the intolerant Australian conviction that everyone was out of step but the Australians; there was the quiet immovable strength of the Orient – regardless of anyone or anything, without discussion or debate they would do it their way.[11]

The relationship of national movements to the new organization and the inner workings of the national movements regarding the role of students were discussed at length. National autonomy was preserved as "it was emphasized that the I.F.E.S. was in no sense a hierarchical super-organization which would interfere with the National Evangelical Unions but was essentially more a fellowship of likeminded National Evangelical Unions for mutual strengthening and for evangelism throughout the student world."[12]

The second question was also complex: what organizational role should be granted to students? One can only guess at the tone of the debates summarized by Lowman: "The Americans present felt that the British were trying to impose IVF's way of working on the USA, including a national student committee. The British, on the other hand, found it very hard to see how a genuine movement of students could exist without one."[13]

Woods recalls that "simplistic, activist Canada and USA were eager to get things going with a full fanfare of publicity, but conservative Europe wanted to move carefully, deliberately and with little public notice."[14] The foundation was communicated through Church newspapers, letters and telegrams. The same meeting nominated Woods as part-time General Secretary, whose role would be to link together the IFES movements, travel the world to encourage

---

was the Archbishop of Sydney, Howard Mowll, who had been president of CICCU the year after it broke with SCM." Lowman, *Day of His Power*, 79.

11. Lowman, 80.

12. "Minutes of the First Meeting of the General Committee of the IFES" (Phillips Brooks House, Harvard University, Cambridge, Massachusetts, 18 Aug. 1947), 4, BGC Box #193.

13. Lowman, *Day of His Power*, 80. Lowman builds essentially on Johnson's and Woods's recollections.

14. C. Stacey Woods, "IFES History Draft" (unpublished manuscript, Lausanne, 1977), 4.

the emergence of new national movements, and strengthen existing ones. Inaugurating a tradition of honouring people who supported its cause and recognizing his credentials in student work, the General Committee invited Hallesby to become the first honorary president.

Another interesting point for our work is that those involved with IFES showed a marked historical awareness from the very beginning, concerned to pass on the legacy of their actions. The 1947 minutes note that it was "proposed that Dr. D. Johnson should prepare a history of the IFES so that the public might be informed of its origin, character and basis of operation. It was noted that Dr. Johnson had material on hand regarding these matters."[15] Johnson indeed wrote *A Brief History of the International Fellowship of Evangelical Students*, but it was published only some twenty years later, in 1964. The fact that, so far, IFES histories have been written only by Anglo-Saxon writers[16] is significant in that it explains the importance given to the 1911–19 events in Britain and the relationship of CICCU with the SCM recounted above.

Constitution

Based on the IVF Britain constitution and the 1935 constitution of the International Conference of Evangelical Students, the 1947 constitution was painstakingly crafted by the delegates, who had to consider the concerns of many different prospective members. I highlight here three major aspects of the constitution.

Objectives

The objectives of IFES are stated in the second clause:

> Seeking to awaken and deepen personal faith in the Lord Jesus Christ and to further evangelistic work amongst students throughout the world.
>
> Strengthening the National Evangelical Unions and providing for fellowship on a worldwide and regional basis.

---

15. "Minutes of the Meeting of the Retiring Executive Committee of the IFES" (Phillips Brooks House, Harvard University, Cambridge, Massachusetts, 18 Aug. 1947), 3, BGC Box #193.

16. Johnson and Lowman from the UK; Lineham (unpublished) from New Zealand.

Arranging at regular intervals united and regional international conferences.[17]

The emphasis on the personal aspect of the Christian faith is unmistakable, as is the absence of any mention of social concern. This priority is illustrated in a comment by a former CICCU and OICCU member writing to explain to a fellow ecumenicist about the "Conservative Evangelicals":

> The Conservative Evangelical says with St. Paul "Woe is me if I preach not the Gospel," and, having made due provision for the studies which are his prime reason for being at a university and the physical and social recreation necessary for health, he aims to give what time he can to Bible Study, prayer and personal evangelism. Thus, when the College Chaplain or his minister or the secretary of the S.C.M. or a denominational society comes to him and says "I admire your zeal – I share your desire to evangelise – but shouldn't we also do X, Y and Z?," the Evangelical honestly answers "I haven't time." To this the retort comes "If you don't study the problems of faith and order, of the church and society, how can you present the Gospel in a relevant way?" "But don't you see" replies the C.U. member, "that you are falling for the chief temptation of the intellectual Christian talking about preaching the Gospel instead of preaching it?"[18]

Ecclesiology

Ecclesiology did not seem to concern the meeting delegates. They came from different churches and had to set aside confessional differences. The constitution mentions the church only twice. The first mention is part of the doctrinal basis, which states that IFES affirms belief in "the fundamental truths of Christianity, including," among ten other points, "the One Holy Universal Church which is the Body of Christ and to which all true believers belong."[19] Note that what matters here is the church invisible, which frees its members to associate with whomever they see fit. The second mention of the church is

---

17. "Constitution of the International Fellowship of Evangelical Students" (Aug. 1947), sec. 2, BGC #193.
18. Martin H. Cressey, *The Conservative Evangelical in the Ecumenical Movement* (London: Student Christian Movement, 1960s), 3.
19. "Constitution" (Sep. 1935), pt. 4.

the provision that "the Fellowship is not committed to any particular form of Church order inasmuch as it is interdenominational."[20]

Non-Collaboration

A clause on non-collaboration, derived from the 1924 British IVF constitution,[21] was approved: "The International General Committee and the International Executive Committee may arrange joint activities in the name of the Fellowship only with those religious organizations whose basis of faith and purposes are equivalent to those of the Fellowship."[22]

Occasioning numerous debates over the years, the clause aimed at preventing any association with the WSCF. It was called upon at the first meeting, where "it was decided that the student movements of Finland and South Africa, which at present have expressed a desire to maintain relationship with the WSCF, should be invited to become associate members of the I.F.E.S.,"[23] for "it was impossible for us to permit a National Evangelical Union to have full standing as a member of the I.F.E.S. while maintaining affiliation with the WSCF."[24] This pattern of opposition characterized the relationship between IFES and ecumenical circles in the 1950s.

IFES considered itself a fellowship oriented to mission, as did the WSCF, yet its theological fundamentals were stricter. It accepted ecclesiological differences within that doctrinal framework and defined itself in opposition to other approaches deemed liberal. The logical consequence of applying a principle of non-collaboration would be the reality of Christian witness on campus that could not demonstrate unity – at least structurally. This was a major point of contention between IFES and WSCF, as the very existence of IFES threatened the supposedly unified WSCF front.

---

20. "Constitution" (Aug. 1947), sec. 5.

21. It reads: "That in connection with the Conference no joint-meeting shall be arranged with any religious body which does not substantially uphold the truths stated in the Basis of the Conference." Constitution reprinted as Appendix 2 in Johnson, *Contending for the Faith*, 262. In WSCF circles, this clause was well known, as this quote from Rouse demonstrates: "Fidelity to its principles in most countries is held to require non-co-operation with any movement which does not accept all its theological beliefs in their entirety, and this has made it a divisive factor in the universities." Rouse, *World's Student Christian Federation*, 293.

22. "Constitution" (Aug. 1947), sec. 9.

23. "Minutes of the First Meeting of the General Committee of the Fully Constituted IFES" (Phillips Brooks House, Harvard University, Cambridge, Massachusetts, 23 Aug. 1947), 3, BGC Box #193.

24. "Minutes of the First Meeting" (23 Aug. 1947), 3.

They Were Not Alone: The WSCF and the Early Years of IFES

If the official confrontation with SCM circles could, broadly speaking, remain marginal to the British context at the beginning of the twentieth century, the rapidly globalizing post-war era would prove to be a very different context to minister in. The local SCM branches affiliated with the World's Student Christian Federation found a new impetus with the ecumenical momentum that was to culminate in the 1948 foundation of the World Council of Churches (WCC). The immediate after-war period saw new IFES national movements being officially structured, and, on several occasions, these movements were founded in direct opposition to local WSCF groups, leading to tensions and discussions. The main question asked was whether it was conceivable for Christian witness on campus to be divided at the very moment when churches seemed to be coming together.

Three important fracture lines emerge from a careful reading of the WSCF archival sources on IFES. These lines are somehow similar to those of the 1910–19 SCM-CICCU story but are articulated against the backdrop of the ministries of the two organizations on the global scene. In what follows, the main *theological*, *ecclesiological* and *missiological* divergences will be presented in some detail, because this will allow for a better understanding of how IFES's theology was perceived by the other major actor in student ministry at that time. And if the "priesthood of all believers" is never mentioned as an underlying point of contention, it nevertheless hovers over many of the discussions.

A word of context first. The WSCF circles did not start looking into IFES when the latter was officially founded in 1947. Internal discussion protocols show that WSCF were worried about the prospect of IFES's emergence on a global scale, having witnessed the interwar conferences sponsored by the British IVF.[25] Faced with the imminent official launch of IFES scheduled for August 1947, the Executive Committee of the WSCF commissioned its General Secretary, Scotsman Robert Mackie, to draft a position paper titled "The Relationships of National Student Christian Movements and the W.S.C.F. to the Inter-Varsity Fellowship of Evangelical Unions." This paper, containing the General Secretary's personal assessment of IFES, and some excerpts of correspondence and of WSCF national movements' reports on their relationships with IFES movements, was subsequently refined and amended

---

25. Robert Mackie affirms that he "was assured personally by an I.V.F. leader in 1936 that there was no intention of forming a *world* organisation." Robert C. Mackie, "The Relationships of National Student Christian Movements and the W.S.C.F. to the Inter-Varsity Fellowship of Evangelical Unions," private document for use within the WSCF and not official pronouncement (Geneva: World Student Christian Federation, Sep. 1946), WSCF Archive 213.16.39/2.

over almost ten years. Confronted with the rapid growth of IFES worldwide, the WSCF attempted to organize a joint consultation in the 1950s, but all attempts remained unfruitful because of IFES's Executive Committee (EC) advising its General Secretary to turn down such invitations. The situation must have been considered serious, however, since the WSCF convened a global consultation on IFES in March 1956 in Switzerland, with a view to preparing an official position paper to be distributed to the WSCF after its General Committee convened in the summer of the same year.[26]

A "Symposium for the use of Student Christian Movements and Their Leaders"[27] was eventually made available within WSCF circles in 1957. This document is among the last stored in the IFES files in the WSCF archive.[28] While "this consultation was unable to formulate recommendations for practical action, [it] did the fruitful work in several commissions which tried especially to define the differences between IVF and SCM and to review the SCM position and program in that light."[29] This last symposium and the documents produced in preparation for the consultation are serious documents that show the earnestness with which the WSCF leadership aimed to understand IFES and its position over almost twenty years. These preparatory and final

---

26. Stacey Woods was, however, consulted about the appropriateness of inviting a certain speaker to the consultation. Philippe Maury, Letter to Rev. Sverre Magelssen (14 Feb. 1956), WSCF Archive 213.14.76/2. No reply from Magelssen could be found and his name is not on the attendance list. It is, however, remarkable that he had been an insider of IFES, being on its Executive Committee until his resignation in 1955.

27. World's Student Christian Federation, "The Relationships of the World's Student Federation and Student Christian Movements with the International Fellowship of Evangelical Students and Inter-Varsity Fellowships," Symposium for the use of Student Christian Movements and Their Leaders (Geneva: World Student Christian Federation, 1957), WSCF Archive 211.16.39/1.

28. In addition to the internal documents (minutes, correspondence, national reports, summaries of discussions, IFES publications), the WSCF archive boxes on IFES also file several academic papers examining the differences between the two movements, notably Verna Claire Volz, "The InterVarsity Christian Fellowship and the Lacks in the Student Christian Movement Program Which Its Rise Reveals" (Master's essay commissioned by the Program Commission of the National Intercollegiate Christian Council [YMCA], Union Theological Seminary, 1945), WSCF Archive 213.14.66/1; Ruth E. Shinn, "The International Fellowship of Evangelical Students (Inter-Varsity): Its Role in the Ecumenical Life of Christian Student Movements" (Bachelor's thesis, Yale Divinity School, 1955), WSCF Archive 213.16.39/2; David Foster Williams, "A Comparison of the Work of the Student Christian Movement and the Inter-Varsity Fellowship as Each Is Found in Latin America" (Master's thesis, The Biblical Seminary in New York, 1959), WSCF Archive 213.16.39/1.

29. World's Student Christian Federation, "Relationships," 3.

documents will be the basis of our analysis,[30] which aims at understanding how IFES was perceived by another ministry with similar aims but a different theological outlook.

Theological Particularisms

> One of the main contributions of the I.V.F. to the University is a definite witness to a particular dogma. He who accepts it is a Christian; he who does not do so, is not. Facts or ideas which do not conform to this teaching are regarded as false, or are kept in another compartment of the mind.[31]

WSCF papers, in either informal notes or official statements, contend that the main problem with IFES theology is its "particularity," meaning that it was either not inclusive enough, of members of other churches, or not up to date enough. An example in this regard is the difficulty encountered by WSCF to make sense of IFES's theology, which WSCF considered to be the heritage of a bygone conflict:

> *Although it is simply foolish to dub the I.V.F. position "fundamentalist," there are certain characteristics which, when put together, produce a strangely rigid position. I confess that any definition still escapes me. The I.V.F. would assert that they take no preconceptions to the Bible and add nothing to it. They are particularly keen on textual study, and the leaders are certainly not afraid of engaging in radical reflections. But everyone else, be it Karl Barth, or C. H. Dodd, who deals faithfully with the Bible, but does not speak of it, or understand it, exactly as the I.V.F. leaders do, is tinged with "liberalism." It is no good pointing out that in flogging "liberalism" in Federation circles, they are largely flogging a dead horse; it is no good pointing out that no one goes*

---

30. The present work is to my knowledge the first to make use of the WSCF archival sources to study IFES. Consequent on the observation that no significant difference is made in the WSCF reports between "SCM" and "WSCF," we have used SCM/WSCF and IVF/IFES interchangeably, despite the fact that, strictly speaking, the "IVF" groups analysed in the documents refer mostly to British groups affiliated or soon to be affiliated with IFES, and that IFES member groups in North America, for example, were rather called "IVCF." No mention is ever made of other names such as "GBU" for France or "GBEU" for Switzerland, despite the fact that they were in existence, were founding members of IFES and also were regularly in contact and conflict with local WSCF-linked local groups.

31. Mackie, "Relationships" (Sep. 1946), 8.

to the Bible without any preconceptions and adds nothing to it. A past controversy has become frozen, and cannot be dissolved.[32]

The relative anti-theological stance of the general IFES leadership appears to have exasperated the WSCF who would have liked to "move on," but the relationship of each movement to theological history was to be an enduring and serious matter of disagreement. On the one side was the WSCF's weariness of strong doctrinal statements out of necessity to remain conversant with the language of the time. On the other was IFES's concern to cling to what it considered to be the "deposit of the faith." WSCF circles affirmed that "while the SCM has grown in theology as the churches have largely, the IVCF's position has changed little since the end of the century,"[33] but IFES leaders were prompt to affirm that theirs was the orthodox stand:

> We would urge you to ignore the view so frequently put forward between the Wars that a strong doctrinal position necessarily leads to the reverse of unity. Church history does not lend its support to such a view, except that there has been a pseudo-unity in times of sterility. As a matter of practical politics, our impression is that the Roman Church has gained a great deal in recent years by asserting its dogma strongly. We sincerely believe that a reunion of Christendom is impossible apart from a strong doctrinal position which in the very nature of things will need to be as congruous as possible in all essentials with that prescribed by our Lord and the Apostles. Without the reassertion and reacceptance of a Biblical Theology, the completion of the ecumenical task, even if it were possible, would be ineffective or even dangerous.[34]

---

32. Robert C. Mackie, "The Relationships of National Student Christian Movements and the WSCF to the Inter-Varsity Fellowship of Evangelical Unions and the International Fellowship of Evangelical Students. Memorandum 2" (Geneva: World Student Christian Federation, Aug. 1947), 4, WSCF Archive 213.16.39/2; emphasis added. This word of linguistic caution does not seem to have trickled down to the basis of the movement. In August 1957, the IFES Executive noted that "after considerable discussion concerning the religious situation around the world and the identification of the IFES with an erroneous definition of Fundamentalism and Separatism, *it was agreed that the IFES must take the position that it was a separatist student movement in the present world situation and not apologize for this fact. To be conservative and biblical in its ecclesiastical thinking.* It was also agreed that an informative, positive statement regarding the IFES, its doctrinal position and emphasis, with special emphasis on definitions, would be of help to young pioneer student movements or groups which are under pressure from the SCM." "Minutes of the Meeting of the Executive Committee of the IFES" (Branksome Hall, Toronto, Canada, 31.8–3.9 1956), 3, IFES e-archives; emphasis added.

33. Volz, "InterVarsity Christian Fellowship," 37.

34. Douglas Johnson, Letter to Greer (22 Apr. 1943), 2, WSCF Archive 213.13.94/7.

Given the normally strong aversion of Johnson to Catholic theology, it is interesting to see him appeal to Catholicism to support his views on the importance of dogma in his organization. Furthermore, the appeal to "Church history" is a frequently recurring pattern in IFES history that is, strangely enough, seldom, if ever, substantiated. Thus, one is left to speculate whether an implicit reference is made to the strength of the Reformers' convictions or to whomever else may have loomed large in the perception of those involved with IFES.

Whereas those connected to IFES affirmed that their doctrinal basis – to which we shall turn in more detail below – was "just" a contemporary rewriting of some of the most fundamental truths, WSCF actors countered that IFES leaders had added to commonly held views – particular views connected with their respective theological taste. Strictly speaking, the WSCF analysis is correct: from its adopted version in 1947 to this day, the IFES constitution states in its introduction to the doctrinal basis that "the Doctrinal Basis of the Fellowship shall be the fundamental truths of Christianity, including . . . [then follow the eleven points of the DB]."[35] As the earlier history of the SCM-IVF Cambridge controversy has shown, the doctrine of the atonement was a contentious point.[36] What is interesting, however, is that even if the British IVF was possibly the most influential in shaping IFES, the doctrinal basis of the world organization introduced a clause on the church which, even if quite minimalist in scope, would respond to a reproach voiced in 1943 by Mackie to Johnson:

> were we to expand it I doubt if we would expand it as you have done, since we do not believe that your statement is fully Biblical either in its emphasis or in its phraseology. We would instance its failure even to mention the Church, and its enunciation of a particular theory of the Atonement. If there is to be a doctrinal basis, let it be a good one.[37]

---

35. "Constitution" (Aug. 1947).

36. At the 1956 meeting, this point was discussed again and the conclusion was that "IVF does not have an adequate doctrine of the atonement. It is legalistic. There is a legal element in justification, but the personal living union with Christ in all aspects overcomes the legalism; and . . . there is a strong holiness train in IVF at points, and emphasis on holy living which cannot be dismissed merely as a working out of religiosity." Peter Kreyssig, "The Reality of the New Life in Terms of Conversion, Regeneration, and Sanctification," Summary of address given at the 1956 WSCF Ecumenical Consultation (Céligny, 1956), 2, WSCF Archive 213.16.39/2.

37. Robert C. Mackie, "Draft Letter Enclosed in Confidential Memorandum on the Relationships of the WSCF and IVF Britain," letter to Douglas Johnson (Apr. 1943), 5–6, WSCF Archive 213.16.94.

The positivist stance towards doctrine that was characteristic of those connected to WSCF is, furthermore, evident from the contention that the attachment of those at IFES to their doctrinal basis was to be attributed to a lack of maturity: "I wonder how many of your old members who are now in the Christian ministry can accept your present Basis without mental reservations. Do you consider it to be impossible of improvement?"[38]

If the reply to the last question was negative in the 1940s as the founding IFES was still unfinished, it turned out to be rather positive later on, as the doctrinal basis has not been significantly amended since IFES's foundation meeting.[39]

Coherent with the refusal to engage in the ecumenical encounter, IFES's membership policy would be more restrictive than that of the WSCF. The reasons were not pragmatic, however, but rather theological. In an articulate analysis worth quoting at length, Robert Mackie frames the differences thus:

> Acceptance of a variety of interpretations of Christian truth is one of the essences of ecumenicity. Here the formulation of the names of the two international bodies expresses a fundamental difference between them. The I.F.E.S. applies the word evangelical to the students who are its members, whereas the W.S.C.F. applies the word Christian to the community into which students are welcomed. This is broadly true also on the national scale. This difference means that the membership of the national fellowships in I.F.E.S. is restricted to an evangelical definition, whereas the national movements within the W.S.C.F. are, for the most part, open to all students who seriously desire to participate in the life of a Christian fellowship.[40]

Nothing is surprising in this quote: the same logic at work in refusing the ecumenical movement based on a diverging ecclesiology, theologically motivated, would in the general ecclesial world prevent unity in the student world. The logic is impeccable, but the prospects of more mutual understanding then were correspondingly weak. What is not mentioned, however, and gives the impression that they were sectarian, is that IFES groups were always encouraged to be open to anyone who wanted to attend their meetings – as the logical consequence of a missionary group by nature. It was – and still

---

38. Mackie, "Draft Letter," 5–6.
39. Except for a 2007 amendment taking on more inclusive language.
40. Mackie, "Relationships . . . Memorandum 2" (Aug. 1947), 4.

is in most cases – the leadership positions that were restricted to those who would sign the doctrinal basis and agree with IVF's aims and purposes, which were much stricter than those of the SCM. Before we turn to the question of the ecumenical movement, however, it is important to note that sociological factors were at play: WSCF authors regularly pretended that the theology of IFES was essentially the result of their minority status, of lesser academic credentials and of a lack of intellectual integrity. The embattlement rhetoric found in IFES documents amply verifies the first thesis, while the two other dimensions were overstated mainly for the sake of differentiation. In any case, such attitudes did not make diplomacy easier.

Ecumenical Diplomacy: IFES Refusal of the Ecumenical Movement

The very essence of the ecumenical movement was to bring churches closer to each other, fostering mutual understanding and recognition.[41] This is why the appearance of IFES on a world scale could not but be a problem for ecumenical circles: it seemed to be yet another split of the already very diverse Christian world if indeed "the division between the Intervarsity and SCM is no less a division in the life of the Church and division between particular denominations."[42] The reason for the "split" or for the appearance of a new movement was apparently the cause of some soul-searching in the WSCF:

> We must first of all acknowledge that the growth of a parallel Christian organization among students, and its spread to country after country, must be to some extent a judgement upon the Student Christian Movements affiliated to the World's Student Christian Federation. If there is a division in the Christian witness in the universities, we share in the responsibility of that division. If another presentation of Christian truth has had greater appeal, there must have been something defective in ours. If another fellowship seems more compelling to students, then ours must lack certain essential features.[43]

---

41. Space does not here permit even a cursory history of ecumenism. For the time frame of this work, see John Briggs, Mercy Amba Oduyoye and Georges Tsetsis, eds., *A History of the Ecumenical Movement*, vol. 3, *1968-2000*, 3 vols. (Geneva: World Council of Churches, 1986).

42. "Report of the Commission on the Student Christian Community in the University," Working groups of the 1956 WSCF Ecumenical Consultation (Céligny, 1956), 1, WSCF Archive 213.16.39/2.

43. Mackie, "Relationships" (Sep. 1946), 4.

While the question is not at the forefront yet, a missiological motive is present. Beyond the reality of divided church ministers or student workers lurks the question of the appeal of each movement to its main public: the student population. The rapid growth of IFES would continue to be a major source of concern in SCM circles.

In fact, in almost every discussion paper, letter, minute or other document mentioning the existence of IFES at the same time as WSCF movements, the same argument comes to the fore: there should not be a divided witness. Whereas those at IFES probably would have agreed that a divided witness was not welcome, agreement on the solution could not be easily reached because of the roots of the division: while WSCF understood the church to be inclusive of all people confessing to be Christians, IFES affirmed the necessity of theological agreement, and, even more, theological purity, for common witness. One sees the puzzlement in Maury's reporting that

> I was always impressed by the fear shown by IFES members that heresy in some sort would enter into their midst, or, broadly speaking, into the life of the church. Each time I discussed with them what the dangers of ecumenism are, I got the answer that in the ecumenical movement there are people with whose faith they cannot agree. This I think they will say about the Federation also.[44]

Maury further concedes that "there are in the Federation people with whose faith I myself do not agree, and whom I consider as heretics,"[45] but it does not really concern him, since his understanding of the church does not rest on theological agreement.[46] This strong ecclesiological divergence, to which we shall soon turn in more detail, hindered any possibility of a merger of the two movements, much to the dismay of the WSCF General Secretary, who concluded that the IVF

> is against the ecumenical movement as at present known. It believes it is wrong and that it must be opposed whether secretly or openly. The I.V.F. believes that we cannot achieve the measure of understanding we have achieved, without compromise of

---

44. Philippe Maury, "Document IV and Additional Notes of the 1957 WSCF Symposium," letter to South African Student Christian Association (Dec. 1954), 5, WSCF Archive 211.16.39/1.

45. Maury, "Document IV," 5.

46. And indeed, this tolerance of heresy within the WSCF was a line in the sand for IFES. As Boyd summarizes, "The SCM was in effect being regarded as a heretical body, which could be approached only in proclamation of the gospel, not by sharing in Bible study." Boyd, *Student Christian Movement*, 85.

faith. For example, the I.V.F. is anti-sacerdotal and will have no truck with "Catholic" views or practices. Consequently, any constructive relationships between Protestants and Orthodox, still less Protestants and Roman Catholics, are a fundamental betrayal of the evangelical faith. Indeed within Anglicanism and Lutheranism there may be the same betrayal; and anything that is High Church is contrary to the Gospel.[47]

The very evangelical character of IFES could not then be easily set aside for cooperation: for IFES to renounce its theological distinctiveness would have undermined its very foundation. One could even analyse the conflict between the WSCF and IFES as a proxy war between the WCC and the World Evangelical Alliance, even if the latter is almost never mentioned in the documentation.[48] There were two views of what it means to be "church," and therefore two approaches to student ministry. It is to a deeper analysis of the ecclesiological arguments advanced by the WSCF that we now turn.

WSCF and IFES and Their Relationships to Church Authority

> As a matter of fact, I am rather convinced personally that the basic difference between the IFES and the Federation lies rather in our conception of an attitude towards the Church.[49]

Two main arguments are put forward by the WSCF: the first is that the church is the community, called by God, to which all who call themselves Christians belong; the second, that while IFES affirmed that it was not a church, its disregard for established ecclesiastical authorities, coupled with its promulgation of a statement of faith, practically amounts to operating like a new church, or at least a denomination – this second point being an unpardonable sin in the view of the WSCF. Maury summarizes the situation thus:

> Our Christian unity with one another is the result not of theological agreement, nor even of mutual love, but of the eternal love of God for us. If we fail in preaching the gospel of Salvation, or fail in living that gospel in personal, social, and racial relations, we oppose the unity which God has founded in Jesus Christ, but

---

47. Mackie, "Relationships . . . Memorandum 2" (Aug. 1947), 5.
48. Lane Scruggs, "Evangelicalism and Ecumenism: The World Evangelical Alliance and Church Unity," *Fides et Historia* 49, no. 1 (2017): 85–103.
49. Maury, "Document IV," 3.

> we do not nullify it. The Church of Jesus Christ is one, not as in a mere achievement of Christians, but as the fullness of him that filleth all in all. Men have divided the church and so have torn apart and distorted the truth of God, but the truth remains in the church, which is still recognizable by faith through the existing churches.[50]

Maury's analysis blends together soteriological, missiological and ecclesiological arguments in a case to which IFES would reply that their understanding of mission and church differed. Maury understands IFES well, however, if we consider Johnson's contention that "our definition of the 'ecclesia' takes the New Testament form, that is, the fellowship of all true believers. In the long run, we are sure that the friends of the ecumenical union have everything to gain and nothing of value to lose by adhering thoroughly to a New Testament definition of the Church."[51]

The evident consequence of this understanding of the church as an assembly of "true believers"[52] led IFES, as we have seen above, to develop very early its doctrinal basis as a way of defining not only its ministry but also who was to be "in" and who was better kept out. Thus, the inclusiveness of the WSCF rendered cooperation unlikely, as Woods had intimated to Maury shortly before the WSCF consultation. In a rare moment of apparently distancing himself from the EC, Woods is reported as saying that

> the thing which made cooperation or unification impossible at the present time was the attitude held by a number of IFES members on the conception of the Church and of the Christian community, namely community based on theological agreement, while in the Ecumenical Movement it is based mostly on common recognition that God in Jesus Christ is creative of the Church.[53]

From what can be read from other sources directly penned by Woods, this looks like a tactical manoeuvre from his side. It might, however, hint at the

---

50. In Robert C. Mackie, "Statement on the Relationship of the Federation with I.F.E.S.," official position paper, 1957 Symposium for the Use of Student Christian Movements and Their Leaders (Geneva: World Student Christian Federation, 1949), 5, WSCF Archive 213.16.39/1.

51. Johnson, letter to Greer, 3.

52. Point J of the doctrinal basis affirms that IFES believes in "the One Holy Universal Church which is the Body of Christ and to which all true believers belong." "Constitution" (Aug. 1947), 2.

53. Philippe Maury, "Memorandum on IFES. Report on a Meeting with Stacey Woods" (Chicago, 21 Dec. 1955), 1, WSCF Archive 213.16.39.

fact that his own approach was possibly more pragmatic than that of other IFES Executive members.⁵⁴

IFES's idea of the church as a community based on theological agreement cannot properly be understood without considering IFES's very Protestant ethos. Individuals can reach theological convictions as a community, but when considering the question of membership, it seems logical to conclude that an individual needs to have reached his or her conclusion prior to joining IFES. This theological persuasion can, of course, be the fruit of a life in a church community theologically close to IFES, but it seems unlikely to be able to understand it without a certain degree of individualism. This "priesthood of the believer" allows the student to be "fit for membership." Most of those at WSCF who were actively in contact with IFES leaders at the senior level were Protestant, some having grown up in evangelical households; this would have rendered them prone to the idea common among Roman Catholics, that Protestants are irremediably individualistic. Yet this is exactly the same argument that WSCF would make against IFES: that its theology was too individualistic, even liberal, as the following rather ironic excerpt from Maury's long letter shows:

> At various times when I have had discussion with IFES leaders and members I have been impressed both by a certain lack of concern on their part for the visible reality of the church – I mean our historic churches – and by what *I might call, at the risk of shocking some of my IFES friends, a very liberal conception of the Church.* On the first point, *I always had a feeling that IFES placed its emphasis more on the importance of individual faith, individual obedience, individual piety, than on the participation in the community of the Church. Even more, I was surprised by the lack of concern for the various signs of the life of the Church.* I am thinking, for instance, of the historic confessions of faith of the Church, of the visible authorities of the Churches, and of the life of local congregations. (In some cases it goes as far as a certain lack of concern for sacramental life, but I know that this

---

54. Maury further reports that "Stacey Woods on his side told me that while he personally would be really concerned in achieving this sort of *rapprochement* and even unity, he could not in the present circumstances do any thing except very slowly and with great caution, in view of the divisions which exist within I.F.E.S. itself, between what we might call the open and rigid elements. While it seems that the American group for instance would be much more open to ecumenical contacts . . . on the contrary, the British and the Norwegian and Dutch movements represent at the present time the most rigid groups in I.F.E.S." Maury, "Memorandum on IFES," 1.

> is not universal.) To be specific, *I would strongly criticize IFES on two separate issues: in many cases it does not really feel responsible for bringing its members into active participation in the life of the Church*; and in the second place, *by calling upon its members to subscribe to a doctrinal statement in the form of a confession of faith, it really substitutes itself for the church, and even behaves as if it were a new denomination or confession*. I think at this point there is definitely a considerable difference between the Federation and IFES.[55]

It is indeed ironic to deem IFES's position "liberal" in the face of IFES's constant contention that their very emergence had been necessary because of theological liberalism. Besides the sacramental question easily explained by the large number of Low Church elements within IFES, the question of the students' and graduates' membership of churches was indeed a matter of constant concern for IFES.[56] As a young graduate would write a few decades later, "Evangelical teaching on how the body of Christ is manifested through its individual members can hardly be faulted. But something else needs emphasis. Every Christian graduate must see the concern expressed in Scripture for the individual local church."[57] What is striking is that more and more articles appeared on the topic of student integration in local churches in the later years of IFES, but there were fewer in the time contemporary to the WSCF consultations. This does not mean, however, that IFES's writing did not demonstrate, early on, a regular concern to encourage students to be part of local communities:

> The Christian group is not a church, lacking among other things the maturity of true elders and the means of practising the ordinances; nor does it witness directly to "society at large." The student, as a member of "society at large," should be a member of

---

55. Maury, "Document IV," 4; emphasis added.

56. Which does not mean that it was always easy for SCM students either. Tatlow tells the story of the foundation in 1912 of "The Auxiliary of the Student Movement of Great Britain and Ireland" – of which he assumed the chairmanship – which had two aims: "To unite in a fellowship of intercession and giving former members of the student Christian movement. To assist members to pass into active service in the Christian Church." Tatlow, *Story*, 728. Bruce analyses this creation as an implicit acknowledgment that the churches were too "narrow" to accommodate the young graduates. Bruce, "Sociological Study," 267.

57. Swee-Eng Aw, "But When I Left College I Couldn't Fit into a Church," *In Touch* 1 (1984): 3.

a local church and his membership of the Christian group should not be regarded as a substitute.[58]

The second charge in Maury's letter is much more substantial ecclesiologically, however, than the reference to individualism: "By calling upon its members to subscribe to a doctrinal statement in the form of a confession of faith, it really substitutes itself for the church."[59] To the eyes of the WSCF General Secretary, it was evident that the doctrinal basis of IFES was in fact establishing a new church. In the same vein and in unequivocal terms, the "Commission on Truth and Doctrine" of the 1956 consultation posits that "the formulation and acceptance of doctrine is the task of the churches."[60] Equally clear had been the reported response of an SCM delegation to the first North American IVCF missionary convention in 1946[61] to a local staff worker's point that the doctrinal basis was simply a contemporary outworking of the Reformers' doctrine:

> Our reaction is that even if these points can be found in the doctrinal statements of the churches, a student group is not the body to formalize and apply the rules, particularly when the most authoritative courts of the churches named were not consulted and would not agree to the process.[62]

The gulf could hardly be deeper: on one side is a student movement that relies on churches to define doctrines and is happy "to bear humbly the burden of Christian disunity";[63] on the other, another movement that considers it necessary to fix in writing its core beliefs to ensure a satisfying common ground for ministry.[64] The doctrinal statement is once again the field of a running battle between IFES and the WSCF:

---

58. James Johnston, "A Biblical Philosophy of Student Witness," *IFES Journal* 2 (1966): 8.

59. Maury, "Document IV," 4.

60. "Report of the Commission on Truth and Doctrine," Working groups of the 1956 WSCF Ecumenical Consultation (Céligny, 1956), 1, WSCF Archive 213.16.39/2.

61. Later, the Urbana conventions.

62. Hilda Benson, Rev. Candy Douglas and Rev. Gerald Hutchison, "Extracts from a Report on the Conference for Missionary Advance, Toronto, 1946" (Toronto: World Student Christian Federation, Jan. 1947), 11, WSCF Archive 213.16.39/2.

63. Mackie, "Statement," 9.

64. One aspect overlooked by the WSCF analysts, however, is that IFES requires national movements applying for membership to submit letters of recommendation from local pastors to ensure that these new movements are known by the Christians in the country. This requirement demonstrates respect for the local church communities.

> The reason why the Federation does not hold any detailed doctrinal basis and does not ask its members to subscribe to a personal statement of faith is our conviction that the confession of faith is properly one of the marks of the Church, and we do not wish our members to confess their faith except within the fellowship of their particular church in which they've been baptized and received.[65]

What is at stake here is a question of non-negotiables. For IFES as well as for the WSCF, witness is the priority. For the latter, however, the unity of Christians on campus will be the most effective argument for others – who cannot beforehand be classified in Christian/non-Christian categories – to consider the Christian faith. For IFES, it is the *compelling content of the faith* (doctrine) that will convince non-Christians to consider the Christian faith. From there ensue ecclesiological convictions: unity with the actual, local churches to witness and submission to their authority, versus unity of doctrine across local churches, gathering "all true believers" for witness.[66] Eventually, the ecclesiological question also becomes a question of power and authority:[67] to the freer spirit of those at IFES answer the more clerically minded WSCF advocates.[68] Formed in an attempt to settle the question, the WSCF official statement is unequivocal: "In the Federation we seek to be loyal to the teaching and traditions of our own churches, knowing that there is a truth of God which

---

65. Maury, "Document IV," 4–5. Even if most of the documents tend to give the impression of a very clear relationship between the WSCF and the churches, it was noted at the 1956 consultation that the issue remained complex: "Because the SCM's present understanding of its relation to the church is not entirely satisfactory, we ask [for] a continuing clarification of this question. One place where this might be done would be in connection with the revision of the objects of the WSCF constitution." "Report of the Commission on the Student Christian Community," 1.

66. "The Federation sees evangelism inescapably bound to ecumenicity because the scandalous division of the church denies its message of redemption and reconciliation to the non-Christian world. The Fellowship of Evangelical students sees in ecumenism a confused and dangerous diversion from the task of a clear witness to Jesus Christ." Shinn, "International Fellowship of Evangelical Students," 31.

67. Talking about the American context, a senior US WSCF official had a similar analysis: "On a student generation which may be characterized, if I may generalize, by a lack of conviction, commitment and community, this effort has proved to be very appealing to many students. I react to the growth of I.V.F. as a judgement on much organized, i.e. ecclesiastically dominated or sponsored, student work." Roger Blanchard, "Concerns of Proposed Ecumenical Consultation" (c.1955), 54, WSCF Archive 213.16.39/2.

68. The relationship of IFES theology, even if very implicit, to J. N. Darby's understanding of the apostasy of the church should not be overlooked. Given the number of influential Brethren members in IFES's early senior leadership, it is hardly conceivable that this would not have been somewhat important.

they partially represent. We do not seek to build up a sect with a Creed of its own."69

The charge of organizing a sect is violent and reflects the power struggles at work in the conflict between IFES and the WSCF. While the documents of the latter seldom mention their connections to the WCC, SCM groups were mainly linked to established mainline churches, even in the Majority World where they often inherited the former colonial structures. Once IFES comes on the scene, it cannot but represent a challenge to the leaders. As Stackhouse aptly summarizes, there is a closer connection between established churches and culture than with "sectarian" or "separatist" movements:

> A "church" is a denomination that enjoys status in the culture, participates in the culture, and indeed manifests something of proprietorial interest in the culture. It includes many whose allegiance is only nominal and typically comprises a variety of views and practices (remnant of the "territorial church" idea) as part of its stature as a broadly "accepted" and "accepting" denomination. The "sect," by contrast, enjoys no status in the culture but rather consciously separates itself from it. It is made up only of "believers," only of those who consciously join it and who maintain its intellectual and behavioral discipline.70

Conversely, against the reliance on established church authorities to delimit doctrine, Woods has a more direct approach that evidently betrays his own Brethren origins. Instead of appealing to historical tradition, he appeals to the history of "the common man":

> Through the ages God the Holy Spirit has given sincere men of God a *common* understanding concerning all vital and essential truth. From the early days of the church to this hour, God has given a *common* understanding, a *common* interpretation, a *common* conviction concerning all fundamental matters of Christian faith and practice. This interpretation is not a personal subjective judgement, but it *has that measure of objective authority which comes from the common voice of men of God through the ages.* Wherever the Bible is held to be the authoritative word of God, and wherever there has been a humble dependence upon the light

---

69. Mackie, "Statement," 9.

70. John G. Stackhouse, *Canadian Evangelicalism in the Twentieth Century: An Introduction to Its Character* (Toronto: University of Toronto Press, 1993), 13.

and guidance of the Holy Spirit through that word, true Christian doctrine has emerged, and God the Holy Spirit has led sincere Christians to a *common* understanding of his mind and will.[71]

The idea of "sincere men" to whom God has revealed himself throughout history is very important to Woods: there is a community, but this is really an "imagined community"[72] of the faithful, a "church of all true believers" and not an institution. It is a fascinating blend of individualism and community which the first IFES General Secretary (GS) presents. Writing in the periodical of the American IVCF, the tone is quite populistic,[73] yet not simplistic: at the core of his plea is a profound conviction that God reveals himself to individuals and that the church comes subsequently.[74] Moreover, this is strongly resented by WSCF circles, as the following analysis of this quote by Shinn shows. For her, Woods

> does not define in any historic terms which are the men throughout the ages to have held these truths, the doctrinal truth held by those fragments of the church with whom Woods and IFES agree. It would seem that Woods has begun with the Protestant emphasis on freedom to read the scriptures under the guidance of the Holy Spirit.[75]

Here we find a combination of the charges of individualism and theological particularism. The idea of having people read the Bible for themselves and not rely on clerical supervision seems to be a stumbling block in Shinn's eyes. And hence, whereas Woods and his colleagues saw themselves as the heirs of orthodox theology, they are accused of being the representatives of only "those fragments of the church." The logical consequence, for Shinn, is theological ostracism:

> Then he has given to his insights . . . a sole validity and authority – a right to cast others aside as not Christian – as arbitrary as the

---

71. C. Stacey Woods, *What Is Biblical Christianity?* (IVCF USA, n.d.); quoted in Shinn, "International Fellowship of Evangelical Students," 14, emphasis in Shinn's original.

72. In reference to Benedict Anderson's seminal work, *Imagined Communities: Reflections on the Origin and Spread of Nationalism* (London: Verso, 1983).

73. For an illuminating discussion on the connections between American culture and theology, see Nathan O. Hatch, "Evangelicalism as a Democratic Movement," in *Evangelicalism and Modern America*, ed. George M. Marsden (Grand Rapids: Eerdmans, 1984), 71–82.

74. Woods was a graduate of Dallas Theological Seminary. His personal dispensationalism may have surfaced or at least been understood by some of his conversation partners.

75. Shinn, "International Fellowship of Evangelical Students," 15.

authority a high churchman claims on historic grounds for his doctrine. To take a crucial example, Woods would claim as a common understanding, as the only understanding given sincere men of God through the ages, the substitutionary doctrine of the atonement.[76]

There is nothing new in this affirmation from someone connected with WSCF that the substitutionary doctrine of the atonement is too marginal in theology to be made a litmus test of Christian fellowship. However, what is rare is to see a hint at what theological alternative was held by the WSCF leaders. Directly under the words quoted above, Shinn refers to Gustaf Aulén's influential book *Christus Victor*,[77] pointing towards the preferred model of atonement in WSCF circles.[78] There is, however, no real theological discussion: IFES's view on the atonement is – in line with Aulén's argument – deemed individualistic and therefore incompatible with the missiological concerns of the day.[79]

Woods was well aware of the criticism raised at IFES's position and engaged with it in clear terms. His position, however, is much less concerned about local expressions of church life than with the theological soundness of those within his fold. One year after the WSCF consultation, Woods writes that

> in the face of the criticism that the evangelical union is independent or is unrelated to the Church, the evangelical union should assert its true oneness with the historic Church of Jesus Christ in university evangelism, *a oneness which is no mere externality* but which is inherent in the life and biblical witness of the evangelical union. In like manner those churches which truly witness to that "faith once for all delivered to the saints" could most helpfully assert

---

76. Shinn, 15.

77. Gustaf Aulén, *Christus Victor: An Historical Study of the Three Main Types of the Idea of the Atonement* [Den Kristna Försoningstanken], authorised trans. by A. G. Hebert (London: SPCK, 1931).

78. This is coherent with the more general concern of the WSCF and WCC milieus for political theology and for the fight against structural injustices.

79. This does not mean that Woods was oblivious to Christus Victor theology, as the following quote shows. He does not, however, mention structural sin, even if it could possibly have been subsumed under "the flesh and the devil" in Woods's mind: "At Calvary, Christ, the last Adam, Christus Victor, as well as putting away sin by the sacrifice of himself and dying as our substitute, dealt with the cosmic issue of sin. He became victor over the world, the flesh and the devil, and by right of moral and spiritual conquest legally defeated Satan. And so this world once more became God's." C. Stacey Woods, *Some Ways of God* (Downers Grove: InterVarsity Press, 1975), 33.

their spiritual unity with the evangelical unions in universities around the world.[80]

Here as well, the language is clear-cut. There is either theological unity with "the historic church of Jesus Christ" or oneness "which is mere externality." Whereas those at WSCF see theological diversity as an asset, Woods and his colleagues see it as a threat, quoting Jude 3, a New Testament verse often found in IFES documents. The concern to prevent heresy within IFES was puzzling for members of WSCF like Maury, who would counter that "the Church is the body of Christ brought together by his redemptive action. Of course there is heresy and unbelief in the church."[81]

Engaging the Student World: Missiological Differences

During the 1956 consultation, one last serious point of disagreement between the WSCF and IFES emerged: the missiological question of the relationship between student groups and the world. But before examining the lines of separation in detail, and lest the reader be left wondering if SCM movements were the proponent of some "secular theology" solely interested in "the world," and IFES, in "pietistic" approaches to evangelism, it is essential to underline that at least until the mid 1950s, both movements had a very clear sense of their calling to witness – to do mission – on campus. In a statement which all IFES leaders would have wholeheartedly signed, the Commission on "Student Community in the University" affirms that "Christian fellowship cannot exist for itself. God gives it to bear witness in the world to his Salvation of the world. Fellowship and mission are inseparable. Without mission, fellowship ceases to be Christian"[82] The same is true of a rather rare consideration of the necessity of parachurch organization, again penned from Maury to his South African addressees:

> The only justification for the existence of movements which keep together Christian students or school boys and girls come out apart from other members of the church, the reason why there is a need for student Christian movements apart from local congregations

---

80. C. Stacey Woods, "Evangelical Unions and the Church," *IFES Journal* 10, no. 3 (1957): 5; emphasis added.

81. Maury, "Document IV," 5.

82. "Report of the Commission on the Student Christian Community," 1.

arises, to my mind, only from the need for a particular instrument to evangelize universities and schools.[83]

As we have seen above, the WSCF considers IFES's theology and practice to be too other-worldly. This analysis seems to stem from IFES's concern for doctrinal purity, expressed in its insistence on doctrinal agreement and non-cooperation policies. Consequently, the WSCF prides itself on engaging the student world in a much more thorough way. It is as if clarity on doctrine and engagement with the world were incompatible:

> The IVF stresses purity of life and of doctrine in order for evangelism to be effective. The Federation tends to stress fluency in the world's language in talking with the students in his world; and seeks to use this language with honesty and integrity. Federation discipline is one of love (identification) and integrity. Actually, the real difference is one of emphasis.[84]

Corresponding to its inclusiveness, the WSCF theology presumes salvation to be a potentially very broad, if not a communal, process. Conversely, IFES movements, coherent with evangelical theology's stronger focus on individual piety, tend to target individual students rather than the wider university community. Put briefly in the words of one WSCF analyst, "the fundamentalist group makes the demands in doctrine and discipline but raises no questions about the society of which they are part."[85] In the same vein, John Deschner, later moderator of the WCC's "Faith and Order" commission, submits that

> the IVF addresses itself to the student himself, as an individual, as a descendant of Adam.[86] The Federation tries to address itself to the student in a concrete situation, to speak to his problems and the form which his discipleship should take in the University. The difference is in method rather than principle.[87]

This difference in method has, however, far-reaching missiological implications. Either a student group considers itself an integral part of a student community and its members therefore have to commit to the arduous task

---

83. Maury, "Document IV," 8.

84. John Deschner, "Evangelism," Summary of address given at the 1956 WSCF Ecumenical Consultation (Céligny, 1956), 2, WSCF Archive 213.16.39/2.

85. Volz, "InterVarsity Christian Fellowship," 19–20.

86. Here the underlying assumption is again the debate on the personal (substitutionary) versus the more communal (Christus Victor) doctrine of the atonement.

87. Deschner, "Evangelism," 1.

of carefully understanding the terrain of their witness in order to reach it relevantly; or they consider university life to be rather accidental and, at least in part, immaterial to the way the Christian message is lived and conveyed. Thus, the WSCF Commission on Evangelism reported in 1956 that

> the whole SCM life and program have to be seen in the light of their concrete setting within the total University community. God has called the SCM to make its Christian witness relevant and challenging to all students and teachers, and to the special responsibilities of the total Christian community in the University.[88]

This statement and the overall tone of the report imply that this was a major difference between the WSCF and IFES, and it is striking to find very few such articulate positionings on the topic of witness and the university community in contemporary IFES documents. Interestingly, the 1970s would see much more of this concern emerge and be advocated for, once the SCM movements had significantly lost in influence.[89] The WSCF takes great pains to underline the necessity of "speaking a Christian voice in the university community." Exemplary in this respect is the following excerpt from the same report which, even without providing many concrete details, nevertheless shows a remarkably contextualized approach, addressing not only students but also teachers and research:

> *The Gospel must be so proclaimed in this setting that it may lead toward the full commitments of persons, making them Christian students and Christian teachers – Christians who find, in their common academic life and daily work of teaching, study, research, a vocation to which God has called them. The task of the student Christian community should not, therefore, be conceived in isolation from academic work, but as having an integral relation to it.* It is not concerned with evangelism plus thinking out intellectual implications, but with evangelism of persons in and through their intellectual life, as well as through the emotional and other aspects of their lives. This demands forms of Christian witness wherein the Lord of Truth can speak his word of judgement, redemption, and illumination in the University community's pursuit of truth,

---

88. "Report of the Commission on Evangelism," working groups of the 1956 WSCF Ecumenical Consultation (Céligny, 1956), 2, WSCF Archive 213.16.39/2.

89. Preston, "Collapse of the SCM"; Lehtonen, *Story of a Storm*.

challenging persons to full commitment and Christian vocation there. *Christian witness, concretely made in the University setting, should serve both to renew and to sustain intellectual ferment which is essential to the rational character of the University.*[90]

The concern and care for the university as an institution of higher education is striking and rarely found in IFES documents of the same period. In those IFES documents, interest in the university is almost always subsumed to the need to reach its population in a friendly manner, but the approach is still very much one of "proclamation." To this, the WSCF – either in implicit rejection of IVF's "mission weeks" or as a general observation – adds that

> we believe that the direct proclamation of the gospel . . . is an essential activity of the Federation. It is done in worship services, through University admissions, through Bible study, and through any other form of witness to which the Federation may be called. . . . This being said, *we would insist, on the other hand, that in our secularised universities many students will never be reached by so-called direct evangelism. We have to live among them simply as men among men, convinced that the new life that Christ has started in us should make us not less, but more fully human, sharing in the interests and problems of our fellow students.*[91]

This concern for the problems of students on campus – broadly speaking a sociopolitical concern – should have programmatic implications, as Maury contends, giving a rough ride to IFES groups:

> In most cases, the program of an IVF group will give much less attention to political and social questions than that of an SCM in similar situations. One could say that IVF often tends to take a "non-political" stand, which SCM will criticize as "de facto conservative" and as "pietistic." . . . Unless I am completely wrong, I would think that one of the major differences between IVF and SCM lies in their different understanding of evangelism in the world. While in the Federation we have much emphasized the evangelistic significance of our "presence" in the world, in IFES evangelism often amounts to a call to get away from the world. While in the WSCF we have emphasized the place of political

---

90. "Report of the Commission on Evangelism," 3; emphasis added.
91. "Report of the Commission on Evangelism," 2; emphasis added.

and social action in evangelism, IVF members look at political and social questions with a conscious or implicit suspicion, as temptations and threats to Christian purity.[92]

Here again, the rebuke is severe: not to commit to social activism means to support the status quo. Although in fact it was not true regarding many social questions, as demonstrated by the sole example of Stacey Woods's stand on racial integration, a very unpopular position at the time of his tenure in IVCF USA,[93] it was indeed standard policy not to get involved in political debates. David Adeney, with his multicontinental ministry experience, explains that

> *the IFES does not allow itself to become entangled in the social and political problems of the day. It is inspired by one passion, "to preach Christ." It does, however, recognize that its members must be aware of the problems in the university and society in which they live.* They are called to be "in the world, but not of the world," and their Christian witness will involve them in opposition to that which is evil and [in] practical sympathy and compassion for those in need around them. They cannot isolate themselves from the sin and suffering of their fellow men. Their emphasis upon fellowship with the Risen Lord and determination to know nothing save Christ and Him crucified should deepen their love for those to whom they are sent to serve in the name of the Lord Jesus.[94]

Adeney, having served in Britain, the US and China, could not be insensitive to the necessities of caution in political matters.[95] Nevertheless,

---

92. Maury, "Document IV," 11. This strong judgment of IFES had, however, been somewhat mitigated in the discussion following the report of the 1956 Commission on Evangelism, which concluded, "It was pointed out that the IVF, as seen in its publications, probably has more interest in culture than might be expected." Deschner, "Evangelism," 3.

93. MacLeod, *C. Stacey Woods*, 112–14. In an intriguing report, however, the WSCF General Secretary offered a rather positive assessment of Stacey Woods's sensitivities towards social issues: "I found him most open and most stimulating and challenging in many ways. I was particularly impressed by his openness, something very new for me in IVF, to political questions. The way in which he spoke about the social and political revolution of our time, the attitude he took concerning the sectarian offensive of extremists of I.C.C.C. and other such groups and the dangers they represent in Asia with the identification they call for between Christianity and anti-communism, was something very interesting and encouraging." Maury, "Memorandum on IFES," 2.

94. David H. Adeney, "Student Work in Southeast Asia," *IFES Journal* 12, no. 1 (1959): 9; emphasis added.

95. He himself had to leave China after the Communist takeover. See David H. Adeney, *China: Christian Students Face the Revolution* (London: Inter-Varsity Press, 1973); and Carolyn Armitage, *Reaching for the Goal: The Life Story of David Adeney – Ordinary Man, Extraordinary*

the accusation of pietism was a frequent one that Woods had probably heard voiced several times. Later, once retired, he would have more time to reflect upon the question, referring to the same Bible passage as Adeney to provide a socio-theological analysis:

> A frequent mistake of *some sincere but insecure evangelical Christians* is to exaggerate the doctrine of the Christian's separations from the world. They mistakenly interpret Christ's prayer in John 17:16: "They are not of the world, even as I am not of the world." They fail to see that the application of this prayer is found in verses 15 and 18 of that same chapter. Christ prayed that his own may be kept from the evil of this world, but they are sent out by Christ into the world in the same manner and under the same conditions and with the same ministry as the Lord himself had been sent by God the Father.[96]

Furthermore, it is clear from the list of experts convened at the 1956 consultation and from other documents that the WSCF's engagement with IFES practice and vision was almost entirely confined to the realities of North America and the British Isles. It is therefore noticeable that in his history of the American movement, written after he retired from IFES leadership, Stacey Woods affirmed in rather unequivocal and, for that matter, even more concrete language than the WSCF report above that

> *nothing is more tragic than when either a student or a member of the faculty fails to play a full part in the life of the college or university but lives in a Christian ghetto and has social and personal participation only with the local InterVarsity chapter and/or a local church. Christian students and faculty are a genuine part of the university community with all the privileges, opportunities and responsibilities that the university provides.* For a student to fail to participate in the life of the university is to receive but a truncated education at best. . . . For effective campus witness and "friendship" evangelism, a Christian student, in addition to fully and actively participating in the local Inter-Varsity chapter, should be active in at least one other college society. He should

---

Vision (Wheaton: OMF Books, 1993).

96. C. Stacey Woods, *The Growth of a Work of God: The Story of the Early Days of the Inter-Varsity Christian Fellowship of the United States of America as Told by Its First General Secretary* (Downers Grove: InterVarsity Press, 1978), 64; emphasis added.

seek a position on the staff of the campus newspaper or in student government. Here he or she may exert an influence for Christ as well as making friends with those who may in the end attend some evangelistic Bible study group. Such a position also can be of enormous assistance in arranging for public meetings in the university where the gospel can be presented or an apologetic lecture delivered. Various social clubs and athletic clubs provide a natural contact between Christians and non-Christians without any compromise in life or witness.[97]

In light of this lengthy passage, it is thus clear that the line of demarcation between the WSCF and IFES was the practical outworking – *prioritization* – of missiological differences based on diverging theological premises. Given the relatively strong influence of (pre)millennialism in IFES circles – a theological aspect to which we shall return[98] – the necessity to preach the gospel was seen to be more urgent in light of Christ's imminent return than any far-reaching social engagement. Looking back on what has been examined so far, we can hence suggest that the situation was much more nuanced than Maury would have liked us to believe in his summary:

> I would say that we are here divided on a very important issue, that of the relation between the church and the world. . . . I am even sure that there is among WSCF members much disagreement on such matters. But it seems to me that we agree at least recognizing that we simply cannot evade the issue, that the world is really the place of our obedience, as well as the object of God's love, and that we are therefore called to love it (even if it means to struggle against it) and never to escape from it.[99]

---

97. Woods, *Growth of a Work of God*, 65; emphasis added.

98. We should not forget that the period contemporary to the debates examined in this chapter was the complex beginning of the Cold War, a period of intense geostrategical tensions likely to fuel apocalyptically minded imaginations.

99. Maury, "Document IV," 11. Even if the WSCF appears absolutely certain of the missiological superiority of its approach, it does not mean that they see it as being without innate dangers as well. Volz's early, but almost prophetic, warning points towards a potential lack of interest in the church on the part of students and other church members entering into social activism: "If we are really critical of our liberal Christianity we see that students and others often are turning to secular social or political groups, from the motivation gained in their church experience and background. They see the church only as it is so often seen obviously, a compromise society against the decadent order from which they wish to revolt. They could understand the Christianity which followed Christ, but do not see the church as anywhere near that." Volz, "InterVarsity Christian Fellowship," 19–20.

5

Good News for a World of Revolutions? The 1960s

The 1950s were marked by confrontations with the WSCF which did not significantly alter IFES's self-understanding. It is now time to turn to the eventful 1960s. Numerous authors have noted important changes in the social atmosphere of the decade, especially from a religious perspective.[1] Gebara's summary of the feelings of the day will remind the reader of the context in which the following developments in IFES history took place:

> Anti-authoritarian demonstrations of all kinds became the guideline of the new world order and a reference point for alternative forms of human coexistence. Terms such as freedom, participation, responsibility, democracy, citizenship, and social justice were a constant part of our vocabulary and dreams. The right to be different, to break with the established norms, to create one's own group, one's own art, music, or sexual life, were elements that kept being found in many places.[2]

Similarly, Woods reported to the IFES 1963 meeting that IFES was at a crossroads:

---

[1]. For a thorough account for the West, see McLeod, *Religious Crisis*. Other important treatments include Sydney E. Ahlstrom, "The Radical Turn in Theology and Ethics: Why It Occurred in the 1960s," *Annals of the American Academy of Political and Social Science* 387 (Jan. 1970): 1–13; Robi Morder, "Années 1960: crise des jeunesses, mutations de la jeunesse," *Matériaux pour l'histoire de notre temps* 74 (2004): 62–69; Callum G. Brown, "What Was the Religious Crisis of the 1960s?," *Journal of Religious History* 34, no. 4 (2010): 468–79.

[2]. Ivone Gebara, "The Movement of May 1968 and Theology in Latin America," *The Ecumenical Review* 70, no. 2 (23 Sep. 2018): 266–67.

> because of growth and acceptance there was the danger of complacency, coldness and ineffectiveness; that in the world today there were changing patterns of world evangelism, particularly in relation to traditional forms of the foreign missionary enterprise; that evangelism must be the task of every national movement, and that, above all, today was a call for a fresh commitment, a life of sacrifice and a new commissioning from God.[3]

That the GS would issue a warning against *complacency* reflects his pioneering spirit and concern about losing the adventurous spirit characteristic of the early days: IFES now totalled twenty-six national movements.

Theology, as well as practice, needed some rethinking. James Houston, one of the founders of Regent College, the influential Vancouver evangelical seminary founded in 1968,[4] recalls that in the wake of the student revolts and the crisis around the Vietnam War,

> everybody began to see things more holistically. We were looking for connectedness and life. The technocratic mindset and the impact of living with science and scientism – there was a strong reaction to that. Their reductionism was cheating us. There came to be a greater desire for theology to be something that should produce wisdom, that should produce healing of the soul and caring of the soul, as well as teaching of the soul. And this is what spiritual theology was purporting to do, to be more holistic, more integrated.[5]

The IFES leadership needed to adapt to a new context to ensure the organization's fitness for the new times. Revolutionary challenges had been

---

3. "Minutes of the Meeting of the Sixth General Committee of the IFES" (Nyack, New York, 1963), 27, IFES e-archives.

4. Regent has played an important role in the history of IFES because of the many staff members who have studied theology there, mostly during sabbaticals. The 50 percent discount on tuition fees for IFES workers is a strong incentive, especially for applicants from the Majority World. See Regent College, Admissions & Finance, "Tuition Discounts," accessed 14 July 2020, https://www.regent-college.edu/admissions-finance/costs/tuition-discounts.

5. Mark Filiatreau, "Honouring Our Elders: Dr. James Houston, Founder of Regent College," BC Christian News, June 2001, https://web.archive.org/web/20090519095349/https://canadianchristianity.com/cgi-bin/bc.cgi?bc/bccn/0601/supelders. Hutchinson and Wolffe note that under Houston and "with the later addition of Jim Packer, Regent would have significant influence in funnelling British influences into American evangelicalism and developing a worldwide network of graduates (on the IVCF model)." Hutchinson and Wolffe, *Short History*, 197.

met for some time already by IFES movements, most notably in China, where students had been under significant pressure by the Communist authorities.[6]

As mentioned earlier, the Chinese IVF had been a founding member of IFES in 1947, before being shut down by the Communist authorities. This first-hand experience of a student movement going through a period of revolution and facing significant challenges might explain to a certain degree the level of cautiousness expressed by IFES leaders towards revolutionary endeavours. In fact, David Adeney, British missionary to China and later Associate General Secretary of IFES with responsibilities for the Far East, penned a vivid, and for the most part first-hand, account of what the Chinese students had had to go through prior to and immediately after the Communist takeover. The booklet was published in 1973, Adeney having become vice-president of IFES in the meantime. Whereas the overall depiction is clearly historical, the author's insistence on the political challenges experienced by the Chinese students seems to indicate two broader purposes.

The first one was essentially that of discouraging potential student interest in the benefits of Communism, depicted as not only a religion but "a dynamic missionary movement aspiring to the conquest of the whole world,"[7] attempting to essentially provide substitutes for Christian doctrine and practice. Hence to the Western readership who might have been tempted to follow the sirens of Communism as a valid meaning-giving and promising solution to the problems of the day, Adeney depicts a totalitarian approach to life and a call to full surrender to the tenets of a new "faith." As Adeney's biographer notes, student ministry had become increasingly difficult in China:

> young people were expected to write the stories of their lives and beliefs, criticizing themselves and then subjecting what they said to criticism from their fellows. The new leaders saw personal reform as the route to wholehearted support of the revolution. Christian students who dared express their beliefs in the study groups were severely chastised for holding to outdated customs, even worse for following a religion espoused by the hated imperialists. With purpose, the indoctrination consumed huge chunks of the day, leaving scant time for Christian meetings. Slowly Christian freedom was being strangled.[8]

---

6. The vivid story is told in Adeney, *China*.
7. Adeney, 41.
8. Armitage, *Reaching for the Goal*, 121.

The methods employed by Communist leaders indeed bear striking resemblance to evangelical practices of journaling and repentance. But the struggles were not confined to doctrinal matters. The linking of social transformation and evangelism was a crucial one and, as usual, approaches dissimilar to that of IFES were questioned in no uncertain terms:

> like the apostles, Christian students had more faith in the transforming power of Christ than the success of any political change. Non-evangelical groups such as the YMCA, persuaded that social change rather than spiritual change was China's pressing need, openly opposed this stand and in so doing deepened the Evangelical's isolation.[9]

This brings us to Adeney's second obvious purpose: a plea against cultural isolationism given the necessity of holistic Christian witness. In a depiction resembling an edifying sermon, Adeney reminds his readership that quietism is not a possible approach to social turmoil such as a revolution:

> There was no freedom of silence in Communist China. Christian students were never allowed to keep quiet when matters of religion were being discussed. They were expected to take part in group discussions, and they were bound to express their opinions of the teaching that was given. If they were known to have a religious background, they were compelled to answer questions designed to ridicule the Christian faith. *Of course, many of the questions that were asked were not new, nor are they confined to communist countries.* Christians were constantly taunted with the charge that Christianity is unrealistic: "You Christians talk about the importance of love, but how can you solve the economic problems of this world through charity? Damn your charity, we want justice!" *Christians who had been mainly concerned about preaching the gospel of salvation to individuals found that they now had to explain the relevance of their message to society as a whole. They were expected to have a Christian worldview.*[10]

The challenges facing Chinese students served as an example of the challenges other students might face elsewhere at any time, which explains Adeney's plea for in-depth intellectual engagement with the issues of the day:

---

9. Armitage, 118.
10. Adeney, *China*, 56; emphasis added.

It is important that Christians honestly face the criticism that comes from the non-Christian world. *Too often we have lived in a ghetto-type existence, out of touch with many of the challenging questions which are being discussed in student groups around the world*. If reading is limited to a small range of evangelical authors, there is little incentive to face the burning questions of our day or to understand the thinking of a vast number of people whose outlook is diametrically opposed to the Christian view of life.[11]

Questions about the relevance of the Christian faith for real-life problems were obviously not confined to Communist China but characterize many of the discussions carried out within IFES in the 1960s.

The Two Ways of Listening and Assertion

Commenting on student protests in the late 1960s and early 1970s, IFES publications mostly present two possible approaches: listening or asserting.[12]

Listening to the World?

As the events around 1968 show, WSCF circles were keen on listening to what the world had to say to Christians, even if this meant a harsh critique. This was no novelty in ecumenical circles; listening to the world had long been on the agenda, as the following excerpt from 1953 shows:

---

11. Adeney, 63; emphasis added. Adeney was not alone in advocating thoughtful engagement with Communist doctrine. An ad hoc working group during GC 1963 had notably recommended that IFES members coming into contact with Communism were to "understand and admit the shortcomings and crimes of nominal Christianity which have indirectly contributed to the rise of communism. Despite total incompatibility between Christ and communism show warm, Christlike love to the individual adherent. Love is stronger than hatred. In criticizing certain aspects of communism, we should also clearly express our support of social progress and justice." "Report on the Working Party Held on Suggestions for Our Behavior toward Communism" (Nyack, New York: IFES General Committee 1963), 1, IFES e-archives, GC 1963 minutes, Appendix H.

12. This framework renders synthetically the main approaches which can be found, even though, in reality, more nuances were present within the fellowship. An articulate categorization à la Niebuhr is not, however, found in the archives. The earliest documented reference to this classic (published in 1951) is made in 1988, where the EC minutes note that "A copy of *Christ and Culture* by Richard Niebuhr is to be circulated to members of the Committee if possible." "Minutes of the Meeting of the Executive Committee of the IFES" (London Bible College, Northwood, England, Aug. 1988), 11, IFES e-archives. The idea of "letting the world set the agenda" was never part of the IFES picture.

> In order to proclaim the gospel of Jesus Christ, Christians should be able to see what is actually happening in the world of today. Because the order which God introduces in Jesus Christ embraces all people and the whole of human life, judging and saving, the Christian mission is a concern for people seen in relation to God and to one another. It cannot be merely a concern of people in one aspect of their lives (e.g. "the spirit" rather than "the body") or for people out of relation to one another. It must therefore reckon with social and political structures, because it must reckon with people as they are in their actual daily life. Christians themselves are God's people only in this kind of world, and are not an enclave separated from the world.[13]

Contextual awareness, receptivity of contemporaries, was high on the agenda, and exemplary of this missiology was the famous *Honest to God* by Bishop Robinson in 1963, notably published by the British SCM.[14] The book's main aim was to "reveal the unsatisfactory imagery which Christian theologians had commonly used to talk about God,"[15] trying to discredit the conservative vocabulary with which theologians close to IFES were associated. For the Anglophone world, Packer responded in clear terms with *Keep Yourselves from Idols*,[16] and for Francophone countries, Blocher wrote a scathing review in the same vein.[17] Viewed from conservative circles, the social impact of the book was significant, as McLeod points out:

> Liberals like Robinson fatally opened the way for doubt and a massive growth in agnosticism. The debates which he sparked off enabled doubters "actually to admit their unbelief" and alienated many of those who had accepted Christianity in a passive and unreflecting way. He quotes one ex-church-goer as saying that "now the parsons are contradicting everything they have said."[18]

---

13. "Minutes of the WSCF General Committee" (Nasrapur, 1953); as quoted in Potter and Wieser, *Seeking and Serving*, 163.

14. John A. T. Robinson, *Honest to God* (London: SCM, 1963).

15. Michael Walsh, "The Religious Ferment of the Sixties," in *World Christianities c.1914–c.2000*, ed. Hugh McLeod, vol. 9 of *The Cambridge History of Christianity* (Cambridge: Cambridge University Press, 2006), 306.

16. J. I. Packer, *Keep Yourselves from Idols* (London: Church Book Room, 1963).

17. Henri Blocher, "Lu et commenté: Dieu sans Dieu," *Chantiers* (1965), 26–30.

18. Hugh McLeod, "The Religious Crisis of the 1960s," *Journal of Modern European History* 3, no. 2 (2005): 207.

The very idea of "admitting one's unbelief" was utterly foreign to IFES rhetoric. As the sixties were swinging, Woods was still General Secretary and going out of his way to deplore the changing mood of the times, stressing the incommensurable differences between Christians and the world:

> The Christian has an utterly different standard of values from the non-Christian. He thinks differently, he reacts differently, he has a different set of value judgments. His life is lived in the perspective of eternity; whereas the unconverted man lives only in the context of time. The unconverted man is of this earth, and the Christian man is essentially an eternal, spiritual, heavenly being.[19]

The reader notices a sense in IFES of being embattled. Robinson's rhetoric was seen as the exact opposite of what they aspired to. Accepting this new framing of theological existence would have amounted to a capitulation, endangering the existence of IFES. Correspondingly, the first response to the times was a reassertion of the truth, but with a strong sense of context. *Mediating* the gospel was seen as a one-way movement, and not much could be learned from the world.

Asserting the Truth in Context

Aware of the changes that were happening, Woods's assessment was of "an exploding world population, a declining ratio of professing Christians in the world, to say nothing of the proportion of those within Christendom who are truly regenerated."[20] He deplored a growing secularism and the loss of influence of the church, together with the problem that "many Evangelicals, particularly graduates, in an effort to find acceptance in the current sociological-scientific society, will continue to compromise their biblical Christianity."[21] The historical narrative of the "slippery slope" of the SCM was resurfacing. However, the IFES assessment of WSCF theology was not only the result of internal prejudice and propaganda. Stacey Woods tells the story of a study carried out by Yale Divinity School to examine

> the essential difference in ethos between the Inter-Varsity Christian Fellowship in Canada and the United States – burgeoning,

---

19. C. Stacey Woods, "The Medium Is the Message," *IFES Journal* 21, no. 1 (1968): 9.
20. C. Stacey Woods, "God's Initiative and Ours," *IFES Journal* 1 (1966): 3.
21. C. Stacey Woods, "Perspectives and Priorities in the 1970's," *IFES Journal* 23, no. 2 (1970): 2.

growing student Christian fellowships – and the Student Christian Movement (World Student Christian Federation) which was already showing signs of decline. I fully expected that this difference would be seen as our doctrinal position regarding Scripture. Not so. The conclusion was that Inter-Varsity consciously depended upon the Holy Spirit, upon his leading and enablement. We believed in supernaturalism, in contrast to the Student Christian Movement, which was judged to be much more naturalistic and humanistic.[22]

The problem was missiological and sociological: how would IFES best *mediate* what it considered the "core gospel" to its audience in a rapidly changing world? Woods advocated for a reaffirmation of biblical faithfulness, but also the idea that adherents of IFES might, after all, belong to a small minority group of faithful remnants, contextually flexible. Woods's overall tone was pessimistic, as the following report exemplifies:

I think all of us are conscious of a growing confusion, both in doctrine and in practice in the evangelical world, as well as pressures from the ecclesiastical world and the secular world. Questions such as the biblical doctrine of evangelism, the true nature of regeneration and conversion, the doctrine of sanctification, are instances of this confusion. There is the danger of succumbing to quick and simplistic methods which appear to guarantee longed-for results in great numbers. In some respects, Evangelicals seem to be stronger numerically and to be exercising a wider influence. Yet on the other hand, our influence upon the ecclesiastical world situation seems slight and there is little response to the message of the Gospel on the part of the secular world. We do not seem able to arrest to any appreciable extent the moral and ethical rot and decay which are destroying the Western World. Our greatest need is for a God-given revival.[23]

The reader notices a disillusioned disorientation. Woods had started student ministries in the 1930s when Christian influence was still powerful,

---

22. Woods, *Growth of a Work of God*, 145.

23. C. Stacey Woods, "Report of the General Secretary to the Seventh General Committee of the IFES" (Wuppertal-Barmen, Germany, 1967), 4, IFES e-archives, EC 1967 minutes, Appendix B.

but he felt that everything was going downhill.[24] Yet Christian influence in the world was not declining everywhere. Even in Europe, Christianity was still very influential in the immediate post-war period,[25] and such a well-travelled man could have noticed that many leaders of the decolonization movements were Christians, as were members of the US civil rights movement. What he saw, however, was that "numbers of countries are closing their doors to professional foreign Christian propaganda and evangelism."[26] So while Woods was adamant that national IFES movements were much more local initiatives than foreign imports, he nevertheless deplored the lost possibilities of sending "professionals" for ministry. The appeal to professionals is particularly interesting because it went against the grain of Woods's otherwise strong emphasis on student initiative:

> Student initiative and responsibility does not mean that only students do the teaching, preaching, evangelizing in the university. Constantly these students call in assistance in terms of graduates, teachers and pastors. However, the burden of witness to the unconverted student body is assumed by the Christian students themselves. They must take the initiative in intercession, personal witness and organization. They must think and plan and prepare. It is their vision, their God-given task.[27]

That an older man would affirm the duties and responsibilities of younger students in such strong terms could have smacked of paternalism to external observers. It nevertheless reflects the contextual flexibility of IFES's approach to student ministry: the conviction of earlier and later leaders that Christian ministry needed to be carried out by students was unabated. Having *direct* access to God, students would know how best to *mediate* him in whatever circumstances they found themselves. In the words of Voelkel, long-term associate of IFES in Latin America,

---

24. He would write in 1975 that "we have a new lifestyle. Society has become permissive and indulgent. A frightening increase in violence, cruelty, brutality and crime is deeply troubling. Relationships between men and women, husbands and wives, parents and children are no longer what they were in the 1940s." Woods, *Some Ways*, 21.

25. Many in-depth studies explore the ebb and flow of Christian influence in the post–World War II era, notably Grace Davie, *Religion in Modern Europe: A Memory Mutates*, European Societies (Oxford: OUP, 2000); Detlef Pollack and Gert Pickel, "Religious Individualization or Secularization," in *The Role of Religion in Modern Societies*, eds. Detlef Pollack and Daniel V. A. Olson (New York: Routledge, 2008), 191–220; Callum Brown, "Religious Crisis."

26. Woods, "God's Initiative and Ours," 3.

27. C. Stacey Woods, "Student Work: Strategy and Tactics," *IFES Journal* 1 (1966): 14.

change has dislodged students from their traditional framework. As never before, they are open to new ideas and a cause worthy of their life and death. It seems very likely from glimmers here and there that change has actually prepared them to hear Christ's call – to become His eternal revolutionaries.[28] This is our moment to act. Laborers are all too few in this growing important segment of society. May God raise up a vast army of bold harvesters to do the job![29]

The balance between preaching and listening was not considered an easy task. But the pendulum between doctrinal assertion and listening to the world was not the prerogative of evangelicals only. The 1960s were also marked, in the religious world, by the Second Vatican Council, meeting from 1962 to 1965 and aiming at an *aggiornamento* (update) of the Roman Catholic Church. Particularly relevant to our subject is the greater emphasis on reading the Bible and on the use of vernacular languages in the celebrating of the Mass. Willaime contends that the increase in individualism, characteristic of the 1960s, was concomitant with intellectual engagement and hence a "Protestantisation of religious feelings":

> The development of ecumenism is inseparable from the evolution of contemporary religious sentiment and of religious organisations themselves. The individualisation and intellectualisation of religious feeling, linked to the rise of the intellectual strata and the cultural level of the population, and the questioning of authority patterns, have favoured an evolution which, in some respects, can be interpreted as a "Protestantisation" of religious feeling (the transition from Latin to the vernacular, the promotion of the laity, liturgical reform, the greater importance given to the Bible, a certain de-clergyfication of the figure of the priest, and the use of the language of meaning rather than that of substance).[30]

---

28. Voelkel put an interesting quote from Nikolai Berdyaev as an epigraph to his book: "The Christian is the eternal revolutionary who is satisfied by no regimen of life because he seeks the Kingdom of God and His righteousness, because he aspires to the more radical transformation of men, of the society, and the world."

29. Jack Voelkel, *Student Evangelism in a World of Revolution*, Contemporary Evangelical Perspectives (Grand Rapids: Zondervan, 1974), 37.

30. Jean-Paul Willaime, "La précarité protestante: sociologie du protestantisme contemporain", *Histoire et Société* 25 (Geneva: Labor et Fides, 1992): 163–64.

This tension of legitimation between hierarchical authority and self-appointment to the ministry is a recurring question for parachurch ministries. Yet IFES cannot be understood apart from a profoundly individual dimension of faith and missionary calling, even if neither is sealed off from the theological debates of the day.

Ultimately, the currents were too strong for either "opposition" or "capitulation" to be a sustainable position, and it took the theological acumen of John Stott, whose influence was growing within IFES,[31] to propose a typical *via media* between two main approaches for Christians in relation to the world. Stott's summary of the positions commonly held at the time is shown in the nearby table.

Traditional "ecumenical" approach	Traditional "evangelical" approach
God's first concern is the world.	God's prime concern is the salvation of human souls.
God's actions in the world primarily aim at establishing his peace (shalom).	God's actions are manifested in the conversion of individuals.
Mission means the church "discovers in the world" what God is already doing, sometimes through political revolutions.	Mission means the church proclaims the gospel, mostly through preaching.
The church is to "join with Christ" in his fight against social injustice.	Social activism is too closely linked to the "social gospel" and should be avoided.

For Stott, simply to retreat from involvement would be unbiblical, because it would mean forgetting that "God did not create souls but body-souls called human beings, who are also social beings, and that he cares about their bodies and their society as well as about their relationship with himself and their eternal destiny."[32] Yet it would be equally unbiblical to adopt a purely this-worldly perspective confusing theological liberation with the spiritual needs of human beings. Hence, for Stott,

> the whole church is called (and every member of it) as much to involvement in the world as to separation from it, as much to "worldliness" as to "holiness." Not to a worldliness which is unholy,

---

31. Based on John Stott, *Christ the Controversialist* (Downers Grove: InterVarsity Press, 1970), 188–89. One of the theological distinctives of Stott was his ability to mediate between diverging positions within evangelicalism.

32. Stott, *Christ the Controversialist*, 188.

nor to a holiness which is unworldly, but to "holy worldliness," a true separation to God which is lived out in the world – the world which he made and sent his Son to redeem.[33]

Debates and discussions held in IFES over the following decades can be read against the backdrop of possible attitudes on the continuum outlined by Stott.

Excursus 1: The Racial Question

Asserting doctrine was not always easy. The 1960s also saw the question of racial relations become more and more acute and in 1963, the Executive was motioned to take a stand on the question. The prompting came from Chandapilla, the Indian GS, who "felt that the IFES should take a strong stand against racial discrimination in any manner because such discrimination is both unchristian and sinful. Furthermore . . . there should be an undertaking from member movements that no form of discrimination should be permitted within their movements."[34]

The issue was not easy to settle since the DB says nothing about race and ethnicity. The issue was more a question of policy than of actual practice. Woods had adamantly opposed segregation in conferences even against some of the US board members,[35] and IFES General Committees (GCs) convened leaders from as many countries and ethnicities as there were member movements.[36] How would the Executive react to a new situation without compromising the usual stance of not getting involved with "non-essentials"? Indeed, "there was considerable discussion in which the question was raised as to the wisdom of the IFES passing resolutions and it was noted that if it passes a resolution on one issue it should in being consistent pass resolutions on many issues."[37] Whereas condemning racial discrimination was unlikely to have troubled EC

---

33. Stott, 190.

34. "Minutes of the Meeting of the Executive Committee of the IFES" (Uppigard, Norway, 30 Sep. 1965), 24, IFES e-archives.

35. MacLeod, *C. Stacey Woods*, 112–14.

36. Chandapilla's move appears to have been more tactical, in the face of WSCF activism, than addressed to in-house controversies, for one looks in vain in the IFES archives for much engagement with racial questions. The fellowship being global, it would have been difficult to sustain any overt racism. This does not mean that no systemic or veiled racism could have been at work – notably in some asymmetric relationships – but it was never defended as a tenable option.

37. "Minutes of the Meeting of the Executive Committee" (1965), 24.

members given their own cultural awareness, their concerns were broader: the WSCF was known to issue statements on political matters, and IFES wanted to remain distinct from such entanglements. As a middle way, the EC suggested that articles should be written in the *IFES Journal* and that possibly one Bible study at the 1967 GC should be devoted to the question. Then, instead of an official resolution which could have been binding and even potentially offensive to some donors, the EC passed a modest motion:

> the Committee affirms its adherence to the Scriptural principle expressed in Galatians 3:28: "There is neither Jew nor Greek, slave nor free, there is neither male nor female, for you are all one in Christ Jesus." Throughout its history the IFES has consistently demonstrated the reality of a fellowship in Christ which knows no racial barriers and by the grace of God it will continue to do so; not by passing resolutions, but by maintaining within and between our unions a close fellowship in the Gospel open to all races represented in the universities.[38]

Such a clear but humble motion within a committee would not suffice to settle the question once and for all. Especially acute was the question of South Africa, which occupied many hours of discussion in Executive and General Committee meetings. There was the question of apartheid, but also that of the membership of the different national movements, one of which was also a member of the WSCF, again prompting the IFES leadership to tackle the perennial question of double membership.[39] Whereas IFES traditionally did not want to make political statements, it was forced to consider the question because of the relationship between Christianity and apartheid. As Bentley-Taylor, special envoy of the GS, noted in 1967, the question was missiological:

> In general, apathy prevails; in the eyes of most African students Christianity stands discredited by the political situation, while European students, even in the Christian Union, are unaccustomed to cordial personal relationships with those of other races; and both parties risk the wrath of their group if they try to break out of the ring in which they are caught.[40]

---

38. "Minutes of the Meeting of the Executive Committee" (1965), 24.

39. The question of the South African movements and their relationships to the WSCF and IFES would provide enough material for an entire book. For an introduction to the history of the challenges, see Lowman, *Day of His Power*, 272–78.

40. David Bentley-Taylor, "African Diary, Part II," *IFES Journal* 20, no. 3 (1967): 28.

As the later history of IFES shows, the question of ethnic relations has kept returning to the foreground, not only in relation to racial issues, but also in questions regarding nations and citizenship. Some movements are still separated along language or cultural lines, and if they are not two administrative entities, they may have several divisions of their ministries focusing on black, Latino or Asian students, such as in InterVarsity USA for example.[41] In any case, the challenge issued by Escobar many years later would not leave much room for doubt:

> IFES has been a movement that pioneered new partnerships through international teams. But national student movements will have to work for better multiracial and multicultural integration at home before they try it abroad. Mission on our doorstep is the new training ground for the new partnerships that will also carry on mission around the world.[42]

Excursus 2: Neutral Grounds and a Castle

From its beginnings, the correspondence address of the IFES International office was the same as Stacey Woods's domicile or office spaces rented in close vicinity to his home. This made sense at the beginning of IFES, because Woods was still the acting General Secretary of IVCF Canada as well as of IVCF USA.[43] However, the situation became uncomfortable as IFES expanded because "certain governments mistakenly equated an American office with a loyalty to American foreign policy."[44] Hence it was decided to move to neutral Switzerland, but diplomatic care was taken; as Woods recalls, "the only stipulation made was that if the move was to be to Switzerland, because of the location of the World Council of Churches and the World Student Christian Federation, the office should not be in Geneva."[45] Even if getting accustomed to French-speaking Switzerland would not prove easy for Woods, the new location, now safe from the politically loaded association with the United

---

41. InterVarsity, "Our Ministry," accessed 10 March 2016, https://intervarsity.org/our-ministry.

42. Samuel Escobar, "A New Time for Mission: Plenary Address to IFES WA 1999" (Hyundai Learning Center, Yong-In, South Korea, 23 July 1999), 4, IFES e-archives.

43. Woods resigned from IVCF Canada in 1952 and from IVCF USA in 1961.

44. Lowman, *Day of His Power*, 359.

45. Woods, "IFES History Draft," ch. 2, p. 7.

States, would soon become a rallying point for IFES staff reporting and seeking advice. Woods himself would later boast that

> visitors were constantly amazed at the very modest, frugal central offices a growing international movement maintained. It was, however, by these strict economies that funds were available for global expansion and it was the general conviction that as little as possible should be spent in overheads and as much of each dollar given be sent abroad for student evangelization.[46]

The move to Switzerland was not only for political reasons but also financial, allowing for more funding to be flexibly allocated, as Woods recalls: "Having our base in Lausanne, Switzerland, resulted in increased Swiss contributions. The British IVF was then responsible for underwriting the costs of the African work, handing it over to IFES in 1973."[47]

Furthermore, in the mid 1960s IFES acquired Schloss Mittersill, a medieval castle in the Austrian Tyrol, as an international training centre for IFES. For Woods, such a training centre was a dream come true and he put significant energy into the project. Numerous memorable regional and international training events, as well as General Committees, took place in the castle. The centre, which ran into innumerable management and financial issues, was eventually sold in 2009.[48] Its heyday, however, was in the 1980s especially because of its strategic geographical location: it was much easier to get Eastern European students to Austria than it would have been to most other Western countries.

Whither Missions?

In the 1960s, the world of missions was subjected to intense scrutiny, which did not spare IFES. Whereas "among mainline Protestants, self-criticism of paternalistic mission practices led to new mission theories of 'partnership' from the 1960s onward,"[49] IFES members took notice of the changes without

---

46. Woods, ch. 2, p. 9. Personal explorations by the writer of this work at the different locations in Lausanne where Woods and the IFES office were based confirm the modesty – even depressing character – of the quarters chosen: nobody would have guessed that a growing international organization was operating from these insignificant apartments.

47. Appendix J to "Minutes of the Meeting of the Executive Committee" (1988), 1.

48. For more on Schloss Mittersill, see Alex Williams, *Holy Spy* (Budapest: Harmat, 2003); MacLeod, *C. Stacey Woods*, ch. 15.

49. Dana L. Robert, *Christian Mission: How Christianity Became a World Religion* (Hoboken: Wiley & Sons, 2009), 71.

changing their overall approaches to mission. Having been founded later than many other missionary organizations and operating out of a federalist framework, IFES was more contextual and emphasized local leadership more than many older ventures.

In this regard, Woods's account of IFES's pioneering work in Africa in the wake of decolonization is illuminating. In the late 1940s, it was apparent that the foundation of numerous new universities in the newly independent nations of Africa represented an extraordinary potential for growth for IFES. However, they were not alone in the field and the old conflicts with the WSCF soon resumed in the form of a "proxy war." In Woods's account,

> quickly the World Student Christian Federation moved to head off the possibility of the formation of any evangelical student movement in these new universities. The doctrine of ecumenical unity was proclaimed. University authorities promised not to permit a second Christian movement on their campuses. In some cases, university chaplains were appointed to control student religious activity. The World Student Christian Federation sent out its own staff to Africa.[50]

The era of decolonization opened up competition for student movements on the African continent and ecumenical circles seemed to have decided to avert the divided witness that the Western universities had shown so far. IFES was relatively powerless in the face of such pushback: "The door seemed shut fast to the IFES. But unknown or unrealized by us, God had his own strategy. He had his own 'fifth column' in these same universities with their widespread campuses and impressive buildings."[51] Not much was left to chance, and in the same way as the former settlers were to "serve" the colonies, "as the call went out for a teaching staff for these new institutions, Christian graduates, largely from Great Britain and all formerly active in local evangelical unions, had applied and received lecturing appointments."[52]

There was a deliberate approach of putting allies in place within the universities, making it much easier for local IFES groups to emerge with the help of these lecturers. In a fascinating exercise in storytelling, Woods presents the situation thus:

---

50. Woods, *Some Ways*, 54.
51. Woods, 54.
52. Woods, 54.

Quite naturally they did what any other Christian lecturer or professor would have done. On a Sunday afternoon these men invited students, many of whom had had their secondary school education in missionary schools and some of whom were Christians, to their homes for a Bible exposition, or as it is known in England, a Bible "reading." This was followed by questions, discussion, prayer, tea and biscuits. Some of these students were converted. Spontaneously on their own initiative they banded together, formed Christian Unions and applied for recognition as student societies. There was no propaganda from the outside. The IFES was never mentioned. In the face of such student initiative and responsibility, the authorities had little alternative but to grant the requested recognition.[53]

The "quite natural" aspect of these initiatives might be overstated. These invitations were rather the result of thorough strategic reflection aimed at fostering the emergence of evangelical groups. As Johnson explains, "We put up all our graduates overseas to the idea of getting students together for prayer and Bible study; leaving the initiative in the hands of the students, except for the jobs they hadn't the time to do."[54] The fascinating aspect of Woods's and Johnson's affirmations is their comments that the local groups emerged "spontaneously" and that there was "no propaganda from the outside." There might not have been poster advertising or shiny launching ceremonies. However, that these IVF-UK graduates were instrumental in encouraging these groups to "band together" is proof enough of the importance of support for these "indigenous" groups.

IFES leaders were not ready to question the relevance of every Christian's calling to missionary witness, including internationally. This was also in line with the WCC's motto of "mission in six continents," adopted in 1963. Accordingly, "missionaries should be appointed to go from anywhere to anywhere, according to need."[55]

The same year, one of the eight national movements welcomed into IFES was a federation of burgeoning movements, the Pan African Fellowship of Evangelical Students (PAFES), founded in 1958. This infusion of African blood into the life of IFES brought new questions, one of which was the relationship of

---

53. Woods, 54–55.
54. As quoted in Lowman, *Day of His Power*, 242.
55. Robert, *Christian Mission*, 72.

foreign missionaries to newly independent countries. The GC minutes record a long discussion in which "delegates from almost every nation represented" took part. They affirmed the "need to rethink the entire task of world missions with the realization that in many countries foreign missionary activity as we have known it will be restricted."[56] Questioning the role and conduct of missionaries was legitimate, but not the universal validity of the missionary mandate. In congruence with the traditional evangelical missionary ethos, the motion was accepted that

> the Executive Committee or a group of its appointees, including representatives from Africa, Asia and Latin America (that is, areas of the world where western missionaries have become politically *personae non gratae*), should reconsider the continuing role of western missionary effort in the light primarily of the universal commission, though not without reference to political situations, in order that western Christians may know how their brethren in these countries wish them to continue to fulfil the Lord's command and that missionary endeavour from western sources be redirected if need be.[57]

That the British delegates moved the motion can be seen either as an implicit acknowledgment that their former leadership in Africa was being questioned and that they were ready to put it on the line; or as a way of keeping the upper hand in the process of discernment. Exchanges were free of neither controversy nor power plays, as even a cursory look at the minutes of the GC shows. Some movements appear much more often than others as spearheading the charges against change, potential theological moves or rapprochement with other organizations. Some leaders gain influence over other leaders and national movements or undermine certain special ministries that they would not see as fitting into the overall priorities of the fellowship. In any case, the discussion about the role of foreign missionaries was far from closed in 1963. Indeed, Chua was later to recall that his "baptism into IFES was at the General Committee in 1967, where there were fierce ideological conflicts. Most of the delegates returned home depressed rather than refreshed."[58] Interestingly, the debates were rather those of staff members than of the student constituency –

---

56. "Minutes of the Meeting of the Sixth General Committee" (1963), 29.

57. "Minutes of the Meeting of the Sixth General Committee" (1963), 30.

58. Chua Wee Hian, "IFES General Secretary's Report 1991" (Wheaton College, Wheaton, Illinois, USA, 27.7-4.8 1991), 3, IFES e-archives, GC 1991 minutes, Appendix D.

only 35 percent of the delegates were students.[59] Not everyone was happy with the committee's procedures, however. As the minutes note,

> Asian delegates who attended the last two General Committee Conferences feel that there is a danger of giving a wrong impression concerning the nature of the IFES. So much time is spent on discussing organisational and constitutional details that the sense of being a true fellowship in the Spirit is obscured. It appears to us that the business sessions tend to be dominated by some delegates whose insistence upon the minutiae of organization has deflected us from discussing the really important issues. We feel the need for spending much more time in prayer, sharing and *facing up to the tremendous opportunities and difficulties in our individual countries.*[60]

This critique represents a rather rare highlighting of the differences in perception between the West and the rest. With an intriguingly mixed-feelings voice, Bentley-Taylor, emissary of the GS and an important voice in the fellowship, reported from the 1967 GC meeting that

> when missionary work passed under review, the Europeans sat back and the note struck by the Asian, African and South American speakers was unmistakably critical. It was suggested that many have rejected the western interpretation of Christ, rather than Jesus Christ Himself. There was a call for more non-professional missionaries, Asians as well as Europeans. A demand was heard for fewer missionaries but of higher quality, for a change in their role, with more emphasis on training others, and the European was reminded of his duty to his own land and continent. Some felt that missionaries had failed to enter the most strategic areas of a nation's life, in particular that in Latin America almost nothing had been done in educated circles and in cities, so that today's low educational standard among Christian preachers was repellent to students.[61]

---

59. "Minutes of the Meeting of the Executive Committee of the IFES" (Casa Moscia, Ascona, Switzerland, 30.8–3.9 1968), 14, IFES e-archives.

60. "Minutes of the Meeting of the Executive Committee" (1968), 3; emphasis added.

61. David Bentley-Taylor, "The Seventh IFES General Committee: An Appraisal," *IFES Journal* 20, no. 3 (1967): 11–12.

For somebody who spent the eight years from 1966 to 1974 touring especially "pioneering fields,"[62] it was a rather abrasive assessment, and he indeed went on to note that he had hoped "that one non-European would be found to voice the balanced truth of missionary sacrifice and achievement."[63] Sifting through imperialism and sacrifice as motivational factors for mission was a complex task. It was not easy for Europeans to take the critique without cynicism, as, contrary to ecumenical circles, they had not been confronted with the famous 1971 call for a "moratorium on missions" by Kenyan theologian Gatu, whose address was unmistakably clear. For the reader to grasp the context in which IFES was operating, it is important to quote this well-known text:

> I am going to argue that the time has come for the withdrawal of foreign missionaries from many parts of the Third World, that the Churches of the Third World must be allowed to find their own identity and that the continuation of the present missionary movement is a hindrance to this selfhood of the Church. . . . I started by saying that the missionaries should be withdrawn from the Third World for a period of at least five years. I will go further and say that missionaries should be withdrawn, period. The reason is that we must allow God the Holy Spirit to direct our next move without giving Him a timetable. The Gospel will then have a deeper and more far-reaching effect than our mission Christianity has provided so far.[64]

While not calling for such a moratorium, evangelical leaders in close association with IFES had expressed a somewhat similar view a year earlier in the 1970 Declaration of Cochabamba:

> We recognize our debt to the missionaries who brought us the gospel. At the same time, we believe that a theological reflection relevant to our own people must take into account the dramatic reality of the Latin American scene and must make an effort to

---

62. See his anecdotal memoir: David Bentley-Taylor, "Adventures of a Christian Envoy" (photocopied manuscript, London, 1992), IFES Archive, Oxford.

63. Bentley-Taylor, "Seventh IFES General Committee," 11–12.

64. John Gatu, speech at the Mission Festival, Milwaukee, USA, 1971, published in *Church Herald*. Quoted in Bengt Sundkler and Christopher Steed, *A History of the Church in Africa* (Cambridge: CUP, 2001), 1027. The address prompted a prolonged debate in missionary circles. See "The Moratorium Debate," *International Review of Mission* 64, no. 254 (1975): 148–64.

identify and remove the foreign trappings in which the message has been wrapped.⁶⁵

This nuanced appraisal of missionary activity runs contrary to many contemporary narratives which see Western missionary presence in a much dimmer light.⁶⁶ The concern was overtly missiological: IFES leaders believed in the same gospel and in the importance of sharing it with their fellow citizens, yet (Western) cultural elements needed to be removed to allow for more contextual appropriation. The influence of the Latin American IFES workers on the future shape of evangelicalism is further evidenced in the statement adopted at Lausanne 1974, which posited that "a reduction of foreign missionaries and money in an evangelized country may sometimes be necessary to facilitate the national church's growth in self-reliance and to release resources for unevangelized areas."⁶⁷

The assessment from several IFES Majority World leaders suggested that IFES had provided them with a framework of relative freedom, which allowed them to develop their own contextual Christian ethos. In 1977, Escobar was already aware of the need to correct narratives when he affirmed that

> our student movements have been exposed in university and through some theological literature to sociological analyses of missions that have created a generally negative attitude. I feel it is necessary to correct it. Of course, many students in our movements have also suffered the effects of a naive fundamentalist approach to missions, relations between missionaries and nationals, etc. I consider it an important task to establish links between the missionary enterprise and our movements, to inform about needs, to challenge with the biblical command to see the world with a missionary vision.⁶⁸

Similarly, Brown would boast in 1997 that, in his eyes, IFES had contributed ahead of its time missiologically:

---

65. "Evangelical Declaration of Cochabamba: At the Founding Meeting of the Fraternidad Teológica Latinoamericana, December, 1970," *Journal of Latin American Theology* 11, no. 2 (2016): 186.

66. Robert, *Christian Mission*, 93.

67. Lausanne Movement, "The Lausanne Covenant" (1 Aug. 1974), para. 9, https://www.lausanne.org/content/covenant/lausanne-covenant.

68. Samuel Escobar, "Report of the IFES Associate General Secretary at Large" (Oxon, England, 28.9–3.10 1977), 2, IFES e-archives, EC 1977 minutes, Appendix E.

IFES has helped the development of new models of mission. Fifty years ago, the idea of autonomous movements led by nationals joining together to further the cause of the gospel was unique. It freed global mission from the controls of western churches and organizations, and emphasized values such as respect for local Christians, national ownership and the fair sharing of resources. Today, such things are taken for granted in most missionary agencies and training institutions.[69]

These developments were the consequence of the conviction that all believers have *immediate* access to God and can theologize in the contexts in which they are placed to *mediate* their faith to their environment. This represents challenges also to the fellowship in which these believers *participate*: a challenge of mutual listening and respect.

Staying Firm through the Storm of 1968

The year 1968 marked a milestone in the history of student ministry. IFES did not hold any global event. Conversely, the WSCF met in Finland for a student conference, immediately followed by its Federation Assembly in Uppsala, Sweden. Both meetings were troubled: some plenary speakers were not allowed to address the students, and a revolutionary spirit also characterized the WCC's meeting.[70] In Lehtonen's words, the atmosphere of the time was such that "students looked for liberation from paternalism and authoritarian and hierarchical structures. Democratization of the university society and some forms of socialism were apparent goals."[71] McLeod also notes a reorientation in students' concerns, highlighting that "as the political temperature reached a boiling point in 1968, student Christian organizations were torn apart, as

---

69. Lindsay Brown, "IFES Jubilee," *Highlights* (Dec. 1997), 2.

70. The centenary historical account of the WSCF is intriguingly quiet on this turbulent time and attributes most challenges to financial difficulties; see Potter and Wieser, *Seeking and Serving*, which does not mention IFES one single time. Conversely, the WSCF General Secretary between 1968 and 1973 wrote a detailed account of the events, notably published by an evangelical publisher because the editors of the official history did not want to publish his account; see Lehtonen, *Story of a Storm*, xix. In the most recent WSCF history, Boyd offers a detailed and nuanced account including critical voices; see Boyd, *Student Christian Movement*, ch. 6.

71. Lehtonen, *Story of a Storm*, 58.

many members decided that working for the revolution was the top priority and everything else was an irrelevant sideshow."[72]

Space does not permit an extensive and fair account of the WSCF-WCC events. However, whatever perspective the reader takes on the events recounted by several attendees of these meetings, they were significant for IFES, marking the disappearance of the WSCF as an effective institutional competitor. After 1968–1972, the WSCF was considered by IFES and other analysts as only a shadow of its former glory. In the WSCF General Secretary's own sombre words, "the Federation left the responsibility for evangelism to the churches' more heavily institutionalized ministries and to a number of evangelical Student organizations."[73] Bruce goes as far as calling this period the "collapse of the SCM,"[74] while Chua would warn that

> with the semi-demise of the SCM in many countries, there has been a tendency for some of our more established movements to be complacent and to strive at respectability. However, several movements have become aware of this danger and have called members to fresh commitment to Jesus Christ and to the proclamation of His Gospel.[75]

If Westerners deplored significant losses from the Christian churches, others were encouraging their fellow workers to stand up to the challenge. Illustrative of this is one of the regular surveys of the world situation published in the *IFES Journal*:

> We are living among new pagans. Christian students and professors in all universities, in Paris and in Makerere, in Djakarta, Rio de Janeiro and Columbia, have to face this fact which unites them: they stand as a minority among non-Christians. But these pagans among whom we live do not resemble the brands classified in religious textbooks. Very often, they are old Christians, old Moslems, old Buddhists, but they are also a new kind of men and women, transformed by the new society which is being born.[76]

---

72. Hugh McLeod, "The Crisis of Christianity in the West: Entering a Post-Christian Era?," in *World Christianities c.1914–c.2000*, ed. Hugh McLeod, vol. 9 of *The Cambridge History of Christianity* (Cambridge: CUP, 2006), 339.

73. Lehtonen, *Story of a Storm*, 325.

74. Preston, "Collapse of the SCM."

75. Chua Wee Hian, "Report of the General Secretary" (Schloss Mittersill, Austria, 1974), 1, IFES e-archives, EC 1974 minutes, Appendix A.

76. Paul D. Fueter, "New Christians for New Pagans," *IFES Journal* 21, no. 3 (1968): 1.

Qualifying the world as populated by "new pagans" was a daring rhetorical framing aimed at motivating the IFES troops. How were staff members to motivate Christian students without pushing them? The issue of paternalism, albeit loosely defined, was also treated in a significant issue of the *IFES Journal*. The author – a staff worker in Latin America – stressed the difference between religious paternalism, assumed to be wrong, and the IFES approach to leadership, which he felt was much more genuine and effective for witness on campus. In his starkly expressed contrast,

> religion in this culture for centuries has meant going to the "padre" to confess your sins, find out what God's will is, and have a Mass said for your beloved dead in purgatory. Is it any wonder that in regard to the things of God, many students feel "unworthy" to attempt leadership and tend to wait for "the professionals" to do it?[77]

Without developing his critique much further, Hanks offered his fellow staff members some strategic points to "slay the dragon of paternalism."[78] They were to

> enrol in university, encourage prayer at the university, encourage Bible study at the university, emphasize biographical leadership studies in the Bible to tackle the model of the *caudillo*, and last but not least, to encourage pastors in their ministry to students. . . . If you can help and encourage pastors to develop a ministry of Biblical expository preaching, of sympathetic prayer for their "rebel students" in the university, you may accomplish more than by your direct ministry on campus.[79]

The IFES leadership tried to walk on the narrow path of tradition and novelty: never did the world seem to set the agenda, but neither was IFES watertight to the significant changes in the mood of the day. This difficult exercise in tightrope walking lasted a long time: the 1971 GC saw numerous doctrinal and missiological tensions discussed.

---

77. Tom Hanks, "Paternalistic – Me?," *IFES Journal* 21, no. 1 (1968): 2.
78. Hanks, "Paternalistic," 3.
79. Hanks, 5.

Traditional Doctrines for Turbulent Times: General Committee 1971

If 1968 was a turning point for the WSCF, the 1971 IFES General Committee was similarly a time of heavy exchanges. Doctrinal tensions were numerous. Papers were circulated and discussed on the authority of the Bible, but matters of procedure also occupied the delegates to a significant degree. The 1971 GC also represented the dusk of the era of the founding fathers: Woods was the outgoing GS, and vice-president Lloyd-Jones made his last major appearance as Bible expositor. His expositions served as a sort of theological testament and are summarized thus by Catherwood:

> "What, then, is to be our method in defining what an Evangelical is? The method, of course, is primarily Biblical. The great slogan of the Reformation, *sola scriptura*, has always been the slogan of the true Evangelical. The Evangelical starts with the Bible. He is a man of the Book. This is his only authority and he submits himself in everything to this." He went on to remind his audience in the third lecture, having quoted from the IFES basis of faith that he had helped to draw up some twenty-five years earlier: "Scripture is our *sole* authority . . . our only authority."[80]

The tone was set: in a time of theological and social turmoil, the traditional evangelical stance was to be kept unabashedly. It is evident that a confrontation with the mood of the time had not been avoided: student unrest was still happening in many countries and the "social question" was not confined to ecumenical circles. Neither was the question of authority which, according to a strikingly negative but nevertheless published report of the student training which had taken place directly prior to the GC, was really the stumbling block of the day, as was the link between theory and practice:

> The well-known men who brought the morning messages did not expound biblical texts as much as expound their applications of certain biblical truths. . . . For the mature groups, the less structured exposure to God's Word was the fellowship needed after an intensive day. But some of the younger groups floundered either in subjectivism or virtual indifference to the selected texts. Perhaps this should be a warning for us: At a time when we are strongly reinforcing our enunciations of our biblical position and vigorously encouraging production of biblical literature, we must

---

80. Christopher Catherwood, *Martyn Lloyd-Jones: His Life and Relevance for the 21st Century* (Nottingham: Inter-Varsity Press, 2015), 51.

simultaneously provide in training courses maximum initiation into personal examination of the Bible on a practical level.[81]

At the GC meeting, besides these habitual Bible expositions and exemplary of the contextual awareness of the IFES leadership of the time, the following discussion papers were submitted to several working groups:

1. Student Unrest: Its Causes, Characteristics and Cures
2. Christianity and Other Religions
3. The Salvation of the Individual and the Place of Social Work in Christian Service
4. Authority, Permanent Truth and Changing Standards
5. Christian Morality in a Non-Christian Society[82]

Bürki's paper on "Student Unrest" is particularly interesting as a window into the thinking of the rising generation. Having astutely noted that "student unrest and rebellion has been a university tradition ever since universities came into existence,"[83] he gives the reasons for the recent unrest as, in his view, essentially threefold:

> (a) the student's prolonged dependence on his family, (b) a sharpened consciousness and critical attitude as a result of intellectual pursuits, (c) the prestige of youth in society, a relatively late phenomenon, which increases their sense of irritation faced with their actual powerlessness in decision-making.[84]

For Bürki, essential to the emergence of this impatience towards felt powerlessness in questions of authority was a crisis in the status of reason, as he further notes:

> The crisis of authority has its parallel in the crisis of autonomous reason. The conviction of the meaninglessness of academic studies and the dehumanising effect of analytical methods in the human sciences in the face of personal and social needs drives

---

81. "Instruction, Imitation, Initiation: A Composite Report (IFES Training Course, Mittersill, 1971)," *IFES Journal* 25, no. 3 (1971): 16.

82. "Minutes of the Meeting of the Eighth General Committee of the IFES – 1971" (Schloss Mittersill, Austria, 28 Aug. 1971), 23, IFES e-archives.

83. Hans Bürki, "Student Unrest: Its Causes, Characteristics and Cures," seminar paper (Schloss Mittersill, Austria, 1971), 1, IFES e-archives, GC 1971 minutes, Appendix J.

84. Bürki, "Student Unrest," 1.

students (a) to "escape from reason" (F. Schaeffer) and from society into experimenting with drugs, transcendental meditation etc. (George B. Leonard, *Education and Ecstasy*), [and] (b) to engage in revolutionary movements of different kinds.... "Student unrest reflects the complex situation of alienation in present-day society with its youth subculture, pluralistic value system, polarisation of movements."[85]

By citing socio-economic factors and noting the "complex situation of alienation in present-day society with its youth subculture, pluralistic value system, polarisation of movements," Bürki's main goal was to try to provide a Christian perspective on the unrest and what an adequate response from IFES groups might be. Taking the example of a study carried out by the Japanese IFES movement KGK which showed that students tended to be motivated by a strong sense of despair, Bürki went on to note that the situation of unrest could possibly mean difficulties for Christian groups, as the fundamental tenets of the faith were attacked for being essentially anti-human: "faith in the only Redeemer from sin, obedience to the Lord of all, keeps man in bondage."[86]

What Bürki offered to counter the charge was, on the one hand, renewed awareness of the seriousness of the situation together with the stringency of the accusations levelled at Christians, but, on the other hand, a calling back to the fundamentals of the faith.

In a development worth quoting at length, Bürki outlined his proposed approach:

> Christians need to adopt a truly critical and prophetic attitude towards believers and conditions within the Church, the university and the world as a whole. We must squarely confront the present utter hopelessness and refuse the falsehood and deception of the so-called healing process of alienation itself. We have particularly to analyse the presuppositions of the different tenets of the new theological liberalism and its social ethics, and expose them to the comprehensive nature of the Gospel.[87]

Sensitive engagement together with forceful affirmation was the prescribed cure for the student unrest. Whereas the WSCF circles advocated *dialogue* as

---

85. Bürki, 1.
86. Bürki, 2.
87. Bürki, 2.

their preferred way of engaging the world, Bürki was adamant that a solely dialogical method would not bear lasting fruit:

> In the training of students we must re-affirm and use the antithetical method whereby the Bible teaches its truth. The New Testament denotes this method by the word *katekesis* (1 Cor. 14:19; cf. Deut. 6:7) which excludes *dialektike* as method of teaching Biblical truth. This does not mean that "dialogue" is of no value in evangelism; it means that the ultimate truth about God, man and the world can only be understood if we accept the authority of the Bible as the Word of God, e.g. if Biblical revelation is the final framework for our reasoning.[88]

Lastly, Bürki also briefly touched upon the actual involvement of IFES student groups in the protests and agitation taking place on their campuses. One cannot but read a certain nervousness in the linking of participation and observation with Christian witness, a nervousness which is found in many other later IFES documents as well:

> Christian student groups which, on the one hand, have been practically involved in student strife and which on the other have tried to carry out the objectives of the Christian fellowship in a narrower sense, have been greatly blessed. If Christian students had formed separate groups besides the Christian Union to give direction to acute campus problems in a responsible way and carry it out, then their witness to Christ might have been more effective. If such specialised groups are formed within the Christian Union the witnessing activities of the union tend to lose their vitality. Whether this loss is a necessary consequence needs to be investigated. It is important to clarify the relation of purpose and means in such separate (or specialised) groups. They should have the full support and fellowship of the whole Christian Union and of the churches.[89]

No written record of the discussions which took place after the presentation of the papers is preserved, but it is safe to assume that they were tense, as, when the delegates asked for the papers to be distributed to a wider circle within IFES, "Prof. Wisløff drew attention to the fact that these papers were not in any

---

88. Bürki, 2–3.
89. Bürki, 3.

way official papers, and that disagreement had been expressed at certain times during group discussion of these papers."[90] This indicates a certain unease from some senior leaders towards an emerging new generation of leaders. As the aforementioned critical report pointedly noted: "We are not merely thinking, praying beings. We are also feeling, deciding, acting persons. Imagine 'old' Christians (e.g. staff workers!) going through a revolution."[91] New leaders were indeed emerging, as the following developments show.

As a result of these many discussions, the attendees resolved to request the Executive to write an introduction to the IFES doctrinal basis in line with the previously explored assertive approach.[92]

In a world of revolutions, the idea that students themselves were the key local agents of worldwide mission was strengthening and rendered even more relevant in the wake of decolonization. From then on, the relationship of indigenous mission to international structures and theological currents was a marked element of the IFES identity.

---

90. "Minutes of the Meeting of the Eighth General Committee" (1971).
91. "Instruction, Imitation, Initiation," 16.
92. See below, "Theological Analysis," p. 211, and A Firm Basis, p. 189.

6

When the South Comes North: The 1970s

The 1970s were a period of intense theological reflection in the Majority World, deemed a "Golden Decade."[1] It is crucial to briefly survey the salient aspects of the time since an essential part of Latin American evangelical theological developments occurred through the work of several IFES senior staff workers, most notably Escobar, Padilla and Arana.[2] Moreover, in 1972, after twenty-five years in office, Woods handed over the baton of GS to Hong Kong-born Chua, a sign of the growing power of non-Western figures in the senior leadership and also some new teachings.[3]

The surge in major theological figures from the Majority World meant for the wider evangelical constituency an intense questioning of its theological premises. This new group of influential figures was in part the result of IFES's practice of letting local leadership develop. This at least was the way both Padilla and Chua would present it to North American students at the 1973 Urbana Conference:

---

1. Daniel Salinas, *Latin American Evangelical Theology in the 1970's: The Golden Decade*, Religion in the Americas Series (Leiden: Brill, 2009).

2. All three had been the main movers of the foundation of the Latin American Theological Fraternity (FTL) in Cochabamba in December 1970 where they had already clashed with Peter Wagner of Fuller Seminary over hermeneutical questions. See MacLeod, *C. Stacey Woods*, 220–21. For the work of the FTL, including numerous archive documents, see "FTL: Fraternidad Teológica Latinoamericana," accessed 27 July 2020, https://ftl-al.com/.

3. Chua showed deep interest in the relationships students entertained with their families, for example, hence bringing to the table the question of family loyalties in the context of communal cultures, a consideration long overdue in IFES's teaching on evangelism. For teachings and anecdotal stories, see Chua Wee Hian, *Getting through Customs: The Global Jottings of Chua Wee Hian* (Leicester: Inter-Varsity Press, 1992).

> Each movement is independent. Each works its own program. Each is to follow the Lord's leading. We do not have any "canned" methods of evangelism and do not lay down the program for anybody. We try to help the students by giving them training, especially regarding the study of the Scripture.[4]

Conversely, as Hutchison and Wolffe suggest,

> Western Evangelicals had tended to send overseas their worker-missionaries rather than their theologians. Their faith in the sufficiency of the cross also meant that Africans, Asians and others needed to work out for themselves what being a Christian in this place actually meant. In return, Westerners who encountered this new dynamism were challenged to the core as to how to deal with their own Eurocentric, Enlightenment traditions.[5]

This encounter did not happen smoothly everywhere.[6] In what follows, the common history of IFES and the 1974 Lausanne Congress will be presented, but it is important to set it in the proper context of theological engagement with the complex circumstances of post-war Latin America.

Coming to Terms with Marxism: Latin America and Misión Integral

> The evangelical university movement, often overlooked in the historical record of Protestantism, has come to contribute its restless, cutting-edge thinking to efforts to express the evangelical faith in terms applicable to conditions on the continent.[7]

The concept of *integral mission* is possibly the biggest theological and missiological contribution of IFES to the church, at least at the end of the twentieth century. Its originator, C. René Padilla, challenged the theological

---

4. Chua Wee Hian and C. René Padilla, "God's Work in the World Today," in *Jesus Christ: Lord of the Universe, Hope of the World; Urbana 1973*, ed. David M. Howard (Downers Grove: InterVarsity Press, 1974), 168.

5. Hutchinson and Wolffe, *Short History*, 187.

6. Alister Chapman, "Evangelical International Relations in the Post-Colonial World: The Lausanne Movement and the Challenge of Diversity, 1974–89," *Missiology* 37, no. 3 (2009): 355–68; Michael Clawson, "Misión Integral and Progressive Evangelicalism: The Latin American Influence on the North American Emerging Church," *Religions* 3, no. 3 (2012): 790–807; Brian Stanley, "'Lausanne 1974': The Challenge from the Majority World to Northern-Hemisphere Evangelicalism," *Journal of Ecclesiastical History* 64, no. 3 (2013): 533–51.

7. Lic Edgar Alan Perdomo, "Una descripción histórica de la teología evangélica latinoamericana (Segunda de dos partes)," *Kairos* 33 (2003): 94–95.

world of the day primarily because of his experiences working with students throughout Latin America.

Universities in Turmoil

IFES was not alone in thinking about the issues of the day. Kirkpatrick notes that "reports from ecumenical SCM staff workers are strikingly similar to those of IFES staff."[8] Essential for understanding the context was the complex situation of Latin American universities in the 1960s and 1970s. The student population had surged to numbers previously unheard of;[9] Bürki noted that "while until 50 years ago university education was an economical luxury, it has now become an economic and national necessity."[10]

Arana[11] described Marxist groups in Latin America as "the most active and militant groups in the universities [who] present a particular attraction by their aim to change life into something worthy of human beings."[12] This represented a significant challenge for Christians, because they were not considered natural allies of the revolutionary spirit of the day:

> It is an undeniable fact that for millions and millions of Latin Americans today the voice of the church is not the voice of God nor are her interests the interests of their respective countries. They look upon her as a symbol of the past, as the remains of an era which must be left behind with all the fanaticism, injustice, and intolerance which characterized it.[13]

How would Protestant and evangelical theologians, university-educated and therefore not belonging to the poorest, rise to the challenge if, as Gebara recalls, "the poor called the institutional church into question and brought about a new movement in theology. Many Protestant theologians and

---

8. David C. Kirkpatrick, "C. René Padilla and the Origins of Integral Mission in Post-War Latin America," *The Journal of Ecclesiastical History* 67, no. 2 (2016): 362.

9. "The total number of graduates between 1940 and 1950 numbered only 62,584, while in the year 1960 alone, the university had over 70,000 students." Kirkpatrick, "Origins of Integral Mission," 356.

10. Hans Bürki, "The Confrontation of Evangelism with Ideology," *IFES Journal* 1 (1967): 25.

11. Peruvian Presbyterian pastor Arana was Associate General Secretary (AGS) for Latin America.

12. Pedro Arana, "Evangelization in the Latin American University," *International Review of Mission* 63, no. 252 (1974): 508.

13. C. René Padilla, "Student Witness in Latin America Today," *IFES Journal* 2 (1966): 14.

communities were also called into question"?[14] Voelkel recalls the following anecdote about Samuel Escobar:

> Knowing that Samuel had once been strongly attracted to Marxism, I asked him, "What persuaded you to follow Christ?" Samuel reviewed his student days. The Communists had fired his imagination to serve his country and meet the social needs of his people (a vision that he had never received in his own Protestant church). However, he soon observed that most young men went through a process. Won through altruistic idealism to the Communist cause, the majority slowly became corrupted as they began to taste power. Samuel saw that the basic selfishness of the individual is a problem that Communism does not have the power to solve. This solution he had found only in Jesus Christ.[15]

The scene was set for new approaches.[16] But hard questioning came first.

Traditional Answers Falling Short

> The greatest practical issue facing the Christian student in Latin America today is not whether or not the wearing of lipstick is permissible to a Christian girl, but what course of action he is to take in the presence of the prevailing social problems and of the ideologies which purport to be able to solve them.[17]

As Padilla and Escobar often said repeatedly, their impeccable evangelical pedigree had not prepared them for the challenges they encountered.[18] Nor did Woods seem to be fully aware of the difficulties he would encounter when

---

14. Gebara, "Movement of May 1968," 265.

15. Voelkel, *Student Evangelism*, 46.

16. A noted answer from the Catholic and mainline Protestant sides was the development of liberation theology. The name of the movement, notably published in English by SCM, is taken from Gustavo Gutiérrez, *A Theology of Liberation*, trans. Caridad Inda and John Eagleson (London: SCM, 1988). Throughout the later history of IFES, those concerned about the integral mission approach championed by Padilla and Escobar regularly accused them of being (Marxist) liberation theologians, a cardinal sin in most of their adversaries' eyes. See C. René Padilla, "The Roads to Freedom: Liberation Theology," *In Touch* 2 (1979): 7.

17. Padilla, "Student Witness," 11.

18. For first-hand accounts of the history of the IFES work in Latin America, see Samuel Escobar, *La chispa y la llama: breve historia de la Comunidad Internacional de Estudiantes Evangélicos en América Latina* (Buenos Aires: Ediciones Certeza, 1978); Samuel Escobar, *La chispa y la llama: Volumen II* (Buenos Aires: Certeza Unida, 2022).

in 1958 he challenged Padilla's aspiration to undertake further studies, thus delaying his beginnings as a staff worker. As Padilla recalls, "'Well,' he [Woods] said, 'you don't need more studies. Why don't you just go? You'll learn more by doing.' [I] say, 'Well, Stacey, just give me time.' And I'm glad I stayed."[19] Yet upon returning to Latin America from his studies at Wheaton College, Padilla found himself "lacking a social ethic. My years of studies in the United States had not prepared me for the sort of theological reflection that was urgently needed in a revolutionary situation!"[20] Escobar similarly argued, in a groundbreaking booklet in 1972, that the contemporary situation was taking

> Evangelicals by surprise with questions for which we do not have answers, for we should have thought about them years ago. In the churches, the generation gap is clear proof that this is so, and some of our best young people are leaving in search of the answers elsewhere.[21]

The debate over the adequacy of Western evangelical theology became a constant of the following decades. Indeed, IFES maintained an ambiguous relationship with the "powerhouse" of global evangelical activism, the Billy Graham Evangelistic Association (BGEA), for in their eyes, "a battle for the church in Latin America was being fought between the liberal, ecumenical promoters of the social gospel, and conservative Evangelicals like themselves who emphasized personal conversion to Christianity as the solution to both individual and social sin."[22]

Many young IFES staff workers struggled with the theology promoted by many Western missionaries, which gave no answers to the questions of the students, as it consequently risked dividing lives into sacred and secular spheres: "Take the case of the Christian student who has grown up surrounded by the care of believing parents. He has managed to divide his life into two

---

19. "T2. Oral History Interview with René Padilla," transcript of audio tape, vol. 2, 361 (Wheaton College, 1987), 2, https://archives.wheaton.edu/repositories/4/archival_objects/238467.

20. C. René Padilla, "My Theological Pilgrimage," in *Shaping a Global Theological Mind*, ed. Darren C. Marks (Aldershot: Ashgate, 2008), 130.

21. Samuel Escobar, "The Social Impact of the Gospel," in *Is Revolution Change?*, ed. Brian Griffiths, IVP Pocketbook (London: Inter-Varsity Press, 1972), 84.

22. Clawson, "Misión Integral," 791. The CLADE 1 Conference held in 1969 was organized by the Billy Graham Evangelistic Association, notably promoting Peter Wagner's *Latin American Theology: Radical or Evangelical?*

neat compartments: 'the sacred,' including an assortment of church activities, and 'the secular,' comprising everything related to his studies."[23]

Another inadequacy the IFES workers observed was the missionaries' apparent lack of personal, long-term commitment necessary in ministry to university students:

> A great portion of the present world population (especially among university students and intellectuals) becomes increasingly suspicious of any slightest hint of indoctrinating practices. They will test on purpose the genuineness of the Christian's interest towards them. Much of the so-called follow-up problem reveals a lack of true concern for the total life of other persons.[24]

If the Latin American IFES staff workers challenged theological fundamentals – going so far as to call fundamentalism a "distortion of orthodoxy,"[25] their commitment to scriptural authority remained unabated. They affirmed that "the need of the hour is to turn to the Word of God in submission to the Holy Spirit. It involves returning to the Bible and to the Lord who reigns through it, as well as calling into question our 'evangelical traditions' in light of written revelation."[26] Given the importance of hermeneutics in the history and theology of IFES, the following story told by Padilla is worth quoting at length:

> Upon returning to Latin America as a staff worker with the IFES, the questions posed by university students and others forced me to see that the historical-grammatical approach to hermeneutics was a good and necessary step, but it was not enough. The fact was that if I was to help Christian university students to witness to Jesus Christ in a context of injustice and poverty, it was not enough to teach them to study the Scriptures with the focus on the message in its original contexts. I had to help them relate biblical teaching to human life in all its dimensions.[27]

The methods of these IFES workers did not go unchallenged. Students and student leaders were trying to *mediate back* their experiences to church leaders,

---

23. Padilla, "Student Witness," 16.
24. Bürki, "Confrontation," 26.
25. Samuel Escobar, "Social Concern and World Evangelism," in *Christ the Liberator*, ed. John R. W. Stott, Urbana 70 (Downers Grove: InterVarsity Press, 1971), 104.
26. "Evangelical Declaration of Cochabamba," 187.
27. Padilla, "Theological Pilgrimage," 130.

but this was not always well received: "There was very little understanding on the part of the leadership. Usually, the pastors would not be very open to the idea of . . . an interdenominational student group."[28] Some also expressed their support, but it was, overall, an arduous and lengthy task to pioneer and strengthen IFES groups. Padilla recalls:

> It would not be unfair to say that to some missionaries, perhaps many [chuckles] missionaries, the student movement was a sort of a threat. We were discussing social issues. You could not . . . do anything else than that. I mean . . . you had to discuss social issues, and try to begin to understand or at least explore the whole question of the relationship between the gospel and social justice. You see, in the midst of a revolutionary situation you cannot spiritualize the gospel.[29]

Interestingly, little of the intense missiological reflection that was starting to be done within IFES, especially in Latin America, got a wider audience through the *IFES Journal*. The publication was discontinued in 1972 because "it was generally felt that the *IFES Journal* was not meeting the needs of students."[30]

A New Theology for a New Era

The new theologians who were growing within IFES had to face two fronts simultaneously. At times, the ministry of IFES was considered dangerous by Christians because of the novel answers given to issues evangelicals were not used to addressing. But it was also considered a danger by revolutionaries who considered especially *evangelical* Christianity to be a foreign import. As Padilla recalls,

> we were probably the only ones that were trying to provide a Christian social ethic to the students and help them think through questions related to our own concrete situation of poverty and injustice. We were often attacked by Marxists who said that we were, well, paid by the CIA or that kind of thing. And yet, on the

---

28. "Interview with René Padilla," 2, 2:3.
29. "Interview with René Padilla," 2, 2:5.
30. "Minutes of the Meeting of the Executive Committee of the IFES" (Sanden Bjerggard, Denmark, Sep. 1972), 17, IFES e-archives. Losses in readership were attributed to the lack of publicity and the old-fashioned layout.

other hand, we were accused by good brethren and sisters for being Marxist.[31]

The theological response had to try to fend off rebuttals from friends and foes alike, which proved to be a long-lasting exercise in maintaining equilibrium. Perhaps the most significant new theological response that IFES workers developed was what would soon be called "Integral mission." This was a critical reflection of liberation theology, which they knew first-hand, Arana having attended Gutiérrez's summer courses which became his magnum opus.[32] Contrary to what some critics claimed,[33] the inspiration for this approach to missionary witness was not borrowing from liberation theology. It shared a deep concern for the poor – famously termed the "preferential option for the poor" – but also insisted on *gospel proclamation*.[34] Kirkpatrick offers a sharp summary of the integral mission developed by the IFES staff workers:

> The proclamation of the gospel (*kerygma*) and the demonstration of the gospel that gives itself in service (*diakonía*) form an indivisible (indissoluble) whole. One without the other is an incomplete, mutilated (*mutilado*) gospel and, consequently, contrary to the will of God. From this perspective, it is foolish to ask about the relative importance of evangelism and social responsibility. This would be equivalent to asking about the relative importance of the right wing and the left wing of a plane.[35]

Some of the most detailed articulations of this new missiology were publicly presented at the Lausanne Congress. In the field, integral mission was promoted during camps organized for students: Bible studies and discussions took place in the mornings and service to poor neighbourhoods in the afternoons. In the universities, traditional evangelistic talks were often supplemented with talks tackling urgent issues of the local students from a scholarly point of view and proposing Christian approaches. Indeed, "students who may never be

---

31. "Interview with René Padilla," 2, 2:5.

32. David C. Kirkpatrick, *A Gospel for the Poor: Global Social Christianity and the Latin American Evangelical Left* (Philadelphia: University of Pennsylvania Press, 2019), 35.

33. Notably Richard Quebedeaux, *The Worldly Evangelicals* (San Francisco: Harper & Row, 1980).

34. "We also believed that, to reach the conclusion of this *preferential option*, it was not necessary to depend on Marxist sociology with its one-size-fits-all prescription for different contexts." Pedro Arana, "Towards a Biblical Public Theology," *Journal of Latin American Theology* 11, no. 2 (2016): 35–59.

35. Kirkpatrick, "Origins of Integral Mission," 368.

persuaded to attend a church or even a Bible study held in a classroom may, however, gladly attend a lecture dealing with a contemporary issue from a Christian perspective."[36] These innovative talks were often published as booklets or mimeographed documents and reached a relatively large audience.[37]

Hence, a critical missiological insight for reaching the specific public of university students was supported by IFES's commitment to student leadership. In Padilla's vivid depiction of a student worker's job description, contrasted with that of a foreign missionary, the picture is clear:

> Suffice it to say that his [the IFES staff worker's] main task is the training of disciples among the students that they in turn may become living witnesses within the university. Naturally, he is to teach not only by word, but also by example. Otherwise, he is a functioneer of the Gospel. But he is far from fulfilling his commission unless he fully recognizes that there is no better evangelist among students than those who are students themselves, and that the continuous intervention of "full-time" student evangelists may produce immediate statistical results but in the long run will be inimical to the development of responsible leaders.[38]

Student Missiology for the Benefit of the Church

> IFES in Latin America pioneered a new style of being Evangelical which was penetrating in its social criticism and unusually conscious of the dangers of religious imperialism.[39]

At this point, the reader might wonder about the relationship of the development of integral mission to the idea that the "priesthood of all believers" is essential to understanding the ministry of IFES.

Archival evidence – which was increasingly insistent on the importance of local church involvement – leads the historian to conclude that if leaders need to insist on something, it means that either their constituency needs

---

36. Padilla, "Student Witness," 21.
37. Possibly the best known of these published series of talks are Samuel Escobar, *Diálogo entre Cristo y Marx y otros ensayos* (Lima: AGEUP, 1969); Samuel Escobar, C. René Padilla and Edwin Yamauchi, eds., *Quien es Cristo hoy?* (Buenos Aires: Ediciones Certeza, 1971).
38. Padilla, "Student Witness," 19–20.
39. Stanley, *Christianity in the Twentieth Century*, 536.

to be reminded of a certain aspect; or that the other players and potential competitors need to be reassured in the face of growing concerns; or both. IFES was tapping into a reservoir of human resources that church leaders were similarly targeting. Similarly, IFES students and staff might have found their involvement in student mission more fulfilling than that in their local churches.

In any case, the very fact that it was the Lausanne Congress that significantly fostered the global influence of major IFES actors shows that their reflections were considered helpful for a vast array of church and parachurch ministries worldwide. Because of the tentative yet somewhat avant-garde nature of student ministry, they could think ahead of many church leaders and hence served the church through their thinking. As Padilla appreciatively notes,

> time for theological work as such was limited, but one can hardly exaggerate the importance that the IFES emphasis on the development of autochthonous national student-led movements had for those of us who were privileged to serve as student workers. *We were given freedom to think and to creatively respond to the demands of the time without feeling compelled to conform to a ready-made imported program.* As a result, the *IFES in Latin America became a seedbed of a theology rooted in Scripture yet at the same time deeply aware of the need to spell out the practical social implications of the biblical message for the life and mission of Christians as individuals and as communities* in the region.[40]

This could explain the ambiguous nature of the relationship IFES staff workers in Latin America, whose thinking we explored, maintained with mission leaders. They were natives of the continent. Their approach was decisively "missionary" in nature. They considered that they had a message to proclaim and incarnate, and that their task was not only to "join in" with the revolutionary forces. Yet, because of their insistence on local incarnational leadership, their relations with missionaries were at times tense and critical. However, this never amounted to downright rejection: much to the contrary, Escobar and Padilla often highlighted the importance of foreign missionary service to developing the gospel in their region. Similarly, Chua was adamant that "new leadership" and "a massive infusion of new blood" were essential for a breakthrough. "I am not anti-Western, nor have I any grudge to hold against

---

40. Padilla, "Theological Pilgrimage," 132; emphasis added. For more on Padilla's ecclesiology, see chapter 12.

any missionary society."[41] In this connection, Robert notes the importance of evangelical organizations rejecting the call for a "moratorium on missions." It instead seems to have focused their energies and, consequently,

> Christians organized themselves into an independent network to evangelize the "unreached peoples," the millions of non-Christians who had never heard the name of Jesus Christ. This mission movement of conservative Christians rejected the idea that the end of western colonialism required the end of cross-cultural missions.[42]

It was a reaction to the WCC's perceived failure to keep the church's mission clearly defined theologically and missiologically[43] which prompted a group of influential evangelical leaders led by Billy Graham to convene an alternative world summit in Lausanne in 1974.[44] The congress marked an important step in IFES's influence on the global evangelical stage. In Kirkpatrick's assessment, "the global Evangelical student movement provided avenues for intellectual exchange that crossed the wide boundaries of 'conservative' and 'liberal,' and 'West' versus 'Majority World.'"[45]

When IFES Changed the Theological World: Lausanne 1974

In 1972, the Executive Committee discussed the potential involvement of the GS Designate, Chua Wee Hian, and of Samuel Escobar, at the time Regional Secretary for Latin America, in the EC of the coming Lausanne Congress on World Evangelism.[46] Others have written the history of this congress and its lasting influence on the evangelical world.[47] Given the later influence of those

---

41. Chua Wee Hian, "Breakthrough in the Seventies," *IFES Journal* 23, no. 2 (1970): 11.
42. Robert, *Christian Mission*, 72.
43. Walsh states that this orientation to social problems at the expense of theology was, among other factors, the result of the influence of the new WCC GS, Eugene Carson Blake. See Walsh, "Religious Ferment," 314.
44. Stanley, *Christianity in the Twentieth Century*, 210.
45. Kirkpatrick, "Origins of Integral Mission," 354.
46. It was not the first such congress. Graham had convened a similar congress – albeit with much smaller Majority World representation – in Berlin in 1966. Escobar, Padilla and Woods had participated, if not spoken. The effectiveness of the IFES speakers at the 1974 event could in part be attributable to experience gained in Berlin.
47. Notably Chapman, "Evangelical International Relations"; Robert J. Schreiter, "From the Lausanne Covenant to the Cape Town Commitment: A Theological Assessment," *International Bulletin of Missionary Research* 35, no. 2 (2011): 88–90, 92; Clawson, "Misión Integral"; Lars Dahle, ed., *The Lausanne Movement: A Range of Perspectives* (Oxford: Wipf & Stock, 2014). In

associated with IFES in the Lausanne Movement – "90% of World Vision leaders in Africa are said to be IFES graduates and nearly 40% of the 2010 Lausanne Congress had an IFES background"[48] – it is remarkable that the participation of senior IFES staff in the first congress was debated at length within the IFES EC. In the eyes of some senior IFES people, the foreseeable participation of Roman Catholics in the congress meant the risk of public doctrinal compromise.[49] Wary of such possible association, board chair Oliver Barclay withdrew early from the congress.[50] In an exercise in balancing arguments rarely recorded in other minutes, the committee notes that

> the pros would include having an IFES "voice" and "presence" in this worldwide body. It would also reaffirm the IFES commitment to worldwide evangelism and missionary enterprise. Besides, the presence of IFES staff would also generate goodwill to evangelical participants at the Congress. It was also noted that many of the aims of the Congress overlapped with those of the IFES. The cons would include the appearance of doctrinal compromise and additional workloads.[51]

An international body theologically very close to IFES convened a meeting. Several senior staff wanted to be part of it, yet encountered strong resistance,[52] possibly also in the light of a recent GC having affirmed that "in

---

terms of composition, the attendance was essentially made up of "experts": "Less than 10 per cent of attendees were lay, whereas Graham had hoped for one-third: for an Evangelical gathering, the preponderance of professional ministers was staggering. More encouraging was the fact that half of all those attending were under the age of forty-four." Stanley, "Lausanne 1974," 540.

48. Daniel Bourdanné, "Foreword," in *Influence: The Impact of IFES on the Lives of Its Graduates* (Oxford: International Fellowship of Evangelical Students, 2015), 9.

49. "Minutes of the Meeting of the Executive Committee" (1972), 8. The minutes further note that the relationship between the Billy Graham Association (the main organizer of the Lausanne Congress) and Hans Bürki (at the time Associate General Secretary at Large) was tense following the Berlin Congress.

50. "Minutes of the Meeting of the Executive Committee" (1972), 15. For a more detailed account of the internal controversy within IFES about the participation of IFES workers at the congress – notably Woods's attempts at preventing Escobar and Padilla giving plenary speeches – see Kirkpatrick, *Gospel for the Poor*, ch. 1. When the congress took place, Woods was not GS any more.

51. "Minutes of the Meeting of the Executive Committee" (1972), 16.

52. The withdrawal of the board chair could have put significant pressure on the GS Designate and his staff. Graham's crusades in the Philippines in 1962 had caused significant tensions with the local IFES IVCF; the felt risk was that collaboration might "compromise the evangelical testimony of the IVCF of the Philippines." "Minutes of the Meeting of the Executive Committee of the IFES" (Lunteren, The Netherlands; Wuppertal-Barmen, Germany, 27.8–1.9 1962), 21, IFES e-archives.

the light of past experiences ... member movements should not engage in any cooperative efforts with any organization, even evangelical, without prior written agreement."[53] Zald's astute analyses of church conflict highlight the personal and contextual factors at play in similar discussions. The sociologist notes that

> first, conflict in the larger society and concern about various aspects of social change is imported into the organization through the interests or value preferences of lay members and professional staff. To the extent that the religious organization is not sealed off from the larger society through insulating ethnic and communal structures, it is difficult for the church to avoid becoming embroiled.[54]

In this case, the latent "conflict" was the connection of evangelism to social involvement. As Clawson notes with the benefit of hindsight not available to the IFES board at the time,

> though originally conceived as a challenge to the World Council of Churches' emphasis on social concerns rather than personal conversion, the relationship between evangelism and social problems quickly became a recurring and prominent theme at Lausanne, due in large part to provocative and widely discussed plenary addresses given by Samuel Escobar and René Padilla.[55]

As explored above, the ministry context of Latin America was significantly different from that of essentially middle-class British and American universities, and engagement with social issues was not an optional extra for most Majority World IFES staff. Zald further relates this involvement to the essentially "ideological" character of an organization like IFES. Thus,

> members and staff can easily justify organizational involvement in the issues of the day (unlike members of a bowling club or the staff of a dry cleaner, for instance).... The grounds for joining may be theological, ecumenical, or more purely practical....

---

53. "Minutes of the Meeting of the Seventh General Committee of the IFES" (Wuppertal-Barmen, Germany, 1967), 14, IFES e-archives.

54. Mayer N. Zald, "Theological Crucibles: Social Movements in and of Religion," *Review of Religious Research* 23, no. 4 (1982): 328.

55. Clawson, "Misión Integral," 795. Merely challenging the WCC would have been difficult, given that about 40 percent of the congress's participants were members of churches themselves involved with the WCC; see Chapman, "Evangelical International Relations," 361.

> But once joined, the actions of the coalition partner, the interdenominational organization, filter back and commit the denomination to activities it might not have desired, which in turn creates internal conflict.[56]

In the end, "over 80% of the speakers were staff, ex-staff and leaders of IFES and our national movements."[57] Given the concerns previously voiced, it is striking how influential IFES became on the evangelical missionary scene. For the GS, this was the crowning of year-long efforts in teaching, publishing and relating to churches. The crux of the matter was first theological but also methodological, as Chua notes:

> It was evident that our stress on teaching students and graduates the whole counsel of God and relating the gospel to every dimension of life had reaped a bountiful harvest. One was humbled to think that God had used our men to be the avant-garde of evangelical theology and practice. So in an unprecedented way, the IFES has been catapulted into a position of unsought prominence.[58]

Given the common insistence in IFES writings on the importance of training the church and society leaders of tomorrow, whether this prominence was indeed unsought is debatable. That said, the passage quoted above is rare archival evidence showing that IFES leaders also saw themselves as a theological avant-garde.[59] If warnings against contemporary liberal theology and concerning tendencies in churches abound, it is noticeable that IFES does not seem to have been very deliberate in fostering "pure" theological reflection alongside issues related to evangelism broadly conceived. This can be understood as a decisively "practical theology" approach, where theology grows out of the missionary encounter of staff workers with students. Hence the insistence that contextual approaches and indigenous and student leadership are missiologically relevant. The Lausanne Congress is one of the rare events for which scholars have expressly noted the influence of IFES:

---

56. Zald, "Theological Crucibles," 328.
57. Chua Wee Hian, "Staff Letter 15" (Oct. 1974), 1, BGC Box #5.
58. Chua Wee Hian, "Staff Letter 15," 1.
59. One of the reasons why those connected with IFES might have felt particularly at ease at the congress was its serious character. Chua proudly notes that "long before the Congress began, we pressed the Committee to insist that all participants should do their homework thoroughly so that intelligent discussion would take place at Lausanne. Over 70% of the participants submitted answers, criticisms and questions on the plenary papers. This was an all-time record for any international Congress!" Chua Wee Hian, 1.

In the long run, the significance of the Lausanne Movement – and affiliated organizations such as the World Evangelical Alliance and the International Fellowship of Evangelical Students – was not just that it re-engaged North American Evangelicals in cross-cultural missions, but that it gave momentum to the proliferation of non-western missionary movements in the 1980s and 1990s.[60]

In the vein of articulate missiological reflection, the two plenary addresses which caused the most enthusiasm and outrage were indeed presented by two IFES staff workers: René Padilla on "Evangelism and the World" and Samuel Escobar on "Evangelism and Man's Search for Freedom, Justice and Fulfilment."[61] Stanley also goes as far as saying that "just as Vatican II must be judged to have made an irreversible difference to the worship, theology and cultural stance of the Roman Catholic Church, so it can fairly be concluded that after Lausanne world Evangelicalism would never quite be the same again."[62] For Stott, the main missiological takeaway was that "now there is a willingness among Evangelicals to accept that if mission (which is God's first and the Church's second) is what God sends his people into the world to do, then it includes social as well as evangelistic activity."[63]

The IFES leadership was aware of the changes happening in the theological world and was correlating them to the world of university students. As Chua noted in 1975,

> from the mid-sixties up to 1970 we witnessed a period of student unrest and revolution. Today we find students on our campuses in a more sober and reflective mood, and subsequently more open to the gospel. Surely this is a time for both sowing and reaping. During the past 4 years, several of our movements have developed healthy and wholesome approaches in total or comprehensive evangelism. The gospel is related to the "whole person" and the young disciple is instructed and incorporated into a life fellowship. However we need to pray that God will raise up more students

---

60. Robert, *Christian Mission*, 72.

61. Kirkpatrick supposes that one of the reasons Padilla was invited to deliver a speech which was known to have polemical potential was the fact that he was a Wheaton College graduate. Kirkpatrick, *Gospel for the Poor*, 20. For a more detailed analysis of the two addresses, see appendix 1.

62. Stanley, "Lausanne 1974," 550.

63. John Stott, "The Significance of Lausanne," *International Review of Mission* 64, no. 255 (July 1975): 289.

and staff with the gifts of "evangelists" who could be used in partnership with others to lead students from a position of non-faith to faith in Jesus Christ.[64]

This does not mean that full consensus was achieved within the fellowship, and tensions around the idea of holistic mission would surface time and again. One of the contentious issues debated by the Executive was notably the question of "IFES staff and their public views on controversial matters."[65] One can read between the lines of the involvement of certain individuals in political discussions and mandates, which was one of the "'explosive' items"[66] of the Executive of the late 1970s.[67]

Lasting Changes

Debates were raging both in the world outside IFES and within the organization. Institutionally, IFES stayed firm, but its leaders noticed that changes were necessary. Soon after stepping down, Woods penned an anecdotal story of the early years of IFES, some comments of which can be read as the testament of a strangely disappointed man. Looking back on his frenetic years of ministry, he warned his readership and, no doubt, his successor:

> I fear that we have grown up like Topsy. So often God was ahead of us, opening doors, establishing student witness, and we have had to scramble to catch up with him. Usually we were so busy with the work in hand that we had little time to plan for expansion into other countries.[68]

Given the rapid expansion of the organization, and given its partly self-imposed structural limitations and emphasis on local initiative, it is no wonder that the administration could not follow up on all developments. As Woods's successor, Chua, approached his first decade as GS, he noticed that the way the gospel was presented needed serious reflection: "I do believe that we must provide for more information for our thinking generation. Our contemporaries are besieged with rival views. They will treat Bible texts hurled at them in the

---

64. Chua Wee Hian, "Report of the General Secretary" (Schloss Mittersill, Austria, 1975), 2, IFES e-archives, GC 1975 minutes, Appendix.

65. Chua Wee Hian, "Staff Letter 31" (Nov. 1978), 2, BGC Box #5.

66. Chua Wee Hian, "Staff Letter 31," 2.

67. One of them was the growing numbers of Roman Catholic students participating in IFES groups in Latin America, which caused a lot of debates in the EC.

68. Woods, *Some Ways*, 51.

same way as they would regard commercial slogans! That is, with suspicion and sometimes opposition."⁶⁹

Some effects of the student unrest of the late 1960s were starting to ripple down to a new campus generation, and the enduring Cold War meant that for IFES leaders, the time was one of recovery of a missionary vision, notably also applicable to Western Europe. To quote one final time from Woods, "Today most university students are almost as ignorant of the truth of the gospel as some primitive aborigines. Many are in a worse condition in that, rejecting the little knowledge they have, they have renounced the Christian faith outright."⁷⁰ Hence "older" countries would need some serious attention. In the words of the European Regional Secretary (RS) Kristensen: "Europe should be regarded as a mission field. The established churches in Europe were not interested in evangelism whilst the evangelical churches were inward-looking and often engaged in internal debate and controversies."⁷¹ The growing missiological awareness developed within the ranks of IFES would need to be put into practice, significant changes occur in student training, and what was learned on the hard terrain of student ministry channelled back into the churches. Foreshadowing IFES's new concern for graduate ministry, discussed at length in the 1980s, Escobar foresaw in 1972 that

> the new generation in the churches should be challenged to give themselves to a life of service, to remember that they have been given much and much is demanded of them. This means that an important part of the preparation and training of all young people for Christian living will be to expose them to the need of their own country so that they can help through the backing of their congregations, or by an informed selection of their place of employment.⁷²

Chua, having listened to his predecessor's advice, was busy looking ahead,⁷³ yet not foreseeing that the end of the decade to come would witness the fall of communism and the opening up of a staggering number of new ministry fields:

---

69. Chua Wee Hian, "Breakthrough in the Seventies," 9.
70. Woods, *Some Ways*, 102.
71. "Minutes of the Meeting of the Tenth General Committee of the IFES – 1979" (Hurdal Verk, Norway, 27 July 1979), 12, IFES e-archives.
72. Escobar, "Social Impact," 97.
73. Chua Wee Hian, "Priorities 1" (Apr. 1988), 1, BGC Box #5.

The 80s will soon dawn. The door of opportunity is open for bold advances. We require men of faith, dedication and vision to attempt great exploits for God. We have been witnessing unprecedented changes in the Islamic World. The oil wealth and the thirst for Western technology has prised students and the professional class from their conservative Islamic foundations. This means that Christian business men, university lecturers and engineers have unparalleled opportunities to be carriers of the gospel in these "hard" lands. There is another phenomenon. A large proportion of Muslim students are studying in Europe and North America. These are relatively more open to the gospel and we need people to befriend them and point them to Christ.[74]

---

74. Chua Wee Hian, "The General Secretary's Perspective" (Hurdal Verk, Norway, 27 July 1979), 3, IFES e-archives, GC 1979 minutes, Appendix D.

7

Growing Partnerships: The 1980s

Throughout the 1980s, IFES reflected deeply on its structure, its identity and its ministry priorities. The fellowship grew significantly in Eastern Europe. Former colonies of the Majority World were coming of age and asserting their priorities. Historically significant was the shift, at the time not yet fully grasped, of the centre of gravity of Christianity towards the south.[1] As analysts bluntly put it, "On the Day of Atonement 1973, there were only 17 million Africans who described themselves as 'born-again Christians.' Over the next three decades, that number would grow to more than 400 million."[2] IFES was growing fast, as in 1983, "tertiary work undertaken by IFES added up to 3,000 groups and 150,000 students, whereas the high school work had 5,000 groups and 200,000 young people."[3]

IFES seemed well positioned; its fundamental commitment to national leadership and broad representation ensured that shifts in numbers did not threaten its core convictions. Yet Hutchinson and Wolffe contend that in the 1980s,

> the worldwide collapse in voluntarism – both secular and religious – presented evangelicals with both a challenge (the voluntary society had been their traditional form) and an opportunity to move from interdenominational reaction (particularly reaction to the 1960s moral revolution) to trans-denominational proaction through

---

1. Dana L. Robert, "Shifting Southward: Global Christianity since 1945," *International Bulletin of Missionary Research* 24, no. 2 (2000): 50–54.

2. Hutchinson and Wolffe, *Short History*, 244.

3. "Minutes of the Meeting of the Eleventh General Committee of the IFES" (Ashburnham Place, Battle, England, 27 July 1983), 15, IFES e-archives.

cooperative action regardless of traditional race, class, gender or religious barriers.[4]

Some of the essential levers of partnership were already in place as the ethos of interdenominational and transnational cooperation had been at the core of IFES's functioning since its inception. Questions of the balance of power and financial oversight were discussed at great length during leadership meetings. Illustrative of the remaining imbalance was the fact that, as of 1983, only five out of seventy-five member movements provided 76 percent of the money in the IFES budget.[5] Moreover, unlike the United Nations Security Council, no such thing as "permanent seats" in the EC were foreseen constitutionally, yet new delegates at the 1983 GC were systematically drawn from the countries whose delegates had stepped back.[6] This is important insofar as the fellowship had increased its geographical scope significantly since its foundation. Yet the list of representatives shows that some countries – notably the wealthier – seem to have, either implicitly or explicitly, been deemed too essential to be left out of the deliberations.[7]

In the Majority World, tensions around the connection between missionary organizations and IFES also existed. For example, "in Gabon, the IFES worked through a denominational student movement in the early eighties. Although its missionaries disliked the IFES inter-denominationalism, students caught the vision."[8] However, debates over the role of foreign missionaries were not confined to the (in)famous "moratorium" debate discussed above. As the EC discussed in 1983, IFES was aware that the history of missions was not one of unabated success:

> Missionaries have often made serious mistakes. Most of our countries first heard the gospel in a way that had shocking overtones of cultural or military imperialism. But nevertheless a church was founded. . . . Equally, national workers have sometimes been blind to the pagan or other anti-Christian elements in their own culture. . . . We all need to be helped by one another to be more biblical in our thought and life, and foreign workers are

---

4. Hutchinson and Wolffe, *Short History*, 257.
5. "Minutes of the Meeting of the Eleventh General Committee" (1983), 14.
6. In this case, Canada, Germany and the UK.
7. Some legal requirements, notably in relation to financial flows, could also have played a role in choosing delegates.
8. Peter J. Lineham, "Students Reaching Students: A History of the International Fellowship of Evangelical Students" (unpublished manuscript, 1997), 126.

often a great help here, even when their influence is mixed with cultural blind areas and they need to be corrected in these by the national leaders.[9]

Sanneh's distinction between "Global Christianity" and "World Christianity" seems to capture both the potential and the tensions of this new development and is relevant to an analysis of IFES.[10] "Global Christianity" would refer to an extension of transatlantic, Anglo-Saxon evangelicalism, whereas "World Christianity" rather describes the indigenous appropriation of the Christian faith, wherever it is to be found. IFES official documents and speeches always insist on indigeneity and contextuality; however, the doctrinal basis and other constitutional requirements limit the accepted level of local flexibility and hence might be understood as promoting more of a replication of Western forms than genuine indigenization of student ministry. This tension would take some time to be adequately discussed but was a matter of significant thinking at the end of the century. We shall return to it later.

I cannot pretend to provide an extensive historical account of all events and people who shaped IFES in the 1980s, but the following exploration of important theological discussions should help the reader to get a picture of what was at stake at the time.

1982–83: What Is IFES?

A short document titled "The International Fellowship of Evangelical Students: Who Are We? Why Do We Exist? How Do We Function?,"[11] published in 1982, pictures an organization which is coming of age and trying to reassess itself. One of the first affirmations is that of the evangelical identity of the fellowship, defined as IFES's deep commitment to "defending, maintaining and propagating biblical truths," these truths having been found in the Bible, the entire trustworthiness of which is reaffirmed. In addition to traditional

---

9. Joe Caterson, "Proposals for Effective Partnership in Worldwide Student Evangelisation," plenary discussion paper (Ashburnham Place, Battle, East Sussex, England, 27 July 1983), 3, IFES e-archives, GC 1983 minutes, Appendix R.

10. Lamin O. Sanneh, *Whose Religion Is Christianity? The Gospel beyond the West* (Grand Rapids: Eerdmans, 2003).

11. IFES, "The International Fellowship of Evangelical Students: Who Are We? Why Do We Exist? How Do We Function?" (Discipleship Training Center, Singapore, 17 Aug. 1982), IFES e-archives, EC 1982 minutes, Appendix A. The quotes in the next section are all from this short document.

biblicism, the paper also affirms the centrality of the doctrinal basis.[12] The presentation goes on to detail the mission field and the strategy deployed, notably insisting on student leadership:

> Students constitute the focal point of the IFES and indeed of all National Evangelical Unions. The universities, colleges and high schools represent vast mission fields where students need to be presented with the claims of Christ as man's only Saviour and Lord. *The most effective bearers of the gospel are committed Christian students.* We know that under God Christian students can be greatly used by Him to bear witness to His love in Christ Jesus, to run their own Christian groups and to help their fellow students grow in Him. *IFES related Christian groups are in effect a mission of students to students*; at the grassroots, the local fellowships manifest strong student responsibility and initiative.[13]

This excerpt can be read as a reaffirmation of previous self-presentations. However, the influence of missiological discussions in the wider Christian world about the role of missionaries, the importance of local leadership, and so on, is probably also in the background. This was no novelty as the presentation hastens to add that the IFES founding fathers "recognized the need for international partnership and cooperation. As well as being a forum for new ideas, the IFES is the agency for mutual strengthening and the unique vehicle for member movements to engage in pioneering student work."[14]

This spirit of cooperation was well in line with the context of the 1980s. The document also insists on the ecclesiological aspects of the work of IFES. If some church leaders had difficulty agreeing on IFES's legitimacy, the fellowship boldly affirms that

> another major reason for our existence is the commitment of all National Evangelical Unions to equip their student members for service in God's Church. Systematic Bible exposition and teaching, participation in group Bible studies, personal and corporate involvement in evangelism and follow-up, leadership responsibilities – all these provide students with firm foundations

---

12. See chapter 11 below.
13. Emphasis added.
14. IFES, "Who Are We?," 2.

and useful experience in serving the cause of Christ both during their university studies and on graduation.[15]

What can be read between the lines here is that the training provided by IFES groups would turn out to have a positive influence on churches *because of the theology* taught in the groups. The emphasis on "Systematic Bible *exposition*" is also noticeable since it was never part of IFES's standard student training curriculum to "exposit" the Bible, the term being understood as "preaching."

The theological soul-searching within IFES went further, notably because growing numbers of Roman Catholic students were joining IFES groups. The discussions carried on within the senior leadership and in consultation with the national movements resulted in a major paper presented by Escobar at the 1983 GC and titled "Our Evangelical Heritage."[16]

The Peruvian missiologist first frames the history of IFES within larger currents in the church, asserting that IFES's "development into a worldwide fellowship made up of strong indigenous movements is a process that cannot be separated from the life of the Church at large. It is part of one of the most remarkable missionary advances in history." This is remarkable insofar as many accounts of IFES's existence hitherto tended to focus on "resistance" and "foundations" more than on positivity. Escobar is not blind to these aspects, for he goes on to say that the expansion of the church in the world "has taken place, come wind come weather, in a century where spiritual and social forces seemed to present insurmountable obstacles" – but his framing is decisively positive. Yet, as Escobar perspicaciously notes,

> our heritage is no heavy burden that previous generations have imposed on us to keep us under control. Sometimes the very word "heritage" is disgusting for young people because it communicates that image. But what we see in our own history and in the history of the Church is that these basic tenets of evangelical truth and life have been liberating truths, dynamic elements within movements of renewal that God has used to keep His Church alive in times of crisis or advance. This is how we in IFES understand them.

Escobar highlights three contributions made by IFES in its history which he attributes to the fellowship's faithfulness to its evangelical heritage:

---

15. IFES, 2.
16. Samuel Escobar, "Our Evangelical Heritage: Major Paper Presented at the 1983 General Committee," *IFES Review* 14 (1983): 2–20. Subsequent quotes are from this document.

In the English-speaking countries, it has brought the recovery of initiative for Evangelicals in theological and biblical scholarship, and university life. In some Third World countries, it has opened the university world to permanent evangelism through indigenous movements. It has produced a generation of able leaders in the worldwide evangelical revival who combine missionary fire with biblical scholarship and devotion to truth.

Escobar's analysis demonstrates deep ecclesiological interests. He envisages that faithfulness to the evangelical heritage will allow IFES to continue being an "advancing missionary force and a body of people seriously concerned with the integrity of the gospel – with a definite ministry within the Church universal." This concern is intensely missiological and, as another paper from the same conference notes, thereby justifies priority-setting in recruiting students for missionary engagement:

We affirm that students, staffworkers, graduates and supporters should strive to fulfil national objectives in spreading the gospel in their universities and schools, in building up strong Christians and in equipping them for service in the Church. At the same time they must also be sensitive to God's call to be concerned with student work in other countries, particularly those that need help.[17]

Escobar develops a positive framing of IFES's being "not just a reactionary movement, developed to counteract other student movements in the name of orthodoxy. Rather, it results from a theological concern and a practical sense of mission that stems from truth. It expresses a recurring movement of the Spirit of God in His Church." Escobar takes historical narratives to task, countering accusations that IFES is reactionary *ad extra* and asserting theological reflection over against missionary pragmatism *ad intra*. Escobar seizes the opportunity to challenge the idea that a "heritage" necessarily could be uniform:

IFES has become a truly "international fellowship" and is growing into the realization of all that is meant in those two first words of its name. Each movement has a different historical background and has to live in very different social, political and ecclesiastical conditions. We rejoice together in our common heritage, but

---

17. Caterson, "Proposals for Effective Partnership," 1.

it is taking time and experience to express it in the differing circumstances in which we live.

Hence the move from a traditional doctrinal focus to a more socio-missiological one: Escobar insists that "the student element in our name" justifies potential similarities, yet "when we come to other aspects of our life, we have to learn to acknowledge the differences." Escobar goes beyond merely acknowledging regional discrepancies and, hammering home his point, stresses the ecclesiological implications of his observations:

> A person who considers himself an Evangelical in any one of these countries comes from a very different experience. For instance, different history and consequentially differing ways of living their faith. A British Evangelical could be an Anglican or a Plymouth Brother. The consequences of their evangelical position for their church-life, ministry and even career, can be very different because of the particular history of Christianity in Britain. But take the Peruvian Evangelical, the member of a tiny religious minority in a Roman Catholic culture. For him being an Evangelical means being re-baptized in 95% of the cases. Compare him with the Norwegian Evangelical who almost certainly would be a Lutheran and who would never ask a person who has a conversion experience to be re-baptized. Then think of the special challenges that come for the Singaporean or the Senegalese who live inside a society dominated by a non-Christian religious majority. For them being an Evangelical is not so much separation and distinction from a nominally Christian majority as presence and testimony in a pagan environment.

For Escobar, a solid student ministry serves the church, for "where the Church is dormant or does not have a good ministry, our student movements are having to provide nurture and guidance on the application of truth to daily life." Throughout its history, IFES has been challenged with competing with local churches. Settling the matter in unequivocal terms, Escobar concludes that

> IFES is a Para-Church Movement. Evangelicals are convinced that the Church is important and central in God's plan revealed in His Word. As an evangelical movement IFES stresses that it is not a church. Sometimes we express our role as being "an arm of the Church" in the university. We have insisted that our evangelistic

task is completed when a person who comes to know Christ in a student group becomes an active member of a local church.

Yet Escobar is equally adamant that the church does not possess a monopoly on the truth. Not only can parachurch organizations arise out of the missionary and theological deficiencies of the church, but "it is not the Church that produces Christian truth, it is the other way round: Christian truth produces the Church. In the same fashion, it is not IFES that has produced evangelical truth, but the IFES is the result of evangelical truth, God's Spirit through His Word, in action." This independence of *truth* from the institutional church hence legitimates the existence of IFES and especially its worldwide expansion, for "we exist for a given purpose; we have a mission." Balancing his valuing of contextual adaptation and his rebuke of any form of theological imperialism, Escobar contends that

> as IFES advances to the most remote parts of the earth, national movements face the task of taking our evangelical heritage and putting it to work in their own situation. This is not just salesmanship. We have no final packaged product called "Evangelical Heritage" made in Peru, England, USA or Norway, that has to be sold to consumers on the campuses of the world. It is rather that we have a living truth that living people will grasp and then apply in their very varied circumstances. This will only happen if IFES is a real Fellowship; if there is mutual respect from every national movement to all the others, [and] confidence in the work of the Holy Spirit in every national situation. What we must avoid is any form of cultural imperialism that hides itself under the cloak of "concern for our evangelical heritage."

Figure 1 summarizes Escobar's development.

The major paper and discussion carried out during the 1983 GC show a demonstrable concern for the link between IFES ministry and church ministry. The idea remains that IFES exists because of some shortcomings of local churches. However, IFES is anchored within the bigger picture of "service to the Church." IFES was not thinking in a vacuum, for several of its leaders had been involved in the Lausanne Commission on Co-operation which published a significant paper, the reading of which was recommended by Chua to its leadership.[18] Furthermore, the need to spend time considering

---

18. The report was published the same year; see Lausanne Movement, "Cooperating in World Evangelization."

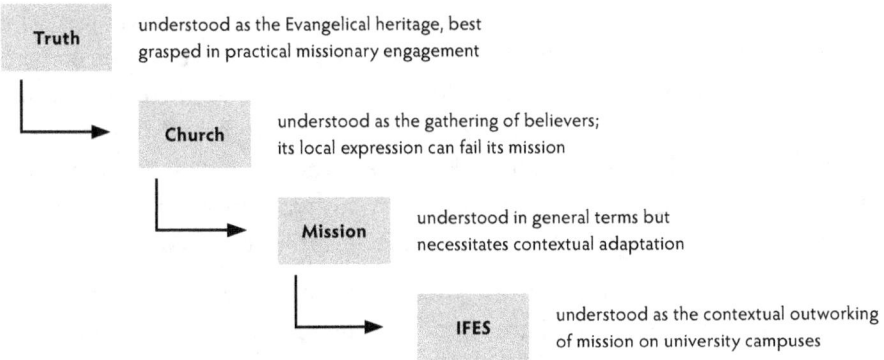

Figure 1

IFES's relationship to local churches was noted as one of the priorities of the incoming EC.[19]

The question of the ecclesial integration of students involved in IFES groups was always a burning one. The IFES leadership discussed the issue at greater length in the 1980s as it became evident that a more deliberate graduate work of some sort was required so as not to "lose" the students in whom so much energy had been invested. This would be a recurring concern for the IFES leadership, rendered even more salient given the need to disciple young professionals who would have to navigate the intricate world of post-communist Eastern Europe. The 1987 GC noted in very self-aware terms that

> an evidence of the effectiveness of our students' work is a growing group of graduates who are serving Christ in the world. *However, it is apparent that there is a high fall-out rate among our graduates in many countries, indicative of the fact that our graduates need continuing help.* At the same time, many movements feel that an effective graduates' work is necessary for the survival and growth of the students' work.[20]

If the organization's strategy, measured against its own criteria, is found wanting, the above is a clarion call for a thorough reassessment. Such observation would cause long discussions in the 1980s and 1990s. It was also observed that IFES had tended to neglect Christian lecturers and professors

---

19. "Minutes of the Newly-Elected Executive Committee Meeting of the IFES" (Ashburnham Place, Battle, England, 27 July 1983), 3, IFES e-archives.

20. "Minutes of the Meeting of the Twelfth General Committee of the IFES" (El Hostel Duruelo, Boyaca, Colombia, 30.8–8.9 1987), 27, IFES e-archives; emphasis added.

in its ministry.[21] While the lack of such "investment" was acknowledged, the importance of the word "student" in the whole IFES rhetoric is evidence enough that such ministry was never conceived of as being part of the organization's "core business." The 1980s nevertheless were a time of intense "strategic soul-searching" as IFES leaders tried to make sense of the contextual developments they were observing. As Chairman Skaaheim noted, ministering to students was still very relevant, given the growing urbanization occurring:

> Mission societies all over the world see the challenge that this situation represents and are already in the process of discussing how to strengthen the mission work in cities and particularly among students. Personally, I think that we will see a dramatic shift in mission strategy. More and more priority will be given to student work and general mission work in urban areas. This also means change of methods. Traditional methods will not be adequate in reaching students with the gospel. Mission societies find themselves in a very demanding position as they have to rethink the whole strategy to find the right way to progress and growth.[22]

Partnerships on a Global Scale

Continuing the methodological "soul-searching" of the decade, the IFES president noted that "we cannot expect to follow the patterns and methods of the early 1900s, but we do believe that there is an unchanging commission."[23] The first time the GC gathered in Latin America, the question of how "foreign" missionaries were to relate to their field was repeatedly voiced in Bogotá, a sequel to the previous GC meeting's discussion of the tension between "national" and "foreign." In the words of the report of a discussion group in 1983,

> foreign workers may not, from a human point of view, be ideal, but then national workers are not ideal either – no one is! The best man to do God's work will always be the man called of God, with

---

21. "Minutes of the Meeting of the Eleventh General Committee" (1983), 18.

22. Anfin Skaaheim, "IFES and a Global Strategy for Mission Work among Students," discussion paper (Yahara Center, Madison, USA, 21 Apr. 1985), 1, IFES e-archives, EC 1985 minutes, Appendix.

23. David H. Adeney, "Light to the Nations: 1987 IFES Presidential Address," *IFES Review* 23 (1987): 4.

Christ-like character and the ability to communicate the gospel and teach the Word. This messenger may be "foreign" because of his race, colour or culture, but his basic qualities as a student worker should help him overcome cultural difficulties.[24]

A few years later, Adeney underlined the significant geopolitical shifts which had occurred in the history of IFES, notably that "in 1934, 99% of the countries of Asia were under colonial rule. Missionaries were almost all Westerners, and the Asian churches had relatively few strong national leaders. Many of my contemporaries were going to similar situations in Africa, India and Latin America."[25] This had changed by 1987, but the former IFES senior staff in Asia still concluded that "perhaps unconsciously we were influenced by an insidious form of national pride related to our British empire background."[26]

This new political constellation would mean for IFES both a challenge and an opportunity. Chua astutely highlighted that "missiologists tell us that 83 nations no longer allow traditional missionaries to work in their countries. Tent-making is and will be the most effective alternative to missionary work."[27] IFES would need to recourse more deliberately to graduates to support its work. As Adeney further commented,

> most of these countries open their doors to teachers, scientists and business people from other countries. Christians with professional skills find unlimited opportunities all over the world to serve in a secular capacity. The Bible is full of examples of different types of people becoming witnesses to the living God. Not only the prophets and prophetesses, but generals and statesmen, farmers and shepherds, midwives and queens, apostles and tentmakers, were all used to proclaim the message of the kingdom of God. IFES is in a unique position to play an important role in the call and training of both the traditional missionary and those who are described in Tetsunao Yamamori's recent book as "God's New Envoys."[28]

---

24. Caterson, "Proposals for Effective Partnership," 3.
25. Adeney, "Light to the Nations," 6.
26. Adeney, 6.
27. Chua Wee Hian, "Major Trends and Developments in IFES" (IFES Executive Committee, 5 May 1988), 2, IFES e-archives.
28. Adeney, "Light to the Nations," 7.

120   The Priesthood of All Students

Correlated with the new political landscape was the question of internal representativeness, which became pressing shortly after the 1987 GC. The issue was the nomination of Chua's successor. A heated discussion occurred at the 1989 EC meeting, during which the question was raised as to why the Majority World candidates were not considered more thoroughly, especially since the 1987 GC had explicitly asked for more non-Westerners to be appointed as IFES staff. Procedures were noted as being designed after the usual procedures of the West, and "it was pointed out that most Two-Thirds World candidates would tend to decline initially and needed to be persuaded to be considered."[29] The whole question caused a considerable stir within the committee, since no non-Western representatives were part of the search committee. "Concern was expressed about the international image of the IFES, what member movements would think and also how the Christian public would react, bearing in mind that the international representation of IFES had always been admired."[30] In the end, Welshman Lindsay Brown was appointed and assumed office until 2007.[31]

Graduate Work

Part of the "strategy audit" which IFES conducted in the 1980s was a re-examination of the standing of graduates. In 1987, significant of a growing ecclesiological awareness, Adeney was rejoicing:

> The IFES is vitally concerned to raise up leaders for the future ministry of the church. After 40 years we are now in a position to see how this purpose is being fulfilled. There is indeed much for which to praise God. I am encouraged when I look back and think of some whom I knew as students who are now holding positions of leadership in the Christian world. Some are pastors

---

29. "Minutes of the Meeting of the Executive Committee of the IFES" (Tao Fong Shan Christian Center, Hong Kong, 25 July 1989), 2, IFES e-archives.

30. "Minutes of the Meeting of the Executive Committee" (1989), 3.

31. It is interesting to note the criteria used to choose a GS as defined by the IEC: "Character: He must be godly. He must have theological stability, insight, firmness, wisdom, maturity of character, integrity, aptitude for reconciliation. He must have proven cross-cultural abilities.... Attitude to Scripture: He must fully accept the Fellowship's position on Scripture. He must be able to teach Scripture and must exemplify the practice of its authority in his life. He must show a biblical (not primarily pragmatic) approach to issues, working from principle and being able to make radical application of Scripture to the questions of the day. Understanding of IFES: He must have a good understanding of IFES ethos and history. He must have a firm commitment to its doctrinal basis and aims, and a passionate commitment to our evangelical heritage, to evangelism and to world mission." Appendix F of "Minutes of the Meeting of the Executive Committee" (1988)," 1.

and leaders in the church, others are serving their generation as teachers or research workers.[32]

As already noted above, the transition from student life and IFES group involvement to "real life" and church commitment had always been a concern of the IFES leadership. In 1988 the situation was considered serious enough by the IEC to commission two separate reports on the question whether IFES should start a dedicated ministry to graduate students. In what follows, we shall focus on the ecclesiological aspects of the considerations debated by the leadership.

It is interesting to note the diverging perspectives presented in the two reports. The first, written by Moïse Napon, delegate for Francophone Africa, makes a strong case for graduate ministry in IFES, while the second, penned by Robin Wells, GS of UCCF, essentially dismisses the idea on account of the priority of student work on which IFES should focus. Both papers were subsequently published in *In Touch*, with a postscript in the form of a response from the GS.[33]

Essentially, Napon affirms that if IFES gets too involved in work among graduates, it runs the risk of supplementing churches. Conversely, not doing enough means taking the risk of letting graduates starve and lose the missionary zeal characteristic of their student days. His conclusion is that the benefits far outweigh the risks. Napon observes three main attitudes among churches towards GBU graduates. The first, historically grounded, is hostility: "Some churches are hesitant or even hostile to the inclusion of intellectuals in their leadership. In colonial days, intellectualism amounted to an incapacity for faith. Therefore even now there are lurking suspicions about graduates and even opposition towards their leadership."[34] The second is especially relevant to our study, for it highlights the issue of lay versus clerical roles. In Napon's words, some churches

> are unaware of the presence of graduates because there are many of them or because of the distinction they make between lay and clergy, and the lay people have no role to play in the church, or ultimately because the graduates do not stand out spiritually and

---

32. Adeney, "Light to the Nations," 4–5.

33. Chua Wee Hian, "Graduate Ministry: A Postscript from the General Secretary," *IFES Review* 26 (1989): 45–48.

34. Moïse Napon, "Ministry amongst Past Members of the GBU" (London Bible College, Northwood, England, Aug. 1988), 4, IFES e-archives.

> therefore they have become nominal members of a church, only attending on Sundays.³⁵

Either the local IFES group had not discipled its graduates well enough for them to sufficiently stand out, or the churches were responsible for their unwillingness to let graduates take up responsibilities. While Napon's impatience with ecclesial leadership is evident, he nevertheless quite clearly questions the effectiveness of the ministry of IFES as well. The last scenario Napon observes is the case where local churches welcome IFES graduates and trust them. But even so, the risk is high that young graduates are pushed to assume responsibilities foreign to the training they have received in IFES groups, and hence are not up to the task.

In addition to these three possible cases, Napon highlights the very specific ethical challenges encountered by young graduates, which may not be commonly discussed in ecclesial contexts. The reflections of the African leader rest on the argument that the continent lacks good lay leaders and that a good doctrine of the church requires that care be given to all its members.

> In Africa where we have a lack of well trained leaders to direct the believing church, and where lay people are encouraged to preach, then it becomes indispensable for us to provide good training in this area. Because of this it is possible for the decision of a lay person to affect the whole life of the church. So GBU graduates need a thorough training so that they can offer a much more effective contribution to a developing church (or a sleeping one).³⁶

While for Napon the lack of good leaders in church in society justifies a deeper commitment of IFES to train and nurture graduates, Wells argues that IFES should focus on its traditional core business: students. The British GS argues that ministry to graduates could be supported on account of the need to "meet the particular and temporary difficulties of graduates in adjusting to the world of work and the life of the church, . . . to stimulate the thinking of graduates who encounter particular questions in their jobs or academic disciplines, [and lastly] to provide general spiritual nurture for graduates."³⁷ Wells goes on to specify that UCCF decided that the first two points fell within the range of their responsibilities, addressed through teaching during university

---

35. Napon, "Past Members of the GBU," 4.

36. Napon, 5.

37. Robin Wells, "A Work amongst Graduates for a Student Movement?" (London Bible College, Northwood, Middlesex, England, Aug. 1988), 2, IFES e-archives.

days and networking in professional groups upon graduation, while the third did not, being the preserve of local churches. Wells then advances his point by appealing to further ecclesiological considerations:

> The main question that has arisen in this relates to the doctrine of the church. It has always been carefully insisted, in IFES movements, that the student work is not a church or in competition with the church. Of course, in no country is the church perfect, and in many countries the churches fail particularly in their ministry to people who have had the privilege of study. But it is also argued that that does not entitle us to establish something which does the work of the churches. General Christian nurture to maturity is the work of the church. And part of the glory of the church is the range of ages, intellectual abilities, etc. to be found there. A graduate ministry can undermine all that.[38]

From a discourse analysis perspective, the recourse to unnamed external instances is striking: it remains for the reader to guess who "always carefully insisted" and where "it is also argued." Wells supposes different understandings of church doctrine between Napon and himself, while he speaks to another reality. As to why a graduate ministry would undermine church work, Wells provides no further argument. It is hence a case, not found very often in archival materials, of senior IFES leaders evidently talking past each other. It is, however, very much in line with the recurring emphasis of Western leaders on "setting priorities" in a logic of shortage of energies and human resources. This is how the following line of argument with which Wells continues is to be understood:

> IFES is set up for ministry amongst students. I suggest we need to keep that as a clear restriction, enabling us to concentrate on that without distraction. Let other agencies do other things, no matter how important they are, and even no matter how useful they are for us – unless they fall explicitly within our primary aim. We need literature for our work, and often literature which no one else can produce. Well, let us do it. But let us not do the work of the churches.[39]

---

38. Wells, "A Work amongst Graduates," 2.
39. Wells, 3.

In sum, while the two visions seemingly clash with each other, one making a case for an institutional approach to graduate ministry while the other wants to let local churches take up their responsibilities, they nevertheless agree on the necessity of nurturing graduate students for their later involvement in church and society. The apparent clash derives from the vastly different contextual realities: Wells speaks out of a British context with established and strong evangelical churches; Napon speaks from the Francophone context of Africa, where evangelical churches mostly exist in Muslim-majority countries and where ecclesiological weakness is more the norm than the exception. Intriguingly, the history of the British context could have supported exactly the same strategy as that advocated by Napon: in a context where evangelicalism is weak, IFES needs to support graduates so that they in turn can support their churches. This is indeed what Wells acknowledges to have been the British strategy of the 1930s and 1940s.[40]

The conclusion of the EC discussion was to task the GS with an official response, later published and essentially stressing the fact that, while graduate ministry was seen as very important, the variety of contexts meant that "a centrally appointed staffworker would not be able to carry out this mandate meaningfully and that regions should be strongly encouraged, through the regional support groups, to consider appointing part-time graduates secretaries."[41]

The logical conclusion for the IFES leadership might have been to decentralize the approach and plainly let regions deal with the matter. Some regions eventually did, and the 1993 long-range plan listed the objective of "fostering commitment among graduates to a continuing student witness in their country and beyond, and to serving church and society.[42] This support was reasserted in 1998, the strategic plan stating that "we will encourage national movements, where appropriate, to appoint staff for this purpose."[43]

The question of graduate ministry was not the only one to occupy the IFES senior leadership in the late 1980s, however. If there were questions about IFES graduates, the atmosphere was also already quickly changing in the student groups. While the IFES leadership always insisted on the importance of student

---

40. Wells, 3.

41. Chua Wee Hian, "Graduate Ministry," 4.

42. Lindsay Brown, "Draft Global IFES Long Range Plan" (Oak Hill College, London, England, 25–31.7 1993), 3, IFES e-archives, EC 1993 minutes, Appendix H.

43. "Second Draft of Global IFES Plan July 1999 – July 2003" (Bischofsheim, Germany, 28.6–3.7 1998), 9, IFES e-archives, EC 1998 minutes, Appendix I.

leadership, they nevertheless noted a shift in the general attitude of student leaders towards responsibilities. Certainly, the General Secretary was positive in 1987, noting that IFES had "invested nearly a quarter of a million dollars in training conferences over the past four years. This is a wise investment!"[44] Nevertheless he deplored that "we rarely find 'charismatic' leaders who are prepared to blaze new trails and who motivate others to attempt great things for God. Our Christian fellowships are increasingly dependent on students who have come from stable Christian homes to serve as leaders."[45] This is a relatively rare example of the growing sense of inadequacy of certain traditional approaches used by IFES among the generation of the 1980s, among both students and younger staff. This unease was also developed at greater length two years later by the IFES training secretary. Debriefing the speakers of the first European Formación training camp, she sounded an intrigued note:

> we are indeed dealing now with a generation of young staff (and even more so of students) who are in many ways the product of our contemporary societies. Staff are not the "self-starters," in many cases, that they used to be. Reasons for this may lie in changes in education, in fragmented family life, in church backgrounds, etc. I see indications of this in the fact that the pastoral dimension of the conference was particularly appreciated along with the more "practical" staff worker and trainer/facilitator sessions. In one sense this is what one would expect and there is nothing wrong with it. However, I sense that it goes hand in hand with less rigorous thought, less commitment to developing a Christian mind, less concern for the doctrinal foundations of our faith. Again, this should not surprise us for it is also a feature of modern society and church life (at least, from my vantage point).[46]

Methodological questions were in the air. Was student leadership still relevant? Were the assumptions of the founding fathers still applicable? How could IFES tackle the challenges of a new generation? As the 1980s were ending, the first concern of the GC 1987 meeting in Bogotá, Colombia, was that of the outworking of partnership within the fellowship.

---

44. Chua Wee Hian, "IFES: The Big Picture," *In Touch* 3 (1987): 5.
45. Chua, "Major Trends," 1.
46. Dr. Sue Brown to Formación 1989 Contributors, 27 Sep. 1989, 1, BGC Box #5.

The One-Another Ministry of Students to Students

As was the case with virtually every significant meeting, IFES leaders reasserted their trust in the leadership of students; even more so at a fortieth anniversary jubilee. In an exemplary quote worth giving at length, Chua asserts,

> Ever since our foundation, our primary focus has been on students. We believe that, under God, evangelical students can be front-line witnesses for Christ on their campuses. *Students possess spiritual gifts and abilities to run their fellowships and to build one another up in the faith.* It is our express aim that, through this on-the-job training and involvement, these students would be trained as leaders. Of course, they need encouragement and input from staff. But, in the IFES tradition, the staff does not dominate and run the student fellowship. They act as trainers or coaches.[47]

While the "coaching" metaphor is a recurrent one and tries to capture the relationship of staff members to student leaders, the explicit affirmation of students "building one another up" is rare. It indicates a fine-tuning of the IFES leadership's theological reflection and an explicit acknowledgment of students' maturity. Emblematic is the publication, one year later in the *IFES Review*, of an article titled "The One-Another Ministry of Students to Students,"[48] penned by two young women who had served as IFES team members in Paris.

The paper aims to "consider ways in which students can exercise pastoral care towards one another within the student group. This commandment of Jesus [to love one another, John 13:34–35] seems to us the foundation of such care." In contrast to more traditional presentations in older articles of the importance of individual piety for efficient witnessing, this paper insists on the revelatory dimension and encouragement potential of Christian communion. Indeed, "God makes his love known to us personally through relationships within the body of Christ by his Holy Spirit. Our faith is worked out in the context of relationships, and the student group can provide a valuable opportunity to work out this relational aspect of our faith." If no deficiency of the church is directly alluded to in this passage, one is struck by the significant, though implicit, overlap between a local church as "body of Christ" and functions here ascribed to the student group. The local group can provide the support rendered necessary by "the increasing disintegration of family life, [leading

---

47. Chua, "Big Picture," 5; emphasis added.

48. Julie Dransfield and Cindy Merritt, "The 'One-Another' Ministry of Students to Students," *IFES Review* 24 (1988): 37–42. Unless otherwise stated, the quotes that follow are from this short article.

to] psychological and emotional obstacles... preventing [students] from fully entering into the healing and restoration which Christ's salvation brings." The article acknowledges the challenges encountered on campus, but also "the temptation within student groups . . . to see Christianity solely as a set of intellectual propositions, rather than as a way of life based on the personal knowledge of God's love for us in Christ." Earlier in the IFES history, readers have encountered such warnings in Woods's writings, yet the antidote there would more likely have been personal Bible reading and prayer. The latter is not forgotten: "There can be nothing more encouraging, faith-building and healing than sharing together in seeing how God is active in our lives in response to prayer"; however, the approach presented here stresses that "it is important that the potential of the student group is maximised, not only by providing an intellectual approach to faith, but by allowing understanding of truth to find expression in tangible ways in Christian friendships." Contextualizing for the realities of student life, the authors go on to highlight the importance of committing time and listening to each other: "We can all think of someone who has helped in our spiritual growth because he or she was prepared to spend time with us."

The church is referred to only in a subsidiary manner, particularly relevant when the pastoral potential of a student group reaches its limit, notably when students face particularly acute emotional crises, in which case "help should be sought from an older mature Christian within the church." Intriguingly the authors continue by suggesting a listening attitude which sounds very akin to "confession-like" events: "It can be a great source of healing simply to allow someone to pour out all that is on their hearts and minds, listening attentively and compassionately. This can help them to clarify thoughts and put them in perspective."

No mention of a "priesthood" of students is made. In contrast, some of the attitudes described and encouraged in the article fall into categories such as mutual pastoral care, petitions to God in prayer and so on. In the end, guidelines for further Bible studies are provided, listing different uses of the word *parakalein/paraklesis*, especially in Pauline writings. Fascinating is the definition of "encouragement": "an informal mutual ministry among Christians, related to prophecy." The article is evidence of the argument of this study that students are considered mature enough to exercise some form of *mediation* between God and each other, that is, some form of *priestly mediation*. We shall return to this topic below for deeper theological investigation.

Besides discussions about representativeness and the best way to envisage a ministry that is faithful to its heritage yet flexible enough to adapt to the new contextual realities, the 1980s were definitely an era of growth. The GS reported in 1988 that no fewer than 270,000 high school and university students were involved with IFES.[49] Similarly, the mood of the time inclined towards large events. The same year, the first quadrennial European Evangelism Conference took place in Würzburg, Germany: "The European organisers had expected 700 students, and nearly 1300 showed up. Jürgen Spiess, General Secretary of SMD-West Germany, spoke of the 'festival mentality' that pervades young people today."[50]

Another of the great trends that would characterize a large part of the future of IFES ministry was the redevelopment of "mission weeks" in the form of lecture series. This also coincided with the appearance of "apologetics" in the IFES parlance. As Lineham summarizes,

> public proclamation of the gospel was difficult in secular Europe, and lectures which presented an apologetic for Christianity were often seen as more appropriate. In the mid eighties a new passion for evangelistic work developed. It began when European staff workers attended the 1984 Oxford Mission. Jürgen Spiess, the new German General Secretary, attended and subsequently told his staff to hold missions on their campuses.[51]

Actually, such lectures had been happening in Germany for a long time already.[52] It was not a new phenomenon, for mission weeks had taken place in many campuses since the beginning of student movements in Europe and elsewhere.

The close of the decade had been marked by intense debates on the nature and orientation of the ministry of IFES, numerous hours and meetings being devoted to strategic soul-searching. Besides regular reaffirmations of the evangelical character and heritage of the fellowship, its ecclesiology was coming of age and gradually becoming more missiologically assertive. On the ground, many national movements were developing. Others were fostering the emergence of movements in lands that gradually opened in the 1990s. The importance of student leadership was as unabatedly stressed as in the previous decades, yet its theological underpinnings were being fine-tuned.

---

49. Chua Wee Hian, "Evangelical Students."
50. Chua, "Major Trends," 1.
51. Lineham, "Students Reaching Students," 57.
52. For the history of the German IFES movement, see SMD, *Rechenschaft geben von unserer Hoffnung: Festschrift zum 50jährigen Bestehen der Studentenmission in Deutschland* (Marburg: SMD, 1999), Hartmut Bärend, *SMD-Geschichte* (Marburg: SMD, 2023).

8

A New World Map to Finish a Century: The 1990s

The last decade of the twentieth century was eventful for IFES, with an unexpected number of new countries officially opening up to its ministry. New nations brought new theological interests, a new weighing of priorities and new relationships, the necessity to reconsider ownership on a larger scale, and the need to adapt the leadership structure to a student generation that was changing significantly. How were the theological fundamentals of IFES to be adapted and owned in a new era, especially in the encounter with Eastern Orthodoxy and Pentecostalism? Moreover, the perennial question of how to define IFES's ecclesiological status came to the fore again. IFES also started to ask itself how to apprehend the university as an institution, as the logical consequence of a steadily growing interest in holistic mission. Many discussions took place during and in between the three GC meetings newly integrated into larger, more representative events called "World Assemblies."

New Nations, New Thinking

Nine out of the ten founding countries were Western. With the fellowship having grown to fourteen times its original size, new balances of interest would come to the surface, and the 1990s saw an intense period of soul-searching. What did "ownership" mean in such a large organization? What would the priorities be, and who would get to decide between them? What strategies would work best with a new generation of students? How would national and denominational loyalties play against theological certitudes?

Eastern Europe

When Eastern Europe officially opened up in the early 1990s, IFES had been "pioneering" student work undercover for many years, the hub of this ministry being Schloss Mittersill in the Austrian Tyrol. As early as 1973, senior leaders would boast that

> during the last four years we have been able to pioneer about twenty to thirty Bible study groups. These have no labels, but God has used IFES special workers and envoys to visit and encourage these students. Our workers are not spies, involved in international intrigue and political espionage. Instead, they are Barnabases encouraging Eastern European students to love and serve the living Lord.[1]

For a ministry that always insisted on its ethos of "indigenous leadership," it might seem bizarre to read so much of "pioneering," as if the Eastern countries had been terra incognita, necessitating exploration. IFES leaders knew that Christianity already existed in Eastern Europe, but they seemed unsatisfied with its state. Williams provides a description which illustrates well how IFES saw its work:

> There had been IFES related student work in some of these countries before the Second World War, but the communists had closed it down, and many church leaders felt there was no need now for anything more than their own, often anemic, church-related youth work. It was the pastors we had to win over to new ideas about students reaching students; they were much more suspicious than any of the students.[2]

Two main areas of difficulty appear from this vivid account: the challenge of political authorities, averse to ecclesial influence and officially serving a state doctrine of atheism; but also the challenge of embattled churches, divided over the ways they wanted to relate, or not, to the State. The question of foreign influence was a concern not only for the State, but also for the local church. The first was worried about political influence, the latter at the possibility of a decline in morality.[3] Furthermore, what legitimacy was possessed by a ministry of students to students, without clerical supervision? As Williams

---

1. Chua Wee Hian and Padilla, "God's Work in the World Today," 173–74.
2. Williams, *Holy Spy*, 13.
3. Williams, 13.

further vividly recalls, the diplomatic fronts were not always neatly separated between "Christian brethren" and "political fools":

> And who were we? Who employed us? Why were we travelling around looking for Christian students? Almost no one knew of IFES and we did not like to explain it in case it sounded like a cover for the proscribed foreign organization which, in fact, it was. However, it was not anti-communist, but trying to establish member movements in the communist countries, and primarily concerned to spawn effective indigenous local networks of students witnessing to their peers about their Christian faith. At that time organizations outside the actual structure of the churches were all forbidden, particularly international organizations.[4]

In these uncertain times, it is understandable that church leaders could fear how potentially more enthusiastic and less mature students might imperil carefully crafted relationships between clergy and State. However, this work among students was mostly done *in collaboration* with church leaders. There was no church-planting strategy but the implicit idea that encouraging students to witness to fellow students would strengthen the church. Hence Williams's candid tone in describing how

> we visited pastors of all sorts of churches in every town in every country which came within our orbit. They did sometimes ask probing questions. They must have often wondered just whose agent we were. But they were unfailingly courteous and often received us with overwhelmingly generous hospitality. The pastors knew the key students in their congregations, the enthusiastic ones, whom we wanted to train and equip to be even more enthusiastic and involved in being Christian witnesses to their peers.[5]

Space does not allow for the recounting of the fascinating stories of people meeting for the first time and being united by a shared vision after a cup of tea and exchange of news about a common acquaintance. The importance of collaboration between mission organizations but also between local churches was regularly stressed. It is arguable that at least during communist times, such a ministry would foster a certain sort of "evangelical ecumenism,"

---

4. Williams, 13.
5. Williams, 132–33.

providing venues for Christians to meet, bypassing traditional divides, whether denominational –

> As fellow Christians we worked together in almost flawless harmony, whether from Brethren, Baptist, Methodist, Lutheran, Reformed or Anglican churches. Divisions which normally separate Christian people into their denominations hardly worried us and never seemed to show. We accepted each other's sincerity to sink our trivial differences and to work together for our great goal, for our great God.[6]

– or even ethnic:

> Yugoslavs with their 12 languages were ethnically mixed and diverse. They would not have flocked to hear a Baptist or Pentecostal speaker, but they flocked to hear an Anglican [John Stott], a foreigner to all of them with no axe to grind, or enemies, only friends. We could all be brothers together because we are all one in Christ.[7]

Critics might wonder if this was all genuinely theological or not more sociological and opportunistic. Students with contacts in the West might increase their chances of travelling or getting access to financial means. Yet stories abound of Christians living under Eastern European communist regimes telling how committing themselves to the Christian faith often had adverse consequences for their employability or their studies, for example.

Ultimately, formerly clandestine student movements were officially registered and the pioneer Polish ChSa welcomed a 2,000-people European Evangelism Conference in 1994.[8]

New Challenges from Tradition: Eastern Orthodoxy

Given the expansion towards Eastern Europe that marked the 1990s, it would be only a matter of time before IFES had to deal with another theological tradition with which it had previously almost never engaged: Orthodoxy.[9] As

---

6. Williams, 50.
7. Williams, 96.
8. Lineham, "Students Reaching Students," 57.
9. Strictly speaking, the traditions in question should be labelled "Eastern Orthodox" or "Greek Orthodoxy." For the sake of readability, "Orthodoxy" will be used as general term in this chapter.

was the case in the previous decade with student members of the RCC, the IFES leadership was slightly in disagreement over the issue. On the one hand, it wished to welcome newcomers into the fellowship; on the other hand, the traditional background of Eastern Orthodoxy was considered to be at odds with the received doctrinal convictions of the organization. The GS assistant for Europe had noted in 1978 that there were "a considerable number of evangelical students continu[ing] to belong to the Greek Orthodox Church. They have come to Christ through one of the many revivals in that church. If we link up with them, this will inevitably upset the evangelical pastors."[10] IFES thus found itself with the tension of mediating between students of aspiring evangelical convictions who remained in their churches, and evangelical pastors, with whom affinity would have been more likely. This was one of the situations where the practical outworking of missiological convictions tends to blur traditional lines of loyalty.

Another challenge for IFES was the fact that Orthodox theology is articulated around core tenets other than traditional evangelical doctrinal statements, which are easier to compare with clear Roman Catholic declarations, for example. This engendered some bafflement in the IFES leadership, as expressed by the GS in 1992:

> Orthodoxy is not the same as Roman Catholicism, and although official Orthodox statements strongly emphasise the differences with Protestantism, *we need to understand precisely what this means.* This is not easy. Matters are made more complicated by the fact that Orthodox theology itself is in a state of flux.[11]

In order to understand the exact issues at stake, the EC commissioned the European Regional Secretary, Jonathan Lamb, to write a memo, which was confidential at the time. The memo offered a contextual introduction, followed by a brief analysis of the theology of Orthodoxy structured around the IFES DB, and finally suggested action points. The essential conclusions of the report as they relate to theology and especially ecclesiology are outlined below.

As often with IFES, the question of the status of Scripture was a first stumbling block, closely intertwined with the question of ecclesial authority:

---

10. Brede Kristensen, "Report of the Assistant to the IFES General Secretary (Europe)" (Raglan, New Zealand, 18 Aug. 1978), 1, IFES e-archives, EC 1978 minutes, Appendix F.

11. Lindsay Brown, "IFES and the Orthodox Church" (Hald Training Center, Mandal, Norway, 28.7–1.8 1992), 1, IFES e-archives, EC 1992 minutes, Appendix I, italics mine.

> Orthodoxy would hold that the scriptures are inspired and trustworthy, and of high authority . . . but not the supreme authority. It represents part of the authority of the church/tradition. In addition, as evangelicals we understand scripture as 66 books, not the apocrypha as some Orthodox may; "as originally given," meaning its Hebrew/Aramaic form in the case of the OT, not the LXX that developed in later tradition; and we would also want to stress that this clause should be understood to mean that the final criterion for interpretation is scripture itself (over against the promise made by converts received into the Orthodox church).[12]

What is particularly striking is the appeal to the boundaries of the Protestant canon, a detail which is an internal tradition that no official document formalizes; the same is true of the refusal to consider the Septuagint as at the same level as other "originals." Finally, hermeneutical methods find their way in drawing lines of distinction. These three main points already amply demonstrate the difficulty of considering the DB to be a sufficient document for IFES: the basis needs constant reinterpretation, mostly in the form of amplification of how it is to be understood, for taken at "face value," nothing in the DB would have properly contradicted Orthodox faith.[13]

Another stumbling block for Lamb relates to redemption. In his analysis, Orthodox believers may well believe in redemption through the sacrificial death of Christ, but "it would be seen to be mediated through the sacramental life of the church, specifically through baptism, eucharist and the mystery of confession."[14] In line with many previous statements, Lamb goes on to restate that "the atoning work of Christ on the cross is central to our understanding of the gospel and of discipleship, [whereas] for some Orthodox, the central points might be incarnation/transfiguration/resurrection."[15] There is a sense of unease here. While not directly stating that the church is not necessary to salvation, the memo effectively plays down the importance of ecclesial involvement, which appears to be somewhat detrimental to evangelical faith:

---

12. Jonathan Lamb, "IFES Movements in Orthodox Countries," Confidential Memo to IFES Team Leaders only (Dimesse Sisteres Retreat Center, Nairobi, Kenya, 31 July 1993), 3, IFES e-archives, EC 1995 minutes, Appendix A.

13. The same difficulty arises upon discussion of "justification," where – notably without naming it – Lamb takes issue with the Orthodox doctrine of *theosis* which he understands to be a mark of synergism including "works of faith" in justification, over against "through faith alone" (DB clause H). Lamb, "IFES Movements in Orthodox Countries," 4.

14. Lamb, 4.

15. Lamb, 4.

"In fact, institutionally, in the church building the ordinary believer is excluded from the area behind the iconostasis. This has substantial theological, pastoral and psychological implications."[16] None of these implications is elaborated further, however; but the fact that Lamb laments the lack of access to the altar is an interesting hint at the underlying assumption that any believer has priestly privileges in this respect. He comes back to it later, adding to his commentary that "we would also wish to raise the issue of praying to the saints, the role of Mary, the special priesthood as opposed to the priesthood of all believers, etc. Sometimes Orthodox people might misunderstand the unique mediatorial role of Christ."[17]

The connection between laypeople and clergy is lurking behind the argument, as is the tension to situate an evangelical parachurch organization in a mostly homogeneous ecclesial landscape. Lamb notes that the belief in "one holy universal church" (DB clause J) "would be affirmed but understood to be the Orthodox Church. There is no 'Vatican 2' in Orthodoxy, and therefore no clear way for the Orthodox to articulate how they see Christians, for example, who are Protestants, evangelicals, etc. It is also linked with the national question."[18] So while Lamb's line of argument seems to downplay the importance of the local church because of its apparent theological shortcomings, he concedes that IFES needs to consider the overall ecclesial context its movements serve in. As had been the case in earlier decades, the question of evangelicalism being a foreign import was lurking in many discussions with church dignitaries who were concerned about "the influx of so many cults and wealthy western missions. [This] is in many senses an understandable reaction, but evangelicals (and also foreign missionaries such as IFES teams) can sometimes come under pressure as a result of this attitude."[19]

This tension between insistence on doctrinal tenets and contextual missiological necessities is best illustrated by Lamb's conclusions:

> It is easy to appear negative or defensive. Rather, we want to be eager to bring the gospel to all students, whatever their background, and we wish to enjoy fellowship with all Christians, including believers from the Orthodox community. . . . We would regard it as an expression of love to be honest about the grave

---

16. Lamb, 4.
17. Lamb, 4.
18. Lamb, 4.
19. Jonathan Lamb, "Orthodox Progress Report" (Centre des métiers de l'électricité, Bingerville, Côte d'Ivoire, 9 June 1994), 1, IFES e-archives, EC 1994 minutes, Appendix K.

difficulties we have with several aspects of the doctrinal position of the Orthodox Church, as expressed above. We would conclude that at the present time there is sufficient confusion over the major gospel issues in the mainstream teaching of the Orthodox for it to be problematic for us to use people active within it in our major leadership roles. . . . Given the fact that we are in the pioneering stage, and given that the need is for wise biblical leadership at every point, we advise very strongly against putting practising members of the Orthodox Church in positions of major influence, where such a person's understanding of doctrine and discipleship could shape the movement's approach to major policy issues.[20]

With these two significant challenges coming not so much from the "world" or other organizations active in the same field of ministry, but from its own ranks – students belonging to diverging church traditions – IFES needed to rethink its ecclesiological status and this question, and that is what occupied many discussions.

Africa and the Majority World

Eastern Europe was not the only area of development for IFES. The 1990s were a sort of "African decade." Africa saw significant growth in the 1980s such that "by 1991 there were conservative estimates that 10% of all the tertiary students in Anglophone Africa were members of Christian Unions."[21] The centre of gravity of Christianity had shifted south, which was not to mean that the centres of power would do the same.

Significant debates about nationhood and its correlates in indigeneity and autonomy could not be avoided. In the early 1990s, a long debate started about whether it was wise to affiliate several movements for any given nation state. Some countries already had several movements (Canada and Switzerland), Belgium was applying for membership and was separated along language lines, and in some countries such as South Korea, divergence of opinion had led to the founding of an "alternative student ministry." In other contexts, the issues were rather ethnic and political, as with the complex situation of apartheid South Africa or Israel-Palestine.

---

20. Lamb, "IFES Movements in Orthodox Countries," 5.
21. Lineham, "Students Reaching Students," 126.

The question was one of unity and diversity. While space does not allow for in-depth exploration of the debates, the following excerpt from a 1998 discussion summarizes the issues well. Sng, EC member and former FES Singapore GS, made a case for unity on biblical and missiological grounds. Having surveyed biblical passages such as Ephesians 4 and John 17, he then stresses that these passages have a clear "missiological dimension. Acknowledging that all believers are bound together in a mystical union in Christ is not enough. This unity has to be seen by others. It must be lived out as a witness to the world. Only then, can the world 'know.'"[22] For Sng, unity must be maintained, for it cannot be taken for granted in a fallen world. The perennial tension between *visible* and *invisible* unity is mentioned again. This unity that needs to be maintained allows for a diversity of functions and approaches, which are contextually relevant, intensely prophetic and culturally shaped. If visible unity was not stressed in the (post-)Christendom West, the Singaporean leader highlights the need for a different approach in countries where Christians are either a minority (Israel) or where the political dimensions of unity bear upon one's understanding of the fundamental unity of human beings (South Africa). Hence the articulation of a working ethos that takes context and culture seriously:

> IFES seeks to encourage students to take responsibility for reaching out to their own campus. In doing so, students are to exercise their gifts, understand their own student culture, and apply Christian thinking in meeting the challenges. Such an approach may lead to a diversity of operation on campus. But within this diversity, practical expressions of unity among all believers must be sought constantly.[23]

IFES had grown, many more movements were coming of age, and the links between power, representation, methodologies and strategies could not be fully discussed apart from contextual sensitivities. For many years, the work in many countries of Africa had been done under the auspices of the PAFES, which was considered as one member of IFES. In the 1990s, autonomous national movements were affiliated separately as part of the newly formed English and Portuguese-speaking Africa (EPSA) region. In 1998, at the height of the discussions, the senior leadership acknowledged that "IFES may be

---

22. Bobby Sng, "Unity and Diversity in IFES" (Senior Staff Consultation, May 1998), 3, IFES Archive, Oxford, SSC 98 papers.
23. Sng, "Unity and Diversity," 3.

too strongly influenced by Western European and North American founding members in the models it adopts for structures."[24] Voices were heard in the South Pacific region saying that the word "evangelical" was concerning and not welcoming enough, while similar opinions were voiced in Africa, where EPSA delegates contended that the doctrinal basis was not inclusive enough. There are no signs in the archives that the fellowship risked implosion during the 1990s, yet one is struck by the growing robustness of the debates carried out and especially by the emergence of strong voices from the Majority World. After all, IFES had boasted about nurturing national leaders and letting them develop a Christian mind adapted to their contextual realities.

Debates about African realities were not based on theological treatises but on field experience. Thus, in 1994, the board listened to two reports on Pentecostalism and the charismatic movement, penned by French-speaking and English-speaking African delegates.

Olofin argues on ecclesiological grounds that IFES groups must be able to welcome believers of all points of view concerning the charismatic question, precisely because IFES is not a church: "The IFES and its member movements *as a handmaiden to the Church* must strive towards providing such a common ground, where charismatics and non-charismatics alike would feel welcome, regardless of the appellation – evangelical."[25] Yet even if IFES groups are not churches but outposts of the local congregations, "our fellowship groups ought to be places where Christ is acknowledged as the true head of the Church, away from our preferred teachers, authors, overseers, pastors, among others."[26]

The "handmaiden" metaphor is a hapax legomenon in the archival evidence indicating the strong importance Olofin attaches to the church, and it contrasts with the pre-IFES days, especially in Western Europe, which were characterized by a rather anti-clerical mood. Members of the clergy were castigated for stifling the pious enthusiasm of young students for the sake of ecclesiastical hierarchies.

Early IFES leaders had insisted on a large degree of formal freedom once a shortlist of doctrinal essentials had been agreed upon. Like any group of individuals coming together around a common cause, they had also built their traditions and structures that were in turn challenged, implicitly on the same

---

24. "Minutes of the Meeting of the Executive Committee of the IFES" (Bischofsheim, Germany, 28.6–3.7 1998), 11, IFES e-archives.

25. Samuel Olofin, "Pentecostals, Evangelicals and Charismatics" (Centre des métiers de l'électricité, Bingerville, Côte d'Ivoire, May 1994), 4, IFES e-archives, EC 1994 minutes, Appendix L2; emphasis added.

26. Olofin, "Pentecostals, Evangelicals and Charismatics," 4.

ground: the right of a believer to have *immediate* access to God. The founding fathers based their belief in the ability of students to know for themselves God's will on the fact that *God had revealed himself in Scripture.* This could be understood *individualistically*, as each believer being his or her own priest. Yet a growing number of Pentecostal students were now arguing that the Bible might *hinder immediacy*. Pentecostal piety was making a case for even more direct access to God: through *unmediated* action, and speaking of the Holy Spirit *from within* the believer. Andria, RS for Francophone Africa, appealed to IFES's self-definition as a reformist movement to remind his colleagues that

> Pentecostal leaders are in agreement with Martin Luther and other reformers who restored the doctrine of justification by faith, and with the Wesleys who restored the doctrine of sanctification. However, they say that now the Lord is using the Pentecostal movement to restore the doctrine of baptism of the Holy Spirit and of fire. We can say that Pentecostalism is concerned about how Christians must believe.[27]

New Challenges from Experience: Pentecostalism

Pentecostalism was not a new phenomenon to IFES in the 1990s, as charismatic gifts had been exercised in local groups for some time already. As early as 1970, Woods had in a characteristically critical tone reported that "in inter-denominational evangelical student unions where speaking in tongues has been practised publicly within the union, usually it has been divisive."[28] This was to be attributed, according to Woods, to the "sinful spiritual pride"[29] of confusing the exercise of speaking in tongues with spirituality. Hence, the logical conclusion of the priority-mindset of the early IFES leader was to make sure that such "paraphernalia" of spiritual life did not disrupt the core activities and stir inter-ecclesial disputes. In Woods's terms,

> because of the inter-denominational character of our societies and the fact that this gift according to the Scriptures is of lesser importance (it is not recorded that our Spirit filled Saviour, the

---

27. Solomon Andria, "Pentecostal, Charismatic, Evangelical: Differences and Distinctives" (Centre des métiers de l'électricité, Bingerville, Côte d'Ivoire, May 1994), 1, IFES e-archives, EC 1994 minutes, Appendix L1.
28. C. Stacey Woods, "Memorandum on Charismatic Gifts" (Sep. 1970), IFES e-archives.
29. Woods, "Charismatic Gifts."

Lord Jesus, ever spoke in tongues), it is recommended, therefore, that this question not be a subject of teaching within a union nor of public practice; rather, that those claiming to have this gift practice it to the glory of God in private.[30]

Yet despite IFES leaders not seeing *charismatic gifts*[31] as essential to Christian piety, many students were experimenting with the essentiality of such practice in their Christian lives. In line with Woods's cautionary words, they were apparently not always welcome, as some years later, in 1978, the IFES board deplored that Pentecostal students were not necessarily joining IFES groups in Latin America but should be encouraged to do so, for "their zeal and boldness in witnessing would be an asset to the Fellowships. At the same time, these Pentecostal students would benefit from a systematic Bible exposition and group Bible studies provided by IFES groups."[32] A missiological tension is palpable here: on the one hand, these "enthusiasts" could kindle new energy in local groups and are notably not dismissed as unchristian; but, on the other hand, they would, according to the IFES leadership, need "proper theological orientation."

The history of the early IFES encounter with Pentecostalism is illuminating because it effectively challenged the core assumption of the IFES leadership that the doctrinal basis would prove sufficient in providing theological orientation for the organization and settle doctrinal discussions. Yet the DB is historically and culturally conditioned. Despite its official labelling as summarizing the "fundamental truths of Christianity," it could not be called upon to mitigate practical tensions resulting from the stress placed on different aspects of Christian doctrine. As was repeatedly proved to be the case, it did not suffice to affirm that "IFES welcomes all evangelicals – Pentecostals and charismatics included – provided they unconditionally confess the basis of faith."[33] Anchoring his observations in cultural history, Warner offers an insightful commentary of the issues at stake:

> Harvey Cox memorably described Pentecostals as "shattering the cognitive boundaries" of conservative evangelicalism, by

---

30. Woods.

31. The expression is here used as a shortcut for charismatic-Pentecostal practices that are not usually practised in more conservative evangelical groups, such as speaking in tongues, prophesying, speaking words of knowledge, etc.

32. "Minutes of the Meeting of the Executive Committee of the IFES" (Raglan, New Zealand, 18 Aug. 1978), 4, IFES e-archives.

33. Andria, "Pentecostal, Charismatic, Evangelical," 2.

privileging the revelatory significance of personal experience.[34] This is reflected in the intemperate denunciations of Pentecostals by some conservatives, who recognized in them a disruptive and dissonant form of conservative piety, shaped more by Romanticism than the Enlightenment.[35]

This "shattering [of] cognitive boundaries" was indeed an unexpected phenomenon, for unlike in the early days of IFES, the challengers could not simply be labelled as "liberal." Resistance to Pentecostalism was not new in evangelical circles, however.[36] In earlier years, IFES had challenged other organizations and churches on doctrinal grounds, yet now it found itself forced to reconsider its own premises in the light of new contextual developments. These premises were frequently reworked, as the next session shows.

Defining the Ecclesiological Character of IFES

The 1990s saw a deliberate effort to arrive at a common-ground communication on how the ecclesial character of IFES was to be defined.

Appealing to the Acts of the Apostles

In 1991, opening his term, incoming GS Lindsay Brown offered the fellowship a programmatic speech titled "The Growth of a Work of God: The Antioch Model."[37] He begins with a traditional presentation of the distinctives of IFES, the first being that IFES is a "Fellowship of international friendships... [where] decisions are reached on the basis of Scripture, in the context of friendship, by persuasion, argument, debate and interaction. That's a risky way to live, but we believe it's the right way for strength of fellowship to be maintained." This relational background established, he affirms that IFES is essentially "grassroots," which means that "we are a student movement with students exercising initiative and taking responsibility"; and lastly, that "national movements remain independent," for "we have a common belief and purpose,

---

34. Harvey Gallagher Cox, *Fire from Heaven: Pentecostalism, Spirituality, and the Reshaping of Religion in the Twenty-First Century* (Reading: Addison-Wesley, 1994).
35. Warner, "Evangelical Bases of Faith," 344.
36. Hutchinson and Wolffe, *Short History*, 202.
37. Subsequently published as Lindsay Brown, "The Growth of a Work of God: The Antioch Model; Address to World Assembly 1991," *IFES Review* 31 (1991): 3–10. All the quotes that follow are from this article.

but employ varying methodologies in fulfilling that purpose. We don't talk in terms of imposing a centralised plan on the rest of the Fellowship."

Brown's speech represents a significant development of the ecclesiological reflection expressed in IFES. It is rare to read such articulate pleas affirming that "we need to have a strong ecclesiology, a strong doctrine of the church." While the term "parachurch" is used loosely in considerations of ecclesiological character, Brown insists that he is "very unhappy with the term 'parachurch' to describe IFES, because the term 'para' means 'alongside' the church, and theologically I've never seen us as such a movement." Instead of seeing IFES as working alongside the church, Brown sees IFES as "*sent out from within the church. . . . We are a part of the church*, obeying the Great Commission of Christ, by going out in mission to a part of the world, the campus, and thence feeding people back into the life of the church."[38]

Brown is aware of the tensions encountered on the field: "Some of our movements may have become very critical and disillusioned out of frustration at the weakness of the church. I know that in some parts of the world, the church is in a desperate state. But it's all we've got. Christ said, 'I will build my church.' He didn't say, 'I will build IFES.'" Consequently, what the new GS encourages his constituency to do is to see itself as an integral element of a more comprehensive picture:

> We must participate in the strengthening of God's kingdom as it is expressed in the life of the church globally. We might lament its weakness, but there's a difference between destructive and constructive criticism. If a church is weak, we have a responsibility to help strengthen it and to ensure that our students and our staff are committed to vigorous, evangelical church life and to building the church of Christ.

Especially in places where Christians were a small minority, IFES needed to entertain relationships with church leaders and could not think of operating on a purely independent basis. Surveying the situation in the Middle East, the EC observed in 1993 that "where the Church is weak, generally student work is also weak."[39] In other places, diverging visions and misunderstanding threatened to undermine some of the ministry of IFES. The EC's "IFES and the Church Task Force" remarked in 1996 that

---

38. Emphasis added.

39. "Minutes of the Meeting of the Executive Committee of the IFES" (Oak Hill College, London, England, 25–31.7 1993), 6, IFES e-archives.

churches can be made uncomfortable by para-church groups like IFES, national movements which are perceived as being "in competition." There is a decreasing commitment by national movements to local church expressions; an increasing separation between Church and national movement. In some countries, groups function increasingly as churches. This shows weak ecclesiology.[40]

It is somewhat ironic for a movement that usually shied away from talking about the church to deplore a weak ecclesiology. As Chua had noted in 1989, remembering his early years as a staff member in Singapore and Malaysia,

twenty years ago, most national movements would not tackle the subject of the church. It was . . . almost like a taboo subject. . . . When we came to the Church, we were asked not to touch it. It was too controversial, people had different understanding and affiliations to local churches, so [if] you want to avoid controversy, you don't discuss the Church, you leave it alone.[41]

The 1995 GC suggested publishing a booklet on the IFES position towards the church. There were questions not only about the relationship of IFES movements to local churches, but also as to whether IFES was involved in church planting. In countries as different as Côte d'Ivoire and Australia, some IFES leaders started to plant churches more fitting with their aspirations than the local expressions already present. Brown adamantly insisted on a logic of partnership, arguing that "while other groups have moved into church planting, IFES encourages students to move into national evangelical churches beyond graduation. IFES is the arm of extension of the local church into the campus, feeding Christian students back into the churches for a lifetime of service."[42] While some in IFES were engaged in church planting, other churches conversely were involved in campus church planting, thereby dividing "students

---

40. "IFES and the Church: Notes Produced by the Task Force Group" (Redcliffe College, Gloucester, England, 30 June 1996), 1, IFES e-archives, EC 1996 minutes, Appendix F3.

41. Chua Wee Hian, "The CU and the Church," audio tape, Formación 89 (1989), IFES Archive, Oxford.

42. "Minutes of the Meeting of the Executive Committee of the IFES" (Urbana, Illinois, USA, 6 Jan. 1997), 7, IFES e-archives. Willmer et al. offer a word of caution about such "partnership talk," arguing that "many parachurch leaders use the language of partnership – especially when they need help from the church. But far too often these sentiments are just rhetoric, and the actions of the leaders give a drastically different message." Willmer, Schmidt and Smith, *Prospering Parachurch*, 179.

into different student groups."⁴³ This second issue occupied IFES movements in the following years, especially in Africa. Hence it is somewhat ironic that IFES saw itself confronted more and more with the potential divisions of Christian witness on campus that the earlier WSCF had accused them of promoting.

More concerning internally was an added phenomenon, perceived as the danger that "some of the staff of some of the IFES movements see the movement as their church."⁴⁴ The combination of so many ecclesiological questions called for a more deliberate settlement, because, only a few years later, Brown lamented that some movements still had "weak links with churches. It may be time for us to reflect in a new way on how IFES links with churches."⁴⁵

By Way of Arrangement

Instead of publishing a booklet on IFES's relationship to the church, the senior leadership opted for a shorter statement summarizing key positions which was made public in 1998. As the sharpest ecclesiological statement to date, it is worth quoting at length. In it, IFES asserts the following:

1. The Church is God's method for reaching the world.
2. All believers are members of the universal Church.
3. There are many and varied expressions of the local church.
4. IFES has distinct postures toward the Church:

    We are not, and refrain from ever becoming, a local church.

    We encourage our staff and students to be involved with a local church along the lines of what we believe to be biblical convictions about doctrine.

---

43. "Minutes of the Meeting of the Executive Committee" (1998), 26.

44. "Minutes of the Meeting of the Executive Committee" (1998), 26.

45. Lindsay Brown, "Report of the General Secretary to the General Committee of IFES" (Kenya Commercial Bank Center, Nairobi, Kenya, 26 June 1995), 6, IFES e-archives, GC 1995 minutes, Appendix D. Intriguingly, in a decade when theological debates and challenges abounded and when academic and strategic reflections shared across the fellowship could have provided perspective, the same report notes that *IFES Review* was discontinued "because of inadequate resources."

> IFES is a mission movement to university students.
>
> Note Distinctive #10 in the IFES Distinctives: "We are not a local church because we say we are not a local church."
>
> Value of the global church expressed in the dynamics of local churches.[46]

Although conceived as a sort of definitive statement on the ecclesiological question, the paper did not settle all issues. IFES affirmed a "desire to have sensitivity to nations that might have student work already out of the 26 that we are looking to pioneer," pointing out that "IFES is looking to build bridges rather than usurp what is going on."[47] If the fundamentally theological conviction that students can be emissaries of the gospel on campus and witness to their fellow students proved to be a strong mobilizing factor for aspiring leaders, the downside of such empowerment could be relational issues with church leadership and, in some cases, immature behaviours:

> IFES needs to look further into the whole concept of modelling. Students tend to have no room in churches. When students come to movements, they find it to be the place where they can come to have room. They often try to be the pastor and preach to express rather than practice humility needed in bible studies. Model passion. We need more models and more creative effort.[48]

At the end of the decade, the summary statements would be direct and clear:

> We are committed to strengthening local churches in countries all across the world. *We do not see ourselves as a para-church movement existing alongside the church, but as a movement which flows out of the church, and subsequently feeds graduates and students back into local churches for a lifetime of service. We see ourselves as an inter-church movement, which acts as an extension of the ministry of the churches.* We are not a one-church movement, we are an interdenominational movement. We do not

---

46. "Minutes of the Meeting of the Executive Committee" (1998), 26.
47. "Minutes of the Meeting of the Out-Going Executive Committee of the IFES" (Hyundai Learning Center, Seoul, South Korea, 14 July 1999), 9, IFES e-archives, EC 1999 minutes.
48. "Minutes of the Meeting of the Incoming Executive Committee of the IFES" (Kwang Lim, South Korea, 26 July 1999), 13, IFES e-archives, New EC 1999 minutes.

elevate any one denomination above others. Our aim is that no one denomination should be dominant within the movement.[49]

Ministering Holistically to the University?

The last significant discussion of the 1990s was a recurring aspiration, voiced at several GCs, to have IFES adopt a more holistic view of its ministry. As the following explorations show, the champions of such an approach often faced an uphill battle.

Two main dimensions of "holistic ministry" can be found in the discussions. The first, more "social," was discussed during the 1987 GC in Colombia, where delegates advocated for more social justice involvement with disadvantaged student populations. Especially in Latin America, the necessity for IFES groups to help their struggling classmates was self-evident.

The second dimension – connecting IFES ministry to the academic-intellectual character of the university – proved intricate to tackle. Board Chairman Ford, commenting on a draft long-range plan in 1992, had pointedly noted that "we are called to 'engage the Campus with the Gospel' and should affirm the value of the university."[50] The foundation would take time to be fully articulated. Training secretary Brown, who had complained about the lack of intellectual level of the Formación 89 participants in a letter quoted above, was adamant in her 1993 report that "we need to regain lost ground in the university, produce Christian thinkers and apologists, and radical Christian disciples who think as people of Christian action and act as people of Christian thought."[51] Brown does not elaborate on why she considered the university "lost ground." However, the reader can assume as a working hypothesis that an embryonic critique at the lack of theological foundations of university education was being voiced. The second, more social dimension was mentioned in the same report, with Brown arguing that "our task is to bear witness to the gospel in the student world. This will mean not simply proclaiming it through personal and public evangelism, but modelling its life-transforming power and its relevance to questions of social justice, poverty, etc."[52]

---

49. "Second Draft of Global IFES Plan" (1998), 5; emphasis added.

50. "Minutes of the Meeting of the Executive Committee of the IFES" (Hald Training Center, Mandal, Norway, 28.7–1.8 1992), 4, IFES e-archives.

51. Dr. Sue Brown, "The Future of Training in IFES" (Oak Hill College, Southgate, London, England, May 1993), 2, IFES e-archives, EC 1993 minutes, Appendix B1.

52. Dr. Sue Brown, "Future of Training," 2.

Seeing the university as more than a "reservoir of people to be reached with the Gospel" necessitated an opening to more than the spiritual dimensions of the student body. This was the case made in a 1994 discussion memo penned by Napon which aimed at establishing the foundations for a full embrace of holistic ministry in IFES.[53] Theologically and historically articulate, despite its brevity, Napon's argument begins with lament:

> The great tragedy is that evangelicals see their priority as saving souls, when in actuality, social action and spiritual ministry are meant to complement, not compete with, one another. Now is the time for the Evangelical Church to integrate spiritual ministry with social action in order to move towards a more "holistic ministry."[54]

This theory of a "Great Reversal" – that most evangelicals had abandoned social commitment to concentrate solely on piety and mission – made by numerous scholars[55] is in most cases only partially correct.[56] The narrative of a theological shift in emphasis is integral to Napon's argument, and indeed, the whole framing of the holistic mission emphasis in IFES could be boiled down to a contest of historical narratives. Napon begins by offering a complex definition of how he understands holistic ministry. For him, it is

> all we do to respond to the physical, spiritual, emotional and social needs of persons, here and now, so as to facilitate the progress of persons towards freedom and wholeness, which will be consummated when our Lord returns. Therefore, man cannot establish Utopia on earth by his sole efforts. The fullness of man can be complete only in the Kingdom to come. This is why the spiritual dimension needs to be emphasized. The Bible asserts, "what value is there if a man gains the whole world and loses his soul, and what can a man give in exchange for his soul?"

---

53. The EC made it its habit to regularly hold discussions about issues significant to student ministry, without necessarily devising policies on that basis.

54. Moïse Napon, "Holistic Ministry" (Centre des métiers de l'électricité, Bingerville, Côte d'Ivoire, May 1994), 1, IFES e-archives, EC 1994 minutes, Appendix LM.

55. See the classic by David O. Moberg, *The Great Reversal: Evangelism versus Social Concern* (London: Scripture Union, 1973). For an informed discussion especially of the American context, see George M. Marsden, *Fundamentalism and American Culture*, 2nd ed. (New York: Oxford University Press, 2006), 85–93.

56. See, for example, Treloar, *Disruption of Evangelicalism*, 252; Kirkpatrick, *Gospel for the Poor*, 7.

(Matthew 16:26). Our ministry should therefore address both the physical (body) and the spiritual (soul).⁵⁷

This development speaks against any accusation that his view is informed more by Marxism than theology: no Marxist would appeal to eschatological, christological disruption to make his or her point. Napon's orientation is missiological. He further offers a plea:

> The great task of the IFES ministry will be to act as a catalyst for the change towards holistic ministry. If only our intellect could manufacture well-balanced programs which address the mind, the body and the soul appropriately, the ministry of IFES will become relevant to the suffering world in our day.⁵⁸

Speaking from the disadvantaged context of Burkina Faso, Napon's defence of holistic ministry was the result of strategic concern for the relevance of IFES ministry on a continent marked by suffering. Hence his conclusion that

> our ministry will be effective and relevant if we break down the dichotomy between the physical and the spiritual, the temporal and the sacred, and rather see man as God created him . . . body and soul, flesh and spirit, two inseparable parts of the same reality. IFES has the international experience, energetic young people, and experienced international graduates to be at the forefront of Holistic Ministry. Take what you have been given and respond with compassion to the human needs that are in God's world.⁵⁹

As usual, the minutes do not record the details of the discussion, but do record that "there was some discussion concerning the historical background to the issue which was not addressed at length in the paper."⁶⁰ Given that biblical history, as well as early church history and the Reformation era, are treated in the short memo, the reader informed of the stories commonly told in IFES historical writings understands that what is here referred to is the early history of IFES and especially its British forerunners in their confrontation

---

57. Napon, "Holistic Ministry," 1.
58. Napon, 3.
59. Napon, 4.
60. "Minutes of the Meeting of the Executive Committee of the International Fellowship of Evangelical Students" (Centre des métiers de l'électricité, Bingerville, Côte d'Ivoire, 29 July 1994), 22, IFES e-archives, EC 1994 minutes.

with the "social gospel" at the beginning of the century.⁶¹ Thereby responding to the challenge,

> Mr Niringiye explained that in the African context "discipleship dos" have at times been restricted to "read your Bible, pray and evangelise" with a lack of emphasis on issues such as family, sexuality, etc. It was noted that holistic ministry is not just an issue for students in the developing world but is also relevant for Western students. The critical issue is how we understand discipleship and stewardship.⁶²

Consequently, one reads in the discourse of the African board members an attempt to use "holistic ministry" as a bridge to broadening the spectrum of what fell within the sphere of responsibility of student ministry, where older terms like "discipleship" had missed the mark. Yet, closing the discussion, Brown

> gave a definition of discipleship as being all of God's truth to all of God's world. Stewardship is the use of all of God's gifts in all of God's world. The application of holistic theology is the application of the whole Bible to the whole man and the whole of society. *We must take care not to be selective in our reading of God's word. He is concerned that when Christians discover a need for social help, they often tend to gradually lose their zeal for evangelism.* A good question to pose is "How can we promote Christian understanding and way of life?"⁶³

Hence the call to holistic ministry was subsumed into a discussion of discipleship. This would occur again during a tense debate that raged at the first GC held on African soil in 1995. Discussing the strategic plan presented by the GS, Columbian and Bolivian delegates expressed their concern "with the lack of emphasis on social issues."⁶⁴ Consistent with his aforementioned conclusion of the board debate of the year before, Brown responded by pointing out that "the phrase 'service in the family, church and society' (as found in the IFES goals) included personal involvement in social change,"⁶⁵ thereby relegating social involvement to the individual sphere.

---

61. See above, chapter 2.
62. "Minutes of the Meeting of the Executive Committee" (1994), 22.
63. "Minutes of the Meeting of the Executive Committee" (1994), 22.
64. "Minutes of the Meeting of the Fourteenth General Committee of IFES" (Kenya Commercial Bank Center, Nairobi, Kenya, 22.6–2.7 1995), 4, IFES e-archives.
65. "Minutes of the Meeting of the Fourteenth General Committee" (1995), 4.

Making a similar point, UCCF UK & Ireland responded as follows:

> To write into the Plan or the goals explicit reference to social action (as integrated with the gospel) is a) a matter of the application of discipleship which may vary from region to region – and should be decided regionally; b) a matter of strong difference as to what the Bible says on the issue – and therefore not a matter of IFES universal agreement; c) adequately covered in the existing goals wording; d) not necessarily in the remit of IFES – IFES has specific goals and does not have to bear the total responsibility of the Church or Christians at large.[66]

Some younger member movements argued on missiological grounds that social involvement was integral to the gospel. Being relevant in their university context meant that social issues could not be thought of as separated from "evangelism." Other, more established movements decided that such involvement would prove detrimental to the unity of the fellowship.[67] If the written response quoted above sealed the discussion at the Nairobi meeting, it would not remain so for long.

With regard to the more *intellectual* dimension of holistic ministry, and significantly shorter, the idea that the university needed more attention was not lost from sight, even if not much was undertaken. In an article celebrating the IFES fortieth anniversary jubilee, Brown quoted Ramachandra as suggesting that "IFES has helped the church to recover its intellectual credibility, stressing the importance of presenting the gospel to confront the ideologies of the contemporary university world."[68]

A decade's worth of discussion hence resulted in a clear commitment to a broad view of the university and to considering the intellectual dimensions of the student world as a strategic institution:

---

66. "Minutes of the Meeting of the Fourteenth General Committee" (1995), 5.

67. The unease seemed widespread, however. The FES Hong Kong GS had also expressed in a written response to the plan – included not in the minutes but in the annexes – that "in order to express the diversity and richesse of this partnership of equals, I propose that different regions should be allowed the freedom to have different emphases or expression of our core values. In fact this trend should be encouraged in order that each region tries to contextualize the goals in a relevant way." "Proposals Presented to the General Committee" (Kenya Commercial Bank Center, Nairobi, Kenya, 22.6–2.7 1995), 1, IFES e-archives.

68. Lindsay Brown, "IFES Jubilee."

> We have full consciousness of the university's strategic importance. We aim to take the university seriously and see it as the primary theatre of service to which God has called us.[69]
>
> We are committed to the promotion of Christian witness among the world's students, and we will make a serious attempt to relate to the university and the challenges of the contemporary student scene, developing where possible creative new strategies for student witness . . . targeting the most influential universities as centres of strategic importance for Christian student witness, and seeking to make a special effort to develop work in those locations.[70]

As the discussions during World Assembly 1999 and in subsequent years showed, it would be at least another decade before commitment in word would be followed by real commitments in terms of staff, publications and events. This story will need to be told subsequently, however.

Pioneering, Empire and Indigeneity

> Our predecessors have pioneered the work with an emphasis on indigenous leadership so that IFES is not owned or operated exclusively out of one country or culture.[71]

Another topic occupied the senior leadership throughout the 1990s: the connection between "empire," "pioneering" and "indigeneity." In internal discussion papers and public meetings, the question was regularly asked how IFES understood the constitutional guarantee of "autonomy" to all its member movements to apply to theological reflection.

Pioneering was essential in the self-understanding of IFES. Its leaders commonly insisted on the need to establish movements in countries where no IFES-connected national movements already existed. In a somewhat ironic fashion, the main goal of this pioneering enterprise aimed at "establishing indigenous movements." The very paradox integral to pioneering from outside something that is meant to be indigenous highlights the tension underlying the whole expansion of the organization. In many contexts, the idea of pioneering

---

69. "Second Draft of Global IFES Plan" (1998), 4.
70. "Second Draft Global IFES Plan" (1998), 7.
71. Barney Ford, "A Shift of Strategy: From Expansion towards Greater Maturity" (Bischofsheim, Germany, May 1998), 2, IFES e-archives, EC 1998 minutes, Appendix E.

"from scratch" could not even be entertained as some Christian student movements already existed. The EC expressed the "desire to have sensitivity to nations that might have student work already . . . [pointing] out that IFES is looking to build bridges rather than usurp what is going on."[72] What IFES aimed at was the existence of movements understanding their mission in ways congenial to other member movements, yet contextually adapted. As Andria affirms, one of the IFES distinctives is "respect for cultural, historical and even theological differences between national movements. Our theology remains essentially evangelical, but it may well be contextualised."[73] The underlying idea is that of an agreed-upon core of distinctively "evangelical" convictions and practices in need of frequent reassertion:

> We have sought in our movements and in our pioneering areas to stress the authority of God's Word and to apply its unchanging truth to our service, witness and relationships. . . . Our founding fathers fought to maintain their evangelical faith; the new generation of students simply inherit this faith.[74]

Besides the difficulty of keeping agreement on an increasingly global scale, an international organization like IFES, by insisting on the "common ground," always risked fostering a high degree of theological and practical conformity. Cultural diversity and local appropriation of the faith, and not only faithful adherence to theological formulas, are essential dimensions of apostolicity. Theology is not developed in a vacuum: as a movement reacting to circumstances and developments in the wider ecclesial and theological worlds, the idea of "story" as a constituting element of the IFES identity is not absent from the leaders' thoughts. As Woods affirmed in 1971,

> each of the national evangelical unions pioneered and established since 1947 has its own particular story of God's work. Each is different. There is no stereotype, but all have a common loyalty to Christ and to His Word. God has helped us from becoming a centralised movement, a rigid organization; we are still an open, free fellowship.[75]

---

72. "Minutes of the Meeting of the Out-Going Executive Committee" (1999), 9.

73. Solomon Andria, "Autonomy and Indigeneity" (Hyundai Learning Center, Seoul, South Korea, June 1999), 1, IFES e-archives, Old EC 1999 minutes, Appendix K.

74. Chua Wee Hian, "General Secretary's Report" (El Hostel Duruelo, Boyaca, Colombia, 30.8–8.9 1987), 2, IFES e-archives, GC 1987 minutes, Appendix B.

75. C. Stacey Woods, "Report of the General Secretary" (Schloss Mittersill, Austria, 1971), 4, IFES e-archives, GC 1971 minutes, Appendix A.

Woods's description resembles Bebbington's quadrilateral core tenets for evangelicalism.[76] Yet IFES's history has evolved with the addition to the organization of new national movements, all of which have their own stories. Niringiye argues that IFES must reflect beyond its 1947 foundation date "on the separate histories that each brought to that moment. It is this convergence of separate narratives forming the one IFES narrative that is at the heart of the ethos of IFES because since 1947, many more narratives have converged, transforming IFES to become what it is today."[77]

Some parts of the early IFES ministry – or of its member movements – developed in the world of colonization. Escobar noted in 1999 that "empires have always been the socio-historical frame for the development of Christian mission as the Pax Romana was in the first century or the Pax Britannica in the nineteenth century."[78] Self-critically connecting the IFES history with the story of "empire" does not mean, however, writing off all the advantages of such association – and paradoxically, the fact that the empire helps in proclaiming the news that individuals can have an *immediate* relationship to God by *participating* in a universal community. On the contrary, Escobar highlights the beneficial aspects of these developments, insisting that

> Protestant missions had a modernizing component in their insistence on Bible translation, literacy, leadership training for the laity, and also in their use of modern medicine and the communication of basic technology. Aspects of globalization such as efficient communication at a global level or facilities for exchange . . . could be neutral factors that Christian mission may benefit from.[79]

As Paul used the imperial Roman road system to spread his message, IFES uses the university system. Ramachandra notes that

---

76. British historian David Bebbington has famously described Evangelicalism as the combination of a quadrilateral of Biblicism, Crucicentrism, Conversionism and Activism. See David W. Bebbington, *Evangelicalism in Modern Britain: A History from the 1730s to the 1980s* (London: Unwin Hyman, 1989), 1–18. "Activism" is implicit in the identity of IFES as a missionary organization and crucicentrism in its traditional evangelical hermeneutics.

77. David Zac Niringiye, "Towards an Understanding of Our Ethos: Some Reflections" (Senior Staff Consultation, 2000), 1, IFES Archive, Oxford.

78. Escobar, "A New Time for Mission," 4. See also World Council of Churches, Commission on World Mission and Evangelism, "Mission in the Context of Empire: Putting Justice at the Heart of Faith," *International Review of Mission* 101, no. 1 (Apr. 2012): 195–211.

79. Escobar, "A New Time for Mission," 5.

one of the many paradoxes we wrestle with in student ministry is that the university itself is not an indigenous institution in many of our countries. It often creates graduates who are alienated from the ways of life of most of their fellow-citizens. The subjects studied, and the way these subjects are taught, often bear little relation to the questions that people ask, the needs of the nation and the ways in which they have learned traditionally. . . . University education has tended to create a brain drain from the rural areas to the urban, and from the global South to the North.[80]

Students often must conform to the expectations of the university – determined mainly by Western canons – in order to succeed academically, and this in turn can undermine their ability to live the gospel incarnationally in their contexts. Ramachandra then observes that, "unable to resolve these dissonances, some students rebel against the whole system that produces such institutions, most divide their lives into self-enclosed compartments, [and] the better off plan to escape."[81]

Highlighting some of the inherent tensions of the association of IFES with the context of "empire" is not a straightforward rebuttal of its practices and discourses, however. IFES's theologically motivated and regularly reaffirmed commitment to the necessary indigenous appropriation of the Christian faith – congruent with the idea of *immediacy* – undermines the idea that Christian mission was solely a colonization process that left no agency to local actors.[82] The very nature of the IFES public – students – implies agency on their part. This "local appropriation of the gospel" – notably not of Christian structures – is at the core of the IFES discourse insisting that "workers serving in pioneer areas or with younger movements should do all they can to hand over full responsibility and leadership to national leaders."[83] Niringiye's summary of the mission of IFES as it relates to indigeneity is worth quoting at length:

The mission of IFES, and therefore of any movement in IFES, is reaching students with the gospel of Christ. A national movement

---

80. Vinoth Ramachandra, "Some Reflections on 'Indigeneity' and 'Autonomy' in IFES" (Hyundai Learning Center, Seoul, South Korea, June 1999), 4–5, IFES e-archives, Old EC 1999 minutes, Appendix.

81. Ramachandra, "Some Reflections," 5.

82. Flett refutes such frequent accounts as too narrow; see John G. Flett, *Apostolicity: The Ecumenical Question in World Christian Perspective*, Missiological Engagements (Downers Grove: InterVarsity Press, 2016), 182–83.

83. Chua Wee Hian, "Staff Letter 9" (Sep. 1973), 1, BGC Box #5.

is founded when this mission becomes indigenous and national in ownership, scope, transmission and expression. There should be in place indigenous and national structures and an infrastructure that embodies this mission and ensures continuity of expression. Since being a student is transitory, it is not enough to speak about the presence of Christian students at a time as evidence of student witness on a campus. There should be a way in which this Christian presence can be continued even after the particular Christian student graduates. And it is not a passive presence, but an active, growing, penetrating, transforming and missionary presence. In Jesus' words, it is being "salt" and "light."[84]

Even as IFES encourages local leadership and ownership, it is likely that in "pioneering situations," IFES could support leaders who will best conform to what they see is expected of them – either in terms of theological formulae or in practices which characterize a "good IFES group," not to speak of more pragmatic aspects such as their mastery of English or another lingua franca. Furthermore, the requirements for affiliations, notably the existence of a constitution and several specific elements of governance, belie the full acceptance that local movements might wish to organize themselves differently. Hence, if the "priesthood of all believers" is meant to allow each individual to relate immediately to God, some areas of ministry seem implicitly better served by replicating a "core package" of structures. This observation also highlights a critical blind spot in the IFES rhetoric: the "gospel" is implicitly believed to consist in a "core package" which can freely be adopted in all cultures.[85]

Despite IFES's strong insistence that what it encouraged was "mere evangelicalism," this was not the way its theology was always perceived, as Olofin remarks for the African context:

> To a large extent therefore the word "evangelical" was seen (and it is still seen) by some, as describing Bible believing Christians, who neither sanction the inhibiting conservatism of the traditions of the mainline churches, on the one hand, nor the liberalism of ecumenism, on the other hand. Also to be truly evangelical was to

---

84. David Zac Niringiye, "Beyond Pioneering," Discussion paper (May 1996), 1, IFES Archive, Oxford.

85. See the remarkable treatment of the question by a missiologist close to IFES, Benno Van den Toren, "Can We See the Naked Theological Truth?," in *Local Theology for the Global Church: Principles for an Evangelical Approach to Contextualization*, eds. Matthew Cook et al. (Pasadena: William Carey Library, 2010), 91–108.

> have very little or nothing to do with the indigenous independent churches that are rooted in indigenous cultures, and sometimes suspected of having links with indigenous pagan worship and practices.[86]

The cultural difficulties Olofin alludes to are not superficial but represent a conflict of loyalty between a foreign label and a local reality. Even as strong a defender of African contextual theology as Andria would write that IFES was to "give strong recommendations to national movements regarding the essence of IFES. Do this in the context of dialogue and reflection, with fraternal love."[87] Andria's conclusions aiming at linking contextuality and commonality, highly appreciated by the EC,[88] proposed a distinction between the *essence* of IFES and its many *faces*. In Andria's words, "IFES is a unique movement with several faces, which just like a family, is united by its essence (its blood), but where each member has his or her own face. There is, therefore, a likeness on the basis of the essence, but the various faces also bring differences."[89] There is no further evidence of this approach gaining traction within the IFES leadership, but this could have been an interesting way of considering the ecclesiological status of IFES: IFES being one of the "faces" of the church universal.

The most thorough examination of indigeneity within IFES is found in a discussion paper presented to the Executive in 1999 and debating the IFES quadrennial plan about to be launched.[90] Ramachandra disputes what he takes to be the naïve underlying idea that "indigenous" is equivalent to "national." Indigeneity "embraces those cultural practices, norms and values that are deemed to be 'home-grown' rather than borrowed from elsewhere." By their very nature, such practices and norms are tough to assess by outsiders. Furthermore, "claims to be 'indigenous' are often the sites of vicious political disputes" where factions compete for the moral superiority they pretend to achieve by defending "a mythical background that predates the advent of foreign oppression." One has to bear in mind, as does Ramachandra, that the question of "culture" is much more complex than simply local customs and folklore, but is the intricate and constantly evolving result of flows of influence on a global scale, most made possible by technology and the media. Essentializing

---

86. Olofin, "Pentecostals, Evangelicals and Charismatics," 2.
87. Andria, "Autonomy and Indigeneity," 2.
88. "Minutes of the Meeting of the Out-Going Executive Committee" (1999), 12.
89. Andria, "Autonomy and Indigeneity," 2.
90. Ramachandra, "Some Reflections," 1. The following quotes come from this short discussion paper.

cultures runs the risk of preserving the outdated myth of "cultural purity." This would, in turn, overlook the fact that "there is a danger that the emphasis on 'indigeneity' (in some missiological and political circles) invariably privileges the voice of conservative elements within the community." These "conservative elements," whose views are potentially easier to grasp by academics trained in Western analytical methods (like most IFES leaders), "do not represent the full scope of experiences in any given context, and treating the community as a homogeneous unit . . . neglects important differences within the community and almost entirely ignores the voices of dissent within."

Ramachandra challenges the idea that the "indigenous" dimension of the work of IFES is limited to questions of governance and methodologies. He argues that "as the Gospel enters into new cultures and subcultures, new questions arise to which those within that particular situation have to respond." This means that

> respect for Christian equality, as enshrined in the IFES Constitution, requires that we create a space in which we all have the freedom to explore the word of God in our own historically particular contexts. We may invite questions, advice, rebuke or correction from the global fellowship. This is a mutual exercise, not one part of the fellowship setting itself up as the doctrinal arbiter for the rest.[91]

Such "advising and rebuking" has happened regularly in IFES, yet it has rarely been fostered, for it runs against the grain of the "deposit of the faith" discourse.[92] Nevertheless, at the end of the century, new challenges arose.

A New Time for Mission: GC 1999

Thinking about and pondering the essentials was much to the fore in the plenary addresses given in South Korea.[93] "Evangelical Essentials," a sort of "theological testament" of John Stott, set the scene, while Samuel Escobar, speaking on "A New Time for Mission," offered a sweeping survey of past

---

91. Ramachandra, 6.
92. See below, chapter 11.
93. As of 1998, the newly revised long-range plan stressed the long-held essentials of the IFES's DB, insisting that "we teach loyalty to doctrinal essentials, which are clearly revealed in Scripture, and agree to remain in harmony and to allow differences on secondary matters. Those doctrines considered to be essential to saving faith are included in our Doctrinal Basis." "Minutes of the Meeting of the Fifteenth General Committee of IFES" (Hyundai Learning Center, Yong-In, South Korea, 23 July 1999), 8, IFES e-archives.

and present challenges facing IFES together with a vibrant call to renewed missional commitment.[94]

Concerned with preparing his audience for the broad scope of his remarks and challenging them from the outset, Escobar started by positing that his "evangelical outlook starts with commitment to the authority of God's Word, and my understanding of God's Word requires cultural awareness."[95] In Escobar's eyes, IFES could embrace new challenges because it had already advanced in turbulent waters, at the forefront of missionary engagement, serving every rising generation. In Escobar's view of IFES history,

> the student movements that came together to form the IFES 52 years ago had a strong tradition of passionate concern for evangelical truth and a deep commitment to world mission. Those origins help us to understand why IFES has been at the cutting edge of Christian mission in this century.

This was theologically fertile ground and a missiologically relevant springboard, as Escobar went on to argue that "faithful testimony for Christ in the hostile atmosphere of secularized campuses prepared these students to be more sensitive missionaries abroad. They had better training than those who had lived within the narrow intellectual confines and protected atmosphere of Christian schools and Bible colleges." These experiences gathered on the field of student ministry had not been concealed, but, in turn, offered back to the wider church. As Escobar further noted,

> it is not then surprising to observe how missionaries and theological scholars who published their first writings in periodicals of student movements by the middle of this century, later on became influential missiologists, breaking new ground for a more biblical understanding of what mission should be. This kind of evangelical ability to deal with secularity is indispensable for a true missionary stance in a post-Christendom era.

In Escobar's eyes, globalization was the main challenge for a missionary organization with a global reach, notably because of capitalism's use of

---

94. Both speeches were subsequently expanded and published: John Stott, *Evangelical Truth: A Personal Plea for Unity, Integrity and Faithfulness* (Downers Grove: InterVarsity Press, 2003); Samuel Escobar, *A Time for Mission: The Challenge for Global Christianity* (Leicester: Inter-Varsity Press, 2003).

95. Escobar, "A New Time for Mission," 2. The quotes that follow are from the same document.

communications channels to take "the latest aspects of Western culture as merchandise to the most remote corners of the world." Escobar was nevertheless no defender of technical backwardness, as he further remarked on the benefits of new technologies and easier communication. IFES was simply following in the footsteps of "Protestant missions [which] had a modernizing component in their insistence on Bible translation, literacy, *leadership training for the laity*, and also in their use of modern medicine and the communication of basic technology."

The speaker was aware of the potential for atomizing forces to fragment an organization as diverse as IFES. Hence his caution that "missionaries will be caught in the tension between globalization and contextualization, and they also have to avoid a provincialist attitude that exaggerates contextualization to the detriment of a biblical global awareness." Changing political landscapes and nationalist claims meant that missionaries needed "to go back to the fundamentals of the Gospel and to disengage themselves from the Western cultural trappings that consciously or unconsciously characterized missions during the imperial era in the nineteenth and early twentieth centuries."[96]

Escobar did not divert from his missiologically informed commitment to involvement in social justice issues:

> Mission projects of this kind are not just the result of a new awareness among Christians about a biblically-based social responsibility. They are also the inevitable response to worsening social conditions that have created many victims, becoming a new challenge to Christian compassion. IFES movements have contributed to the discipling and formation of leadership in many of these projects in which an interdisciplinary approach is required.

Showing a striking ability to foresee developments that would soon take over the world, Escobar made a strident appeal for the reconsideration of

---

96. "Contextualization" is a disputed word among missiologists and theologians more generally. In this work, I use it in the sense indicated by Flemming: "the dynamic and comprehensive process by which the gospel is incarnated within a concrete historical or cultural situation. This happens in such a way that the gospel both comes to authentic expression in the local context and at the same time prophetically transforms the context. Contextualization seeks to enable the people of God to live out the gospel in obedience to Christ within their own cultures and circumstances." Dean E. Flemming, *Contextualization in the New Testament: Patterns for Theology and Mission* (Westmont: InterVarsity Press, 2009), 19. See also Dean Gilliland, "Contextualization," in *Evangelical Dictionary of World Missions*, eds. A. Scott Moreau, Harold A. Netland and Charles Edward van Engen (Grand Rapids: Baker, 2000).

ecclesial and para-ecclesial structures considering the trends he observed in the student world:

> In the new century that will soon begin, new generations of students need to see a Christian presence and hear the Gospel of Jesus Christ on their campuses around the world. They will be less interested in concepts and more open to stories, poems and songs. They will have access to Internet and web pages. Virtual religious experiences will be available to them at the touch of a keyboard. Still, they will be hungry for fellowship and for a personal authentic touch of reality. Christian witnesses will need to be filled by the Spirit who is the one that drives people to mission. They will also have to learn the art of storytelling, to master the complexities of creating web pages, to start and nurture fellowships of committed believers, to engage in service in the name of Christ, to celebrate their faith and to figure out how to serve the Lord in their professions wherever he calls them.

Urging the fellowship to embrace new challenges was coherent with Escobar's enthusiasm for a ministry to which he had consecrated so many years. He concluded his passionate plea by stressing that IFES was well positioned to embrace the challenges ahead because of the solidity of its foundations and the versatility of its approaches, and could take confidence from the fact that "thus far IFES has been a useful instrument for mission."

Deep Debates for the End of the Millennium

> The long-standing debate among Christians about the relation between evangelism and social action seems now to be over. It is widely recognized among us that, as in the ministry of Jesus so in ours, words and works, the proclamation and the demonstration of the Kingdom, good news and good deeds, belong together. The gospel needs to be spread visually as well as verbally. These two things are "like the two blades of a pair of scissors or the two wings of a bird."[97]

Kindled by Stott and Escobar's addresses, the General Committee debated issues of social justice at great length, in terms more strident than those heard

---

97. John Stott, "Evangelical Essentials: Plenary Address to IFES WA 1999" (Hyundai Learning Center, Yong-In, South Korea, 23 July 1999), 1, IFES e-archives, GC 1999 papers.

in 1995. Things were happening on the ground: an Israeli delegate noted that "there are groups who have provided meals for students and residence for students. It's important that we recognize these examples of student mission in our work. This is not just for the sake of this report but for the sake of missions in the world."[98] A Swiss delegate had "been very surprised and happy at the same time to see at this conference the beginning of the social questions," yet also wondered why more space was not allocated to the question in the draft global plan. To this, Brown responded that it had been "a concern not to put too many of the social concerns in the document, as this can be a very nationalist concern. We are cautious [not] to highlight a focus on any particular issues. We can add to this if you wish." The Columbian delegate went further, "respectfully confess[ing] distress regarding the remark that social issues concern just national movements. It may be one way to help the Fellowship understand that national/local concerns do affect us as a Fellowship." To this further remark, Brown said he took the rebuke and suggested a task force to tackle the issue.

The next day, VBG Switzerland moved a motion to "set up a task force to investigate the biblical basis of mission and social justice and its implications on the global student witness of the IFES family." Some delegates responded by endorsing the motion, yet cautioning that many doctrinal elements were in place already, since the "biblical basis of mission [was already] well articulated within the official documents of IFES" (Kenya), or that "we all agree with the theology that all is mission" (Portugal). Others more or less adamantly opposed it, wondering how to relate "the motion at hand and our objectives" (Spain), while others were concerned that "we will sound like the UN or a liberal student movement" (Finland).

The FES Hong Kong delegate articulated the impression that "IFES cannot sweep it under the carpet and I welcome the gentleness of this motion to set up a task force to investigate. I do not see anything to reject in this motion. There is nothing wrong with investigating an issue of biblical mission." In the end this view won the day and the motion was passed.[99] The debate was rekindled in another motion devoted to graduate ministry, moved by the Brazilian delegation, suggesting that

> we will encourage a commitment to wholistic mission among graduates within the Fellowship. We desire to continue contribution

---

98. "Minutes of the Meeting of the Fifteenth General Committee" (1999), 11. The quotes that follow are from the same document.

99. With one vote against and seven abstentions out of a total of 105 votes.

to the discipling and formation of leadership in missionary projects. As long as possible we will provide training in the areas of Christian service and encourage our graduates to consider positions *where they can serve others so that they make a prophetic contribution to the life of their nations.*[100]

Especially the last sentence caused significant discussion, the main point of contention being whether such ministry fell within the realm of IFES or within that of local churches. In one of the tightest votes of any GC in IFES history, the motion was passed.[101]

---

100. "Minutes of the Meeting of the Fifteenth General Committee" (1999), 18; emphasis added.

101. Fifty-seven voted in favour, forty-five against and three abstained.

9

IFES in a New Millennium

For obvious methodological reasons, the formal historical section of this work ends in 2000. Examining the work of people who, for the most part, are still very much alive and well would take the historian into uncharted territory and possibly preclude the advisable distancing necessary for thoughtful and tentatively objective research. Hence this chapter is only a cursory sketch of some of the most salient events and people of the most recent years.

The 2000s were a time of new territories: geographically, the fellowship continued to welcome new national movements. From a technical point of view, emails and websites entered the world of communication. In 2001, the IFES office moved to the old university city of Oxford. In 2007, the first African GS, Chad-born Daniel Bourdanné, was elected. The following year, a new global strategy plan resulting from a consultative exercise with the national movements, "Living Stones," was launched. Featuring prominently the 1 Peter text to which we will come back, it describes IFES thus:

> We are a global community of indigenous student movements, called to engage the University with the good news of Jesus Christ.
>
> Our vision: Students built into communities of disciples, transformed by the gospel and impacting the University, the Church and society for the glory of Christ.[1]

Note that "indigenous" had now made its way into the official IFES identity; so had the notion that the university was to be engaged.[2] Similarly, the

---

1. International Fellowship of Evangelical Students, ed., "Living Stones: IFES Vision to 2020" (2008), 2.

2. The university as an institution for the horizon of IFES began to be more important with the "Engaging the University" symposium organized immediately prior to WA 2007 in Toronto.

church was explicitly acknowledged as the horizon of the fellowship's ministry, marking a significant shift and demonstrating a growing sense of self-assurance on the ecclesiological terrain.

As to student involvement, two important moves marked the 2011 World Assembly (WA) meeting in Poland. The first was a *student gathering* allowing for the deliberately growing number of students attending World Assemblies to meet among themselves and build international connections. The second, following years of lengthy debates, was the inclusion of two student delegates in the IFES Executive.[3] The same year, a global "Scripture Engagement" team was formed to encourage students and staff worldwide to renewed commitment to sustained engagement with the Scriptures.

In 2011, the IFES International Service Centre, as the Oxford office was now called, moved into a jointly owned building with UCCF. In 2013, the "Governance Development" programme launched, aiming to support national movements in developing strong and ethical governance structures. In the same vein, a "Ministry Impact" team formed, helping member movements assess their areas of growth and potential development, and an "Indigenous Support Development" ministry began, supporting national movements in raising funds locally, thereby reducing their reliance upon international support.

In 2015, another significant institutional move was to add a *scholars' track* to the World Assembly gathering in Mexico, marking a continuing interest in nurturing scholars closely linked with IFES movements. Building upon such encounters, the "Big Issues in the University" project, founded by the Templeton Foundation, formally gave new impetus to engaging universities. The same year, a new international office hub opened in Kuala Lumpur, servicing the whole fellowship with IT support.

In 2016 the "Global Leadership Initiative" convened a select group of fifteen promising young leaders from across the globe for the first cohort of a mentoring scheme lasting three years.

The last WA to date was in 2019. The year was eventful, marked by the nomination and then retraction of Chris Clarke from New Zealand to succeed Daniel Bourdanné as GS. More unanimous was the welcoming into IFES of the national movements in Cambodia, St. Vincent and the Grenadines, Solomon Islands, Cayman Islands, Vanuatu, Myanmar, Faroe Islands, Montenegro, Guinea-Bissau, Grenada, and two other countries in Eurasia and Europe not named for reasons of political sensitivity.

---

3. For the sake of transparency, I should add that I was one of them.

Most recently, the "Logos and Cosmos Initiative," aimed at fostering a deeper engagement with theology and the sciences within IFES, was launched in 2020, with the Latin America and Francophone Africa regions as pilot fields. The same year, Englishman Tim Adams was appointed GS, and soon announced that the new strategic priorities, about which the fellowship's leadership had been consulting the whole organization for more than a year, would soon be launched. The "Thriving Together: IFES Ministry to 2030" strategic plan was made official in early 2022.

Provisional Conclusion: History in Writing

The preceding chapters have offered a brief survey of some of the most salient facts, developments and ideas which have shaped the history of IFES. Out of a modest and somewhat adventurous gathering of some senior Christians interested in missionary work in the universities developed an international organization with extensive geographical reach. This historical section was intended to provide the reader with a good sense of the theological and missiological trends which have shaped the identity of IFES. In the next part, I turn to look more closely at the main IFES activities, before examining more substantive theological and missiological resources, to show how this ministry to lay students can be best understood by framing it under the doctrine of the "priesthood of all believers."

Part 2

IFES Activities

10

The Practical Functioning of Student-Led Ministry

So far, the historical part of this work has assumed the reader's relative acquaintance with the activities of an IFES group. However, it is now necessary to present these activities in more detail to map out the theological, ecclesiological and missiological questions that the activities can pose – and the answers which IFES has arrived at.

The core IFES activities of witness, prayer, Bible reading and fellowship presuppose theological convictions about *immediacy, mediation* and *membership.* In 1959, Adeney – later IFES president – outlined the basic tenets of the IFES vision: "To be effective a Christian fellowship on campus must have a three-fold objective: (1) To strengthen the faith of those who are already Christians (2) To introduce non-Christians to Christ (3) To prepare men and women for the service of the Kingdom of God."[1] Thus, IFES students gather based on their personal *immediate* faith, *participate* in fellowship that sustains and deepens it, for the purpose of *mediating* it to their environment through front-line missionary work. All these activities are supported by staff members who *mediate* the authority of the fellowship – albeit to varying degrees – and encourage local groups to remain in fellowship not only with IFES but with the greater Christian tradition through theological engagement and membership in a local church.

---

1. Adeney, "Student Work," 4.

Witness

An essential marker of the evangelical identity is its insistence on sharing the faith. This explains the fellowship's insistence on the necessity and urgency to *evangelize* or *witness*. As Zald observes, religious organizations have an inherent missionary mindset: they hold "theological and ideological beliefs about the relation of individuals and groups to each other, to society, and to the good and just life."[2] Scheitle concludes that

> unless those beliefs call for a complete retreat from the world, the believer is usually inspired and compelled to try and shape the world into the vision described by their beliefs. This is the role of outreach, which consists of four themes or goals: conversion, community, communication, and charity.[3]

More than the term "outreach," the idea of "witness" is fundamental to the self-understanding of IFES groups. The word is used to describe the *mediation* of one's faith to another person. As Jochemsen insists, "witness is a word we use frequently in the IFES and rightly so. It is one of the New Testament words describing an important element of the mission of the church and of the Christian in the world."[4] The "training and equipping" aspects of the activities of an IFES group are essential. As Escobar forcefully puts it,

> groups are formed not as a shelter where the faith of students can be protected, or as cells where the atmosphere of the church is projected into the campus. They are rather points where disciples can grow because they are engaged in mission and in that process their faith is strengthened and understood in a deeper sense.[5]

Witnessing activities take two main shapes: *personal evangelism* and *university mission*. As the name implies, *personal evangelism* describes all encounters where students deliberately share activities and discussions with fellow students to encourage them to consider the gospel for themselves. This can also occur in the context of weekly group meetings, to which IFES students invite their friends. The main thrust of the idea of *university missions* is that

---

2. Zald, "Theological Crucibles," 317.

3. Christopher P. Scheitle, *Beyond the Congregation: The World of Christian Nonprofits* (New York: Oxford University Press, 2010), 40.

4. Henk Jochemsen, "Authentic Christian Witness Demands Authentic Christian Service: Lecture Given at the International Student Conference Held at Schloss Mittersill in August 1989," *IFES Review* 29 (1990): 35.

5. Escobar, "Evangelical Heritage," 9.

the gospel needs to be proclaimed on campus as *public truth* and not only as *private belief*. Barclay's explanation of "university missions" as understood from the early CICCU days has mostly prevailed to this day within IFES and is hence worth quoting in full:

> Missions gave a unique opportunity of presenting the whole Christian message on the authority of God. In Universities the tendency is to regard religious views as just human opinion open to debate and discussion and having no authority other than the transient authority of the current academic fashion. The sermons, and especially the Missions, gave the opportunity to say clearly that God has spoken and to outline what He has said. There was a place for discussion to lead up to a Mission or to persuade people to come to hear preaching. There was a place for it to follow up a Mission afterwards. But the CICCU believed that, unless there is an authoritative declaration of the message as a word from God, we fail our listeners. The Missions focused this concern and made it plain that the CICCU had a message to declare.[6]

Here, the student group is presented as *mediating* between the university and God. Yet this mediation is not *immediate*, in that a speaker is coming. Students do not "preach" at mission weeks. They are expected to "witness" personally. Yet, if the whole point of the "mission" approach is to "convey a message," the student group structurally provides the platform for an invited speaker to "declare the message." At least from an organizational level, there is here no "priesthood of all students." Students setting the stage are at most "priests" to a secondary degree, as they might discuss the talk and thereby the message with their attending friends.

Prayer

As Christian students witness to a fundamentally transcendent reality, prayer is of utmost importance and is closer to the idea of priestly activities. Presenting a portrait of the "ideal IFES student," Woods emphasizes the combination of prayer and the – notably personal – study of the Scriptures:

> In our universities, what is our ideal of a Christian student? Surely it is the inner-directed Christian man or woman, *who has learned to find his resources in God rather than in the collective*

---

6. Barclay, *Jesus Lane Lot*, 128.

> *activity of the group. This student is spiritually weaned and finds his nourishment himself in prayer and Bible study aided by the Holy Spirit.... He has accepted God's law as his rule of life to be fulfilled in the power of the Holy Spirit and on this basis can engage in the task of evangelism with assurance and in dependence upon God alone.*[7]

The individualistic undertones are more evident here than in most of Woods's writings. What counts for the "ideal student" is to rely on his or her *immediate* relationship with God. Still, prayer is not understood solely instrumentally to prepare students to witness. It is also understood as an act of witness per se. Chua affirms this potential, noting that

> non-Christian students are quick to spot qualities like love among Christians and the intimate relationship between the Christians and their Lord, especially through spontaneous prayer. The second element supports the first and the union of propositional and incarnational witness certainly makes an effective thrust in evangelism.[8]

Similarly writing from the Asian context, Adeney links personal piety with questions of leadership, stressing the importance of personal responsibility for one's faith and witness over against the temptation to outsource it to seasoned ecclesial leaders:

> Teaching from more experienced Christians is welcomed, but such help should never cause Christian students to become dependent upon outside teachers and advisors. Through fellowship in prayer together and the student-led Bible study groups young Christians experience the leadership of the Holy Spirit. Non-Christian students may be suspicious of the activities of outside workers and organizations, yet they are bound to be impressed when they see their fellow students enjoying the study of the Word of God and sincerely and earnestly introducing Christ to their friends.[9]

Significantly, Adeney does not link the appeal of the Christian faith to its traditional anchoring or its truthful character, but to its existential, personal

---

7. C. Stacey Woods, "The Inner-Directed Christian," *IFES Journal* 1 (1966): 19; emphasis added.

8. Chua Wee Hian, "Staff Letter 8" (July 1973), 8, BGC Box #5.

9. Adeney, "Student Work," 8.

relevance to outsiders. His argument presumes the desirability of relating to God, but such desirability is in turn assumed from *membership* of a supportive and loving community. This could be interpreted as *indirect priesthood*, for students here mediate God and the communion they enjoy with him not necessarily in propositional terms but in lived experience into which their fellow students are invited. The early IFES leaders also interpreted it as a direct consequence of the "priesthood of all believers." Exemplary of this is Wisløff:

> In one sense all believers are priests. Peter calls the believers "a holy priesthood" (1 Peter 2:5). We who believe in Jesus have in his name the right to go directly before the throne of God with our prayers; we need no priest's substitute and intercessor. All believers stand equal before God. Therefore, we speak of the "universal priesthood of believers."[10]

This sense of *immediacy* with God, here assumed for prayer, is implicit in much of the hermeneutics supporting the work of IFES. Though the importance of prayer was not debated within IFES, diverging views of its exact characteristics existed. For example, Bentley-Taylor noted from one of his African tours that "it had been suggested to them that a real Christian spends five hours a day in prayer, speaks only of Christ and is wholly free from temptation. I was glad of the chance to reconsider these matters with some of the leaders."[11] Similarly, in Latin America, personal prayer was not seen as a panacea: "Evangelicals have discovered the privilege of personal prayer and Bible reading. But in terms of strategic initiative in evangelism, the 'pastor' has often simply replaced the 'padre.'"[12] This shows that regional differences abound in a very diverse fellowship despite a common commitment to core spiritual practices.

---

10. Carl F. Wisløff, *I Know in Whom I Believe: Studies in Bible Doctrine*, Norwegian original 1946 (Minneapolis: AFLC Seminary Press, 1983), 126. Lutheran Wisløff was part of the spearhead of the Pietist movement in Norway. Furthermore, "Wisløff has also strongly emphasized the priesthood of all believers and urged freedom for Christian organizations and societies within the Church of Norway." N. Yri, "Wisløff Carl Fredrik," in *New Dictionary of Theology*, eds. Sinclair B. Ferguson, David F. Wright and J. I. Packer (Downers Grove: InterVarsity Press, 1988), 726.

11. Bentley-Taylor, "African Diary," 31.

12. Hanks, "Paternalistic," 2–3.

Bible Reading

> There is a great deal of evidence within the member movements of the International Fellowship of Evangelical Students that more university students have been truly converted through Bible study than through any other means.[13]

Bible reading has always had an important role in the history of those connected with IFES. Their view of the Bible has shaped practices, vision statements, teachings, advertising and even controversies. It is important to see the connection between how IFES understands the "priesthood of all believers" in IFES and its handling of the Bible. The approach of the Moravian Pietists, Spener and Francke, shaped the way early IFES leaders saw the strategic importance of Bible study in the university context.[14]

Paramount to the idea of a "priesthood of all students" within IFES is the notion that the Bible can be read and understood in an *immediate* fashion. In Adeney's account, this is one of the main differences that IFES brings to the constellation of student ministry organizations:

> In some Christian youth organizations, the students have little opportunity of studying the Bible for themselves. They listen to large numbers of sermons, attend Bible Classes where they may receive excellent teaching, and yet never come to the place where they can discover for themselves the privilege of searching out spiritual truths in their own personal Bible study, or leading a group of their friends into the joys of a group study of the Word of God.[15]

While criticizing such an approach as potentially too individualistic, Greggs astutely notes that the doctrine of the "priesthood of all believers" cannot be appropriately understood outside of the doctrine of Scripture. Indeed, as "biblicism" is a core feature of evangelicalism,[16] it is essential to note that what is said and believed about the Bible is also the result of reading the Bible and not solely of a superimposed hermeneutical principle:

> To say that it is a condition of the principle of *sola scriptura* is to say that it is a doctrine which suggests that all readers of the

---

13. Woods, *Some Ways*, 102.
14. Johnson, *Brief History*, 29.
15. Adeney, "Student Work," 5.
16. Bebbington, *Evangelicalism in Modern Britain*, 2–18.

Scriptures can read the text unmediated by another and hear it as the direct Word of God; and – furthermore – that the text can be read as the direct Word of God unencumbered by the interpretation of a particular mediator or body of mediators.[17]

This is not restricted to evangelicalism, however. Kraemer also links empowerment of the laity to a thorough rediscovery of the Bible:

> In order to regain an "adult Christianity" an immersion in the Bible and its direct, unambiguous way of speaking about God and His centrality is indispensable for the Church as a whole. Especially indispensable for the laity, if they are to be enabled to become what they are often called nowadays: the spearhead of the Church, and not its hesitant rearguard. The first and great commandment: "Thou shalt love the Lord thy God with all thy heart, and with all thy soul and with all thy mind" (Matthew 22:37) is imperative for the whole membership of the Church, not for a tiny part, and the whole membership should accordingly be approached on that basis.[18]

In IFES, the Bible is assumed to be *immediately accessible.* Yet the growing output of literature about the Bible from the presses of national movements or directly sponsored by IFES belies the autonomy of individuals or small groups of laypeople to read the Bible on their own and reach a sufficient understanding.[19] A whole infrastructure supports the backstage of the "direct" encounter with the Bible. The "backstage encounter" is helped by devotional practices, commentaries, dictionaries and (daily devotional) study guides published by many IFES movements. Moreover, the *immediacy* of Scripture has not gone unchallenged, and even if this is not the place to provide a full discussion of the epistemological issues at stake, some of the most salient aspects of the criticism should be outlined, especially as they pertain to the context of student ministry.[20]

Taking one tradition under the magnifying glass, it is interesting to note the commonalities between the *inductive Bible study* approach most often

---

17. Tom Greggs, "The Priesthood of No Believer: On the Priesthood of Christ and His Church," *International Journal of Systematic Theology* 17, no. 4 (1 Oct. 2015): 378.

18. Hendrik Kraemer, *A Theology of the Laity* (Philadelphia: Westminster, 1958), 118.

19. Lowman insists that "it is what scripture actually says – not what we misunderstand it to say – that God says." Pete Lowman, "What Scripture Says, God Says," *In Touch* 3 (1982): 5.

20. For a critical account, see Brian Malley, *How the Bible Works: An Anthropological Study of Evangelical Biblicism* (Walnut Creek: AltaMira, 2004).

advocated within IFES circles, and Torrey's method of study.[21] He writes in the preface of one of his major works,

> this work is simply an attempt at a careful, unbiased, systematic, thorough-going, inductive study and statement of Bible truth. The method of the book is rigidly inductive. The material contained in the Bible is brought together, carefully scrutinized, and then what is seen to be contained in it stated in the most exact terms possible. Exactness of statement is first aimed at in every instance, then clearness of statement.[22]

Torrey goes on to specify that although he makes no direct use of the original languages, his work is "based upon a careful study of the original text as decided by the best textual critics."[23] The premise following which an "inductive" reading of the Bible makes access to its plain sense more probable, over against denominational-shaped readings, is paramount to understanding how Bible reading is conceived within IFES circles.

The corollary of the attribution of a "plain sense" to the Bible is the absence of any *mediator* between the text and the reader. This undermines any clerical mediation between students and the texts they are encouraged to read. There are evident connections between Torrey's approach and the necessities of interdenominational cooperation. The missiological consequences are also evident: if Scripture has a plain meaning accessible to any reader of goodwill, it means that it should be even more evident that students, whose daily occupation is to work towards understanding, should be confronted with the Bible.

Yet the whole approach was also challenged from within IFES. Two somewhat diverging personalities argued against "inductive study" from two different angles. Chronologically first, Woods launched a forthright attack on its populistic dimension. Mentioning what in his opinion was a low-ebb phase in the life of IV-USA, Woods deplored that,

---

21. See Timothy Gloege, "A Gilded Age Modernist: Reuben A. Torrey and the Roots of Contemporary Conservative Evangelicalism," in *American Evangelicalism: George Marsden and the State of American Religious History*, eds. Darren Dochuk and Thomas S. Kidd (Notre Dame: University of Notre Dame Press, 2014), 199–229.

22. Reuben Archer Torrey, *What the Bible Teaches: A Thorough and Comprehensive Study of What the Bible Has to Say Concerning the Great Doctrines of Which It Treats* (New York: Fleming H. Revell, 1898), 1.

23. Torrey, *What the Bible Teaches*, 1.

in spite of efforts to the contrary, straight Bible exposition largely went out the window, and weak inductive Bible study without personal application reigned. This drastic imbalance had a pronounced negative effect. Some seemed to think that any student could lead an effective Bible study. At least the Holy Spirit's special gift of the Bible teacher seemingly was ignored.[24]

From the above quote, the reader can only infer the shift that had occurred through the history of IFES, and which has repeatedly been occurring: the back-and-forth movement between exposition and student-led study. *Immediate* Bible study is not seen as the panacea, and groups at times have appealed to external expertise. In the late 1970s, Chua observed that there were "few regular Bible study groups on [African] campuses, and the African students need to be taught and trained to handle the Word of God for themselves."[25] The GS hence welcomed staff exchanges between movements so that they might benefit from each other's expertise. Whereas this could be negatively understood as a foreign imposition of methods – note the irony of people needing to be "taught" to "do things by themselves" – African movements in this example were not deprived of agency. On the contrary, IFES had a clear mandate to its emissaries, which was "to work themselves out of their jobs."[26]

From a completely different angle, Escobar complained as early as 1970 that "observation of Bible study habits and programmes has moved me to the conviction that an unbalanced emphasis on inductive study, plus the Scofield Bible influence in most of our Bible schools and seminaries, have given people a fragmented view of God's Word."[27] He explained the need to develop teaching materials to help students recover a more global view of the Bible. Such a global view considers the Bible as a formative lens through which the university can be seen and mission contextualized. "Christian thinking" was always on the agenda of IFES. Johnston was convinced that

> as students learn to bring every concept captive to Christ and to apply scriptural principles to the moral and social situations which they encounter at university, so in later life they can provide their fellow Christians with an adequate philosophy of life by thinking

---

24. Woods, *Growth of a Work of God*, 151.
25. Chua Wee Hian and Padilla, "God's Work in the World Today," 170–71.
26. Chua Wee Hian and Padilla, 170–71.
27. Samuel Escobar, "Report of the Associate General Secretary at Large" (Raglan, New Zealand, 18 Aug. 1978), 1, IFES e-archives, EC 1978 minutes, Appendix E.

through, biblically, issues within their own academic discipline or within the political, social or industrial sphere in which they find themselves.[28]

The striking notion in this argument is that this Christian contribution is likely to come *after their time at university* and will distinctively serve *their fellow Christians*. Although implicit, the underlying understanding is that the IFES students will *mediate* their biblically shaped view of the world to the rest of the academic community.[29] The idea of a "priesthood of all Bible readers," never so stated in the IFES documents, rests on a close connection between acknowledging that students' intellectual status should not be forgotten when discussing Bible study. Something happens when a group of young students, whose main job is to understand ideas and processes and develop new skills, gathers around an ancient text to understand it. The group is often interdisciplinary, featuring multiple levels of hermeneutical expertise, theological acumen or religious socialization. If non-Christians attend the study, another level of complexity is added: Christian students share their faith and form a community that witnesses to those individuals attending as "visitors" or "seekers," however they are called. Additional layers of identity can be postulated, such as, for example, a community of a non-Christian engineer and a Christian engineer, which might in some cases prove hermeneutically more fruitful than that of two Christians, one of whom studies literature and the other who studies chemistry. The *mediation* of Scripture is thus intertwined with the simultaneous negotiation of multiple identities at the intersection of academia and the church.

Respect for the authority of the Bible and consensus on the necessity of its study are decisive markers of the IFES identity. Any individual has the right to read the text by and for him- or herself.[30] Yet, as the above has shown, there is a tension between the individual's approach to the text, his or her experience and interpretation of what is read, and what others make of the same text. The community is the place where such multiway exchanges take place in dialogue with the Christian tradition.

---

28. Johnston, "Student Witness," 10.

29. This mediation is supported by a robust infrastructure of books published by IFES movements.

30. Intriguingly, IFES documents seldom allude to the fact that private Bible reading is, historically, a recent phenomenon. This blind spot could be explained sociologically: as the IFES constituency consists of academics, they implicitly locate themselves among the literate elite – thereby forgetting that many people in church history who were pious had no access to a privately owned Bible or to literacy altogether.

Fellowship

> God makes his love known to us personally through relationships within the body of Christ by his Holy Spirit. Our faith is worked out in the context of relationships, and the student group can provide a valuable opportunity to work out this relational aspect of our faith.[31]

The pietistic roots of the organization indeed presuppose the individual's relationship to God through prayer and scriptural engagement. Yet the meetings of student groups create the framework for mutual upbuilding and communal witness. Insofar as students meet regularly to read the Bible, pray and witness, either formally or informally, the community plays the role of a mechanism of checks and balances vis-à-vis the individual and his or her potential to be led astray by his or her own interests.

More importantly, the community is a *mediating community*. The fact that meeting in groups is considered necessary implies that the spiritual lives of students would lack perspective without the encouragement and exhortation of others. Thus, this fellowship has a *mediating* character on two levels: mediation into Christian thinking broadly speaking – in the case of outsiders – and mediation into IFES thinking, the "shared social and theological history"[32] which this work explores. The practice of Bible study in the academic environment hence strengthens beliefs and community. But besides the edification and missionary aspects of Bible study, it also serves as preparation *for the rest of life*.

Bielo highlights the value of regular and sustained dialogical engagement: "There is something to be said for devoting an extended amount of time every week explicitly to the act of dialogue. And there is something to be said for sustaining communities that prioritize open, reflexive, and critical conversation."[33] Such dialogical tradition broadens individuals' horizons, helping them develop skills necessary for a successful life at university. For this dimension to be deliberately fostered, Bible study needs to explicitly include engagement with academic matters in all instances to introduce the dialogic habit of scriptural reasoning to issues pertaining to the university. Still, studying the Bible in a group is no panacea. Woods, constantly worried

---

31. Dransfield and Merritt, "'One-Another' Ministry," 37.

32. James S. Bielo, *Words upon the Word: An Ethnography of Evangelical Group Bible Study*, Qualitative Studies in Religion (New York: New York University Press, 2009), 51–52.

33. Bielo, *Words upon the Word*, 167.

about populism, cautions that "the great danger of group study is that it will be allowed to degenerate into fruitless speculation where personal reaction – 'It seems to me' or 'I think' – becomes the authority rather than Scripture itself."[34]

The community is not only synchronically important but also diachronically and geographically. Such openness harnesses the potential of a worldwide fellowship to edify all the members of the "hermeneutical community" in which "we are enriched together, because we integrate into our own understanding the readings of those among us with a different story. And since their story becomes part of our heritage, their 'evangelical' perspective with 'ours' blends into a 'richer' evangelical."[35]

This brief exploration of the mediating character of the student community highlights that considering the "priesthood of all believers" as an essential theological and missiological key does not in any way compel an individualistic approach to the Christian faith. Much to the contrary, as IFES leaders have always insisted that encountering other Christians and non-Christians is fundamental to one's identity and growth as a follower of Christ.

Despite the strong insistence in IFES parlance on students as leaders, the common experience of its national movements is that some support is necessary for student groups to be sustained over time. It is therefore to the function of staff members that I now turn.

The Complex Role of Staff Members

Staff members are situated at the intersection of church and parachurch ministry.[36] They are professionals yet often not professionally trained, with some theological training but mostly not ordained. They support students, provide teaching, and mentor them as they develop their Christian faith and life during their university years. Summarizing decades of ministry philosophy towards the end of his tenure, Chua noted that

> ever since our foundation, our primary focus has been on students. We believe that, under God, evangelical students can be front-line witnesses for Christ on their campuses. Students possess spiritual gifts and abilities to run their fellowships and to build one another

---

34. Woods, *Some Ways*, 104.

35. Niringiye, "Understanding of Our Ethos," 2.

36. Most of this section has been written with staff members of national movements in mind. Most of the following observations apply to regional and international IFES staff as well. See below, chapter 15, for detailed reflections on the "parachurch" notion.

up in the faith. It is our express aim that, through this on-the-job training and involvement, these students would be trained as leaders. Of course, they need encouragement and input from staff. But, in the IFES tradition, the staff do not dominate and run the student fellowship. They act as trainers or coaches.[37]

Chua's outline of the different functions assigned to staff workers illustrates the implicit "priesthood of all believers" logic at work in IFES: because IFES students have a direct relationship to God (*immediacy*), they can be front-line witnesses (*mediators*) of Christ on their campuses. This takes place in the context of their *membership* of the IFES fellowship as well as in the church. For notably theological reasons, the role of staff workers is subsidiary. Furthermore, despite its universalist undertones, Chua's approach is flexible enough to accommodate regional variations.[38] What is observed here is a missiological concern for the development of students qua students, which took the form of advising staff to remain in the background of student meetings:

> Some groups had felt that over-participation by staff members had led to the students tending to sit back and leave the discussion to the older and wiser person. The students were stirred to think much more of discussing among themselves, though they did appreciate the presence of staff members and the knowledge that if they got into difficulties, they could always refer to them for help.[39]

While theologically motivated, this insistence on student leadership has also proven viable in many contexts where no staff were available to coordinate the work yet. This discussion about the functions of IFES staff members bears a striking resemblance to questions about the roles of office-holders in churches. Greggs's analysis of Ephesians 4 leads him to affirm that "the specific offices and roles of the church are expressions of ministering to the ministry, of serving the servants. It is for the service of the gospel in the world that the church exists, and to equip it for that service and ministry."[40] Such an argument is reminiscent of Kraemer's lines of thinking, articulated many decades earlier:

---

37. Chua Wee Hian, "Big Picture," 5.

38. Space does not permit an exploration of the debates around leadership and culture which were held within IFES, but overall they relate to the day-to-day enactment of the student leadership approach and do not question the validity of the approach.

39. "Minutes of the North Atlantic Zone Committee of the IFES" (Grundtvigs Höjskole, Frederiksborg, Hillerød, Denmark: EC 58 minutes, Aug. 1958), 4.

40. Tom Greggs, *Dogmatic Ecclesiology*, vol. 1, *The Priestly Catholicity of the Church*, Kindle (Grand Rapids: Baker Academic, 2019), 142.

> It is just on the point of enabling the laity to account for the hope and the faith which is in them that the theologians have to meet and strengthen the laity. Provided they let themselves also be taught by the laity. For the laity should in this matter not be seen primarily as the needy, ignorant and helpless, but as that part of the Church that has to carry the brunt of the burden of encounter with the world in and around themselves, and to voice and incarnate the Church's, or better, Christ's, relevance to the whole range of human life.[41]

It could therefore be argued that staff workers also play the role of a priest to the local group.[42] Interesting links can be drawn between the tasks of contemporary staff workers and those of Old Testament priests, as summarized by Anizor and Voss. These priestly functions are judging, teaching, reading and blessing:

> Priests have the honor of continual access to the presence of the Lord in the sanctuary, but they also bear the responsibilities of offering sacrifices for the people, helping them discern holy from profane and clean from unclean, teaching the law, applying its commands to the varying circumstances of Israel's life and blessing the people in the Lord's name.[43]

The "discerning" part is crucial at the university, as students are confronted with numerous new ideas and concepts that may or may not contradict the faith they have been holding to so far. IFES leaders have often encouraged critical examination of what the university teaches to "test everything; hold fast what is good."[44] Besides organizational sustainability, two main concerns preoccupied the IFES leadership: theological faithfulness and leadership. In the late 1930s, Clowney had "argued that staff leadership would be necessary to guard student chapters from falling into theological error."[45] He later said in

---

41. Kraemer, *Theology of the Laity*, 113–14.

42. Of course, only in derivative fashion. Similar connections could be drawn with other ministries described in the NT, notably in Ephesians 4.

43. Uche Anizor and Hank Voss, *Representing Christ: A Vision for the Priesthood of All Believers* (Downers Grove: InterVarsity Press, 2016), 32.

44. 1 Thess 5:21, ESV.

45. Keith Hunt and Gladys Hunt, *For Christ and the University: The Story of InterVarsity Christian Fellowship of the USA 1940–1990* (Downers Grove: InterVarsity Press, 1991), 71.

an interview in 1986, "I was wrong. Students do need instruction and counsel, but leadership develops where students have a real responsibility for witness."[46]

The teaching function occurs through the large number of training events of all sorts organized in the IFES network, be it at local, regional, national or international level, and through the regular one-to-one meetings of staff members with group leaders. As to the contextual application, we have already seen how strongly IFES leaders insist on the need to reflect upon biblical teaching and apply it to the lives of students and ministry on campuses. Equipping the laity for faithful witness and presence is thus a deeply ecclesial act, which also involves the laity serving ministers by confronting them with realities hitherto not properly experienced. In the context of IFES, the learning Kraemer envisaged can happen on two fronts simultaneously. First, students encounter new challenges in their universities, which staff were unaware of and did not consider themselves. Second, through the worldwide encounter of IFES people across boundaries, mostly crossed by laypeople, as we have seen, new questions are raised of the Christian faith as understood by the fellowship. In Flett's summarizing words, "world Christianity opens the theological field because it detaches that discourse from a singular concentration on a constricted history and its attendant range of questions."[47]

Yet IFES had been traditionally sceptical about formal theological training, for historical reasons explored earlier in this work. These reservations also applied to IFES staff. The idea that often prevailed, summarized by Lowman, was that "IFES full-time staff are usually people who have already 'learnt their trade' as active and effective members of a student group and then as staff workers with their national movement."[48] Despite this apparently satisfactory situation, national movements and the IFES leadership voiced their interest in the theological training of their staff members early on. GS Chua was aware that theological needs – notably not precisely defined – were increasing throughout IFES. Framing these needs in broad contextual lines, he suggested that,

> in view of the confused philosophical, ecclesiastical and theological climate of our age, it is almost a "must" for all our movements to have their own theologians. These are men who could advise students, graduates and staff of the current trends of thinking and help them to view these from a biblical perspective.[49]

---

46. Quoted in Hunt and Hunt, *For Christ and the University*, 71.
47. Flett, *Apostolicity*, 245.
48. Lowman, *Day of His Power*, 366.
49. Chua Wee Hian, "The Next Four Years," *IFES Journal* 25, no. 3 (1971): 9.

The debate was framed in the somewhat elusive notion of "raising the calibre of staff,"[50] an issue tackled by devising a humble scheme of scholarships for IFES staff aspiring to theological studies or at least continuing education. The said programme was – at first begrudgingly, then more enthusiastically – green-lighted by the EC. Consistent with its Low Church origins, IFES never considered formal theological training indispensable, not even for its highest representative.

Lastly, the blessing part of a priest's ministry occurs in two ways. First, the staff worker prays for the local group and its leaders. Second, when students meet for fellowship and comfort each other with their faith experience, this can happen when a staff member is present. However, it also happens among students as they are priests to each other: "We shall consider ways in which students can exercise pastoral care towards one another within the student group. This commandment of Jesus seems to us the foundation of such care."[51]

Partial Synthesis

Through this brief survey of the main activities of IFES groups, admittedly synthetic and without full consideration of regional variations, I have shown that the "priesthood of all believers" can function as a helpful theoretical framework to understand the work of IFES. As a missionary organization, it focuses first on witness, understood as *mediating* the gospel to other people who are not yet acquainted with it. Sharing the gospel is an intensely spiritual activity resting on the individual's *immediate* relationship to God, sustained in regular individual and communal prayer. Another focus of IFES groups is Bible reading. These groups are student-led; the underlying conviction is that *immediate* access to Scripture is possible for any lay student wishing to read it. This reading is presumed to occur individually and in the context of the fellowship in which the IFES student *participates*, besides a local church. Local groups are supported by IFES staff members who also, albeit in a subsidiary manner, play some sort of mediating role between the organization and the local group and church tradition. Helping students develop Christian discernment, providing teaching and blessing them are actions closely linked to *priestly* functions.

---

50. "Minutes of the Meeting of the Executive Committee of the IFES" (Charney Manor, Oxon, England, 28.9–3.10 1977), 17, IFES e-archives.

51. Dransfield and Merritt, "'One-Another' Ministry," 37.

This survey leaves some important questions open. If an IFES fellowship functions as a Christian community on campus, we need to question the *ecclesial character* of an IFES group: what should be made of the *dual membership* of students in the local group and in the local church, and, more broadly, in the church universal? Furthermore, despite a voiced commitment to the *immediacy* of one's reading of the Bible, a local fellowship frames how the individual grows in understanding the biblical text. However, this framing can also function as a *mediation* of the received hermeneutical tradition. Are these *priestly functions*? None of these questions is quickly settled, but over the years, IFES has developed a growing corpus of approaches to which I now turn.

Part 3

Ecclesiological and Missiological Reflection in IFES

11

A Firm Basis

> We believe that God has entrusted us with the historic evangelical faith based on the teaching of the apostles, and we dare not compromise in any way when it comes to matters of doctrine.[1]

Having surveyed the history of IFES in part 1, and explored the main activities of the local groups in part 2, I now turn to ecclesiological and missiological reflections within IFES. As I have argued above, theology in IFES has developed chiefly "on the go" as students and staff have ministered in various contexts. Nevertheless, as IFES has often defined itself by conformity to doctrinal standards, it has developed substantial theological and missiological reflection. The first example is a doctrinal basis as key governing text. This basis presupposes that believers have an *immediate* capacity to read for themselves that Scripture essentially says what the basis affirms it says. Yet the doctrinal basis also poses questions about context and indigeneity: how is such a centrally defined document to serve a fellowship spread worldwide that takes pride in respecting local leadership? Furthermore, the basis presupposes *membership* in a believers' church or a personal attitude akin to such ecclesiology.

A close analysis of the developing reflections within the fellowship shows a growing consensus that missiological experiences gathered on the ground paved the way to a *missional ecclesiology* consonant with the premises of IFES's work. I show that such *missional ecclesiology* developed within the fellowship over decades, as illustrated by a sample of a few prominent and representative voices of IFES staff who wrote extensively. The theology of the "priesthood of all believers" which I propose in this work is not explicitly articulated in the IFES documents. Yet the ecclesiological and missiological

---

1. Adeney, "Student Work," 8.

Genesis of the Doctrinal Basis

> When we trace the origin of our member movements, we discover that they owe their existence to the fact that Christian believers, both students and student leaders, took their doctrinal position seriously.[2]

The IFES archives do not document all the details of the DB's genesis. The early 1946 minutes note that some amendments were made to an original proposal, but the "original proposal" does not exist in the archives. Neither is the correspondence alluded to in the oldest minutes. The most likely hypothesis is that Johnson essentially suggested that the British IVF doctrinal basis be taken over, and asked for amendments and suggestions from the delegates.

Johnson remembers that the IVF DB was a joint work of members of the London Christian Unions and graduates from the London College of Divinity.[3] This group, notably not only made of laypeople, drew upon existing doctrinal statements such as the Anglican Thirty-Nine Articles, the Westminster Confession and especially the doctrinal basis of the Evangelical Alliance. But it also notably used the documents produced by the London Women's Inter-Faculty Christian Union. So from the very beginning, women had their doctrinal say in the life of their fellowship and were instrumental in putting doctrinal safeguards in place, as well as insisting on them being signed by members.

After lengthy discussion, the document was fine-tuned and became the DB of the 1928 newly founded IVF Britain. The IVF basis was taken over verbatim by the 1936 Beatenberg Conference.[4] It is also likely the original to which the 1946 minutes refer. Eventually, during the conferences leading to the official founding in 1947, a final revision combining elements of the 1935 International Conference of Evangelical Students constitution and the IVF DB was agreed upon as part of the Draft IFES constitution. The early IFES minutes record many more debates on the fellowship structure than on the shape of the

---

2. Carl F. Wisløff, "The Doctrinal Position of the IFES," *IFES Journal* 3 (1963): 2.

3. See his detailed account in Johnson, *Contending for the Faith*, 109–14, 127.

4. Pierre de Benoît et al., eds., "Invitation to the 1936 International Conference in Beatenberg, Switzerland" (1936), BGC #193.

doctrinal basis, which indicates a high degree of agreement. In what follows, I focus on analysing IFES's own understanding of the DB.

Yet Another Creed? Justifying the Doctrinal Basis

> The existence of the DB expresses the conviction that the divine truth of biblical revelation can be conveyed in frail human words by teaching in the power of the Holy Spirit and that it can be known and received for salvation and sanctification through the illumination of the same Holy Spirit.[5]

Much has been written on the functions and roles of creeds and statements of faith of different organizations throughout the church's history.[6] Woods stresses the doctrinal basis's most crucial role: "The IFES does not regard its basis of faith as a flag to be hoisted to the top of a pole, but rather as an anchor, which though unseen keeps a ship from drifting onto the rocks."[7]

As we shall see, the IFES narrative abounds with references to the DB having safeguarded the fellowship against all odds. As the organization was close to celebrating thirty years of existence, Woods's successor emphasized this: "This basis of faith is meant to serve as an anchor, especially when contemporary theological currents are seeking to sweep evangelical Christians from their confidence and firm stand on God's authoritative revelation through Jesus Christ and through the Scriptures."[8]

The ecclesiological status of the doctrinal basis and its relationship to creeds was early on a matter of contention for critics of the organization, especially church dignitaries: "For a body to issue a doctrinal basis means that it sets itself up as a new church. If it really holds the historic faith, the Apostles' Creed and the Nicene Creed should be sufficient."[9] Conversely, IFES pioneers repeatedly

---

5. Hans Bürki, *Essentials: A Brief Introduction for Bible Study Based on the Doctrinal Basis of the International Fellowship of Evangelical Students* (London: IFES, 1975), 11.

6. For a comprehensive analysis, see Jaroslav Jan Pelikan, *The Christian Tradition: A History of the Development of Doctrine*, 4 vols. (Chicago: University of Chicago Press, 1987–94).

7. Woods, "IFES History Draft," ch. 2, p. 14. Johnson also tells the story of the Scottish professor of anatomy and former Navy volunteer Duncan Blair who used to say about signing the DB: "I regard it as running up my ensign to the masthead in order to show where my allegiance belongs." Johnson, *Contending for the Faith*, 156.

8. Chua Wee Hian, "Foreword," in Bürki, *Essentials*, 7.

9. Ronald Owen Hall, "A Circular Letter from the Bishop to All Clergy to Be Discussed with Anyone Concerned with the FES" (1963), IFES e-archives, EC 1963 papers. Hall had worked with the British SCM prior to his appointment to Hong Kong. The letter was written

stressed that they "never thought that such a statement in any way displaced the historic creeds of the Church."[10] Woods fends off the charge of schism by appealing to the necessities of the IFES mission and its contextual challenges, notably those of the university context and its reluctance to take evangelical theology at face value. Yet, while IFES writers regularly assert that their DB is not a creed but "merely a set of agreed-upon doctrines for common witness," they nevertheless appeal to the function of historic creeds to explain the aims and function of the DB. This is especially the case with the *ex animo* adhesion which is hoped for from IFES members: "Like the great creeds and confessions of the Church, the Doctrinal Basis becomes meaningful and dynamic only when its statements are enthusiastically studied, interpreted and applied."[11]

The IFES line of argumentation can be summarized thus: historically, churches have always reacted to the challenges of their time by issuing summaries of the faith. It is no novelty to issue a doctrinal basis to respond to identified challenges to the faith. The IFES DB is no exception: it responds to the day's challenges but, most importantly, does not propose any new doctrine or anything that would be at odds with the ancient creeds in line with which it is written. Furthermore, the preamble to the DB submits that "the Doctrinal Basis of the Fellowship shall be the fundamental truths of Christianity, *including* . . . ,"[12] which implies that the DB pretends neither to replace any creed, nor to be exhaustive. Finally, since IFES does not consider itself a church but a specific-purpose group, the fact that a core of doctrinal convictions forms the basis of common actions does not suffice to make the fellowship liable to the charge of schism.

A Rallying Point and a Boundary Marker

> Our insistence on the Doctrinal Basis may be the emphasis that has been more closely identified with IFES in some countries. In others it is the demand for personal conversion and the disciplines of a deep spiritual life at the personal and communal level. Around the world and in spite of local variations, "the quiet time" is part of the IFES tradition, and evangelism is conceived as taking people,

---

in the context of Hall's refusal to let John Stott lead a university mission in his diocese. They later reconciled.

10. Woods, "IFES History Draft," ch. 2, p. 13.
11. Chua Wee Hian, "Foreword," 7.
12. "Constitution" (1947), clause 4.

sooner or later, to the experience of personal commitment to Jesus Christ.[13]

Even for somebody usually rather identified as a reformer within the evangelical world, the DB is in these words clearly presented by Escobar as a rallying point.

We have shown how strong the conviction is in IFES that doctrinal unity is paramount. It is also important to stress it in the context of discussing boundaries. At a time of significant geographical expansion of the organization, Barclay found it necessary to stress in 1989 that "we've already seen that to try to unite people on any basis other than the truth is to invite disaster. But the great strength of IFES is that it enables people to cross denominational, national and racial boundaries because of its primary commitment to biblical truth."[14] It is notable that this affirmation is both positive and negative: negative, as aiming at preventing any significant ecumenical move; but positive, in its underlying belief that "truth" will be the rallying point of evangelicals of goodwill around the world, cultural differences notwithstanding.

Committing by Signing

From an organizational point of view, it was never considered sufficient within IFES circles to have a doctrinal basis lying in the drawer of its General Secretary. Therefore, right from the beginning of the fellowship, and in keeping with the custom in IVF Britain, the demand was made for people aspiring to membership or leadership positions to express their agreement by signing the doctrinal basis. In this, the Western, legal, tradition is evident, and it is debatable whether the practice of signing a document is always contextually relevant, especially in the case of oral cultures. So while taking for granted the normal way of signalling one's commitment in writing, Bürki's official commentary foresees the possibility of oral assent only:

> By signing the Doctrinal Basis I attest that I have become convinced that the DB summarises basic doctrines of the biblical revelation which I desire to confess and practise by faith. Of course such a declaration may be made orally before others if one hesitates to sign a paper. In any case, it is essential that one should be personally convinced of the truth by the direct study

---

13. Escobar, "Evangelical Heritage," 8.
14. Barclay, "Guarding the Truth," 32.

of Scripture seeking enlightenment through the Holy Spirit Who reveals Jesus Christ.[15]

This practice of signing a statement did not go unchallenged, however. As so often, Bürki appeals to historical practice: "Some Christians have asked whether it is necessary or even biblical to subscribe *ex animo* to the Doctrinal Basis. In the early church at every baptismal service those who were to be baptised had received catechetical instruction on the gospel and they confessed their faith publicly."[16]

If the IFES leadership strongly encourages assent to the DB on the part of student leaders, it is also clear that signed adhesion is not considered sufficient. In Woods's cautionary words,

> merely then to subscribe to a doctrinal position is insufficient. Just to belong to an association which is doctrinally correct is quite inadequate. The student himself must be doctrinally literate – for himself he must know the truth, for it is by this means alone that he can find his way through the labyrinth of life on earth and be freed to serve his Lord in obedience and fruitfulness.[17]

We noticed earlier that ethical considerations are not explicit in the DB's formula; they are, however, implicit, and here Woods shows his awareness that more teaching is probably necessary. The interesting motif which emerges from this observation will be treated below: it is the conclusion at which the IFES leadership had to arrive in later years – that the DB is not always sufficient in its function as boundary marker and rallying point.

The last area where those connected to IFES are expected to signify their assent to the doctrinal basis – even though they will most likely have done so much earlier in their *cursus honorum* at the national and potentially regional level[18] – is when they assume office at the international level. In addition to

---

15. Bürki, *Essentials*, 19–20.

16. Bürki, 19. The practice of signing the DB was so important to him that he was ready to sign the DB "behind the back" of a student leader, provided he would essentially agree. In 1962, during a meeting of the GBEU Switzerland board, Bürki pushed very hard for the practice to be made policy. The debates were long and tense and Bürki is quoted wondering, "Why would one not be willing to sign? If a young person does not agree to sign, even though he agrees with the basic points, we can sign for him and put it in our registry. This is the basis, not only doctrinal, but also of our work." "Procès-verbal de l'assemblée annuelle du Conseil des GBEU de Suisse romande; Discussion du soir" (Vennes-sur-Lausanne, 24 Feb. 1962), 12, Conseil&Co. 1957–62, GBEU Switzerland Archives.

17. C. Stacey Woods, "Take Heed unto Doctrine," *IFES Journal* 1 (1955): 16.

18. This is no longer uniformly the case, however.

an endorsement for the potential employee from his or her national General Secretary, the Executive "shall receive from the proposed worker answers to a questionnaire which shall inquire concerning Christian convictions, scholastic qualifications and general outlook. There shall in every case be an acceptance *ex animo* of the Doctrinal Basis of the I.F.E.S."[19]

At the intersection of personal agreement and organizational assent is the IFES practice of renewing the expression of allegiance to the DB. This happens on at least two occasions. First, either orally or by signature, individual members of the Executive are asked to signify their agreement with the basis at the beginning of the committee's annual meeting, as the archival records of these meetings indicate. Second, and more ritually perhaps, delegates are asked at the beginning of each quadrennial meeting of the General Committee "to express their wholehearted agreement with the doctrinal basis of faith by standing."[20] The role of the committee chair is regularly mentioned in the minutes: "Prof. Wisløff then read the doctrinal basis of the IFES, and spoke of the importance of this, and emphasized that it was no mere formality. He then invited all present to stand, indicating their full agreement with these principles of faith."[21]

It should be noted that this re-enforcement ritual is the culmination of a cascade of affirmations of the DB. As we have seen, all IFES Executive Committee members are required to affirm the DB in their recruitment process; the same applies to all other office-holders and staff of IFES. If individuals are requested to sign the DB to signify their agreement – and thereby their commitment to a certain degree of doctrinal compliance – the same is also expected from the national member movements. Therefore all the IFES member organizations' DBs are required by the 1947 constitution to be equivalent to that of the fellowship: "National Evangelical Unions . . . shall be understood to mean only those Evangelical Unions which (i) are representative of and draw their members from students of university grade of an entire nation and (ii) *have a doctrinal basis which is equivalent to the Doctrinal Basis of the Fellowship.*"[22] Consequently, it can be assumed that most delegates at any General Committee meeting would have already affirmed the doctrinal basis through their participation in a national movement.

---

19. "Minutes of the Meetings of the Executive Committee of the IFES: Session I" (Institut Emmaüs, Vennes-sur-Lausanne, Switzerland, 10 Aug. 1948), 7, BGC Box #193.
20. "Minutes of the First Meeting" (1947), 1.
21. "Minutes of the Meeting of the Seventh General Committee" (1967).
22. "Constitution" (1947), clause 12a.

While carving an organizational policy within a relatively close group of senior church leaders in 1947 did not go without challenges, it is clear that, in advance, not all potential developments could be envisaged which would go with the enlargement of the fellowship so as to include many more countries. Doctrinal requirements would not always suffice, as the conundrum around the question of the existence of several evangelical student movements in any given country/nation state has shown throughout the story of IFES.

The Executive noted in 1988 that "the Constitution implies that the only rationale for division amongst Christian student movements in a given country is on theological grounds."[23] This is congruent with the primacy of doctrine that we have noted in many instances. Historical realities do not necessarily consider only doctrine, however. Therefore the same Executive also observes that "historically IFES has always accepted the position that some student groups cannot subscribe to an evangelical basis of faith. However, they also recognize that there are distinctive cultural, linguistic and political differences which may mean the existence of more than one evangelical student movement in a given country."[24]

The situation was getting much more complex than the original opposition to WSCF-affiliated groups, whose relevance for not complying with evangelical tenets of faith could be brushed aside. The question could never be solved in a way that would respect the letter of the constitution, and this is why the 1988 committee decided "not to propose changing the Constitution to allow only one movement per nation, as this would mean, for a start, disaffiliating movements from three countries."[25] Finally, the constitutional wording was amended in 1963 to read, "The International General Committee shall have power at its discretion to affiliate a regional association of student movements covering more than one country as if it were a national evangelical Union."[26] This was sufficient to deal with the situations of Ireland, South Africa, the French overseas territories, Sudan, Nigeria and Israel, to name only a representative sample.

---

23. "Minutes of the Meeting of the Executive Committee" (1988), 5.

24. "Minutes of the Meeting of the Executive Committee" (1988), 5.

25. "Minutes of the Meeting of the Executive Committee" (1988), 5. The countries in question were Belgium, Canada and Switzerland, with two movements in each instance, separated along linguistic lines. It should be noted that at the time of the foundation of IFES, the Swiss movements (founding members of IFES), though technically operating separately, had a common General Secretary (Hans Bürki) and were considered one movement. The full, official split occurred in 1962.

26. "Minutes of the Meeting of the Sixth General Committee" (1963), 19.

In another instance of necessary contextual considerations, to say that IFES as an international federation requires its member movements to have a compliant doctrinal basis does not necessarily presume doctrinal colonialism. In a lively account of the 1958 Cochabamba South American Student Conference, where the Latin American national movements came under the umbrella of IFES, missiologist and contextual theology advocate Samuel Escobar recalls that

> in business sessions, delegates hammered out with fire and painstaking parliamentary procedure the doctrinal basis upon which the work would develop. Sometimes two lines of minutes would summarize two hours of heated discussion For example, what was the best way to express our unanimous conviction that justification by faith is essential to our message? IFES was presenting to us their Basis of Faith as a proposal: it was through that discussion that it became *ours*. . . . The deliberations over the name of the Congress, the formulation of objectives and the doctrinal basis were in reality an exercise in expressing the reality of what the groups represented already were.[27]

What this personal recollection underlines is that, questions about the theological possibility of a doctrinal statement being universally valid notwithstanding, the IFES DB has indeed fulfilled that role in many contexts.

As to the institutional positioning of IFES towards other similar organizations, we shall return to it later,[28] but we should note in passing that while in this respect also the DB is IFES's main instrument to prevent its member organizations from being part of other, similar bodies, nothing in the basis itself prevents any individual from entertaining external allegiances.[29]

Marking Boundaries

Whereas the doctrinal basis plays the role of a boundary marker for "officials" in the local groups or in the leadership of a national movement,[30] it should never preclude participation in the regular meetings of a given student group, which is, after all, missionary in purpose. Hammond, aware of contextual

---

27. Quoted in Lowman, *Day of His Power*, 196.
28. See chapter 4.
29. Bruce, "Sociological Study," 152.
30. Regarding national practices, it is assumed that they generally follow the same pattern, given the missionary orientation supposedly congenial to an IFES movement.

variation, specifies that "membership in the Christian Unions is open to anyone who affirms his faith in 'Jesus Christ as my Saviour, my Lord and my God' or – since there are certain local differences of expression – such other short declarations of faith as are in use."[31] The rationale for limiting official membership to those who affirm the DB is a question of power: the requirement to affirm the doctrinal basis functions as a sort of theological "notwithstanding clause." Lowman summarizes thus the issues at stake:

> The heavy emphasis on Bible study at every level, combined with constitutional safeguards obliging leaders to be committed to the doctrinal basis, has tended to produce an environment where student leaders will not drift away from the original vision, but instead become permeated by Scripture and hear the voice of God speaking into their decision-making.[32]

Obviously, to ascribe such an important role to the selection of members presupposes understanding unity as resting first on theological agreement. In Barclay's words, "to try to unite people on any basis other than the truth is to invite disaster."[33] No provision is made for students "belonging before believing," at least not in any leadership capacity.[34]

This selection of members does not apply only to individuals in national movements, but also to national movements themselves for membership of the fellowship. Brown notes with evident relief that

> doctrinal statements of the member movements in the I.F.E.S. are equally if not more explicit. The reason for this is that already suggested: in our day, the trustworthiness of Holy Scripture is being severely attacked, and therefore it must be affirmed and vigorously defended. It is important to see that it is subject to attack from within "Christian" and even evangelical circles, for if it were only being attacked from the outside by admitted atheists,

---

31. T. C. Hammond, *Evangelical Belief: A Short Introduction to Christian Doctrine in Explanation of the Doctrinal Basis of the Inter-Varsity Fellowship* (London: IVF, 1935), 10.

32. Lowman, *Day of His Power*, 357.

33. Barclay, "Guarding the Truth," 32.

34. Grace Davie has popularized the concept of "believing without belonging" to describe the general public's perception of faith in the UK since 1945. See Grace Davie, *Religion in Britain since 1945: Believing without Belonging* (Oxford: Blackwell, 1994). The idea of "belonging before believing" would describe a situation where an individual is welcomed into a student group so as to take (limited) responsibility even before he or she has decided to commit him- or herself to the Christian faith, thereby getting a sort of "trial run" of what it means to be a Christian.

humanists, and theological radicals, this would be a less serious concern to us.[35]

What Brown's words clarify is that the perceived need to elevate the DB to the status of an inescapable boundary marker for IFES arose out of disagreement *among Christians* much more than out of a desire to separate the fellowship from overtly secular influences. How else could be explained the extremely strict constitutional stipulation that "the International General Committee and the International Executive Committee may arrange joint activities in the name of the Fellowship only with those religious organizations whose basis of faith and purposes are equivalent to those of the Fellowship"?[36]

Besides the evident animosity towards any idea of co-belligerence at an institutional level, what is most striking in this clause is that it could be read as allowing for joint activities with non-religious organizations, because the question of an equivalent doctrinal basis would not arise. However, given the strong focus on gathering individuals together for *a common purpose*, it seems very unlikely that the writers of the constitution would have envisaged IFES engaging in activities – social justice, for example – with non-religious bodies. This need not be read as a core opposition to other activities but is congruent with the requirements of constitutional brevity. Since "nothing contained in this Constitution shall give any power to the Fellowship in any way to control the activities of the National Evangelical Unions which shall remain autonomous,"[37] nothing would prevent a national movement engaging in collaboration with other bodies, including religious ones.

Guarding the Deposit of the Faith

> One of Paul's favourite metaphors to describe this responsibility to hand on the essentials of the tradition is that of keeping the "deposit" (ἡ παραθήκη). The reference in I Timothy vi. 20 might accurately be translated "Timothy, guard the deposit."[38]

Despite IFES being historically newer on the scene of student movements than SCM movements, for example, the idea of being somehow uniquely placed to

---

35. Harold O. J. Brown, "The Inspiration and Authority of Scripture," *IFES Journal* 23, no. 2 (1970): 20.
36. "Constitution" (1947), clause 9.
37. "Constitution" (1947), clause 11.
38. Hammond, *Evangelical Belief*, 48.

mediate classical Christianity has been fundamental throughout the history of the fellowship. In the same way that Israel was the depository of God's promises and blessings for the nations, IFES has entertained the idea that it has the same role for the university campuses of the world. Making his own the argument of an address given by Lloyd-Jones in 1961, Johnson wanted to warn the IFES readership that

> there is no inherent guarantee that the I.V.F. will never go wrong or be side-tracked. Eternal vigilance is the price of liberty, and eternal vigilance is the only guarantee of the safety of the I.V.F. as, indeed, it is of the whole Christian Church. You cannot live on the past. You may thank God for it, and you must also learn lessons from it. The most important of these is the vital necessity of continued and continuing vigilance, lest we become something which is a denial of what we were at the beginning and of what, by the grace of God, we have been throughout the years.[39]

The first aspect of the IFES discourse is decisively theological. Following his mentor's steps and commenting on 1 Timothy 6:20 and 2 Timothy 1:14, Johnson underlines IFES's understanding of the importance of a "deposit of faith" which has to be preserved:

> The majority of exegetes are agreed that this is "the deposit of faith," which may also be equated with "the form of sound words" or "outline of the sound teaching" of the Second Epistle. . . . Clearly, the religion of the earliest followers of our Lord resisted any influence or form of development which was not in harmony with such basic doctrines.[40]

The exegetical accuracy of this position notwithstanding, there was a strong anxiety among the early leaders to keep something that might otherwise become lost.[41] Even if Johnson and his colleagues emphasize student leadership, students are not envisaged as greatly influencing how the "deposit of doctrine" is understood. Theirs is the role of witnessing from that message to non-Christians, and of passing on the role of guardians of the faith to the next generation of students.

---

39. Johnson, *Brief History*, 98.

40. Johnson, 101.

41. The combined forces of secularization and decolonization, which marked several periods of IFES's history, might, in part, explain this anxiety.

One of the logical conclusions of such a theological understanding is that IFES will look for leaders who will guard the deposit *in line* with its received understanding.[42] This understanding of leadership formation as "passing on" has shaped how IFES has designed its programmes, set its priorities and invested in events. It is, however, intriguing to note the co-opting of a clearly ecclesial logic – ordination – to the context of laypeople in a parachurch organization. This unapologetic move shows how early IFES leaders inadvertently blurred the lines between church and parachurch when doing so supported their logic and especially their theological convictions. As he stepped down as the IFES theological secretary, Brown left an unheard plea for more investment in what could be called "theological vigilance" or at least in-depth theological training:

> In my opinion, the theological dimension of the I.F.E.S. work will continue to grow in importance as it becomes less and less possible for any church or fellowship, even the young, vigorous, and unspoiled ones, to ignore the constant output of degenerate and apostate thought presented as Christian theology by the surrounding world. *We must never fall into the pattern of merely reacting, of merely being slightly more conservative or less radical than our surroundings, as this will drag us inevitably into the same decline, only a few paces behind the leaders.* For this reason, I think that for the I.F.E.S. to be without the services of a full-time secretary for theological students would be a luxury which it can ill afford. To fail to face the theological dimensions of our common challenge as evangelical students and student leaders is either to slip into anti-intellectualism in this area, or, because we are unwilling to take that turn, to be drawn into the paths of theological and moral relativism and to lose the distinctives of our biblical faith.[43]

Here, Brown argues that some theological oversight is necessary because of the risk of doctrinal degeneration, especially in the theological world. Yet the doctrinal deposit that needs to be preserved needs constant local reappropriation and re-exploration, hence the importance of supporting the

---

42. Johnson comments on 2 Tim 2:2 that "the student leadership of the Christian Unions has . . . been influenced by the conviction that the same principle, the same fidelity and the same character-traits are essential in all who undertake Christian leadership of any kind." Johnson, *Brief History*, 102.

43. Harold O. J. Brown, "Report of the Theological Secretary" (1971), 3, IFES e-archives, GC 1971 minutes, Appendix H; emphasis added.

orthodox evangelical theological students throughout their studies. The unease is evident in Brown's words which are exemplary of an important tension between the local and the central, and between individual and communal access to truth.

Can a Doctrinal Basis Be Reformed?

Having surveyed the genesis of the DB, its core theological tenets and its ascribed and prescribed role in the life of IFES, it is interesting to examine next its relationship to wider theological debates.

Discussing the British case (and being therefore limited to it), Warner identifies five "laws of evangelical bases of faith": increased prolixity (many additions in the process of reviewing the basis); increased conservatism; a surfeit of certainties; non-reflexivity (in terms of contextual situatedness: bases tend to be seen as universally valid); and an ambiguous relationship between evangelicals and fundamentalists.[44] While these might all be applicable to the British context – Warner notes for his first law that in terms of words, the IVF/UCCF basis "used 165 in 1928, 199 in 1974, 311 in 1981, and 324 in 2005" – these "laws" do not equally apply to IFES. In fact, with the notable exception of adopting inclusive language in clause D – going from the "universal sinfulness of all men" to that of "all people" in 2007[45] – the IFES DB has remained remarkably constant in terms of wording.

Similarly, while tensions might occur between different generations of members of a movement if the DB changes,[46] no IFES pioneer would have reservations about signing its current version, unless she or he has undergone a change of theological views.

Conversely, the fourth "law of non-reflexivity" does apply to the IFES DB. The preamble to the DB in the original constitution affirms that "the IFES

---

44. Warner, "Evangelical Bases of Faith," 336–37.

45. "A formal written ballot was taken on the first proposal to amend the doctrinal basis. The motion passed with unanimous agreement." "Minutes of the Meeting of the General Committee of IFES" (Redeemer University College, Ancaster, Ontario, 18 July 2007), 3, IFES e-archives.

46. As is the case with the added revisions of the UCCF basis. While not charitably worded, Warner's "law of a surfeit of certainties" suggests that "those able to sign one iteration of an IVF/UCCF basis may no longer be deemed sufficiently 'sound' after its subsequent revision – [leading] to a third characteristic: the law of a surfeit of certainties. Because there is no conciliar authority, no final and binding arbiter of evangelical orthodoxy, and because Protestant Evangelicalism is intrinsically fractured and fissile, those who demur from a particular basis are more than likely to compose an alternative." Warner, "Evangelical Bases of Faith," 337.

doctrinal basis shall be the fundamental truths of Christianity, including . . ."[47]
In Warner's analysis,

> the twentieth-century bases typically positioned themselves as *ex cathedra*, definitive and durable pronouncements of evangelical certainties. There is no sense of contingency due to the specificity of culture and generation, nor any recognition of the plurality within the tradition that is only too evident to a dispassionate observer of the diverse formulations of evangelical orthodoxy.[48]

A theological analysis of the IFES DB shows its historical situatedness and the fact that it was written in response to a specific context. It does not, however, say so, and the fact that changes are made close to impossible by constitutional provision strengthens the feeling that the pioneers of IFES did not intend the basis to require amendments because of a later theological context. What the history chapters above have outlined, however, is the fact that in the encounter with Roman Catholic, Pentecostal and Eastern Orthodox students, mere reaffirmation of the tenets of the DB did not suffice and called for significant efforts of interpretation amounting to an *official hermeneutic* of the DB.

So far, the analysis of the IFES DB has shown that one of its most fundamental functions is to differentiate the organization from others (a variation of Warner's fifth law). The stakes are therefore high, and despite the aforementioned events showing the inadequacy of the DB to cover all challenges, any attempt at changing the DB is likely to generate a significant debate within the fellowship. Warner astutely suggests that "the symbolic boundaries of pan-Evangelicalism generate a commonality that transcends, at least in part, the diverse social and denominational contexts of its participants. These symbolic boundaries therefore take on a quasi-sacred role and become the immovable touchstones of evangelical legitimacy, the guardians of common identity."[49]

This analysis describes the situation in IFES very well. The DB has been recognized as useful in many very different contexts and, as such, has worked as a powerful centripetal force. Sociologically, qualifying the DB as "sacred" would certainly not fit habitual IFES usage; the official document and many early accounts nevertheless do ascribe to it a somewhat similar role. Analysing

---

47. "Constitution" (1947).
48. Warner, "Evangelical Bases of Faith," 337.
49. Warner, 343.

the relationship of Protestantism to dogmatic formulations, Willaime notes the complexity of the matter and hints at some of the most fundamental differences between classical Protestantism and evangelicalism:

> By making religious truth a matter of interpretation, this model leads to a permanent debate within the religious organization about the religious truth it seeks to convey and thus to *a constant criticism of the formulations adopted*. Ideological authority is, in principle, exercised only by the power of its conviction and rational argument in value. Theological research is formally free, and the theologian is given an important role in the management of religious truth, since it is he who, on the basis of a certain knowledge, will say what is the right line. *The religious organization has only a functional role here: as a second instance in the service of truth, its mode of operation and its distribution of roles have only a relative value and are sociohistorical.*[50]

As this research shows, however, the possibility of "formally free theological research" was not on the horizons of the IFES founders and there is no archival evidence of "constant criticism of the formulations adopted." However, if Willaime is right, the lines between sociology and theology are hence blurred in the case of IFES. Warner concurs, suggesting an important difference between a *sociological boundary marker* and a *theological conviction*: the latter would be "capable of critical evaluation and refinement,"[51] while the former would not. In Warner's terms, a *sociological boundary marker*

> is an unassailable presupposition of symbolic force. To transgress the boundary is near unthinkable, and provokes the strongest reaction. The defence of the boundary is immediate, automatic, and often strident. While such a boundary may well be explained and defended in conceptual, doctrinal, and rational terms, its significance and continuing currency may be better conceived as the ritualized performance, relational and linguistic, of a collective subcultural identity.[52]

This frame of reference is not, of course, that of most IFES writers who would likely disagree with the implied definition of theology as in need of

---

50. Willaime, *Précarité Protestante*, 24–25; emphasis added.
51. Warner, "Evangelical Bases of Faith," 343.
52. Warner, 343.

"critical evaluation and refinement." In Hammond's view, the DB consists of "principles which can be stated with certainty and clarity, although their particular applications in experience offer scope for variety of opinion. The applications also depend to some extent on the nature of the immediate problems."[53]

If the DB is considered to cover all the essentials of the faith, only their application can be contextually adapted, not their essence, and, seemingly at least at the international level, not even its formulations. Yet, contrary to what some critics have regularly claimed of the IFES DB, focusing on "essentials" does not amount to a prohibition of contextual applications of a considerable variety. As Bürki clearly states,

> each study of these doctrines should lead to practical application: what does this mean for me, for us here and now and for the future of our life, our work, our relationships? What behaviour, confession, repentance, praise, obedience, prayer, action or abstention is being conveyed to us by the Holy Spirit through this present study of God's Word? Such findings can be formulated in a very brief form as a manifesto ("a clear and obvious truth that should be made known to all concerned"). Here is also the place and occasion to study biblical doctrines afresh and to apply them in the context of the church, of science, politics, social responsibility, and so on.[54]

While the DB is unapologetically seen as never potentially in need of revision – for instance, nothing significant was made of the question asked in 1971 "Is this basis adequate today?"[55] – that does not mean that it is considered final for all Christians. Bürki sounds an interestingly open note in the following commentary worth quoting at length:

> It is not the function of the DB constantly to add new doctrines according to the debates of a particular generation; rather it summarises the doctrines which are essential for all time, and thus it provides a basis for fresh formulations of creeds, confessions or manifestos which may speak to contemporary issues. For example, issues on racial discrimination, social justice, the struggle against poverty and for peace, need to be confronted and answered with

---

53. Hammond, *Evangelical Belief*, 6.
54. Bürki, *Essentials*, 19.
55. C. Stacey Woods, "The IFES Doctrinal Basis," *IFES Journal* 25, no. 3 (1971): 11.

a fresh exposition and practical application of the doctrines of creation, man, sin, redemption, the law and the gospel.[56]

The enumeration provided at the end shows that already in 1975, the IFES senior leadership was aware of the theological hot potatoes that might surface in the future – or had already been surfacing. Warner makes the astute observation that "the undeniable fact of evangelical pluralism might be expected to lead to a measure of relativism, and a ready acknowledgement of secondary doctrinal specifics."[57] In the case of IFES, while the doctrinal basis, shared practices and experiences, as well as shared personnel in many instances, provide a relatively high degree of commonality, the fact remains that there is no "one evangelical world," and even a cursory glance at the correspondence files of the subsequent General Secretaries shows them playing the role of firefighters between factions, and this more often than they might have wished. No other situation should be expected of a fellowship of such a global scale. However, if all the IFES pioneers hammer their point that their DB, by its focus on *essentials*, is already an "acknowledgement of secondary doctrinal specifics,"[58] even if only by contrast, inscribing themselves into the theological tradition of differentiating between central tenets and *adiaphora*, the reader still might have the impression that "finality and certainty take centre stage, drowning out any intimation of provisionality, contingency, and open-ended critical theology."[59] This is not only an impression since the IFES DB is virtually impossible to change in any fundamental way, for the constitution stipulates that no change in the doctrinal basis can be made "without unanimous agreement."[60] Not only does IFES pledge to keep its doctrinal basis stable, but it did not originally expect national movements to alter their own bases, the 1947 constitution foreseeing that "a National Evangelical Union which changes its doctrinal basis so as no longer to comply with the terms of Clause 4 hereof shall cease to be a member of the Fellowship."[61] As the more recent history shows, this clause has not been activated: several member movements have indeed changed their doctrinal bases fairly significantly – albeit not so as to contradict the IFES DB –

---

56. Bürki, *Essentials*, 12–13.
57. Warner, "Evangelical Bases of Faith," 337.
58. Warner, 337.
59. Warner, 337.
60. "Constitution" (1947), clause 14.
61. "Constitution" (1947), clause 12c.

without being excluded.⁶² The clause was revised in 2015, adding to doctrinal nonconformity another cause for disaffiliation: "The Board may temporarily suspend any National Movement which changes its doctrinal basis in a way that is no longer consistent with that of IFES *or if it brings IFES into disrepute.*"⁶³

Since the DB is not meant to change, the burden of crafting similar documents, implicitly, however, for purposes other than student witness in universities, rests on the shoulders of individuals or subgroups who will then have to account for their respective work. Some countries such as South Africa have followed this possibility and added important complements to their doctrinal basis – which is indeed based on the IFES DB – relating to questions of ethnicity and social justice.

To issue a revised formula or to expand on the original IFES DB would likely be considered undesirable as a Pandora's box susceptible of fracturing a fellowship of independent national organizations aimed at reaching their campuses: so strong is the importance of the DB for uniting the fellowship in the IFES literature. Yet the question remains: the DB was agreed upon by ten founding members with very similar outlooks and essentially similar contexts. The situation at the beginning of the twenty-first century, with 170 member movements, is significantly different. New questions have emerged, especially in the wake of decolonization and the rise in influence of churches independent of international denominations in the Majority World. This observation does not presume any theological wrongness in the DB's affirmations, but questions the adequacy of their formulation for *all times and places*. For example, what is the DB to make of theologically important notions not always so relevant to

---

62. To name but a few: InterVarsity USA has a very different formulation and significant additions; see InterVarsity USA, "What We Believe," 17 April 2017, https://intervarsity.org/about-us/what-we-believe. UCCF Great Britain has expanded several clauses; see UCCF, "Doctrinal Basis," accessed 9 May 2020, https://www.uccf.org.uk/about/doctrinal-basis.htm. SCO South Africa has also expanded several clauses; see "Statement of Faith," Students' Christian Organisation (SCO) South Africa (blog), https://web.archive.org/web/20210621163925/https://www.sco.org.za/statement-of-faith/. AFES Australia and ABUB Brazil have added some precisions; see AFES, "Doctrinal Basis," accessed 21 May 2020, https://afes.org.au/about/doctrinal-basis; ABUB, "No Que Cremos," Aliança Bíblica Universitária do Brasil, accessed 21 May 2020, http://abub.org.br/no-que-cremos. VBG Switzerland has explicitly abandoned its doctrinal basis: "A few years ago, the VBG broke away from its old faith base. Over time, it had become too narrow for the staff. Now the VBG no longer formulates its most central beliefs in its own confession, but agrees with all other Christians on the old [Apostles'] creed." VBG, "Geistliche Leitlinien: In Was die VBG Ausmacht," 25 March 2017, https://wp.vbg.net/spirituelle-traditionen/. Interestingly, the "Spiritual Guidelines," which cover six "spiritual traditions," take very much the form of a doctrinal basis.

63. "Constitution of the International Fellowship of Evangelical Students" (July 2015), IFES e-Archives, clause III.C.1; emphasis added.

the West, such as poverty, racism, colonialism, ancestor worship, polygamy or creation care, to name but the most salient? The question remains as to whether it is missiologically responsible to keep without change such a statement of faith for national movements created potentially more than seventy years after the inception of IFES, in contexts immeasurably different from that of the nineteenth-century British Empire, with vastly larger numbers of universities around the world, representing a growing variety of academic traditions and cultures. Hence, other "essentials" could emerge in other contexts, no doubt in close relationship to the existing ones but maybe stressing other important theological elements.[64]

The fact that no serious attempt to revise the DB has been made so far witnesses to the fact that it has so far been understood as broad enough to express and accommodate the concerns of most member movements.

Having surveyed the more sociological aspects of the DB, it is now time to turn to the relationship of IFES to theology more generally, and the role which the DB plays in this constellation.

IFES, Theology and the DB

IFES and theology have had a complex relationship marked by difficult experiences with university theology. At times, the fellowship's leaders have been very sceptical of academic theology, the alleged liberalizing tendencies of which they have often castigated. At the same time, challenges encountered on the mission field, together with the necessity to define the organization's identity over against other actors in the field or in discussion with church leaders, have necessitated in-depth theological thinking, even if this has primarily been aimed at legitimizing IFES's story and existence. In the words of Hammond, "every human society and joint activity must necessarily be controlled by some degree of common conviction. Prolonged united effort directed to one main end would be impossible without it."[65]

The doctrine of the "priesthood of all believers" does not feature explicitly in any of the formulations of the DB. However, I argue that the claims of the DB have been developed in implicit relationship to this doctrine, which in turn helps make sense of the DB's affirmations. Moreover, the idea that any given

---

64. A *very* tentative list might include the doctrine of reconciliation, the Christus Victor approach to the atonement, the doctrine of *imago Dei*, the doctrine of the kingdom of God, issues relating to mission, political theology and social justice, gender equality, etc.

65. Hammond, *Evangelical Belief*, 5.

believer would be able to deduce from the study of the Bible illuminated by the Holy Spirit a similar core of essential doctrines presupposes each believer's direct access to God:

> It is from one source – Holy Scripture – that all subsequent statements of the Basis have been derived. Only by divine revelation do we know such truths as those concerning the Being of God, the all-comprehending scope of His providence and rule and, also, the nature of His redeeming love to man.[66]

The IFES leaders affirm that these beliefs are not "invented" by *individuals* but rather "received" and in line with the apostolic teaching:

> It is of greater importance that every Christian should seek by his own study to gain an improved understanding of what he believes and why he believes it. It is expected that office-bearers, in addition to the doctrines set out in these ten clauses [of the DB], will accept and teach all else that can plainly be proved from Holy Scripture to have been part of the apostolic teaching.[67]

Believers have *immediate* access to the Bible. This implies that Scripture is the privileged channel of relationship to God.[68] This provides common ground for evangelicals who "comprised not only the unschooled, but also the highly educated whose rationality was yoked to their prior and primary allegiance to the unassailable authority of the Bible."[69] This view of the importance of the Bible pervades IFES writings. It is here that perhaps the clearest, though very implicit, underlying influence of an individualistic understanding of the "priesthood of all believers" is found. If the Bible speaks, any believer can understand it, provided a correct attitude of mind and spirit is manifested. Yet, despite the proclaimed allegiance to the Bible's perspicuity, the fellowship deemed it essential to produce a doctrinal basis, understood as *norma*

---

66. Hammond, 12.

67. Hammond, 10.

68. We could even go further to postulate *membership* in some sort of "Enlightenment community." At least this represents the cultural *milieu* of the early IFES.

69. Such *direct* engagement with Scripture and the unfolding appropriation of doctrine does not occur in an epistemological vacuum. Summarizing recent scholarship on the topic, Warner articulately suggests that "both classical liberalism and Evangelicalism depended upon Enlightenment foundationalism to build a rational reconstruction of Protestant orthodoxy. For liberals, the Enlightenment's liberation of human reason was the prerequisite for a new theology. For Evangelicals, the foundational presupposition within their Enlightenment-shaped theology was biblical infallibility." Warner, "Evangelical Bases of Faith," 341.

normata,⁷⁰ nevertheless held in high importance, as the following statement from 1982 exemplifies:

> We are also evangelical. Theologically this means that we are deeply committed to defending, maintaining and propagating biblical truths. *We affirm the entire trustworthiness of the Bible for all matters relating to doctrine and conduct. We place great emphasis on our Doctrinal Basis.* Student leaders, staffworkers and other officers subscribe to its tenets in writing. As evangelical Christians *we also stress our fidelity to the gospel.* This is worked out as we share and proclaim it enthusiastically and boldly to others.⁷¹

The underlying assumption is that Scripture has a plain sense that is *immediately* accessible to committed readers. In this case, the DB plays the role of a "controlling summary" allowing group leaders and staff to assess how solid – perhaps hear "compliant" – the Bible knowledge of a given student is. From the firm belief that the Bible is *entirely trustworthy*, and that the DB is a "mere summary" of its core teachings, IFES leaders assume the universal validity of the DB.

Even if it is presented as a summary of core scriptural doctrines, the DB is nevertheless also the product of core essential doctrinal concerns of the early IFES leaders who, shaped by their own cultural context, tended to emphasize some doctrines over others – and the most evident example is the affirmation of the "entire trustworthiness" of Scripture, which is not part of any of the old creeds. Neither is the substitutionary explanation of the atonement. Woods was well aware that "this doctrinal basis represented *those truths which were relevant to the university situation* and were *in some places* being called into question by secular scholarship and humanistic thinking."⁷² This statement is important because it highlights the profoundly *reactionary* nature of the IFES DB – a similar comment applies to most creedal statements in church history.⁷³ This interpretation seems to be underscored by the somewhat strange fact that

---

70. Theologians differentiate between normed norms (*norma normata*), which means a norm the authority of which is itself given by a *norma normans,* a norming norm (Scripture).

71. IFES, "Who Are We?," 2; emphasis added.

72. Woods, "IFES History Draft," ch. 2, p. 13; emphasis added.

73. In defence against potential relativizing charges, IFES leaders have often averred that the reactive nature of a doctrinal basis does not automatically disqualify it from long-lasting relevance; e.g. Horn: "All summaries of Christian belief are a balance between the unchanging truth of God on one hand and the pressing circumstances at the time of their compilation on the other. Most of the great creeds (like many of the New Testament letters) were drawn up to combat particular errors. . . . We do not ditch these letters because they come out of a particular

IFES "also" stresses the importance of the gospel, so yet another sub-canon inside the restricted list of points.

We have here a soteriologically based hermeneutic: the Bible cannot properly be apprehended *outside* of a personal relationship with God, hence the emphasis on trustworthiness – a more pietistic category – rather than on "infallibility," a more scientific-rationalist category.[74] On the one hand, this theology stresses that any individual can hear God's word for him- or herself, *mediated* by the Bible read in the context of that individual's own, *unmediated* relationship to God – that is, without others standing between God and him- or herself. On the other hand, IFES insists on the need for a DB specifying the understanding to which faithful reading will lead believers.

Theological Analysis

A complete theological analysis of the IFES DB would justify a work in its own right.[75] In what follows, I will try to interpret a sample of the DB's statements in the light of the contexts in which they originated and how they were debated within IFES.

The first official commentary of the DB at the time of the IVF Britain movement was penned in 1935 by Hammond, and subsequently revised.[76] The main reason for looking in-depth at the IVF DB and not primarily at other national movements' bases is the influence that the British movement had on the insistence on the doctrinal basis: not only were the early pioneers Lloyd-Jones and Johnson British, but so were later influential leaders in the Executive Committee such as Barclay, Catherwood, Wells, Horn and Lowman, who have all written on the importance of the doctrinal basis for the life and integrity of IFES, as has Welshman Brown, long-term General Secretary.[77]

---

historical, geographical, sociological or religious context." Robert M. Horn, *Ultimate Realities: Finding the Heart of Evangelical Belief* (Leicester: Inter-Varsity Press, 1999), 86–87.

74. Holmes's somewhat pointed summary is that "North American Evangelicalism, with a broad commitment to inerrancy, views the Bible primarily as a collection of facts to be believed; British Evangelicalism, stressing instead authority, views the Bible primarily as a collection of rules to be obeyed." Stephen R. Holmes, "Evangelical Doctrines of Scripture in Transatlantic Perspective," *Evangelical Quarterly* 81, no. 1 (Jan. 2009): 53.

75. Readers interested in a detailed analysis can read appendix 2.

76. Hammond, *Evangelical Belief*. The document was revised several times, the last being in Horn, *Ultimate Realities*.

77. Most of these writings are in the form of articles in IFES publications, memos to committees or papers given at meetings. Johnson, Barclay, Catherwood, Horn and Brown have all devoted some pages to the DB in their respective books. For example, see Johnson, *Brief History* and *Contending for the Faith*; Robert M. Horn, *Student Witness and Christian Truth*

The second commentary, *Essentials: A Brief Introduction for Bible Study Based on the Doctrinal Basis of the International Fellowship of Evangelical Students*,[78] resulted from intense discussions held during the 1971 General Committee. This GC unanimously passed a motion reaffirming its

> unqualified adherence to the Doctrinal Basis of the IFES. The IFES is a movement which seeks to obey the authority of the crucified and risen Lord Jesus Christ. Therefore, the IFES acknowledges the authority of Holy Scripture as the Word of God, completely trustworthy in its totality and in all its parts.[79]

A subcommittee suggested "that a short study guide on the meaning of the Doctrinal Basis should be prepared for the member movements."[80] The Executive "agreed that it should not be classified as an official document having the same authority as the IFES Constitution or Doctrinal Basis."[81] Associate GS Bürki penned a brochure not meant "for theological debate, but for individual and group Bible study,"[82] which remains the DB's last published IFES official commentary to date.[83] This approach is interesting as it shows an implicit tension in the organization's relationship to the biblical text: every believer is supposedly able to understand it by him- or herself; no clerical mediation is needed.[84] Yet the fact that the General Committee – constituted essentially of senior staff members of national movements and only marginally

---

(London: Inter-Varsity Press, 1971); Barclay, *Jesus Lane Lot*; Lowman, *Day of His Power*; Barclay and Horn, *Cambridge to the World*; Lindsay Brown, *Shining Like Stars*.

78. Bürki, *Essentials*.

79. "Minutes of the Meeting of the Eighth General Committee" (1971), 19. Before the motion was passed, Stacey Woods, in his capacity of outgoing General Secretary, stated in unequivocal terms that "we must be aware that in evangelical biblical circles in many parts of the world there is a shift from the traditional historical doctrine of Scripture which should cause us concern; he did not imply there was any shift in the IFES or its member movements, but that we would probably be confronted with a certain ferment on the part of some students. We welcome students in our movements who are liberals and who, by God's grace, will be brought to a biblical position. But if in the leadership of IFES there were to be a shift, it could mean the beginning of the end of the IFES. This General Committee represents such leadership" (18). See pp. 85–89 above.

80. "Minutes of the Meeting of the Eighth General Committee" (1971), 20. Excerpts from the report of the subcommittee were published in Bürki, *Essentials*, 49–50.

81. "Minutes of the Meeting of the Executive Committee of the IFES" (Schloss Mittersill, Austria, 30.8–3.9 1973), 22, IFES e-archives.

82. Chua Wee Hian, "Foreword," 8.

83. At the time of writing, it has been out of print for many years and the writer is not aware of plans for republication.

84. Interestingly, Padilla was Baptist and Bürki originally from a Brethren (Darbyist) background.

of students – expressed the need for more explanation is striking. Some sort of "hermeneutical circle," as shown in figure 2, can summarize the process.

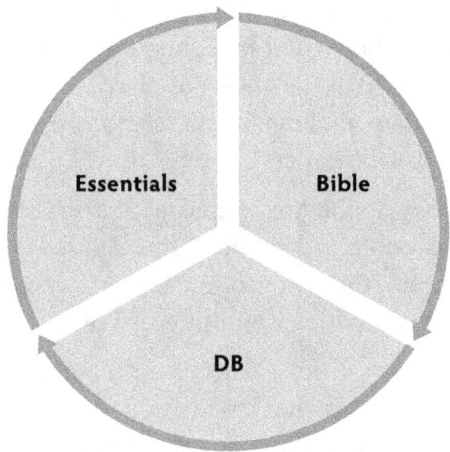

Figure 2

Focusing on Essentials

> The doctrinal basis of the Fellowship shall be the fundamental truths of Christianity, including . . .[85]

Fundamental to how IFES understands its DB is the idea of *concentrating on essentials.* Since the fellowship connects members of different church traditions with diverging specificities, its actors must agree on a common corpus of affirmations.

Hence, the DB can be conceived missiologically: it states what is deemed essential to preaching the gospel effectively and adequately, to reach a specific public in a specific context – the university. Local strategies will be variations on the theme of the eleven affirmations, which are considered sufficient grounds for people to become Christians since they will assure the inscription of the new believers into the essentials of the Christian tradition.

---

85. The text of the DB has remained unchanged since 1947 (except for clause D; see below). In what follows, we quote from Bürki, *Essentials*, 21. See also IFES, "What We Believe," accessed 19 May 2020, https://ifesworld.org/en/beliefs/.

As often in the study of the theology of IFES, the rationale lies behind hermeneutical considerations. IFES pioneers always insisted that the content of the DB was the result of a deductive process. In Hammond's words,

> a sufficient, practical grasp of the basic doctrines does not call for great intelligence, nor will it take long for a determined seeker (with the Holy Spirit as his guide) to discover what the apostles regarded as fundamental in a man's relationship with his Maker and also with his fellow men.[86]

A proper methodology applied to scriptural "materials" bears proper fruit, much like the synthesis obtained by sifting through scientific literature on any given topic. As Lowman, the writer of the hitherto official IFES history and former member of the Executive Committee, posits,

> precisely because the groups' objectives do not necessitate taking up positions on issues that divide equally biblically minded Evangelicals, students from different denominations can labour in partnership and enrich one another. There can be few members of IFES-linked groups who have not gained by this exposure to the different perspectives of other biblically minded believers. In turn, the links created in the student scene serve to build essential bridges within the evangelical community in the following years.[87]

For Hammond, the DB is a solid starting ground, and Christian students should be respectful of each other's views on secondary matters for the sake of common witness. Consequently,

> all officers and members are . . . urged to discourage any attempts within the Unions to proselytize, and to refrain from criticism or disparagement of the denominational views of other members. United opposition to fundamental error will be all the stronger if they are free to differ about secondary matters.[88]

The DB is hence a powerful ecclesiological statement. Being a member of the church "to which all true believers belong"[89] implies creedal agreement to the statements of the basis. Consequently, one could read the DB as

---

86. Hammond, *Evangelical Belief*, 5.
87. Lowman, *Day of His Power*, 337.
88. Hammond, *Evangelical Belief*, 45.
89. Clause J.

summarizing the essentials of a *missionary organization* and the essentials of the faith on which all Christians should agree.

Ecclesiology

> J: The one Holy Universal Church which is the Body of Christ and to which all true believers belong.

The IFES DB acknowledges the existence of the church as a given. However, while the existence of a visible church is implied by the clause, the precision that "all true believers" form it goes beyond common creedal affirmations to imply that "ultimately, only God knows who belongs to Him and therefore to His Church."[90]

Here as in many other clauses, the key to interpreting the DB's view is to mark a boundary between a believers' church ecclesiology – in this case quite distinctly evangelical – and a multitudinist church. Again, personal faith is critical: "All who come to Christ in personal saving faith and acknowledge Him as Lord are made, by their new relationship with Him, members of the one, sanctified, worldwide company of His redeemed people."[91] So while no criteria for church membership are explicitly formulated in the DB, the underlying *believers'* church ecclesiology emerges clearly from the commentary.[92]

Moreover, confessing the church as being essentially *invisible* cannot be understood apart from pneumatology:

> The Bible teaches us that the Holy Spirit dwells both in the local Church and in the universal Church. The one Spirit *animates* the whole Church and is the source of fellowship which unites Christians in the "one body" of Christ.[93]

---

90. Bürki, *Essentials*, 44–45.

91. Hammond, *Evangelical Belief*, 44. Reference is made to John 10:16.

92. On the personal nature of the faith and its implications for bases of faith, Collange comments that "the Church is not always mentioned in our confessions (Salvation Army, Assemblies of God) or is mentioned only incidentally (AEF, GBU . . .). This is due first of all to the 'personal' perspective of a salvation understood in a rather individualistic way, and to the congregationalist perspective of the community linked to it, the Church being then – where it is mentioned – the whole of 'all believers united in the Spirit' (GBU, AEF)." Collange, "Les confessions de foi «évangéliques»," 77. The connection with congregationalism points towards the strong Brethren influence observable in the early IFES pioneers' own backgrounds.

93. Hammond, *Evangelical Belief*, 43; emphasis added. Reference is made to 1 Cor 3:16; Eph 2:20–22; 4:3–4.

Is this "animation" the link between the spiritual reality of the universal church and missionary engagement? The idea is not yet fully articulated, but the seed of a *missional ecclesiology* is evident here. The believer's *(immediate) animation* to be involved in mission presumes *membership* in the invisible church, even without a satisfying local ecclesiological context.

In a development worth quoting at length, Hammond resorts to the notion of a *spiritual priesthood*, of which all Christians are members:

> This community constitutes a body of which Christ is the Head. They form a building or temple which is indwelt by God's Spirit. *They constitute a priesthood* which is to offer the sacrifice of worship. This "people of God" has *the duty to spread the wonderful knowledge of God's saving work*. In this community they are interdependent, or "members one of another." ... Such fellowship is clearly meant to be realized, wherever possible, by every Christian by active membership in a local congregation. The Evangelical Unions affiliated to the Inter-Varsity Fellowship are not to be regarded as such local congregations or "churches." They have a limited purpose in a limited sphere and for a limited period in the experience of their members.[94]

This concise and balanced treatment is one of the most cogent to be found in IFES documents. Hammond's concern for respectful relationships between local student groups and church is remarkable. Note that the "duty to spread" the gospel is explicitly ascribed to the people of God and is not the prerogative of professional ministers only. Students are hence already full members of the church universal and are its legitimate emissaries in the world. This insistence on the invisible church is not, however, to the detriment of local church membership. Speaking of student groups, Hammond is adamant that

> their members should not neglect regular participation in the worship and fellowship of a proper local expression of the Body of Christ. They ought normally to be baptized members, and to partake regularly of the Lord's Supper, in such a congregation. This means that the Inter-Varsity Fellowship would wish earnestly to disclaim any notion that it is, or desires to become, a Church

---

94. Hammond, 44; emphasis added. References given are Eph 1:22–23; 2:20–22; 1 Pet 2:5, 9; Rom 12:5; Eph 4:3, 13–16; Heb 10:24–25.

or Sect. Its functions are purely those of an auxiliary to the mainstream of Church life.⁹⁵

Assuming that the functions of a student group are "purely those of an auxiliary" implies the corresponding belief that students can rely on a supportive local ecclesial environment. However, as the recurring articles and debates on how to best support students transitioning "back" to local churches show, this has never been universally the case. IFES students are encouraged to be members of local churches based on doctrinal agreement: "It is the duty and privilege of its members to encourage one another to work in true communion with any Christian congregation which is scriptural in preaching and practice, and whose members acknowledge the one Lord and confess the one faith."⁹⁶ Shortly after the heyday of ecumenism, Bürki was clear in his warning that "it is necessary also to observe that no encouragement is given in the New Testament to those who would exalt fellowship at the expense of sound doctrine."⁹⁷ As a result, many students have struggled, whether because of leadership or for theological reasons, not to mention the absence of a local church in countries where Christians are a small and sometimes persecuted minority.

Partial Synthesis: Anchoring Truths for a Changing World

It is not easy to do justice to the role of the DB in the history of IFES. I have shown that despite an a priori difficult relationship with theology, IFES has developed its own theology, of which the DB is the earliest, most articulate evidence. The DB presupposes the *immediacy* of a believer's relationship with God, which is a set of eternally, practically acontextual essential truths. This *immediacy* is supported by a firm affirmation of the trustworthiness and perspicuity of the Bible. It postulates that any student anywhere in the world would recognize the same essential truths to be essentials. Besides, allegiance to the affirmations of the DB creates and shapes a community of which students become *members*. This community is not an alternative local church, but the manifestation of the *invisible church* on campus. This believers' church ecclesiology coexists with the underlying assumption, only implicit at this stage, that *mission* is primary in the church's existence – and concomitantly in

---

95. Hammond, 45.
96. Hammond, 45.
97. Hammond, 46.

Christian existence. It is now to the slow development of a *missional ecclesiology* in the thinking of IFES authors that we turn.

12

IFES Authors Discussing Ecclesiology

How should the church be defined theologically? A summary statement like the 1998 "Statement on the Church,"[1] which affirmed the importance of the church while at the same time stating that "we are not, and refrain from ever becoming, a local church,"[2] was long in the making. It rested, among other things, on the ecclesiological work of several figures close to IFES. T. C. Hammond and John Stott were two Anglican clergymen who had a long-lasting influence on IFES students. Jim Stamoolis was theological student secretary for IFES in the 1980s and as such a sort of "in-house theologian." René Padilla was IFES associate General Secretary throughout the 1970s and 1980s, David Zac Niringiye was himself Regional Secretary for EPSA until 2000.

T. C. Hammond: *In Understanding Be Men*

Hammond's *In Understanding Be Men*,[3] first published in 1936, provided IFES circles with a first common work of doctrine destined explicitly for "non-theological students." The book's overall tone is consensual, "somewhat Anglican in ethos and mildly Calvinistic in emphasis."[4] Written at the request

---

1. See above, chapter 8.
2. "Minutes of the Meeting of the Executive Committee" (1998), 26.
3. T. C. Hammond, *In Understanding Be Men: A Handbook on Christian Doctrine for Non-Theological Students*, 1st ed. 1936 (5th ed.; London: IVF, 1960). The aim of the book was to "make accessible to the ordinary reader, if only in an elementary form, the great treasures of knowledge reposing in the volumes of theological thought" (p. v).
4. Warren Nelson, *T. C. Hammond: Irish Christian; His Life and Legacy in Ireland and Australia* (Edinburgh: Banner of Truth Trust, 1994), 133.

of the IVF – he was himself part of its theological advisory committee[5] – this work is interesting from a theological point of view because it shows the interest of IFES circles in doctrine and theology.[6] Practically speaking, "something not too technical was wanted to help students who had recently come to faith in Christ."[7] How could "non-theological" students be provided with enough yet not too much theology to navigate university life and teaching? A detailed study of the book would surely provide more insights, but for our purposes, it is to the treatment of the church that we turn.[8]

For Hammond, "the points on which emphasis is needed are those which concern our common Evangelical Protestant position in contradistinction to extreme forms of Sacerdotalism and other perversions of the Apostolic tradition."[9] Apostolicity refers here to the apostles' teaching and not to a succession of bishops. His definition stresses more the church *triumphant* than the church *militant*, for in Hammond's view, "in its fullest sense, the Church must be described as the 'company of all true believers,' and this includes those who have passed to their rest, as well as true believers who are still living."[10] There is here a very close connection to the IFES doctrinal basis.[11] Yet the church militant is not forgotten, for Hammond concedes that "the Visible Church is the Body of Christ in action in the world, though never in its ideal character, but beset with the limitations of time, space and human infirmity."[12]

Hammond shows his interest in being attuned to students and knows how prompt they might be to use their newly acquired knowledge to question

---

5. Geoffrey Treloar, "Hammond, Thomas Chatterton," in *Biographical Dictionary of Evangelicals*, ed. Timothy Larsen (Leicester: Inter-Varsity Press, 2003), 286–87.

6. Given his tight schedule, Hammond expressed the need for an assistant, who happened to be none other than Douglas Johnson, the future IVF general secretary and a very influential figure in IFES's early years. He was described in the preface of the first edition of *In Understanding* as "a graduate interested in the same project, and who wishes to remain anonymous" (1936, p. vi). See Nelson, *T. C. Hammond*, 89. However, Johnson seems to have been much more than an assistant, being rather the originator of the volume of which he "hammered together a full outline and then approached Canon T. C. Hammond to polish it up and put his name to it." Geraint Fielder, *Lord of the Years: Sixty Years of Student Witness – Story of the Inter-Varsity Fellowship/ Universities and Colleges Christian Fellowship, 1928–88* (Leicester: Inter-Varsity Press, 1988), 61.

7. Nelson, 88.

8. For the broader question of ecclesiology, see Chase Kuhn, "The Ecclesiological Influence of T. C. Hammond," *Churchman* 127, no. 4 (2013): 323–35.

9. Hammond, *In Understanding* (1960), 160.

10. Hammond, 161.

11. It seems that Hammond was heavily involved in writing it, according to Treloar, *Disruption of Evangelicalism*, 199.

12. Hammond, *In Understanding* (1960), 162.

church authorities, for he cautions that it "is a wise general rule for them not to attempt experiments."[13] Hammond advocates respect for the authorities, as long as no conflict of conscience is involved. The "self-determination" of the message of Scripture for an individual's course of action is a characteristic outworking of the doctrine of the "priesthood of all believers," which is here implicitly used to empower people to make their own decisions, yet not in "hasty judgment."[14]

Despite encouraging respect for church authorities, Hammond's consistent reaffirmation that Scripture can be understood *immediately* by students leads him to take to task a view of ministry which he finds biblically unwarranted. For him, Scripture does not support "the two false elements which crept into the medieval doctrine of the ministry and have been revived in recent years,"[15] which he takes to be the hierarchical order of church government and "the assigning to ministers of a mediatorial work as priests."[16] Hammond goes on to say that "Scripture asserts that Christians as a whole constitute a priesthood (1 Pet. 2:5). Scholars agree that sacerdotal terms are not discoverable in Christian writers until the close of the second century. 'Sacrifice is not part of the Christian ministry' (Hooker)."[17]

Furthermore, "any view of the Christian Ministry which makes ordination the occasion for the supposed bestowal of powers of mediation, sacrifice and special judicial powers over sinners is false to Holy Scripture. There is no occasion in the New Testament where the Christian minister is termed 'priest.'"[18] Hammond was also adamant that the concept of "clergy" as a "clerical caste" was "unknown to Scripture,"[19] but went further in his goal to strengthen his audience's resistance to "sacerdotalism":

> The idea that the Christian minister is in any sense a mediator between God and man is "repugnant to holy Scripture." He may be

---

13. Hammond, 160.
14. Hammond, 160.
15. Hammond, 168.
16. Hammond, 168.
17. Hammond, 168. Hammond does not explicitly reference Hooker's *Laws of Ecclesiastical Policy* 5.58.2. It is interesting to note that the first edition of his work read, "Scripture asserts that *Christianity* as a whole constitutes a priesthood." Hammond, *In Understanding* (1936), 207; emphasis added. One can therefore posit either an evolution towards individualization of the understanding of priesthood in Hammond's thinking, or at least the desire to be more precise in his expression.
18. Hammond, *In Understanding* (1960), 171.
19. Hammond, *In Understanding* (1960), 168.

a channel (or medium) through whom God speaks to His people. But there is no hint in Scripture that he is an indispensable link between an individual Christian and his God.[20]

One can easily see the polemicist[21] at work here when the tension is considered between Hammond's stringent refusal of any mediatorial function, while yet conceding the possibility that a member of clergy might be a "medium." He continues that

> the same perversion may be present in subtler forms. The Christian must beware of any obtrusion on the part of a ministry which in any way weakens the glory of our Lord's High Priestly work (see the Epistles) or arrogates to itself any power which Scripture claims belongs solely to Him or the Holy Spirit. While he ought to magnify the office of those commissioned to "feed the flock of God," he must also hold firmly to his own privileges as a member of the "royal priesthood" of redeemed sinners.[22]

Hammond's appeal to the reader to resist church ministers who are potentially controlling is voiced precisely on the grounds of his understanding of the "priesthood of all believers." Since the book became "the basic diet for decades"[23] of IFES leaders, especially given the apparent lack of conservative evangelical literature at the time *In Understanding Be Men* was published,[24] Hammond's underlying rationales have played a significant role.

Hammond did not define "parachurch," but this ecclesiology carefully articulates the relationship between the local church and Christian students. Refusing a "sacerdotal" definition of the church, he strongly insists that every student believer is a member of the royal priesthood and therefore of the church. Yet this *membership* is framed within the limits of an individual conscience shaped by the student's own diligent reading of Scripture and warranted insofar as the local church is essentially a context in which the student is fed by the Scriptures and responding to them. Implicitly for Hammond, the missionary

---

20. Hammond, *In Understanding* (1960), 172.

21. On this aspect of Hammond's work, see Geoffrey Treloar, "T. C. Hammond the Controversialist," *Anglican Historical Society Diocese of Sydney Journal* 51, no. 1 (2006): 20–35.

22. Hammond, *In Understanding* (1960), 173.

23. Fielder, *Lord of the Years*, 61.

24. The book was subsequently translated into several languages. The title of the Spanish edition is especially explicit as to the audience of the book: T. C. Hammond, *Cómo comprender la doctrina cristiana: manual de teologia para laicos* (Buenos Aires: Ediciones Certeza, 1978). See Treloar, *Disruption of Evangelicalism*, 200, for the importance of the work.

calling of the individual emerges out of his or her relationship to God and precedes membership of the local church, the latter being evaluated based on its faithfulness to the former.

John Stott: *One People*

The next work relevant to our exploration is *One People*, the published version of the "Pastoral Theology" lectures delivered at Durham University in 1968 by the Anglican priest Stott.[25] Addressed initially to theological students and focusing on attitudes of the clergy to the laity, the lectures were originally titled "The Theology of the Laity."[26] This book is interesting because of Stott's long association with IFES circles. It was deemed relevant enough for the student world for it to be published by InterVarsity Press, the publishing house of InterVarsity in the United States.

The work surveys the doctrine of the church and focuses on different kinds of relationships which have existed between clergy and laity. Stott comments on how tense these relations have often been and pointedly remarks that lay initiatives which contributed to the missionary movements in the nineteenth century and "were spontaneous, the upsurge of lay energy from below, [were] sometimes tolerated by church leaders only because they had no alternative."[27] Stott concludes that the correct relationship between clergy and laity is neither one of dominion (clericalism) or denigration (anticlericalism), nor of separation (dualism), but service, for "the laity are the Church and . . . the clergy are appointed to serve them, to seek to equip them to be what God intends them to be."[28]

According to Stott, "the chief way in which the clergy are to serve the laity is in helping to teach and train them for their life, work and especially witness (*marturia*) in the world. The *diakonia*, service, of the clergy is subservient to the *marturia* of the laity."[29] The argument rests on functional differentiation and not on apostolic succession.

Stott hence argues for a *missiological* understanding of the church based on the very text from which the "priesthood of all believers" is most often argued:

---

25. Stott explains in the preface that the book *One People* was "a revision and extension" of the lectures. John Stott, *One People* (Downers Grove: InterVarsity Press, 1971), 7.

26. Stott refers several times to an important book published a few years earlier: Kraemer, *A Theology of the Laity*.

27. Stott, *One People*, 10.

28. Stott, 42.

29. Stott, 13.

> The New Testament authors declare, the God who has called us out of the world sends us back into the world: you are a chosen race, a royal priesthood, a holy nation, God's own people, that you may declare the wonderful deeds of him who called you out of darkness into his marvellous light.[30]

Stott does not advocate abolishing clergy but continues, noticing that "God's people . . . are both a priestly people, to offer to Him the acceptable, spiritual sacrifices of praise and prayer, and a missionary people, to declare to others the excellences of their God, the God who has called them into His marvellous light and has had mercy upon them."[31] As an aside, Stott counters Cyprian's identification of the priest with the Old Testament priestly function, arguing that "the Old Testament priesthood has been superseded in the New by the priesthood of all believers, that is, the priesthood of the whole Church."[32]

Christians are called to and equipped for witness in their respective spheres for two main reasons. First, because "in many respects, the laity are in a position to engage in this work far more effectively than the clergy, because 'the laity is the dispersion of the church,'[33] 'immersed in the world,'[34] penetrating more deeply into secular society than the average clergyman will ever get."[35] Second, because witness can only be practised by people by virtue of their Christian calling and not through any delegation to a specific group (clergy), for "there is no possibility of worship or witness by proxy."[36] This has vast consequences for the practice of ministry in ecclesial contexts and in the wider world. It was arguably the concern to see Christians taking care of each other in the process of discovering God's word for themselves that brought Stott also to endorse the practice – at the time relatively new – of small (home)groups operating similarly to student groups on campus. In Stott's own words,

> if it [the growth of homegroups] needs to be explained in terms of human experience, it is probably to be understood as a protest against the dehumanizing processes of secular society and the

---

30. Stott, 17, quoting 1 Pet 2:9.
31. Stott, 24–25.
32. Stott, 29.
33. Stott quotes Kraemer, *Theology of the Laity*, 181.
34. Stott quotes John A. T. Robinson, *Layman's Church* (London: Lutterworth, 1963), 18.
35. Stott, *One People*, 44.
36. Stott, 25.

superficial formalism of much church life. There is a widespread hunger for a life which is genuinely human and absolutely real.[37]

So, for Stott, the laity essentially *is the church* which witnesses in different contexts: in short, *a priesthood of all believers*. If this holds true, then witnessing students *are* the church, they are not *alongside* the church as the word "parachurch" could indicate. Because one of the tasks of the gathered assembly is to equip the laity to be the scattered church and to *mediate* the gospel to their entourage, the laity cannot be autonomous from the church. Stott's concern to teach the laity and encourage students to be missionaries where they are seems to have strongly appealed to the masses of students he was in contact with, especially in later years.[38]

Jim Stamoolis: "Ecclesiology and Mission"

Stamoolis, IFES Theological Student Secretary in the 1980s, penned a brief article relevant to our work.[39] He proposes that "the central defining aspect of evangelical ecclesiology is that the gospel must be personally applied to the individual. It is important to note that saying it must be personally applied does not necessarily mean it must be individually applied."[40] Yet Stamoolis also notes that it is one thing to believe that every student has the *potential* to witness on campus; it is another to think every student is *equipped* to do so. *Training* usually helps bridge the gap. The question is at core missiological and depends on one's comprehension of the mission field. Stamoolis optimistically noted that, at the time of writing, a shift in perceptions was occurring:

---

37. Stott, 73. A good illustration might be given from a student remembering her pioneering years in GBEU Switzerland (she was later with her husband to pioneer IFES groups in francophone Africa): "I had brought my whole family there, little by little, and then my brother went to a camp, several camps, skiing, with us. And he saw young people reading their Bibles every day. He said, 'But that's not true, it's not possible for young people to read their Bibles every day' – he couldn't believe his eyes. He found it sensational. And it's true that it's interesting [that] when you're from the Reformed church [you] approach the Bible in a different way from an old pastor who teaches us *ex cathedra*, and it's true that this is something that works well with young people." Interview with Denyse and Louis Perret, 12 February 2012.

38. For further biographical context, see Timothy Dudley-Smith, *John Stott: A Global Ministry* (Downers Grove: InterVarsity Press, 2001), chs. 10–12; Alister Chapman, *Godly Ambition: John Stott and the Evangelical Movement* (New York: OUP, 2012), ch. 6.

39. James Stamoolis, "An Evangelical Position on Ecclesiology and Mission," *International Review of Mission* 90, no. 358 (1 July 2001): 309–16.

40. Stamoolis, "Ecclesiology and Mission," 310.

> The good news is that the concept of lay witness is finding new life. Part of the reason for the demise of lay witness seemed to be in the presumed need for a heavy apologetic to convince secular man of the existence of God. The enemy of secularism was not one that an ordinary Christian could combat. Therefore, it took a trained professional to be able to present the gospel. In the postmodern age, personal opinion is more acceptable, albeit personal opinion cannot be accompanied by a dogmatic claim to have universal truth.[41]

The allusion to the "priesthood of all believers" is implicit but shows a remarkable degree of flexibility in this context. It is also rendered necessary by the fact that "church" and "witness" do not always fully overlap:

> The Church and, by extension, the local manifestations of the universal Church are the visible expressions of God's activity in redeeming humankind. It is always a mistake to place the boundaries of the kingdom of God as co-terminus to the Church. We do not fully know where God is working or even how he is working in his creation.[42]

On the one hand, if gospel work can occur outside the boundaries of the local church, it can therefore occur in the context of a parachurch group. On the other hand, this means that God might be at work even outside (para-) ecclesial frameworks. Christians might be invited to discern where God is already at work in the world before they join in. Though rarely articulated in IFES documents prior to the late 2000s, this last argument is nevertheless somewhat implicit from the organization's early history. Non-Christian students showing an interest in the gospel, being open to exploring its truth and relevance during their university years and engaging in conversations and activities with Christian students, are witnesses to the work of the Holy Spirit *prior* to the witness of IFES students – or other Christian students.

---

41. Stamoolis, 313.
42. Stamoolis, 313.

René Padilla: "An Ecclesiology for Integral Mission"

In a thoughtful volume published in 2003, Padilla and several of his colleagues offer theological rationales for local practices of integral mission.[43] Most of the foundations of Padilla's reflection, which I present here, were laid during his years as an IFES staff member.[44]

The theologian starts by contending that the confession of Christ as *Kyrios*, Lord of the whole universe, represented a contextualization of the Pauline writing for New Testament readers.[45] Next, he argues that "the integral church is one which recognizes that all spheres of life are 'mission fields' and looks for ways of asserting the sovereignty of Jesus Christ in all of them."[46] This implies an incarnational presence of the believer in all spheres of life, as an agent of the inaugurated kingdom:

> Christian discipleship understood as a missionary lifestyle – the active participation in the realization of God's plan for human existence and the creation, revealed in Jesus Christ – to which the whole church and each of its members have been called, expresses, in a word, the essence of the church's mission.[47]

Padilla further contends that the main impediment to this integral presence of Christians in all their spheres of life lies in the failure of church leadership to empower lay believers to witness without clerical support. In his own rather direct words, bearing close reminiscences of IFES's insistence on lay student leadership,

> integral mission demands the "declericalization" of ministries and a "laicization" of the clergy. In other words, it requires a recognition of the apostolic nature of the whole church. This implies, on one

---

43. C. René Padilla and Tetsunao Yamamori, eds., *La iglesia local como agente de transformación: una eclesiología para la misión integral* (Buenos Aires: Ediciones Kairós, 2003). In what follows, I use the English translation: C. René Padilla, "Introduction: An Ecclesiology for Integral Mission," in *The Local Church, Agent of Transformation: An Ecclesiology for Integral Mission*, eds. C. René Padilla and Tetsunao Yamamori (Buenos Aires: Ediciones Kairós, 2004), 19–49.

44. Padilla's talk at Lausanne seems to have precipitated his departure from the senior IFES team, pressured by the US and UK GSs. This is also hinted at by David C. Kirkpatrick, "Died: C. René Padilla, Father of Integral Mission," Christianity Today, 27 April 2021, accessed 22 July 2021, https://www.christianitytoday.com/news/2021/april/rene-padilla-died-integral-mission-latin-american-theology.html.

45. Padilla, "Ecclesiology for Integral Mission," 24. For a full-length argument along the same lines, see Flemming, *Contextualization in the New Testament*.

46. Padilla, 27.

47. Padilla, 28.

hand, that all members, by the simple fact of being disciples of Christ, share in the commission to go into the world in the name of Jesus Christ, as his witnesses. It also implies, on the other hand, that the leaders are a part of the *laos*, the people of God, just as are all the rest of Christ's followers, no more and no less.[48]

Such a development shows a close connection to Stott's thinking on articulating the roles of laypeople – witnessing – and clergy – equipping. Padilla closes the circle with the "priesthood of all believers":

> All this is in accordance with the biblical doctrine which formed one of the pillars of the Reformation of the sixteenth century, the priesthood of all believers. The classical reformers like Luther and Calvin, however, emphasized the soteriological consequences of that doctrine, namely that a person could have a direct relationship with God without the need for intermediaries.[49]

Lest his readers incline to limit the doctrine to individual consequences, Padilla hastens to add that the magisterial Reformers

> did not pay much attention to the ecclesiological consequences: that all believers are called to Christian ministry, whatever their vocation. In consequence, it was a common idea in the Protestant world that the benefits of salvation could be separated from the responsibility for mission. Integral mission demands the recovery of the priesthood of all believers to the extent that the church becomes a community in which all members, equally, encourage each other to discover and develop their gifts and ministries in those countless areas of human existence which need transformation by the power of the gospel.[50]

Such argumentation underlines the necessity for all Christian students to take the missionary task seriously by virtue of the nature of their Christian faith. The same applies to church leadership.[51] In short, Padilla's theology of the lordship of Christ over the whole earth births his concern for *integral mission*. This leads him to the conclusion that the *whole* church is called to mission wherever its members are found. Consequently, these lay members need to be

---

48. Padilla, 45.
49. Padilla, 45.
50. Padilla, 45–46.
51. Padilla, 47.

equipped and encouraged for their service, which is the church leadership's task. The connections with the logic of student ministry are clear.

David Zac Niringiye: *The Church: God's Pilgrim People*

Published in 2015, *The Church: God's Pilgrim People* is one of the latest works in ecclesiology penned by a former senior IFES staff member.[52] Niringiye acknowledges numerous IFES figures in his foreword, his book representing an important treatment of ecclesiology from a Majority World perspective.

Niringiye's work is more narrative than analytical. Beginning with the Old Testament and painting a grand panorama of biblical history, Niringiye summarizes his thoughts by suggesting there are three marks of a church: "faith, love and hope – as the key features that mark out the new community in Christ as the people of God."[53] The church has its roots in the people of Israel, whose election had the blessing of others in mind: "Moses made it clear that the people of Israel were now God's people in God's mission to restore creation, harmony and community for his pleasure and glory."[54]

Consequently, most of the setbacks experienced by Israel can be attributed to their failure to realize their vocation as God's ambassadors. Niringiye intertwines the situation of Israel with that of the contemporary Christian church. In rather direct words, he suggests that "a lot of the malaise and slumber in the churches today can be traced to the loss of consciousness of the pilgrim nature of our lives, individually and corporately."[55] This "pilgrim nature" is the central metaphor of Niringiye's work and is consistent with the fact that he writes from a Majority World perspective where evangelical churches are often accustomed to being the minority or at least not as privileged as many Western churches.

Niringiye develops a *missional ecclesiology* more interested in the spiritual character of the community than in its programmes. Ethical coherence is presented as an essential marker of the true nature of a given assembly. Commenting on "strong" churches around the world, he says that

> such churches often lose their cutting edge and get conformed to the society around them, worshipping its idols and participating in

---

52. Niringye was RS for EPSA until 2000.
53. David Zac Niringiye, *The Church: God's Pilgrim People* (Downers Grove: InterVarsity Press Academic, 2015), 26.
54. Niringiye, *The Church*, 56.
55. Niringiye, 59.

its greed. They coexist with, and in some cases enhance, the levels of social injustice in their societies. These churches are said to be strong, thriving and powerful, and yet the levels of social injustice are growing. Doesn't that say something about whom they serve and worship? Just as in Israel there was a lot of religion, so these churches are packed with programmes and activities. Yet God's verdict on such churches stands: they are idolatrous.[56]

Niringiye's work features robust social criticism. Despite having worked for many years in IFES, he does not shy away from rebuking fellow evangelicals. For example, having noted that Jesus was rejected by the religious establishment of his day, he asserts that "they are today's ecclesiastical bureaucrats: archbishops, bishops, clergy and pastors are the chief priest and priests; Bible-believing evangelicals are the Pharisees of the time; and theologians of all shades are the teachers of the law."[57]

The key to a rediscovery of the power of the "church project" is, for the author, to rediscover the role of everyone in God's mission. Niringiye distinguishes between "calling" and "assignment":

> Calling is assumed in assignment: it is about being and belonging to Jesus, in God's mission and his kingdom. Assignment is about the location and role within God's mission and kingdom, the particular journey of disciple that is marked out, the particular cross that the disciple must take up in following Jesus.[58]

This is a *theology of the laity*: "To everyone Jesus calls, he assigns a task; everyone who follows has a particular journey with Jesus, growing to know him more on that journey as they live out their discipleship."[59]

What is particularly striking about this research is that there is almost no difference between the vocation of a local church and that of a student group. Making more explicit what was latent in Hammond and implicit in Stott, Niringiye blurs the lines between church and parachurch by not assigning strong significance to clerical roles in his definition of the church. Ultimately, this means that there is no sharp line between the vocation of today's church and that of the people of Israel. Niringiye supports his case by quoting extensively from Wright's exposition of Exodus 19:

---

56. Niringiye, 72.
57. Niringiye, 102.
58. Niringiye, 103.
59. Niringiye, 103.

> The function of priesthood in Israel itself was to stand between God and the rest of the people – representing God to the people (by their teaching function) and representing and bringing the people to God (by their sacrificial function). Through the priesthood, God was made known to the people, and the people could come into acceptable relationship to God. So God assigns to his people as a whole community the role of priesthood for the nations. As their priests stood in relation to God and the rest of *Israel*, so they as a whole community were to stand in relation to God and the rest of the *nations*.[60]

Christians need to realize the transitory character of their situation as *pilgrims* and their vocation to engage their environment: "The Gospels are emphatic that as we follow Jesus, we declare the good news of the reign of God in all we are and do. Sharing the good news about Jesus is integral to being a disciple."[61] Commenting on the early disciples' commitment, Niringiye notes that

> the impact of their witness to the world would not be achieved in withdrawal, but like salt in food and light expelling darkness, it was through their presence, a savouring presence, and by the proclamation of the gospel of the kingdom that they would prevent moral decay and expel the darkness of evil in the world.[62]

This represents a shift in the argument from the earlier IFES rhetoric, which had more of an embattled character. IFES was on campus more to *preserve* and *defend theology* than to *engage the world*. This is coherent with a strong sense of the pneumatological character of the community:

> With the advent of the Holy Spirit at Pentecost God's redemptive activity shifted from working through the particular people and nation of Israel to working among all peoples and nations, "all whom the Lord our God will call," as Peter proclaimed ([Acts] 2:39). The universalization of the gospel of the kingdom of God was immediate upon the coming of the Holy Spirit. At Pentecost the new community, the community of the kingdom of God, was

---

60. Christopher J. H. Wright, *Knowing Jesus through the Old Testament* (Downers Grove: InterVarsity Press, 2014), 92.
61. Niringiye, *The Church*, 111.
62. Niringiye, 109.

> inaugurated – ushered into the world, embodying the presence of Christ in the world, living by his word and his Spirit.[63]

Niringiye displays a strong bent towards *voluntarism*. He observes that diverse communities existed already in New Testament times, suggesting that "the Greek term *koinonia*, which is translated as 'fellowship,' signified voluntary partnership or sharing around a particular interest, vocation or commitment and was in common use. What was novel was the nature and basis of their *koinonia*. Their *koinonia* was the work of the Holy Spirit."[64]

This insistence on the Holy Spirit, not found in earlier IFES discussions of ecclesiology, is noticeable. It indicates the more "tentative" nature of ecclesiological existence in a more fragile environment than the privileged contexts out of which earlier IFES writings arose. However, scepticism towards methodological certainties does not mean a complete overturning of theological tables, as the following excerpt shows:

> Understanding, discerning and obeying: that is what Christian mission is primarily about. One of the biggest problems today is the over-dependence on methods, strategies, institutions and technologies in Christian mission. The challenge before us is to discern the voice of the Holy Spirit amid the noises of our histories, cultures and lifestyles. Priority must be given to Bible teaching and prayer.[65]

The theological foundations Niringiye outlines here go beyond earlier IFES thinking but remain coherent with the foundations: attentiveness to context, growing cultural awareness and the centrality of a Scripture-shaped piety. In the same way that Hammond stressed the importance of scriptural reasoning, Niringiye calls for an engagement with the world logically intertwined with evangelism:

> The first mark, then, of the presence of the Holy Spirit in a community is that the gospel will be continually proclaimed. This is evangelism. It should be noted that the gospel was proclaimed not just to the outsiders; the believers needed to continue to hear the good news expounded, constantly hearing the call to turn

---

63. Niringiye, 122.
64. Niringiye, 122–23.
65. Niringiye, 144.

their entire being towards God and his purposes and continue to follow Jesus.⁶⁶

Fundamentally, then, because the *mission of God* precedes the *mission of the church*, IFES cannot be "sent by the church":

> Where did we get the idea of a "sending church"? It is not the church that sends; the church is sent. It is not the church that sends; Jesus sends by his Spirit. We, the disciples of Christ, the new community, are the sent people of God. Now as then, it is God who sends, and he sends those he has called first as his disciples.⁶⁷

The argument comes full circle: if the people of God carry out the mission of God sent by the Spirit of God, the legitimacy of parachurch missionary involvement is achieved and the distinctions between church and parachurch become blurred to a large extent. Whatever ecclesiastical reservations may arise, students qua Christians can prayerfully discern what God calls them to do. It is even arguable that the campus could in many cases play in the lives of Christian students the same role the exile played in the history of Israel: "Israel, as a people of God, were formed in the exodus; when they lost track of their identity after they settled in the promised land they were taken into exile, from where the remnant rediscovered their identity and mission."⁶⁸ No small number of testimonies of IFES students follow roughly the same lines: they had a rather fundamental Christian commitment amounting to nominalism, for their faith was inherited from their parents. The confrontation with new ideas, the campus culture and other perspectives forced them to revisit their own assurances. In the same way that Stott and Stamoolis called for students to be equipped, Niringiye insists that "insiders" need to be taught as well and are not "ready to go and teach" their classmates – *mediate* the gospel – contrary to what the earliest IFES books and brochures had assumed. Pneumatological discernment and contextual changes force the actors to realign their convictions attentively and constantly with God's prompting. The *immediacy* of the believer's relationship to God is not questioned, but the insistence of these authors on equipping shows that such piety does not automatically generate wise *mediation*.

Hammering home this missiological point, Niringiye insists that the discourse cannot, therefore, continue to be one of "insider versus outsiders":

---

66. Niringiye, 150.
67. Niringiye, 154.
68. Niringiye, 175.

> We have already understood that it is not the work of the Christian community to "bring others" into the fold of Christ; Jesus will bring them. The longing to attain the "whole measure of the fullness of Christ" should compel us to go to the ends of the earth, to other cultures and nationalities, to search for those who belong to him, so that with them our understanding and appreciation of our redemption is enhanced and our experience of Christ deepened. . . . We need all the cultures, all the nations and all the peoples in order to appreciate the multi-dimensional, multi-faceted fullness of Christ. It is the translation of the life of Jesus into the way of life of all the world's cultures and subcultures throughout history that will enable us all to correct, enlarge and focus our own understanding and experience in Christ.[69]

Here, Niringiye goes further than all the preceding authors I have surveyed. He does not suppose that the church "has it all" and "merely needs to communicate it," but understands mission as enriching the church by broadening its horizons and its understanding of God. This does not mean that the church has nothing to say to the world but that the church can still learn. By extension, such an approach is promising for a ministry to the university, a place of discoveries.

To summarize the development in the ecclesiological thinking of IFES authors, we see several argumentative moves: Hammond first distinguishes apostolicity from sacerdotalism, insisting on the primacy of doctrine over clerical office. Stott takes on the baton to tell clergy to equip the laity. Stamoolis insists that work is done outside the church, not only within its walls; Padilla, that the work done has to consider all aspects of life. Niringiye finally insists on the tentative, improvising nature of pilgrims witnessing. What we have here is a sort of paleogenesis of a *missional church ecclesiology*.

Partial Synthesis: IFES as a Theological Enterprise

The IFES story is riddled with debates about the theological legitimacy of its enterprise alongside the church. As I will show in the next part, calling the organization "parachurch" does not solve many of the conceptual problems. It can be helpful as a commonly understood umbrella term, but it also betrays a

---

69. Niringiye, 183.

fundamentally *ecclesiocentric* approach, which is increasingly questioned by the current shape of world Christianity and the secularizing tendencies of the West.

History might be an explanatory factor: because the relevance of the Christian faith was questioned earlier on many university campuses than in the rest of society, IFES had to develop a theology compatible with its ministry environment. From the core missiological conviction that any student can witness to his or her faith on campus and that the university is a mission field in dire need of being reached with the gospel, the fellowship concluded that God's mission is primary over ecclesial structures.

True to their evangelical identity, the fellowship's leaders argued that the Bible was perspicuous and able to be read by all students who would, through faithful study, apply its teachings to their lives and studies.

Yet the Bible was not the only supporting structure to IFES's mission. A missionary organization cannot dispense with theological legitimizing devices. The IFES precursors had developed their doctrinal basis, which, once carefully merged into a common document, provided the newly founded fellowship with a core assemblage of beliefs considered unchangeably essential to the evangelical faith's orthodoxy. Even if the doctrinal basis was never seen as akin to a new creed, IFES indeed was *theologizing*, deciding which beliefs were central to faithfully living out and *mediating* the gospel on university campuses. Furthermore, as the years went by, IFES leaders developed into theologians themselves or called upon recognized theologians to flesh out their theological thinking, either through doctrinal books, Bible study guides or pamphlets.

The missional understanding of the student's vocation on campus and the dispensability of any clerical oversight of students' activities are the most evident supporting elements showing that the "priesthood of all believers" is the implicit rationale for the ministry of IFES. Yet, as the growing literature output shows, this understanding was not – contrary to what many polemicists have argued throughout the last centuries of church history and during the shorter IFES history – individualistic. It starts from the *immediate* access to God, but it is discovered, lived out and refined through one's *participation* in a fellowship with a clear *missional* vision.

Having begun as a "mere" missionary organization creating networks of people with common aspirations to proclaim the gospel on university campuses, IFES matured into a theological enterprise in its own right, offering some of its leaders the venue to systematically explore the theological underpinnings of what was at the beginning a more pragmatic venture: to refine their thinking in the light of international encounters as theological iron sharpens theological iron.

This exploration of how ecclesiological and missiological reflections have developed throughout the history of IFES has shown how the ideas of *immediacy*, *mediation* and *participation*, which I argue to be constitutive of a missional understanding of the "priesthood of all believers," keep surfacing, even if only implicitly. In the remainder of this work, I will show how further theological resources, notably in biblical theology and *missional ecclesiology*, contribute to a fuller understanding of the work of IFES.

Part 4

Theological Resources

> There is never a time . . . when the priesthood of all believers is not crucial in the life of the church – it belongs to the *esse*, not the *bene esse*, of the church.[1]

Having surveyed the historical development of IFES and how its "in-house" theologians framed its work, I turn to biblical and theological materials. I argue in this research that the "priesthood of all believers" is the underlying theological doctrine that best helps make sense of the work of IFES. In this part, I briefly examine the biblical foundations of the doctrine of the "priesthood of all believers." I then draw on a range of theological voices to explore the role of the laity in the mission of the church to show how the "priesthood of all believers" allows for a *missional ecclesiology*.[2] From there, I suggest an in-depth

---

1. Robert A. Muthiah, *The Priesthood of All Believers in the Twenty-First Century: Living Faithfully as the Whole People of God in a Postmodern Context* (Eugene: Wipf & Stock, 2009), Kindle loc. 43–46.

2. A whole range of other ecclesiological implications – especially for church policies – could be drawn from the texts I examine, but they would exceed the scope of this work. See Greggs, "Priesthood of No Believer," 376.

examination of "parachurch," which is the "ecclesiological label" attributed to organizations like IFES. Though widely used, I show that this label does not reflect how IFES leaders have understood their work: for them, their work was the natural, contextual outworking on campus of a *missional* understanding of the church. Following Roland Allen's missiological reflections, we can see student ministry as a *ministry of expansion* of the church. I consequently argue that students *participate* in the *missio Dei* as *priests* and pilgrims in a complex environment. Finally, the argument comes full circle with a reflection on *apostolicity* as an essential character of the church.

13

The Priesthood of All Believers

Here I cover the most salient aspects of the Old Testament (OT) priesthood, notably the link between the priestly order and the rest of the people, and what happened to that function in New Testament (NT) times and the patristic era. The following cannot be understood as even a close attempt at providing an exhaustive survey of all the exegetical and hermeneutical debates on relevant biblical texts. It does, however, aim to survey those elements most helpful for shedding light on the work of IFES. I explore the fundamental text of 1 Peter 2:4–10, which often serves as the NT background for a doctrine of the "priesthood of all believers." I then discuss the thorny question of the link between the collective and individual dimensions of this calling to "serve others."

Old Testament
Priests for the Nation

In the Old Testament, priests are part of the overarching hierarchical structure of Israel, reflecting a "graded holiness"[1] – a stratification of the people according to purity and statutory proximity to God. They were generally understood as serving "as intermediaries between the people and God, and as advisors and leaders of the nation."[2] Priests were also responsible for presenting the people's

---

1. Philip Jenson, *Graded Holiness: A Key to the Priestly Conception of the World*, JSOT (Sheffield: Bloomsbury, 1992).
2. John T. Swann, "Priests," in *The Lexham Bible Dictionary*, ed. John D. Barry (Bellingham: Lexham, 2016).

sacrifices.[3] Yet there is a shift from a more sacrificial understanding of the priesthood towards a more educational one in the post-exilic period.[4] One crucial dimension of their teaching was the distinction between the sacred and the profane,[5] helping the people distinguish what was right before the Lord and giving instructions on proper conduct.[6]

Another dimension of the priestly office, divination, offered divine answers to precise questions asked by the people and delivered oracles, often using the mysterious Urim and Thummim.[7] Anizor and Voss deduce that the common feature of the non-sacrificial elements of priestly ministry

> is their clear public and word-centered orientation. Priests bring the word of the Lord to bear on the entirety of Israel's existence, in the everyday and sacred dimensions as well as the legal and cultic. Priests were the heralds of the will of Yahweh, especially as they interpreted the word for the people and applied it to the difficult and various circumstances of Israel's community life. These priestly practices contributed in different ways to forming a covenantally faithful people by constantly directing the gaze of the community to the very covenantal word that formed it.[8]

Priests, then,

> have the honor of continual access to the presence of the Lord in the sanctuary, but they also bear the responsibilities of offering sacrifices for the people, helping them discern holy from profane and clean from unclean, teaching the law, applying its commands to the varying circumstances of Israel's life and blessing the people in the Lord's name.[9]

---

3. Roland de Vaux, *Ancient Israel: Its Life and Institutions* (London: Darton, 1961), 356; John H. Walton, *Ancient Near Eastern Thought and the Old Testament: Introducing the Conceptual World of the Hebrew Bible* (Grand Rapids: Baker, 2006), 156.

4. Swann, "Priests."

5. Lev 10:10; Ezek 22:26; Hag 2:10–14; etc.

6. Jer 2:8; Hos 4:6; etc.

7. Numerous hypotheses have been put forward about these unknown objects: were they dice? sticks? etc. No scholarly consensus has emerged yet. Cf. Vaux, *Ancient Israel*, 352.

8. Anizor and Voss, *Representing Christ*, 36.

9. Anizor and Voss, 32.

A Priestly Nation

The Old Testament also speaks of a priestly vocation for the people of Israel as a community. Just before the law is formally given, God calls his people to a special relationship:

> Now therefore, if you obey my voice and keep my covenant, you shall be my treasured possession out of all the peoples. Indeed, the whole earth is mine, but you shall be for me a priestly kingdom and a holy nation. These are the words that you shall speak to the Israelites.[10]

Durham interprets these words in this way:

> Israel as the "special treasure" is Israel become uniquely Yahweh's prized possession by their commitment to him in covenant. Israel as a "kingdom of priests" is Israel committed to the extension throughout the world of the ministry of Yahweh's Presence, . . . a kingdom run not by politicians depending upon strength and connivance but by priests depending on faith in Yahweh, a servant nation instead of a ruling nation. Israel as a "holy people" then represents a third dimension . . . : they are to be a people set apart, different from all other people by what they are and are becoming – a display-people, a showcase to the world of how being in covenant with Yahweh changes a people.[11]

Israel is elected explicitly from among the nations to "assume a special function"[12] – that of blessing. In Exodus 19:6, Israel is called a "holy nation" (גּוֹי קָדוֹשׁ – *goy kadosh*). The use of the word גּוֹי is unusual for Israel,[13] yet the same word is used in the calling of Abraham to be a blessing to the nations in Genesis 12:2. This suggests that this election is a missionary calling.[14] In Wright's view, this "key missiological text"[15] has far-reaching implications for understanding God's relation to his people, and Israel's relation to the world:

---

10. Exod 19:5–6.

11. John I. Durham, *Exodus*, Word Biblical Commentary 3 (Waco: Word, 1986), 263.

12. W. J. Dumbrell, *Covenant and Creation: A Theology of the Old Testament Covenants*, 1st ed. 1984, Biblical and Theological Classics (Carlisle: Paternoster, 1997), 86.

13. W. Ross Blackburn, *The God Who Makes Himself Known: The Missionary Heart of the Book of Exodus* (Downers Grove: Apollos, 2012), 93.

14. Dumbrell, *Covenant and Creation*, 89.

15. Christopher J. H. Wright, *The Mission of God: Unlocking the Bible's Grand Narrative* (Downers Grove: InterVarsity Press Academic, 2006), 224. At the time of writing, Wright is IFES vice-president and chairs the Theological Advisory Group.

> The universal perspective . . . is explicit in the double phrases *all nations* and *the whole earth*. Although the action is taking place between YHWH and Israel alone at Mount Sinai, God has not forgotten his wider mission of blessing the rest of the nations of the earth through these particular people who he has redeemed.[16]

Through electing Israel, God aims to accomplish his purposes for the other nations as well. Snyder concludes that "God's plan was that his people would represent him to the world. They would be the channel of his revelation and his salvation purposes. This was God's commission to Israel. Although Israel often was unfaithful and the commission was only partially fulfilled, God's purpose was clear."[17]

New Testament
Christ as the High Priest

The NT presents Christ as the ultimate High Priest, surpassing the Levitical priesthood. Our interest here is to see how Christ's disciples are depicted as a priesthood. Leithart suggests baptism as the channel of this attribution:

> As first-century Jewish converts, once divided into priests and laymen (cf. Acts 6:7), were baptized, a homogeneously priestly people emerged. Baptism formed a new Israel out of the old, molding her into the eschatological race of the Last Adam, the kingdom of priests. It is the efficacious sign of the clothing change of heaven and earth, destroying antique Israelite order and remapping the terrain. It is the "washing of palingenesia."[18]

Leithart makes a critical case in closely linking OT motifs and rites to Christ's work, but this connection can also be made more straightforwardly, for what Leithart leaves open in his exercise in correspondences are the goals of the inclusion of Christians into Christ's priestly ministry. It is not the purpose of the present work to examine the priesthood of Christ in detail but to see its potential link to the "priesthood of all believers." As we shall soon notice,

---

16. Wright, *Mission of God*, 224–25.
17. Howard A. Snyder, *Liberating the Church: The Ecology of Church and Kingdom* (Downers Grove: InterVarsity Press, 1983), 171.
18. Peter Leithart, *The Priesthood of the Plebs: A Theology of Baptism* (Eugene: Wipf and Stock, 2003), 197.

priestly dimensions to the life and ministry of Christians will be only *derivative* and ensue from their being *in Christ*.

1 Peter: An Essential Text for a Controversial Doctrine

When the notion of a "priesthood of all believers" is discussed, the standard go-to passage is in 1 Peter. Scholars debate whether the doctrine can appropriately be based on this passage. In what follows, I argue that the priesthood described in 1 Peter 2 is an attribute of the whole multi-ethnic church, Jew and Gentile. This is a *communal* reality but also shows itself in the actions of individual Christians in the world. This priestly activity is centred on witness – *mediation* – and involves Christians instructing one another and building one another up.

The text offers several ways the letter's addressees will live out the holy living to which they have been called.

> Come to him, a living stone, though rejected by mortals yet chosen and precious in God's sight, and like living stones, let yourselves be built into a spiritual house, to be a holy priesthood, to offer spiritual sacrifices acceptable to God through Jesus Christ. For it stands in scripture:
>
> "See, I am laying in Zion a stone,
>   a cornerstone chosen and precious;
> and whoever believes in him will not be put to shame."
>
> To you then who believe, he is precious; but for those who do not believe,
>
> "The stone that the builders rejected
>   has become the very head of the corner,"
>
> and
>
> "A stone that makes them stumble,
>   and a rock that makes them fall."
>
> They stumble because they disobey the word, as they were destined to do.
>
>   But you are a chosen race, a royal priesthood, a holy nation, God's own people, in order that you may proclaim the mighty acts of him who called you out of darkness into his marvellous light. (1 Pet 2:4–9, RSV)

This text "is notable as representing one of the largest collections of OT images in the NT,"[19] with numerous allusions to Exodus 19. In 1 Peter the audience are addressed as an "elect" people, very similarly to how the people of Israel were constituted a "treasured possession" in the Sinai Desert, having been called "out of darkness."[20] In the same way that Israel's election rested on God's goodwill alone, "the status of Christians depends upon the status of Christ, for they are joined to him."[21]

However, a very significant difference between the calling to life of the first and the second "holy priesthoods" is the inclusion of Gentiles into the latter. In the same way that God elected Israel to be a blessing for the nations, so the new multi-ethnic Christian community is elected in Christ for a particular goal.

Collective or Individual Priesthood?

Does this widening of the priestly calling to a larger group entail a "priesthood of all believers"? Snyder answers positively and insists that

> in the Old Testament, *some* of God's people were priests: now *all* are priests, fulfilling the original design. In the Old Testament, *some* people were special servants of God: now *all* believers are servants of Christ. In the Old Testament, *some* people were occasionally gifted by the Spirit for special tasks: now *all* God's people receive gifts of the Spirit.[22]

Other commentators question whether the functions of the OT priests can be transferred to *individual* Christians. Greggs, for instance, notes a tendency to individualize the doctrine at the expense of its communal aspects. In relatively strong words, he assesses that

> the priesthood of all believers has an easy habit of becoming a discussion of the priesthood of each believer, individually and independently, in which each of us is considered our own priest. In that way, the doctrine falls victim to the very thing it seeks to avoid: individuals appropriate the very thing which in the

---

19. Paul J. Achtemeier, *1 Peter: A Commentary on First Peter*, Hermeneia (Minneapolis: Fortress, 1996), 150.

20. 1 Pet 2:9.

21. Edmund P. Clowney, *The Message of 1 Peter*, The Bible Speaks Today (Leicester: Inter-Varsity Press, 1988), 83.

22. Snyder, *Liberating the Church*, 179.

work of Christ ends, and which is only continued as the believer participates in the body of Christ, in the whole life of the church.[23]

Greggs also affirms that "the idea of priesthood is never applied to an individual in the NT (beyond those who are temple priests) except Jesus Christ."[24] Similarly, Achtemeier[25] insists that

> the point of this verse [1 Pet 2:5] is not the priestly status of each individual Christian, nor the idea that each is to function as a priest for his or her fellow Christian. The priesthood in this context can be understood only as corporate with a function that, as the parallel with 2:9b suggests, includes a witness to all humanity.[26]

However, even if we accept that 1 Peter is not referring to individuals, the question remains: how could Christians exercise priestly prerogatives *as a community only* and not as individuals? The rest of the epistle underlines in several ways the importance for Christians to conduct themselves "honourably among the Gentiles, so that . . . they may see your honourable deeds and glorify God when he comes to judge."[27] Clowney hence argues that "Peter is concerned about the holiness of God's temple not only when Christians are assembled for worship, but in their daily lives as well."[28] The most obvious of these priestly activities seems to be the *mediation* of God towards others. Even Green, who finds in these verses no "basis for the Reformation doctrine of 'the priesthood of all believers,'"[29] because of the communal character of the priestly house, nevertheless somewhat confusedly asserts that "emphasis falls therefore not on the priestly role of believers within the community of believers, but on the priestly identity and role of the community of believers in the world-at-large."[30] After all, what are Christians doing when they "proclaim the mighty acts of him who called [them] out of darkness into his marvellous

---

23. Greggs, "Priesthood of No Believer," 377.

24. Greggs, 381.

25. Achtemeier interacts with a variety of scholars, yet always insisting that "such priestly functions as the Christian had . . . were as a member of the Christian community, not as a separate individual, as though each were somehow a priest." Achtemeier, *1 Peter*, 165.

26. Achtemeier, 156.

27. 1 Pet 2:12.

28. Clowney, *1 Peter*, 88.

29. Joel B. Green, *1 Peter*, The Two Horizons New Testament Commentary (Grand Rapids: Eerdmans, 2007), 61.

30. Green, 61.

light"[31] if not *mediating* God's works and person to the people they are engaging with?[32] This engagement presupposes that *any Christian* can discern how his or her faith can be articulated in context. This *sensus fidei* is grounded not only in pneumatology[33] but also ecclesiology: "The church lives through the participation of its members, the laity and the ordained, and is constituted through them by the Holy Spirit. This is the ecumenical consensus. What is disputed is how this occurs."[34] A significant cause of dispute is the link between communality and individuality in the expression of the priesthood. Hiebert warns in pointed words that

> *the priesthood of believers is not a license for theological lone-rangerism.* We need each other to see our sins, for we more readily see the sins of others than our own. Similarly, we see the ways others misinterpret Scriptures before we see our own misinterpretations. Along the same line, we need Christians from other cultures, for they often see how our cultural biases have distorted our interpretations of the Scriptures.[35]

Hiebert's thinking looks like a thoughtful contextualization of Luther's thinking. "Mutual correction" is an essential part of IFES groups' freedom in studying the Bible without clerical oversight; it is furthermore an essential element of the life of the fellowship as movements correct each other in their hermeneutical practices as well. Greggs also contends at great length that one of the essential dimensions of church life is to move individual Christians from focusing on themselves to caring for others in the community:

> The form which the church takes as it is created as an event of the act of the Holy Spirit of God is the form of Christ. As the Spirit frees the individual to live simultaneously for God and for the other (freeing her from her *cor incurvatum in se*), the individual is freed to participate in the body of Christ, and more

---

31. 1 Pet 2:9.

32. For the debated Qumranic influence on the notion of "community" in 1 Peter, see J. Ramsey Michaels, *1 Peter*, Word Biblical Commentary 49 (Waco: Word, 2004), 96.

33. See World Council of Churches, "Baptism, Eucharist and Ministry," Faith and Order Paper no. 111 (Geneva, 1982), 16, https://www.oikoumene.org/resources/documents/baptism-eucharist-and-ministry-faith-and-order-paper-no-111-the-lima-text.

34. Veli-Matti Kärkkäinen, "The Calling of the Whole People of God into Ministry: The Spirit, Church and Laity," *Studia Theologica* 54, no. 2 (2000): 150.

35. Paul G. Hiebert, "Critical Contextualization," *International Bulletin of Missionary Research* 11, no. 3 (1987): 110; emphasis added.

specifically in the particular form of Christ's priesthood in which orientation towards the Father (vertically) and towards the world (horizontally) exist simultaneously.[36]

Hence personal relationship to God, personal witness and communal missionary existence are closely intertwined and provide a series of internal checks and balances. If we suppose a student ministry organization to be essentially a branch or an arm of the church on campus, these doctrinal provisions apply and should not be any more concerning to church leaders than other activities of their congregants. Hence the student organization's calling is essentially the same as that of the church: to love God and neighbour and serve both. Engagement lies at the heart of the Christian calling, which follows what the people of Israel were meant to do as a "display-people":[37]

> The royal priesthood of believers exists to declare God's *aretas* (Greek: excellencies, virtues, mighty acts, praises). . . . As both worship and evangelism, the Lord's saved ones proclaim and celebrate the *aretas* of God, particularly his promised and fulfilled redemptive acts. Therefore, as those brought by new birth into a priestly community, believers are to walk in holiness and obedience while abounding in good deeds and announcing the Lord's mighty works. These are the sacrifices – the acceptable sacrifices – of the royal priesthood.[38]

This proclamation, understood as a logical consequence of Christ's election and salvific work for believers, consists obviously in witness and worship as a constituent of the "spiritual sacrifices" which Christians are called to offer. Here seems to lie an expansion of Israel's original calling as God's people. As Green tells us, "in Peter . . . 'praise' is expanded to include not only vertical language (worship) but also horizontal (proclamation) and has been given a particular content."[39] There is thus a whole range of applications for understanding the implications of the "priesthood of all believers." Holy living – the consequence

---

36. Greggs, *Priestly Catholicity*, 48.
37. Durham, *Exodus*, 263.
38. Anizor and Voss, *Representing Christ*, 48.
39. Green, *1 Peter*, 62. I have not found scholarly commentaries on the contrast between proclaiming God's *aretas* and the importance of the reputation of God in the Old Testament, a reputation which was not held highly by the people, as Malone notes, taking "Ezekiel 36:20–23 [where the prophet] lambasts the Israelites for the influence their behaviour has had on Yahweh's reputation. Four times in four verses he is concerned that 'my holy name' has been 'profaned among the nations.' We must recognize that this is the cultic language of the tabernacle and its priests; 'to make/pronounce profane' (*ḥll*) is the opposite of 'to make/pronounce holy' (*qdš*)."

of election; worship – bringing sacrifices; and witness – declaring the praises of God: these are the most evident, arguably all in a missional light, if we agree that "all four titles originally given to Israel ('chosen race,' 'royal priesthood,' 'holy nation,' 'his own possession') are now applied to the multi-ethnic church, bringing to mind the gracious initiative of Yahweh to call and rescue his people."[40]

Ministry to the Gentiles

Paul also links his ministry of proclamation and teaching to a priestly activity, notably saying that he has written boldly to the Romans "because of the grace given me by God to be a minister of Christ Jesus to the Gentiles in the priestly service of the gospel of God, so that the offering of the Gentiles may be acceptable, sanctified by the Holy Spirit."[41] Paul hence extends priestly activity from the sole context of the people of God to witnessing to Gentiles. For Dunn,

> there can be no question, therefore, that Paul here described his ministry in priestly terms. That, however, should not be taken to indicate that he thought of himself as a priest in a special way distinct from the ministries of other believers. . . . The whole imagery of priesthood has clearly been transposed entirely out of the cult and applied in its transformed sense to Paul's ministry of preaching the gospel to Gentiles.[42]

Paul seems to imply here a priestly mediation between himself, the Gentiles and God. Notably, Paul ventures into this ministry "because of the grace given me by God," which is possibly an allusion to the election language observed in Exodus 19, underscoring the 1 Peter passage.[43] The "acceptable" sacrifice[44] of which he writes here also strongly resonates with the "spiritual sacrifices acceptable to God through Jesus Christ"[45] that Christians are to bring to God

---

Andrew S. Malone, *God's Mediators: A Biblical Theology of Priesthood*, NSBT 43 (Downers Grove: InterVarsity Press, 2017), 139; for more references see Malone, *God's Mediators*, 137–40.

40. Anizor and Voss, *Representing Christ*, 48.

41. Rom 15:15–16.

42. James D. G. Dunn, *The Parting of the Ways: Between Christianity and Judaism and Their Significance for the Character of Christianity*, 1st ed. 1991 (2nd ed.; London: SCM, 2006), 107.

43. Conversely, Malone rejects an individualistic interpretation, alleging that Paul "would hardly identify himself with an exclusive (and potentially defunct) priestly caste." Malone, *God's Mediators*, 174.

44. Rom 15:16.

45. 1 Pet 2:5.

individually as well as *corporately*. As to the nature of the relationship between the Gentiles and the sacrifice, Wright is not sure whether Paul is thinking

> of "the offering made by the nations," the eschatological tribute of the nations in the form of the worship and praise that these Gentile believers now give to the living God instead of to their previous idols? Or does he mean "the offering *that consists of* the nations," seeing the nations themselves as the offering, that Paul is making to God as the fruit of his evangelistic/priestly ministry? Whichever is the exact meaning, it is clear that Paul sees the whole Gentile mission as the fulfillment of Old Testament prophecies regarding the ingathering of the nations and the worship that will ascend to the God of Israel from the nations in the process.[46]

One final observation is relevant to a "priesthood of all believers": the idea that Paul's message is addressed not solely to the leaders of the Roman congregations, but to all *participating* in these churches, for as the apostle puts it, the Romans "are full of goodness, filled with all knowledge, and *able to instruct one another*."[47] Paul puts a high value on the ability of the congregants to build each other up and exhort each other to ministry, not limiting this task to ordination, training or gender, for instance. Dunn interprets this as implying that

> *all ministry and service on behalf of the gospel can be considered as priestly ministry*, the new covenant equivalent of the ministries of grace (charisms) reserved in the old covenant for those specially anointed. By applying such cultic language to such non-cultic ministry on behalf of the gospel, Paul confirms that the cultic barrier between sacred and secular has been broken down and left behind.[48]

Patristic Era

Early Christians did not often come from the priestly class of Israel and, in fact, it took some time for the very concept of "layperson" to be developed

---

46. Wright, *Mission of God*, 526.
47. Rom 15:14; emphasis added.
48. Dunn, *Parting of the Ways*, 107; emphasis original.

in Christian literature.[49] Clement of Rome, arguing how the Jews organise themselves, underlines that "the priest is given his particular duties: the priests are assigned their special place, while on the Levites particular tasks are imposed. The *layman* is bound by the *layman*'s code."[50] This first mention of laypeople in the church is linked with a new interpretation of the very structure of the church. Clement first interpreted the ministry of church leaders "along the Jewish-sacerdotal lines of the OT (the priesthood of Aaron) (1 Clem. 43–44), even introducing for the first time the distinction between clergy and laity."[51]

Whereas he agrees with Clement being the first to introduce the formal distinction between clergy and laity, Lightfoot does not find a sacerdotal stance in Clement's writings.[52] He suggests that until Cyprian, "a Sacerdotal view of the Christian ministry [had] not been held apart from a distinct recognition of the sacerdotal functions of the whole Christian body."[53] Before Cyprian, neither Clement, Tertullian nor even Origen developed a special sacerdotalism of their own. They rather insisted on the priest acting *as a representative* of the general priesthood, not in a personal capacity, thereby underlining that the priesthood of the clergy differs "from the priesthood of the laity only in degree, in so far as the former devote their time and their thoughts more entirely to God than the latter."[54]

If Cyprian "represents the beginning of the decline of the emphasis on all believers as a royal priesthood and the concurrent rise of the ministerial priesthood's prominence,"[55] he was soon to be followed by other church fathers, in no unqualified manner, however:

> Vain shall we be if we think that what is not lawful for priests is lawful for laics. Are not even we laics priests? It is written: A kingdom also, and priests to His God and Father, has He made us. It is the authority of the Church, and the honour which has

---

49. George Huntston, "The Ancient Church, AD 30–313," in *The Layman in Christian History*, by Stephen Neill and Hans Ruedi Weber (London: SCM, 1963), 28–56.

50. 1 Clement 40.5, in Cyril Charles Richardson, ed., *Early Christian Fathers* (Philadelphia: Westminster, 1953), 62; emphasis added.

51. Vittorino Grossi, "Priesthood of Believers," in *Encyclopedia of Ancient Christianity*, ed. Angelo Di Berardino (Downers Grove: InterVarsity Press, 2014), 3:304.

52. Joseph Barber Lightfoot, *Saint Paul's Epistle to the Philippians; A Revised Text* (London: Macmillan, 1888), 254.

53. Lightfoot, *Epistle to the Philippians*, 257.

54. Lightfoot, 258.

55. Anizor and Voss, *Representing Christ*, 62.

acquired sanctity through the joint session of the Order, which has established the difference between the Order and the laity.... Therefore, if you have the *right* of a priest in your own person, in cases of necessity, it behooves you to have likewise the *discipline* of a priest whenever it may be necessary to have the right of a priest.[56]

What stands out from Tertullian's expositions is that the attribution of priestly prerogatives to laypeople should remain exceptional and should not be understood as constitutive of their Christian estate. Yet, even if many early church writers were reluctant to let the laity exercise priestly roles, examples show that laypeople did actually take up the challenge[57] – first in worship, as can be seen from biblical examples[58] as well as from early Christian manuals and the aforementioned letter of Clement.[59] What is more, it is possible to track down a role for the laity in the constitutions and discipline of the churches: they elected their presbyters and deacons and could also revoke their election and speak absolution of sin to their fellow church members. Linked with this was also the possibility for laypeople to teach for mutual edification and to give reasons for their hope in a surrounding culture that was averse to their faith.[60] Lastly, early Christians in the diaspora are reported to have made a lasting impression on pagans with their attitude to their fellow citizens during plague epidemics, when they took care of many people and showed ethical conduct in line with their beliefs, an attitude displayed by both clergy and laity.[61]

These examples show the importance of the shift completed from the OT understanding of the priesthood characterized by a high degree of stratification, towards an apprehension of the priestly dignity of *all* Christians. This shift occurred for theological as well as for missiological reasons:

The application of the concept of sacerdotal dignity to all Christians, in the light of Christ (the anointed one), was also an

---

56. Tertullian, *On Exhortation to Chastity* 7 (ANF 4:54).

57. The following section draws heavily on Huntston, "Ancient Church," especially pp. 30–52.

58. "When you come together, *each one* has a hymn, a lesson, a revelation, a tongue, or an interpretation" (1 Cor 14:26); emphasis added.

59. Williams mentions the Greek *prospherontes* as the descriptor of laypeople in early churches. In Huntston, "Ancient Church," 33.

60. It is interesting that the famous "call to apologetics" is also found in 1 Peter. See 1 Pet 3:15, which calls upon all addressees of the letter and not only church leaders.

61. Stark provides convincing evidence of such conduct: Rodney Stark, *The Rise of Christianity: A Sociologist Reconsiders History* (Princeton: Princeton University Press, 1996), especially pp. 73–94.

apologetic response to the pagan mediations with the divinity proposed at the beginning of the mystery religions (although only in Christ is such a mediation possible) and Greek philosophy, which considered God completely inaccessible (in Christ, however, every person is offered the opportunity to draw near to God). In the context of the priesthood, understood as the possibility of relating to God through the mediation of Jesus Christ, Christian antiquity knew a diversity of ministries that, on the concrete level, reflected the hierarchical structure of the church, esp. the triadic structure of deacon-presbyter-bishop.[62]

Partial Synthesis

The Bible presents us with a generous, creator God electing people to be a blessing for others: first, individuals such as Abraham, but then the whole people of Israel. The institution of the priesthood is a tool to structure how the elect people relate to God, and this clergy exists to *mediate* between God and his people, to instruct and teach Israel, and to sacrifice on their behalf. Yet the whole people of Israel are also called "a priestly nation" and are supposed to channel God's blessing to their surroundings. The logic continues with the institution of a new covenant in Jesus Christ who inhabits all the priestly functions outlined in the OT and calls out a people, the church, who participate in his continuing work. *Participation* in this new people implies *mediating* God's blessing to the world, as individuals and communities. The New Testament, and especially 1 Peter, witnesses a widening of the priestly prerogatives to the *whole* people of God.

---

62. Grossi, "Priesthood of Believers," 3:304.

14

Dogmatic Reflections: Laypeople in the Church

Having surveyed biblical-theological materials, I now turn to selected theological sources that will build a theology of the laity necessary to understand student ministry. I have deliberately chosen to look outside traditional evangelical sources to show that what I argue in the last part of this work does not rely exclusively on evangelical thinking but on a growing ecumenical consensus in the twentieth century.

Roman Catholic Teachings

Vatican II had a significant effect on the theological developments of the twentieth century and was contemporary to the early years of IFES, showing that the question of the role of laypeople in the church was a topic that transcended denominational boundaries. In subsequent years, further Catholic documents discussing mission increasingly went in the direction of a *missional ecclesiology*. I now turn to a brief survey of some of these texts.

All Are Called

Vatican II insists that all members of the church "are impelled to carry on . . . missionary activity because of the love with which they love God and by which they desire to share with all men the spiritual goods of both its life and the life to come."[1] The insistence is on personal calling and collaboration with

---

1. Pope Paul VI, "*Ad Gentes*," Decree on the Mission Activity of the Church (Rome, Vatican II, 1965), sec. 7.

ecclesial hierarchy. John Paul II similarly adds that "because of the one dignity flowing from Baptism, each member of the lay faithful, together with ordained ministers and men and women religious, shares a responsibility for the Church's mission."[2] The "lay faithful" are defined to "mean all the faithful except those in Holy Orders and those who belong to a religious state sanctioned by the Church."[3]

A tension runs through most encyclicals relevant to our study: the calling of all members of the church by virtue of their baptism is underlined, while at the same time their separation from ordained ministers is stressed. The work of laypeople is in no way dispensable, however: "Each member of the lay faithful should always be fully aware of being a 'member of the Church' yet entrusted with a unique task which cannot be done by another and which is to be fulfilled for the good of all."[4] The main difference between ordained ministers and laypeople is that

> the lay state of life has its distinctive feature in its secular character. It fulfils an ecclesial service in bearing witness and in its own way recalling for priests, women and men religious, the significance of the earthly and temporal realities in the salvific plan of God. In turn, the ministerial priesthood represents in different times and places, the permanent guarantee of the sacramental presence of Christ, the Redeemer.[5]

There is an urgency to minister in society because "if lack of commitment is always unacceptable, the present time renders it even more so. It is not permissible for anyone to remain idle";[6] but this urgency cannot dispense with the importance of the sacraments for the Catholic Church. This sacramental aspect of the ministry is hard to find in any Protestant discussion of "parachurch" organizations.

The Nature of the Church

Closely related to the above is the discussion on the church's nature, especially its missionary purpose. This purpose goes hand in hand with the status of

---

2. Pope John Paul II, "*Christifideles Laici*," Post-Synodal Exhortation on the Vocation and the Mission of the Lay Faithful in the Church and in the World (Rome, 1988), sec. 15.
3. Pope John Paul II, "*Christifideles Laici*," sec. 9.
4. Pope John Paul II, sec. 28.
5. Pope John Paul II, sec. 55.
6. Pope John Paul II, sec. 3.

the church in the world. *Ad Gentes* hence affirms that "the pilgrim Church is missionary by her very nature, since it is from the mission of the Son and the mission of the Holy Spirit that she draws her origin, in accordance with the decree of God the Father."[7] In missiological terms, the *missio ecclesiae* derives from the *missio Dei* and is eminently Trinitarian. This carrying out of God's mission is *apostolic*. As *Apostolicam Actuositatem* states,

> The Church was founded for the purpose of spreading the kingdom of Christ throughout the earth for the glory of God the Father, to enable all men to share in His saving redemption, and that through them the whole world might enter into a relationship with Christ. All activity of the Mystical Body directed to the attainment of this goal is called the apostolate, which the Church carries on in various ways through all her members.[8]

This eminently *missional* understanding of the apostolate is made even more explicit when framed by the notion of sharing in Christ's office.

Sharing in Christ's Office

Tightly linked to the definition of the apostolate, we have the insistence on the fact that

> in the Church there is a diversity of ministry but a oneness of mission. Christ conferred on the Apostles and their successors the duty of teaching, sanctifying, and ruling in His name and power. But the laity likewise share in the priestly, prophetic, and royal office of Christ and therefore have their own share in the mission of the whole people of God in the Church and in the world. . . . They are consecrated for the royal priesthood and the holy people (cf. 1 Peter 2:4–10) not only that they may offer spiritual sacrifices in everything they do but also that they may witness to Christ throughout the world.[9]

This quote underlines the missionary aspect of the "priesthood of all believers" in the context of the Catholic Church. This is illuminating, because it runs against many of the polemics we read in Protestant and evangelical

---

7. Pope Paul VI, "*Ad Gentes*," sec. 2.

8. Pope Paul VI, "*Apostolicam Actuositatem*," Decree on the Apostolate of the Laity, Vatican II decree (Rome, 1965), sec. 2.

9. Pope Paul VI, "*Apostolicam Actuositatem*," secs. 2 & 3.

writings on questions of priesthood and witness. The main difference between the confessions might then be much more a question of ecclesiological government – the relationship of the laity to the hierarchy, to which we shall return – than of dogmatical theology or even of missiology.[10]

Christifideles Laici further insists that "the lay faithful participate, for their part, in the threefold mission of Christ as Priest, Prophet and King. This aspect has never been forgotten in the living tradition of the Church."[11] We might read this insistence on history as a slight polemical affirmation targeting non-Roman Catholic traditions. Yet this also shows a robust contextual awareness, which can also be seen in the diverse vocabulary used:

> In recent days the phenomenon of lay people associating among themselves has taken on a character of particular variety and vitality. In some ways lay *associations* have always been present throughout the Church's history as various *confraternities*, *third orders* and *sodalities* testify even today. However, in modern times such lay *groups* have received a special stimulus, resulting in the birth and spread of a multiplicity of group forms: associations, groups, communities, movements. We can speak of a new era of group endeavours of the lay faithful.[12]

The pope does not define any of these groupings[13] but underlines the *differentia specifica* of the Roman Church in the same section. He connects the priestly mission of Christ to the Eucharistic sacrifice, a move which other traditions would not necessarily accept: "The lay faithful are sharers in the priestly mission, for which Jesus offered himself on the cross and continues to be offered in the celebration of the Eucharist for the glory of God and the salvation of humanity."[14] What other confessions might agree with, however, is the missional dimension to this otherwise liturgical argument. There is broader common ground in the idea that Christians *participate* in Christ's mission. As *Ad Gentes* affirms, missionaries are

---

10. If this is pragmatically true, dogmatically speaking the RCC sacrament of Holy Orders, whereby a priest is inducted into acting *in persona Christi*, implies an ontological change which sets the RCC priesthood apart from that of any other confession: "the character imprinted by ordination is for ever. The vocation and mission received on the day of [a priest's] ordination mark him permanently." "Catechism of the Catholic Church," para. 1583, accessed 23 February 2023, https://www.vatican.va/archive/ENG0015/__P4Y.HTM.
11. Pope John Paul II, "*Christifideles Laici*," sec. 14.
12. Pope John Paul II, sec. 29; emphasis added.
13. See the short description in Pope Paul VI, "*Ad Gentes*," sec. 6.
14. Pope John Paul II, "*Christifideles Laici*," sec. 14.

God's coworkers ... who raise up congregations of the faithful such that, walking worthy of the vocation to which they have been called ..., they may exercise the priestly, prophetic, and royal office which God has entrusted to them. In this way, the Christian community will be a sign of God's presence in the world.[15]

So, on the one hand, the Catholic Church encourages laypeople to engage in society but, on the other hand, it wants to make sure nothing goes against the hierarchy.[16] Several indirect exhortations to compliance are needed, leading the historian to suppose underlying issues concerning precisely these points. *Apostolicam Actuositatem* insists that the laity should do this "in communion with their brothers in Christ, especially with their pastors who must make a judgment about the true nature and proper use of these gifts not to extinguish the Spirit but to test all things and hold for what is good (cf. 1 Thess. 5:12,19,21)."[17] Oversight is deemed necessary to ensure the proper orientation of lay activism.[18]

More closely linked to the concern of this research is the Magisterium's insistence on the necessity to contextualize missionary work for the different social milieus of a given society. From a wealth of articulate materials, the following section presents only a sample.

Contextualizing for the Spheres of Society

Vatican II begins by noticing that the "apostolate becomes more imperative in view of the fact that many areas of human life have become increasingly autonomous."[19] From there unfolds the need for an "apostolate in the social milieu, that is, the effort to infuse a Christian spirit into the mentality, customs,

---

15. Pope Paul VI, "*Ad Gentes*," sec. 15.
16. Pope Paul VI, "*Apostolicam Actuositatem*," sec. 19; "*Ad Gentes*," sec. 23.
17. Pope Paul VI, "*Apostolicam Actuositatem*," sec. 3.
18. *Christifideles Laici* offers an insightful list of criteria to assess lay organizations: "*Primacy given to the call of every Christian to holiness*, as it is manifested 'in the fruits of grace which the spirit produces in the faithful.' ... *The responsibility of professing the Catholic faith*, embracing and proclaiming the truth about Christ, the Church and humanity, in obedience to the Church's Magisterium, as the Church interprets it.... *The witness to a strong and authentic communion* in filial relationship to the Pope, in total adherence to the belief that he is the perpetual and visible center of unity of the universal Church, and with the local Bishop ... in the particular Church.... *Conformity to and participation in the Church's apostolic goals*, that is, 'the evangelization and sanctification of humanity and the Christian formation of people's conscience.'... *A commitment to a presence in human society*, which in light of the Church's social doctrine places it at the service of the total dignity of the person." Pope John Paul II, "*Christifideles Laici*," sec. 30.
19. Pope Paul VI, "*Apostolicam Actuositatem*," sec. 1.

laws, and structures of the community in which one lives, which is so much the duty and responsibility of the laity that it can never be performed properly by others."[20] This concern for the limitations of ordained ministers to reach out to people can be read in all the documents studied here and, interestingly, provision is made for specific groups to meet as an incarnation of the church in a given place:

> The laity who engage in the apostolate only as individuals, whether for the reasons already mentioned or for special reasons including those also deriving from their own professional activity, usefully gather into smaller groups for serious conversation without any more formal kind of establishment or organization, so that an indication of the community of the Church is always apparent to others as a true witness of love.[21]

In this context, young people "must not simply be considered as an object of pastoral concern for the Church: in fact, young people are and ought to be encouraged to be active on behalf of the Church as leading characters in evangelization and participants in the renewal of society."[22] This is not only a question of recruiting fresh blood for church mission, but a sign of in-depth missiological thinking. John Paul II also insightfully notes that "in the life of each member of the lay faithful, there are particularly significant and decisive moments for discerning God's call and embracing the mission entrusted by Him. Among these are the periods of adolescence and young adulthood."[23] Sociological analysis drives the harnessing of young people for mission:

> Their [young persons'] heightened influence in society demands of them a proportionate apostolic activity, but their natural qualities also fit them for this activity. As they become more conscious of their own personalities, they are impelled by a zest for life and a ready eagerness to assume their own responsibility, and they yearn to play their part in social and cultural life. If this zeal is imbued

---

20. Pope Paul VI, sec. 13.

21. Pope Paul VI, sec. 17. Later, John Paul II was also to note that "groups, associations and movements also have their place in the formation of the lay faithful. In fact they have the possibility, each with its own method, of offering a formation through a deeply shared experience in the apostolic life, as well as having the opportunity to integrate, to make concrete and specific the formation that their members receive from other persons and communities." Pope John Paul II, "*Christifideles Laici*," sec. 62.

22. Pope John Paul II, "*Christifideles Laici*," sec. 46.

23. Pope John Paul II, sec. 58.

with the spirit of Christ and is inspired by obedience and love for the Church, it can be expected to be very fruitful.[24]

From this ensues a call to engage all spheres of society, and more specifically culture, for "the lay faithful are never to relinquish their participation in 'public life,' that is, in the many different economic, social, legislative, administrative and cultural areas, which are intended to promote organically and institutionally the common good."[25] The line of argument can thus be summarized as follows: the church has been called into existence by God and its purpose is to witness to God in every sphere of society. Because the calling is extended to all church members by virtue of their baptism, all laypeople are called to engage their respective societal spheres. Strategic thinking necessitates considering young people in particular, because of their future influence. Incidentally, *Ad Gentes* also notes that there are laypeople "worthy of special praise . . . who in universities or in scientific institutes, promote by their historical and scientific religious research the knowledge of peoples and of religions; thus helping the heralds of the Gospel, and preparing for the dialogue with non-Christians."[26]

Lastly, *Ad Gentes* calls for missiological reflection on culture. Even if this call to value culture is addressed primarily to aspiring priests, it is nevertheless remarkable:

> Let the minds of the students be kept open and attuned to an acquaintance and an appreciation of their own nation's culture; . . . let them consider the points of contact which mediate between the traditions and religion of their homeland on the one hand and the Christian religion on the other.[27]

Christians as a Royal Priesthood: Hans Küng and Others

> Nowhere in the New Testament does it say that the primary responsibility for accomplishing the purpose of God in the world rests in the hands of the "official ministry." The primary responsibility is always upon the shoulders of those "called to be

---

24. Pope Paul VI, "*Apostolicam Actuositatem*," sec. 12.
25. Pope John Paul II, "*Christifideles Laici*," sec. 42.
26. Pope Paul VI, "*Ad Gentes*," sec. 41.
27. Pope Paul VI, sec. 16.

saints," the *laos theou*, "the people of God." Thus, in religion it is the layman who must do most of the work in the world.[28]

I have briefly surveyed some major official Catholic teachings that shed light on a "priestly and missionary" understanding of student ministry. In what follows, I turn to the work of a few other theological voices, notably Hans Küng, who have pushed further towards a "theology of the laity," in order to articulate a priestly understanding of the whole people of God. This articulation has some preliminary consequences for practical theology, missiology and missionary practice. Such consequences have not automatically been drawn, as Snyder argued in 1983:

> Protestants have always held, at least theoretically, to the doctrine of the priesthood of believers. For the most part, however, this doctrine has been understood soteriologically rather than ecclesiologically. That is, it has been understood to mean that all Christians have direct access to God without the mediation of a human priest. But the implications of this doctrine for Christian ministry have seldom been drawn out. Perhaps the reason is that these implications radically call into question the clergy-laity split by asserting that all believers are priests and therefore ministers.[29]

Christ as Only High Priest and Mediator

> All human priesthood has been fulfilled and finished by the unique, final, unrepeatable and hence unlimited sacrifice of the one continuing and eternal high priest.[30]

Küng complains about the fact that, too often, ecclesiologies have tended to overemphasize offices and therefore to assume the implicit equation *ecclesia = hierarchia*. Hence "they failed to realize that all who hold office are primarily (both temporarily and factually speaking) not dignitaries but believers, members of the fellowship of believers."[31] To Küng, an individual is first either a Christian or not, and the ontological status of priests is determined by their standing as Christians and not as members of the clergy. Thus, the church is

---

28. Findley B. Edge, "Priesthood of Believers," *Review & Expositor* 60, no. 1 (1963): 16.
29. Snyder, *Liberating the Church*, 169.
30. Hans Küng, *The Church* (New York: Sheed & Ward, 1967), 363.
31. Küng, *Church*, 363.

founded not upon the offices, but upon Christ himself. Küng then offers a rapid synthesis of the main biblical teachings about the priesthood,[32] concluding that "there is only one single mediator, and that is Jesus Christ."[33] If Christ is the sole mediator and if his work is not to be imitated or replicated, it follows that this applies to all Christians: "Since Christ is the unique high priest and mediator between God and all men, all men who believe in him have immediate access to God through him."[34]

What are Christians to do with this privileged access? Küng ascribes to the general priesthood the function of *mediation*. For Küng, the implications of the "priesthood of all believers" are never only private, but always to be understood as a service from and to God.[35] Christ is the sole mediator between people and God, but through the Christian's communion with Christ,

> all believers are absorbed into the mediating work of the one and only mediator. Their function is to mediate between God and the world, by revealing the hidden works of God and making effective his acts of power. Hence every Christian is a priest of God, by being a witness to God before the world.[36]

This statement has powerful implications for mission because it anchors the Christian's work in the world in the divine commissioning, and even if Küng acknowledges that the New Testament does not use mediatory language, Christians are messengers of God's eschatological act of salvation.[37] To speak of Christians as being drawn into Christ's mediatory function, however, also prevents them from identifying only with Christ and feeling totally estranged from their fellow human beings. If priesthood means service, one has to be concerned for the well-being of all humans. This also unfolds in another eminently priestly activity – prayer; for "every Christian is a priest for the world, by having free access to God in faith and by being able to appear before God on behalf of others and intercede for them."[38]

Summarizing his whole development on the general priesthood, Küng states that it consists "in the calling of the faithful to witness to God and his

---

32. Küng, 431–32.
33. Küng, 368.
34. Küng, 369.
35. Küng, 381.
36. Küng, 381.
37. Küng, 369.
38. Küng, 381. Küng refers notably to Phil 2:15; 1 Thess 5:5; 1 Tim 2:1.

will before the world, and to offer up their lives in the service of the world."[39] This reads very similarly to Luther arguing in his well-known treatise that "a man does not live for himself alone in this mortal body to work for it alone, but he lives also for all men on earth; rather, he lives only for others and not for himself."[40]

This, so Küng argues, is how God creates fellowship among Christians, as they witness from his works and are encouraged by the knowledge that they can count on each other's support in all matters, including the fight against sin and the bearing of each other's suffering.[41] To put it in even shorter terms: "Each one knows that he appears before God on behalf of others, and knows that others appear before God on his behalf."[42] Such an attitude requires doctrinal conviction to bear fruit in the daily lives of individuals. There is a *missional*, outward move from the church into the world, "from being worship within the community to being worship within the everyday secular world."[43]

Participation in Christ's Work

However, the priesthood of all believers cannot be understood as a sort of "endowment" that is given upon baptism and remains the believer's own possession to use individually. Much to the contrary: the priestly vocation of the Christian is exercised as the consequence of his or her *participation in Christ's work*, and never independently of it. This aspect seems not to be "ecumenically controversial,"[44] because of the broad agreement on this consequence of salvation for Christians across confessional lines. This means, in Root's words, that "the Christian is priest and king only as fellow-priest and fellow-king with Christ. In the context of the emphasis on the union of Christ and the Christian . . . this 'fellow' status is an expression of the Christian's participation in Christ."[45]

---

39. Küng, 381.

40. Martin Luther, from "On the Freedom of a Christian" (1520), in *Selections from His Writings*, ed. John Dillenberger (Garden City: Doubleday, 1961), 73.

41. Küng, *Church*, 381, building on Gal 6:2.

42. Küng, 381.

43. Küng, 381.

44. Michael Root, "Freedom, Authority, and the Priesthood of All Believers," in *Critical Issues in Ecclesiology: Essays in Honor of Carl E. Braaten*, eds. Alberto L. García and Susan K. Wood (Grand Rapids: Eerdmans, 2011), 93.

45. Root, "Priesthood of All Believers," 94.

As we shall see later, there are numerous missiological consequences to the affirmation that "this participation in Christ is not just participation in the results of his work. Rather, the Christian is taken into Christ's work."[46] This participation in the body of Christ is not solely individual but intensely communal, as Congar also argues: "To the extent that the life that is in Christ is communicated to us, we become the very body of Christ. We become the members and, all together, the body of Christ the king, priest and prophet."[47]

Partial Synthesis

The theological writings explored above are admittedly only a sample of the material that exists on the topic of the place and role of laypeople in the church. Yet despite differences in background, a remarkable consensus emerges from these different voices.

God chooses *all believers*. An important dimension of this dignifying calling is that believers are to *witness* to their environment and call others to have a relationship with God – that is, like the OT priests, to *mediate* God to others. This is the basis of the doctrine of the "priesthood of all believers." Church traditions tend either to stress the individual aspect of this calling or insist that it is primarily exercised in the community. Yet this relationship of *individuals* with God is made possible because of Christ's *mediation* and is notably expressed through *participating* in the church. The texts surveyed here are fundamentally in agreement that the church exists to further God's mission. Consequently, the church's personnel – the clergy – are supposed to facilitate that mission. Church traditions diverge with regard to the exact link between clergy and laypeople, mostly on the question of authority structures and, implicitly, the exact "borders" of the church. Yet they agree on the fact that becoming a *member* of a church – either voluntarily by choice or by being born into it – means participating, albeit only derivatively, in Christ's own and unique *priestly* work. True to the logic of the incarnation, this work is always *contextualized*, as Christ reaches people wherever they are and so the church is called to reach them, notably through the witness of laypeople in all spheres of society which members of the clergy do not necessarily reach.

Based on these considerations, Christian students, as laypeople called by God, can legitimately engage in contextual witnessing activities. For this

---

46. Root, 93.
47. Yves Congar and François Varillon, *Sacerdoce et laïcat dans l'église* (Paris: Vitrail, 1947), 13.

purpose, they have often gathered in specific organizations outside the walls and hierarchical orders of traditional ecclesial structures. It is now to the ecclesiological status of "parachurch" organizations like IFES that I turn.

15

Missional Ecclesiology

The above explorations on the life of the church raise questions about how IFES as an organization relates to the church. How can an ecclesiology consonant with the notions of *immediacy*, *mediation* and *participation*, which I argue frame a robust understanding of student ministry, be developed? In this chapter, I explore the notion of "parachurch," which usually describes structures operating outside the hierarchical oversight of habitual church structures yet engaging in activities recognized as somehow falling within the orbit of the "church." In the chapters that follow I then question the missiological legitimacy of such a notion on several grounds: missionary experience (Roland Allen), missiology proper (*missio Dei*) and contemporary reflections on the ecclesial situation of Christian minorities (pilgrimage and priesthood in the post-Christian world) and on a renewed understanding of what constitutes "apostolicity." This whole questioning of the legitimacy of the parachurch turns out to be answered in a promising manner by a *missional* understanding of the church which undermines the separation of church and "parachurch." As this chapter explains, I think the word misleadingly reflects a certain structural ecclesiocentrism. Yet, because it is so widely recognized as an "umbrella" term, I will use it for the sake of simplicity.

The Nature of Parachurch Organizations

Part 3 of this work has surveyed how IFES leaders themselves have understood the ecclesiological status of their "parachurch" organization.[1] Yet such a relationship has often been contentious in missiological and ecclesial writings.

---

1. In what follows, "parachurch" refers to "a parachurch organization," for the sake of brevity.

So far in our explorations, we have assumed what a parachurch organization is more than we have defined it. In what follows, I survey a sample of analytical definitions of the parachurch phenomenon, highlighting the difficulty of defining it to articulate its specificities, and the tensions with church structures that often arise.

Defining "Parachurch"

> Everyone seems to have a vague sense of what is being talked about and might be able to throw out a name or two as illustrations. But are we talking about a single type of organization? If not, what exactly does this umbrella term contain?[2]

Surveying the literature on parachurch, which notably does not feature any widely recognized standard work, means encountering various definitions covering a spectrum from the most essentialist to the most functionalist. Parachurch organizations are defined primarily regarding their relationship to the church. Since Protestants do not have the structure of the Catholic Church, no account of the nature of parachurch has secured widespread agreement in Protestant circles.[3] Yet the development of Protestant and evangelical parachurch organizations did not occur in a vacuum, especially in the West. The Catholic Church developed an elaborate reflection on the topic because of the emergence of numerous lay organizations, generally known under the umbrella name "Catholic Action." These associations were founded mainly by laypeople seeking to work in specific areas of society, and at times they presented an ecclesiological challenge to the Magisterium.[4]

In his major work, Scheitle outlines numerous definitional issues with the notion of "parachurch":

> The prefix "para-" could be defined as something existing "beside" or "alongside" of a related entity. However, it could also be defined

---

2. Scheitle, *Beyond the Congregation*, 10.

3. Notably, the World Council of Churches' "Baptism, Eucharist and Ministry" document does not mention para-ecclesial groups in its discussion of ministry and ordination, for example.

4. For more on Catholic Action, see Gerd-Rainer Horn, "Catholic Action: A Twentieth-Century Social Movement (1920s–1930s)," in *Western European Liberation Theology*, ed. Gerd-Rainer Horn (Oxford: OUP, 2008), 5–43. An important part of Catholic Action was its student branch. See notably David Colon, "Face aux églises: un siècle d'organisations d'étudiants chrétiens," in *Cent ans de mouvements étudiants*, by Jean-Philippe Legois and Alain Monchalbon, ed. Groupe d'études et de recherches sur les mouvements étudiants (GERME) (Paris: Syllepse, 2007), 217–26.

as something "beyond" or "aside from" a related entity. The difference is subtle, but it represents the crux of the problem. Is the parachurch sector a partner working cooperatively alongside churches and denominations or is it a rogue agent working beyond the reach of them?[5]

Essentially, what is at stake is the legitimacy of already existing structures. As Stackhouse observes,

> this term *parachurch* is seen by some as implicitly derogatory, and with good reason. It suggests that the "true" Church is represented only in local congregations and whatever political structures link those local congregations together into denominations. Every other Christian organization is somehow just "alongside" this true Church: It is merely "parachurch."[6]

Even if "*merely* parachurch," the existence of the term implies that the activities of these organizations nevertheless fall somewhat within the domain of ecclesial activities – and I would argue that this "somewhat" is best understood within the framework of a *missional ecclesiology* which can be home to a large array of activities. This is how White adds precision to the definition of "parachurch":

> The local Church is broad, concerned with the total person, ministers in a geographical locale to a wide spectrum of ages and needs, and is narrow in doctrinal interpretation. The para-local church society is usually *narrow in purpose, specialized in tasks, narrow in the age of those involved, broad in doctrinal tolerations, crosses denominational lines* (except for denominational para-local church structures), and often is *geographically scattered*.[7]

This is one of the most articulate definitions which does not play church and parachurch against each other. Much to the contrary: for White, "a key question for local church and para-local church agencies is, are they performing a biblical function that builds up the body of Christ?"[8] Yet this seemingly easy way of assessing the parachurch is more intricate than it appears, for

---

5. Scheitle, *Beyond the Congregation*, 33.

6. John G. Stackhouse, *Evangelical Landscapes: Facing Critical Issues of the Day* (Grand Rapids: Baker Academic, 2002), 27.

7. White, *The Church and the Parachurch*, 84; emphasis added.

8. White, 81. Note that White uses "para-local" to underline the "alongside the church" aspect of parachurch organizations in order to avoid the sense of being "beyond."

two reasons. First, can methods fully be seen in separation from aims? And second, how far can parachurch achievements be assessed as to whether they "build up the body of Christ" if we consider not only the number of people committed to one or other structure, but also the tensions that often arise between local churches and the parachurch? As Willmer underlines, "what makes the parachurch such a lightning rod of controversy is that *its subordinate role is often questionable*."[9]

More missiologically positive, Niringiye observes that the purpose of a parachurch organization "fits into the overall mandate of the Church. Consequently, these organizations often state that they exist to serve the local Church. *They are Church-related in Mission, but not structurally or Church based.*"[10]

Niringiye hence suggests a relationship of *mission* and not of structure. In the same vein, Willmer et al., in one of the few in-depth treatments of parachurch organizations, affirm that the usefulness of the word lies precisely in the common purpose of churches and parachurch, despite structural differences: "The word *parachurch* has come into existence and has caught on so well precisely because it is a useful word to describe these Christian organizations that *work beyond the church yet often work for the same goal – the advancement of the Gospel.*"[11] The tone is eminently positive, valuing the contribution of parachurch structures, but what does "beyond" mean here? The debate runs the risk of being reduced to mere structural questions of leadership and power. Would a renewed insistence on "the priesthood of all believers" sign the death warrant to ordained ministry?[12] If one thinks of the church as defined in terms of that hierarchy, it creates a problem: how do these independent organizations relate to the church? If, however, the church itself is considered in terms of voluntary association – that is, if "church" names the gathering together of believers for worship and service – then the question becomes one of the relationship between different parts or forms of church, as parts of one body of which Christians are *members*. At the intersection of theology and sociology is *voluntary participation*.

---

9. Willmer, Schmidt and Smith, *Prospering Parachurch*, 13; emphasis added.

10. David Zac Niringiye, "Parachurch Organizations and Student Movements" (Christianity in Africa in the 1990s, Edinburgh University, May 1990), 4–5; emphasis added.

11. Willmer, Schmidt and Smith, *Prospering Parachurch*, 25; emphasis added.

12. Space does not permit an exploration of the whole theology of ordination. Since the great majority of IFES leaders have not been ordained, it has not been a major point of debate in the organization's history.

Church Members Taking on Mission

Many authors trace parachurch initiatives back to "the Spirit [who] chooses to work through some members of the body of Christ in a different way than through others. The charisms are not uniform but multiform, and therefore there is a diversity in ministry even though there is a oneness in mission."[13] The Lausanne Movement, recognizing this tension, notes that "the tendency of the 'establishment' to control individual initiatives runs the risk of *quenching the Spirit*. On the other hand, the tendency of voluntary organisations to insist on their independence runs the risk of *ignoring the Body*. It is the age-old tension between authority and freedom."[14]

Ecclesiologically speaking, the *voluntary principle* is closely related to a *believers' church* ecclesiology, following which "the church is first and foremost the gathered community of believers who, based on their personal confession of faith in baptism, have announced their voluntary entrance into the community."[15] Laypeople have the right to approach God *directly*. Since they are called to witness wherever they are, they can also organize themselves adequately. Correspondingly White, hinting at the core argument of the present research, affirms that

> under the new covenant, the believer has *direct access and individual responsibility* to God *without the intercession of an earthly priest*. This *priesthood* brings a new freedom for the believer both in worship and in service. It is the cornerstone of the ministry of every believer. Thus, the believer *as an individual and the believer in fellowship with other believers has personal responsibility to obey God's commands* about evangelism, discipleship, serving others, helping the poor and so on.[16]

There is then significant common ground between international volunteer networks and the church universal. On this logic, if participation in the local church is based on a legitimately personal, voluntary choice, then the

---

13. Donald G. Bloesch, *Life, Ministry, and Hope*, vol. 2 of *Essentials of Evangelical Theology* (San Francisco: Harper & Row, 1979), 108.

14. Lausanne Movement, "Cooperating in World Evangelization," ch. 1; emphasis original.

15. Fernando Enns, "Believers Church Ecclesiology: A Vital Alternative within the Ecumenical Family," in *New Perspectives in Believers Church Ecclesiology*, eds. Abe J. Dueck, Helmut Harder and Karl Koop (Winnipeg: CMU, 2010), 113. Exploring all the ins and outs of this ecclesiological tradition would explode the boundaries of this work. For a classical, detailed historical survey, see Donald F. Durnbaugh, *The Believers' Church: The History and Character of Radical Protestantism* (New York: Macmillan, 1968).

16. White, *The Church and the Parachurch*, 80; emphasis added.

parachurch makes no difference. IFES leaders have indeed presupposed that students have the right to gather and witness within and outside an ad hoc structure organized in a way closely related to Christians gathering in churches and chosen according to criteria other than the parish principle. Indeed, "if the church has its *radical basis* in *personal faith* in God, then it must be a voluntary association. As a *free, autonomous community* it cannot be controlled by the state, or by princes or kings or civil government."[17]

Hence Brackney sees parachurch organizations as "a particular group of voluntary associations of Christians whose purpose is directed at a stated task, relying heavily upon laypersons and *independent of any accountability to an institutional church structure*, but that may assume functions historically associated with the church."[18] Because some "parachurch" organizations structure themselves to a high degree, Brackney wants to call them "Quasi-Voluntary Associations" – under which he counts InterVarsity (USA).[19] Yet this category again takes the "hierarchical element" as decisive. As a group of humans gathered for a common purpose, IFES has also generated its own hierarchical structure, however decentralized its leaders say it is. Structures like IFES not only facilitate mission but also shape it by equipping people for mission and providing accountability structures. There is accountability within a parachurch structure, and to the extent to which its members are members of the scattered church, they are anchored in the reality of the church universal even if they do not always evidently defer to traditional ecclesial structures. The Lausanne Movement notes that "all are agreed that specialist functions require specialist organizations (e.g. for Bible translation, student evangelism and cross-cultural missions)."[20] The same logic applies to student organizations, which can recruit "specialists" for their tasks. Yet since students are also members of local churches, tensions surrounding their involvement in IFES groups – or similar associations – often amount to a question of loyalty between the church and the parachurch. This becomes even more complex when the issue of spiritual and emotional support is raised, which even makes some parachurch organizations a

---

17. Roger Haight, *Comparative Ecclesiology*, vol. 2 of *Christian Community in History* (London: Bloomsbury, 2014), 278–79; emphasis added.

18. William H. Brackney, *Christian Voluntarism: Theology and Praxis*, Faith's Horizons (Grand Rapids: Eerdmans, 1997), 136.

19. Brackney, *Christian Voluntarism*, 137.

20. Lausanne Movement, "Cooperating in World Evangelization," ch. 1.

major thorn in the side of churches. Their local component provides them the opportunity to form the same intimate social ties on which churches thrive. They begin to provide the same social and psychological benefits that make churches more appealing when it comes to activities like worship and fellowship.[21]

University ministries work with people transitioning from home, from one city to another, between different ages of faith. Parachurch support structures might simply have a broader appeal to them at a certain stage of life. Brackney suggests an interesting combination of interwoven factors, adding leadership to the picture we have drawn so far:

> Individual involvement in parachurch organizations has been so rewarding for some and so expansive for many of its leaders that it becomes a primary outlet for religious interests and participation. . . . It *is easy to see how the parachurch can become the definitive form of Christian identity for dedicated members.* Time sacrificially given, funds regularly contributed, opportunities for spiritual service, ceremonial recognition of leadership, public perceptions of high levels of "Christian commitment," and careful nurture of voluntary commitment with attendant theological rationale all define a new category called "para church Christianity."[22]

This way of settling an intricate tension does not satisfy Hammett, who adamantly wants the relationship between church and parachurch to be a "servant-partnership" model. For him,

> if ministry performed by a believer-priest is done in the context of a parachurch group that operates as an arm or extension of the church, then the authority conflict is sharply reduced, if not eliminated. The exercise of one's priesthood is placed in the proper context, as a part of the church's ministry.[23]

Whereas this line of argument is congruent with his overall case that parachurch organizations "possessing a status subordinate to that of the church . . . [should] defer to the church, honor the church . . . [and] accept

---

21. Scheitle, *Beyond the Congregation*, 55.
22. Brackney, *Christian Voluntarism*, 143–44; emphasis added.
23. John S. Hammett, "How Church and Parachurch Should Relate: Arguments for a Servant-Partnership Model," *Missiology* 28, no. 2 (1 Apr. 2000): 205.

[their] ministry under the authority of the church,"[24] this does not seem to solve anything, for, as we shall see shortly, one of the reasons for the emergence of the parachurch is precisely a failure – either real or perceived – of the church to exercise a given ministry. According to Hammett, current parachurch leaders would be better waiting for the local church leadership to greenlight, support and oversee their actions before they "go to work." The crucial question here is also what is understood by "church," for if a local church fails in its *missional* vocation, the loyalty of believers is ultimately higher and goes to the church universal. Stott concludes that "since Evangelicals desire in all things to be guided by the Bible, we should be able to grade specialist activities thus: independence of the church is bad, co-operation with the church is better, service as an arm of the church is best."[25]

It is obvious that local church leaders might deplore the fact that the student part of their constituency sees in the parachurch "the definitive form of Christian identity," because this raises vast ecclesiological debates and questions the way parachurch leaders have presented Christianity if their members do not feel the need to be part of a local church community. Notably, it is to the "priesthood of all believers" that White appeals to solve the leadership tension between church and parachurch:

> Finally, we note that participation in a para-local church society causes one to function in at least two authority structures. These will occasionally be in conflict. But to have conflicting authorities – work, family, government – is not unusual. In conflict, the believer-priest is individually responsible for deciding which authority takes precedence.[26]

Partial Synthesis

The above discussion has shown that many of the difficulties arising from the definition of "parachurch organization" exist because most descriptions focus on structural questions. From the prefix "para-," many commentators assume that the parachurch is subordinate to the church. The question of the legitimacy of parachurch structures over against ecclesial structures is often

---

24. Hammett, "Church and Parachurch," 200.

25. Lausanne Movement, "Cooperating in World Evangelization," ch. 1. Stott wrote this chapter, the "Theological Preamble."

26. White, *The Church and the Parachurch*, 85.

posed. Yet this is unsatisfactory, mainly because, as we have seen, many of these organizations have arisen out of missionary concerns which, at core, are ecclesial, for they reflect a missional understanding of the church's mission. Christians have assembled voluntarily to carry out the missionary task – and out of these voluntary structures, fully-fledged organizations have emerged. Consequently, what is required is a more constructive *ecclesiological* approach to the parachurch phenomenon, and it is to this that I now turn.

Towards an Ecclesiology of the "Parachurch"

Speaking of parachurch organizations as voluntary associations and exploring issues of leadership and loyalties is helpful, but it explains their existence more on sociological than on theological grounds. I now turn to two important ideas proposed to legitimate the emergence of these structures – the *deficiency approach* and the *innovative approach* – before suggesting a *rejoinder* to both approaches.

The Deficiency Approach

The first important hypothesis for the emergence of "parachurch" structures explains their existence by the supposed failure of the local church to fulfil its missionary vocation. The underlying assumption of this understanding is the *immediacy* of the relationship of individual Christians to God:

> *We know from Scripture* that it is God's will that people and nations everywhere should be reached with the gospel. So committed Christians across the centuries have felt free, *under the Spirit's guidance,* to use their God-given reason and creativity in organizing and using whatever structures are necessary to carry out God's purposes in fulfilment of the Great Commission.[27]

This argument draws a line between "Christians" and "committed Christians" who have seen a lack and engaged in filling the gaps by calling into existence new structures, as if the church was not sufficient to accommodate the "Great Commission outreach." Note the emphasis on "Scripture" and on guidance from the "Spirit," which are both potentially opposed to (failed) church

---

27. Warren W. Webster, "The Messenger and Mission Societies," in *Perspectives on the World Christian Movement: A Reader*, ed. Ralph D. Winter (Pasadena: William Carey Library, 1981), 764.

leadership. Hence, at the intersection of "voluntarism" and the identification of "deficiencies" in the church, we find the historically fertile ground of "Free Church." Bloesch notes that the thinking of Philipp Jacob Spener[28] was very influential in the development of later Free Church ecclesiology; the famous notion of *ecclesiola in ecclesia*[29] was congruent with Luther's ideas. In this view, "every Christian is given the privilege of teaching others, of chastising, exhorting, and converting. Every believer should be concerned about the personal salvation of his fellow human beings and should devote himself to prayer on their behalf."[30] This development took place against the backdrop of the perceived failure of the clergy of Spener's time to live up to the standards of piety Luther had envisaged. A later heir of Spener's views, who had a strong influence – even if indirectly – on early IFES leaders,[31] was Brethren-founder Darby. Thinking the clergy of his time corrupt, he saw himself as a reformer. Lay preaching would supplement the clerical failure to be faithful; "Christians should preach to those ready to perish and [so Darby] was critical of those who restricted their evangelism in order not to offend their superiors."[32] In the same way, Brackney argues that the parachurch meets a potentially new need: "One of the primary functions assumed by parachurch organizations is to provide for new outlets of mission work. In this regard, the parachurch takes to itself a function historically assumed by the church."[33]

Such a view has far-reaching ecclesiological consequences, notably for the responsibility of a local church towards its constituency – in short, *a theology of the laity*. White does more than allude to this aspect when he boldly affirms that

> it seems that one of the goals of world evangelization should be to get more people doing more ministry more of the time. The "more people" must involve the equipping and sending of the laity. Yes, sending, not just building them up. But systems for sending by a local church are largely restricted by a formal schooling

---

28. Exposed at length in his landmark pamphlet *Pia desideria oder herzliches Verlangen nach gottgefälliger Besserung der wahren evangelischen Kirche, nebst einigen dahin abzwekenden christlichen Vorshlägen* (original in 1675; Leipzig: Köhler, 1841).

29. D. Martyn Lloyd-Jones, "Ecclesiola in Ecclesia," in *Approaches to Reformation for the Church*, vol. 4, Puritan Papers (Hartshill: Tentmaker, 1965).

30. Bloesch, *Life, Ministry, and Hope*, 115.

31. Most notably, Douglas Johnson and Hans Bürki.

32. Neil Dickson, "'The Church Itself Is God's Clergy.' The Principles and Practices of the Brethren," in *The Rise of the Laity in Evangelical Protestantism*, ed. Deryck Lovegrove (London: Routledge Chapman & Hall, 2002), 218.

33. Brackney, *Christian Voluntarism*, 138.

requirement. Para-local church groups have consistently broken through this barrier by equipping and sending the "unlearned and uneducated" to minister full-time. We still need full-time people. But our current formal educational systems are only a part of the preparation. The New Testament pattern is more "learning by doing."[34]

As I will argue in the last part of this work, such "faithful improvisation" is what is called for in the constantly changing environment of the university, with its demands and challenges.

Circling back from theology to sociology, Scheitle assumes a "market" of religious goods available, in which "the rise, fall, and rise again of the parachurch sector represent a continuous narrative in the changing structure of the religious market."[35] In this view, a parachurch organization is simply filling a gap by offering potential clients religious *goods and services*[36] that local churches might not be able to provide. Hence the proliferation of organizations trying to tackle the same needs.

The idea that "parachurch" structures arise because of the deficiencies of ecclesial structures, only briefly exposed here, rests on the assumption that *mission* is fundamental to the church's purpose: this is essentially a *missional ecclesiology*. Framing the debate in such terms, however, explains some of the tensions which arise between church leaders and parachurch leaders: sociologically speaking, a "competitor" arises, questioning long-held theological fundamentals – for example, a certain *mediatory* role for the church – and ecclesial traditions – for example, the subordination of the laity to the clergy. The logic behind this *deficiency approach* is that, had the church taken its missionary vocation seriously enough, structures like IFES would not have emerged. Implicitly, then, parachurch organizations would represent a regrettable development wasting the church's precious human and financial resources. In this approach, church leaders can condescend to tolerate "parachurch" organizations for a time, but they would rather they dismantled themselves and "got back" to the clergy's authority. This summary, admittedly pointed, nevertheless highlights the most negative approach to the parachurch. Yet another, more positively missiological, view is possible – one which rests on the need for new approaches in a changing world.

---

34. White, *The Church and the Parachurch*, 163.
35. Scheitle, *Beyond the Congregation*, 21.
36. Scheitle, 6.

The Innovative Approach: New Wineskins and Dual Structures

The idea that the parachurch represents a necessary innovation is paradigmatically expressed in Snyder's "wineskins argument" presented at the Lausanne 1974 Congress. Snyder distinguishes between the church as biblically understood and auxiliary ecclesiastical structures "which did not exist in New Testament days, but which have grown up through church history."[37] Instead of playing missionary structures and church off against each other, he affirms that

> the Church is itself a missionary structure, and any group of missionaries may be a legitimate embodiment of the Church. This means there can be no question of the Church versus "missionary structures." Where missionaries are, there is the Church, and their missionaries are responsible to demonstrate the reality of Christian community.[38]

Snyder thus undermines the idea that the parachurch could be conceived as "beyond" or "outside" the church, but boldly anchors parachurch structures within a broadly conceived church: "Whereas the Church itself is part of the new wine of the Gospel, all para-church structures are wineskins – useful, at times indispensable, but also subject to wear and decay."[39] This strengthens the legitimacy of the parachurch and relativizes its contingent status.[40]

Two major ideas underscore this understanding of parachurch structures. The first is theological and relates to a profoundly Protestant understanding of the link between truth and organization, as Willaime, in an analysis quoted earlier, has astutely observed in the context of the Reformation:

> Ideological authority is, in principle, exercised only by the power of its conviction and rational argument in value. Theological research is formally free, and the theologian is given an important role in the management of religious truth, since it is he who, on the basis

---

37. Howard A. Snyder, "The Church as God's Agent in Evangelism: Conference Presentation," in *Let the Earth Hear His Voice: Official Reference Volume, Papers and Responses*, eds. International Congress on World Evangelization and J. D. Douglas (Minneapolis: World Wide Publications, 1975), 356.

38. Howard A. Snyder, "The Church as God's Agent in Evangelism: Working Paper," in International Congress on World Evangelization and J. D. Douglas, eds., *Let the Earth Hear His Voice*, 341–42.

39. Snyder, "Working Paper," 337.

40. Like others, Haight states in his *summa* that all forms of church are actually contingent; see Roger Haight, *Ecclesial Existence*, vol. 3 of *Christian Community in History* (London: Bloomsbury, 2014), 33. If this is correct, then diminishing the value of the parachurch because of its contingent flexibility is misguided.

of a certain knowledge, will say what is the right line. *The religious organisation has only a functional role here: as a second instance in the service of truth, its mode of operation and its distribution of roles have only a relative value and are sociohistorical.*[41]

As Protestantism submits the formulations of the faith to biblically informed criticism – often carried out by laypeople – ecclesial structures can be evaluated against the backdrop of their faithfulness to what has been identified as the church's mission. Here, *participation* in the church implies that Christians, by virtue of their *immediate* relationship to God through Scripture, can criticize the way in which the gospel is *mediated* to the world, within and outside the gathered assembly. Loyalty to the church is shown by biblically assessing its functioning and, if necessary, by reforming it.

The second major idea builds on Winter's "Two Structures of God's Redemptive Mission."[42] Winter's primary argument is that the New Testament describes and prescribes the function of the church but not its form. The church, essentially modelled after the Jewish synagogue and including "old and young, male and female,"[43] is the first of his "two structures," and it resembles the later parish church. The second is derived from Paul's own "missionary band," for the apostle was,

> true enough, sent out by the church in Antioch. But once away from Antioch he seemed very much on his own. The little team he formed was economically self-sufficient when occasion demanded. It was also dependent, from time to time, not alone upon the Antioch Church, but upon other churches that had risen as a result of evangelistic labors. Paul's team may certainly be considered a structure.[44]

This formal flexibility of the early church raises questions about practical theology: to what extent can forms be adapted to function and task? Camp summarizes Winter's position as implying that if only *functions* are prescribed in the NT, "it is theologically legitimate to change the form of the assembly from synagogue to church to diocese. Similarly, it is scripturally acceptable to change the form of a missionary band to a monastic structure or to a mission

---

41. Willaime, *Précarité Protestante*, 24–25; emphasis added.
42. Ralph D. Winter, "The Two Structures of God's Redemptive Mission," *Missiology: An International Review* 2, no. 1 (1 Jan. 1974): 121–39.
43. Winter, "Two Structures," 122.
44. Winter, 122.

agency, in as much as the function remains the same."⁴⁵ Winter argues that the two structures have operated more or less successfully throughout church history in the form of *modality* (local church) and *sodality* (missionary band), defined as follows: "A modality is a structured fellowship in which there is no distinction of sex or age, while a sodality is a structured fellowship in which membership involves an adult second decision beyond modality membership and is limited by either age or sex or marital status."⁴⁶

Yet Winter is taken to task by Willmer et al. for making too close a connection between medieval orders and parachurch ministries because the latter "make no claims to offer a spiritual life that is deeper than the spiritual life of a Christian who attends church faithfully. These groups simply offer avenues of service."⁴⁷

Such critique risks reducing the success of parachurch structures to their practical value and presupposes only functional interest from their members. Yet ministry cannot be separated from "spiritual" life. It is logical to conclude from various training events, spiritual literature and overall teaching that IFES students are indeed called to "a deeper spiritual life" including witnessing – what others call "religious goods." In student ministry, these "goods" are targeted towards their audience, taking special care to be contextually relevant to university life. It is precisely this contextual relevance, together with a reduction of theological tensions, that considering the parachurch as a transient structure allows. Snyder summarizes the benefits of such an approach:

> (i) That which is always cross-culturally relevant (the biblically-understood Church) is separated from that which is culturally bound and determined (para-church structures). Thus, one is free to see the Church as culturally relevant and involved and yet not as culturally bound. (ii) One is free also to modify parachurch structures as culture changes, for these are not themselves the

---

45. Bruce K. Camp, "A Theological Examination of the Two-Structure Theory," *Missiology* 23, no. 2 (1995): 201.

46. Winter, "Two Structures," 127. Brackney explains the relative success of Winter's thesis by its closeness to common narratives in Protestant circles: "Winter's typologies have received wide attention in the Protestant missiological community, particularly among the independent and evangelical organizations, because he asserted that the sodality principle was recovered in Protestantism and is best exemplified in the modern voluntary associations of the missionary movement." Brackney, *Christian Voluntarism*, 131. One could push the cultural analysis further and explore the relationship of "voluntary agencies" with the modern notion of "individual agency" almost consubstantial with "modernity" (as the nineteenth-century context of most voluntary organizations might imply).

47. Willmer, Schmidt and Smith, *Prospering Parachurch*, 27.

Church and therefore are largely culturally rather than biblically determined. (iii) Finally, this distinction makes it possible to see a wide range of legitimacy in denominational confessions and structures. If such structures are not themselves the Church and are culturally determined, then whole volumes of controversy and polemics lose their urgency and become merely secondary. Widely varying confessions are freed (at least potentially) to concentrate on that which unites them: being the people of God and carrying out the evangelistic task – while relegating structural differences to the plane of cultural and historical relativity.[48]

If, then, an organization like IFES has mission as its *raison d'être*, then from the point of view of *missional ecclesiology*, in which "where missionaries are, there is the church," the main way of distinguishing parachurch from "church" will be by arguing that the form of mission it pursues is inherently limited relative to the broader *missional calling* of the church, because it focuses on students only. If, as Snyder says, "missionaries are responsible to demonstrate the reality of Christian community," one of the ways in which an organization might be inherently limited relative to the missional calling of the church will be if it somehow cannot "demonstrate the reality of Christian community." The argument runs the risk of circularity: parachurch leaders accuse the local church of being missionally deficient while the latter rebukes the first for being narrow-minded in their ecclesiology.

This argument of dual structures is eminently more positive towards parachurch structures, underlying their importance in the *contextualization* of mission in the world. Yet the perennial question of authority remains if these structures are still considered to be *para*-ecclesial and not fully ecclesial in nature. A promising way out of this riddle might be to consider the relationship of the parachurch to the local church in the same way denominations relate to the church universal.

A Rejoinder: From the Double Nature of the Church

A more recent proposal explores the relationship between the participation of Christian students in parachurch organizations and in local churches.

---

48. Snyder, "Working Paper," 338. Opposing the "biblically-understood" church, deemed "always relevant," and parachurch structures seems a shortcut, for even "biblical understanding" is culturally conditioned.

Debanné[49] draws a parallel between ecclesiology and Christology. Having acknowledged the "legitimacy issue" that parachurch organizations often suffer in the eyes of church leaders, he contends that this issue is the result of an ecclesiological blind spot: forgetfulness of the primacy of the universal church over the local church. This presupposes "a Christology that would emphasize the human nature of Jesus without fully appreciating his divine nature: a doctrine of the Church that does not take into account the two natures of the Church, local and universal, inevitably leads to concrete situations that do not correspond to God's plan."[50]

In contrast, Debanné contends that valuing the concreteness of the local is

> liberating and energizing for the believer. It is the bearer of a seed of creativity and new initiatives: it allows each member of the faithful, man or woman, to be prepared in his or her local Church to take his or her place in the worldwide work of Christ inside and outside that Church. It makes him/her capable of becoming an autonomous actor (because he/she is dependent on Christ) in initiatives for the Kingdom of God.[51]

This autonomy is relative. Debanné notes that any Christian will be a member of a local church and should do everything in his or her power to remain in good standing with the church's leadership. However, the key to his argument is that the church leadership has responsibilities to the whole Christian community. This argument rests on the fact that "we see Peter, for example, ascribing to the Church being built around Christ the same prerogatives and responsibilities as those ascribed to the community of Israel (royal priests, a holy nation, a people redeemed [by God]), 1 Pet. 2:4–10; see Ex. 19:5–6)."[52] The connection with the idea of the "priesthood of all believers" is evident. Debanné argues in strong terms that "the new convert becomes a member of the universal Church before becoming a member of a local church, in the way that baptism in the Holy Spirit (conversion, regeneration:

---

49. Debanné was GS of the French-speaking GBUC (Groupes Bibliques Universitaires et Collégiaux du Canada) working in Quebec from 1999 to 2014.

50. Marc Debanné, "L'étudiant chrétien, l'Église locale et les mouvements chrétiens étudiants: comment démystifier la place du «para-Église» ?," *Théologie évangélique* 14, no. 1 (2015): 25.

51. Debanné, "L'étudiant chrétien," 26. Enns also alludes to the doctrine of the two natures: "Universality and particularity are two sides of the same coin, just as the believed and experienced church are two sides of that one coin, as is the incarnated Christ." Enns, "Believers Church Ecclesiology," 124.

52. Debanné, 26–27.

the invisible reality) precedes water baptism (the visible manifestation)."[53] This argument is consistent with the primacy for truth already noted in most IFES writers. The same logic is at work for ecclesiology:

> The primary reality of biblical ecclesiology is the universal Church. It must therefore also be the primary principle of the believer's theological understanding of the Church. Even if local Church life will fill most of their time and energies (this will be the case for most Christians), they will only be able to live this local Church life correctly if they understand it in the context of the universal Church, of which it is a local manifestation.[54]

Debanné also goes to great lengths to debunk the concerns of certain church leaders that parachurch organizations might show a lesser concern for doctrine because of the contingencies of missionary work. For him, the fact that many organizations have a doctrinal statement demonstrates the opposite and is a sign of maturity and faithfulness, because "mission outside" is eminently riskier doctrinally than "church life." For him, "it is necessary to understand the specific role of inter-church works in the body of Christ: to join to the proclamation of the truth in a given missionary context a work of unity that goes beyond the local churches and denominations, according to the Lord's twofold demand."[55]

This line of argument is rare in IFES-related publications, but it fleshes out more clearly than many other documents the way many IFES leaders have legitimized their work. While parachurch organizations can indeed become sectarian, denominations run the same schismatic risk by putting too strong a focus on their own denominational distinctives. Debanné hence draws upon the primacy of the missionary calling of the Christian to highlight that "the Lord's call to faithful evangelisation gives us no choice, whatever the type of structure in which we work: we must stand in a gap where the two risks are always present."[56] The conclusion Debanné draws from this missiological observation is that the term "parachurch" should be abandoned in favour of "inter-church" in order to dispense once and for all with the derogatory and

---

53. Debanné, 28. This counters Haight's contention that "if the church is a free association, then the primary reference for the term 'church' insofar as it is an organized community is the local church." Haight, *Comparative Ecclesiology*, 279.

54. Debanné, 28.

55. Debanné, 42.

56. Debanné, 42.

implicitly sectarian resonances of the word, for "members of the Body are not defined by the risk they face."[57]

Overall, Debanné reads like a peaceful rejoinder to the "deficiency approach" and the "necessary innovation" approach, yet grounding his ecclesiological argument for abandoning the notion of "parachurch" on Christology and the primacy of the individual's relationship to God. For Debanné, this relationship *precedes* involvement in the local church. Hence what used to be called "parachurch" is, plainly, "church." Theologically speaking then, the *immediate* relationship to God of individual *members* of the church universal shapes their *missional* orientation, for which they gather in what could be called a *branch* of the church – in our case, a "campus branch" or, to use a missiologically sounder term, an *incarnation* of the church.

If all the above explorations are true, there is not much left to prevent a parachurch like IFES from being called "ecclesial." This depends on a distinctively *missional ecclesiology* on which not all church traditions are agreed. Yet there is another dimension of ecclesial existence that needs tackling: what is the "parachurch" to do with the sacraments?

About the Impossibility of Being Church: The Question of Sacraments

> How shall we understand the spreading parachurch organizations? Some are designed to supplement and assist churches. While others appear to be churches in all but name.[58]

Being firmly anchored in evangelicalism, the theological self-understanding of IFES has traditionally put less weight upon sacramental theology. As Protestantism usually acknowledges baptism and Eucharist/Communion, it is on their practice that the few debates carried out in IFES circles focus. Traditionally most IFES groups have celebrated the sacraments only exceptionally, even if they are an important part of ecclesial life. It is one of the strongest ecclesiological arguments allowing differentiation of a Christian Union from a church. Illustrative of this understanding of the exceptional case is Woods's anecdote of a student camp in 1949:

> A problem arose when the Islamic student who had confessed Christ asked for baptism. We told him that this should be done in a church, but his reply was, "I don't know any church, I've

---

57. Debanné, 43.
58. Edmund P. Clowney, *The Church* (Downers Grove: InterVarsity Press, 1995), 100.

never been in a Christian church." *So, after some consultation and prayer we broke every rule of interdenominational student work by having a public baptism* in the sea conducted by M. Gaston Racine, a much beloved speaker. Quite a crowd of the public gathered around as the young man stood in the sea, gave his testimony and then was baptised in the name of God the Father, Son and Holy Spirit.[59]

These "rules of interdenominational student work" are nowhere formalized. Yet the fact that Woods alludes to such a concept shows his understanding of the respective tasks of local churches and student groups. This topic was discussed at length in the Lausanne Movement and the aforementioned Lausanne Occasional Paper 24. This *summa* of evangelical thinking on parachurch quotes from an unpublished paper by holiness preacher Paul Rees. He argues for the importance of the *notae ecclesiae* [marks of the Church] in the discussion around parachurch organizations, which for him are different from denominations: "Denominations at least owe their existence, and are answerable, to assemblies of believers among whom may be found the *notae* of church reality."[60] These *notae* go back to Calvin affirming that "wherever we see the Word of God sincerely preached and heard, wherever we see the sacraments administered according to the institution of Christ, there we cannot have any doubt that the Church of God has some existence."[61] Here, the parachurch seems to be found wanting.

Clowney also elaborates on the protestant Reformer's "biblical and spiritual understanding of the Church's attributes"[62] which has consequences for the definition of a student group:

> The limitation of the parachurch group is that it lacks some of the marks of the church. It needs denominations because it does not provide the ordered structure of office, worship, sacrament and discipline that a denominational church offers. Because such groups are not churches, they do not dismiss members to churches or receive them from churches, and rightly find no difficulty in recruiting members of denominational churches.[63]

---

59. Woods, "IFES History Draft," 13; emphasis added.

60. Lausanne Movement, "Cooperating in World Evangelization," Appendix A, §2.

61. John Calvin, *Institutes of the Christian Religion*, trans. Ford Lewis McNeill, The Library of Christian Classics (Philadelphia: Westminster John Knox, 2011), IV.1.9.

62. Clowney, *The Church*, 101.

63. Clowney, 107.

It is fascinating that *not being a church* could be seen as providing a "missiological advantage." A student group can provisionally dispense with issues of church discipline and questions of denominational loyalties that are so hard for outsiders to understand. A local student group cannot be a church for these authors because it does not celebrate the sacraments. Whether the "Word is sincerely preached" in student meetings varies significantly between more participatory cultures and more hierarchical ones.

In any case, IFES leaders were not oblivious to these questions. Hammond's early "theological treaty" written for IFES-like groups briefly comments on the *notae* following the creedal framework of *unity, sanctity, catholicity* and *apostolicity*. These characteristics arguably can be found in each student group. Hammond indeed suggests that "the true Church of Christ is to be found everywhere where he and the Holy Spirit are enthroned in men's hearts. Hence the true church is the whole congregation of Christian people dispersed throughout the whole world."[64] The student group is no substitute for involvement in a local church, as Hammond hastens to caution that "students, however, particularly those who are in residential universities, need to be even more on their guard against the neglect of Holy Communion than of public worship in general."[65]

One of the earliest explanations of IFES's relationship to the sacraments[66] is indeed found in the context of describing the marks of a true church. In a passage worth quoting at length, Johnson offers his definitely "Low Church" understanding of the sacraments and takes the opportunity to explain ecclesial differences:[67]

> With all orthodox Christians they [the member movements of IFES] would set great value on the possession of a true Christian ministry; and fulfil the functions of a servant of Christ. But they must take their stand on the Reformers' insistence that (whatever mechanical aids are employed for the preservation of due order) *the successors of the apostles are clearly defined in the New Testament in relation to their beliefs and character.* They are

---

64. Hammond, *In Understanding* (1960), 163–64.

65. Hammond, 182.

66. In most evangelical circles, the Lord's Supper and baptism would usually be called "ordinances" rather than sacraments. For theological clarity, "sacrament" will be used throughout.

67. It is worth underlining that this passage is an integral part of the first official IFES history commissioned and approved by the Executive. It can therefore be considered somewhat authoritative.

described in Scripture as those who faithfully proclaim the Word of God,[68] and administer the two sacraments according to Christ's holy ordinance. There must, similarly, be no compromise with any of the administration of the Lord's supper which includes the idea of a repeated sacrifice (except that of "the sacrifice of praise"), *or of a priestly sacerdotal or mediatorial function to be performed by the minister.* The Bible, again, is quite unequivocal at this point. Christ, by His death on the cross, has "made there (by His one oblation of Himself once offered) a full, perfect, and sufficient sacrifice, oblation, and satisfaction, for the sins of the whole world; and did institute, and in His holy Gospel command us to continue, a perpetual memory of that His precious death, until His coming again."[69] The corollary of this is that Christians no longer need any other atoning sacrifice, and since their great High Priest has been appointed the sole Mediator between God and man, Christians have no need of any other mediatorial priesthood. To re-introduce any such thought into the Church of God is an unnecessary misunderstanding. More seriously, it must be regarded as an affront to the all-sufficient Mediator and sole Priest at God's right hand.[70]

This development shows how congenial to the theologizing of early IFES leaders the idea of a non-mediated relationship to God was. This was theological and ecclesiological, notably connected with a strong emphasis on the substitutionary dimension of the atonement. These views of the early IFES leadership could not be expected to be fully shared by every leader of every national movement, given the numerous traditions represented. Given the lack of unity on specific topics like the sacraments, should leaders keep their personal opinions quiet, or voice them? Did unity require silence, or should enlightened differences be expressed? Illustrative of this kind of tension is the following recollection of Indian IFES board member Enoch talking about his early years in UESI (the Union of Evangelical Students of India):

> We had to work out our policy on [all] sorts of issues. One of these was our stand as an interdenominational movement, on

---

68. Quoting 1 Timothy 2.
69. Johnson gives reference to the Communion Service in the Book of Common Prayer of the Church of England, which summarizes 1 Pet 2:24, 25; Eph 2:13–18 and Heb 9:11–28.
70. Reference given in footnote to 1 Tim 2:5; Heb 6:19–9:28. Johnson, *Brief History*, 104–5; emphasis added.

doctrines on which Evangelicals differ, such as baptism. There was a suggestion that we should not talk about baptism in E.U. [Evangelical Union = UESI student group] meetings, except to Hindu converts, and even when asked individually we should refuse to state our views [lest] students be carried away by a senior's opinion. I had difficulty accepting this and refused to agree to it. I felt that every individual must have the liberty to express his own convictions when occasion demands, provided he does not try to get converts to his own point of view.[71]

Whereas in national movements, sacramental questions could be addressed contextually following the local leader's sensitivities,[72] the question of Communion in particular was raised for IFES conferences, for arguably in the context of a growing ecumenical sensitivity, international conferences had seen an aspiration to celebrate Communion. The mandate to the Executive to examine the question came from the Scandinavian delegations. After long discussions spanning several years, the committee adopted the following guidelines, which are the last such policy to date:

(i) It must not be taken for granted that Communion Services are suitable for all international conferences of IFES.

(ii) Where participants of conferences tend to identify the Communion Service as a church function, it might be better not to hold such services.

(iii) Member movements do not have to follow the pattern and practice of Communion Services held at IFES international conferences as this might conflict with the consciences of some conference members.

---

71. H. Enoch, *Following the Master* (Mumbai: GLS, 1977), 75.

72. Escobar's vivid depiction of the contrasting situations within the fellowship is worth quoting: "For instance, the idea of having the Lord's Supper or Communion after an evangelical student camp in some European countries, can raise the tremendous debates about ministry and sacraments that have divided Christians since the Reformation. On the other hand, in Africa or Latin America it is the most natural thing for Lutheran, Baptist, Pentecostal and Christian and Missionary Alliance students to have Communion as an expression of their evangelical experience in a camp. Again the solemn and beautiful experience of the Lord's Supper at the Urbana missionary convention of the IVCF in the USA would be unthinkable, in that kind of inter-denominational situation, for some European Evangelicals." Escobar, "Evangelical Heritage," 5.

(iv) At international conferences, careful announcements must be made concerning the nature of the service and the possibility of abstaining must also be stated.[73]

In more recent years, acknowledging "ecumenical developments," some movements have officially opened the way for local student groups to celebrate the Lord's Supper. Exemplary of this are the SMD Germany guidelines which stipulate that "at events there is a basic rule that the Lord's Supper should be instituted by theologians or the SMD leadership if possible. . . . The purpose of this rule is to ensure that the Lord's Supper is administered by people who are theologically and 'liturgically' trained."[74]

When local groups can celebrate Communion, the requirement that the celebration should preferably be led by somebody who has been theologically trained is ecclesiologically diplomatic. However, it does not take full consideration of what the "priesthood of all believers" means. Muthiah boldly asserts that

> ordination must no longer be held as a requirement for those who would administer the Lord's supper. Since 1) all believers are gifted by the Spirit; 2) all charisms are of one nature; and 3) all believers should be ordained, no particular charism or office uniquely qualifies a person to administer the bread and the wine. It might be wise for a community to draw upon individuals who are mature in their faith and who embody the fruit of the Spirit to lead the community in the breaking of the bread and the drinking of the wine. But such selection would be based on embodied faith rather than on charisms or office.[75]

Lastly, Debanné also argues that from a biblical-theological perspective – notably from 1 Corinthians 12 and Ephesians 4 – the NT describes "interchurch ministries" (apostles and prophets) that reach beyond the walls of the local church. He concludes that "even if, according to the NT, the marks and organization of the Church (with sacraments, teaching and discipline) are

---

73. "Minutes of the Meeting of the Executive Committee of the IFES" (Oak Hill College, London, England, 20 Sept. 1976), IFES e-archives.

74. Gernot Spies and Achim Schowalter, "Der Hochschul-SMD-Leitfaden zur Feier des Abendmahls in SMD-Gruppen" (n.d.). This is an internal training document.

75. Muthiah, *Priesthood of All Believers*, Kindle loc. 1927.

centred in the local Church, there is no passage stating that they would be 'limited' in a strict sense."[76]

Partial Synthesis

> The church took shape around the originating impulse of God in Jesus toward the kingdom of God in history and finds its *raison d'être* in continuing to mediate God's empowerment and supply the social basis for this mission.[77]

Our brief survey of the notion of "parachurch" has explored the building blocks of the definition of this phenomenon. We have seen that the *voluntary principle* underscoring it presumes the primacy of the individual's *immediate* relationship to God, based on which the local church is assessed. Given evangelicalism's insistence on *mission*, many Christians have found the church lacking in its commitment to take its missionary calling seriously. Such is the *deficiency* explanation for organizations like IFES, which exist "beside" traditional ecclesial structures. While helpful for understanding "parachurch" historically, this approach risks diminishing the value of what so-called parachurch organizations have achieved throughout church history.

Others have argued that because of the necessity to contextualize the *mediation* of the gospel message in the world, parachurch structures were simply a structural innovation akin to "new wineskins" and coherent with developments already present in NT writings, notably the existence of the stable *modalities* and the more flexible *sodalities*, two structures collaborating in mission. A rejoinder position was offered, proposing that in the same way Christology articulates the two natures of Jesus Christ as both divine and human, so ecclesiology can articulate two natures for the church, the first being the church universal and the other the local church. In this last view, because all Christians are *members* of the universal church, the "parachurch" is only an "incarnation" or "branch" of the church universal outside the walls of the traditional local church. The parachurch then plays a vital role in the overall calling of the church.

Despite their disagreements, all these perspectives assume the centrality of mission to the definition of the church. This, in turn, underscores a *missional ecclesiology* legitimating so-called "parachurch" structures because their

---

76. Debanné, "L'étudiant chrétien," 32.
77. Haight, *Ecclesial Existence*, 106.

activities fit the brief of a "mission" which is broadened to become the heir of Israel's calling to be a display-people of God's redemptive calling. Despite being widely used as a linguistic shortcut, the term "parachurch" is therefore misleading. It reflects an outdated hierarchical, ecclesiocentric vision of the church which is not congruent with the primacy of mission over structures.

16

A Ministry of Expansion? Roland Allen's Missiology and IFES Ministry

To articulate the connection between biblical theology, ecclesiology and missiology in student ministry, the work of pioneer missionary and missiologist Roland Allen (1868–1947) is helpful and illuminating.[1] Allen explored the priesthood of laypeople in the missionary context in a short book probably penned in the late 1930s but published only in 2017: *The Ministry of Expansion: The Priesthood of the Laity*.[2] In what follows, I present some of the most salient aspects of Allen's reflections insofar as they shed light on how IFES ministry can be missiologically understood.

I have found no explicit references to Allen in the IFES archives or published documents related to IFES. Yet parallel lines of thinking run between Allen's reflections and how IFES leaders have conceived of their work. High Anglican missionary-priest Allen insists on the importance of the sacraments and episcopal ordination and discusses his status as a geographically distant envoy. Conversely, IFES leaders insist on the importance of the Word, reflect on authority issues more generally (either doctrinal or with regard to ecclesial leaders) and discuss the ideological "remoteness" of many aspects of campus life. While Allen's public arguments differ from those of IFES, many of his

---

1. For more on Allen, see Hubert Allen, *Roland Allen: Pioneer, Priest and Prophet* (Grand Rapids: Eerdmans, 1995); Steven Rutt, *Roland Allen: A Missionary Life* (Cambridge: Lutterworth, 2018); Steven Rutt, *Roland Allen II: A Theology of Mission* (Cambridge: Lutterworth, 2018).

2. Roland Allen, *The Ministry of Expansion: The Priesthood of the Laity*, ed. J. D. Payne, Kindle (Pasadena: William Carey Library, 2017).

ideas highlight the difficulty of drawing sharp lines between what is "in" the church and what is "outside" it or "beside" it.

Allen articulates his missiology around "apostolic principles," which Rutt summarizes thus:

> Planting the indigenous Church through short-term itinerant evangelists; establishing the Church in apostolic order – the Scriptures, a basic creed, the ministry, the sacraments; self-governing churches which ordain locally trained leadership to administer the sacraments frequently; self-supporting churches which manage their own affairs; and self-propagating churches which empower the laity to influence the culture as a missionary body, are reiterated today for ongoing missiological discussion.[3]

These principles run through most of the theology of IFES. Somewhat blurring the lines between church and parachurch, with one important caveat the description applies to the practices of IFES: high regard for the apostolic tradition – understood as teaching and not as succession; a basic creed – the doctrinal basis; self-governing student groups and national movements which appoint locally trained leadership and manage their own affairs; self-propagating national movements (sometimes helped in the pioneering phase by other IFES movements); and overall the empowerment of the (student) laity throughout the process. Only the sacramental dimension is less prominent in IFES.

Confidence in the Laity

Based on a biblical-theology approach, Allen's central missiological idea is that of *expansion*, a process he assumes to be *spontaneous*:

> I mean the expansion which follows the unexhorted and unorganized activity of individual members of the Church explaining to others the Gospel which they have found for themselves; I mean the expansion which follows the irresistible attraction of the Christian Church for men who see its ordered life, and are drawn to it by desire to discover the secret of a life

---

3. Steven Rutt, "Roland Allen's Apostolic Principles: An Analysis of His 'The Ministry of Expansion,'" *Transformation* 29, no. 3 (2012): 237.

which they instinctively desire to share; I mean also the expansion of the Church by the addition of new churches.[4]

Allen displays impressive confidence in the laity, warranted by a firm trust that the Holy Spirit leads any Christian, irrespective of his or her training or seniority.[5] Thus, many years prior to developments in missional ecclesiology, Allen proposed a "simple concept in theory, but a complicated reality to achieve due to Western church expectations."[6] Such expectations, especially "related to ordination and the Eucharist," caused Allen to write his short book.

As with many of his writings, *The Ministry of Expansion* frequently has polemical undertones. Based on his experience as a missionary, Allen took exception to the theological arguments of many of his contemporaries, arguing that they were not taking full consideration of the situation on the mission field. The theologians of the day, said Allen, were embroiled in a Christendom mentality which could not do justice to the needs and specificities of foreign lands where churches were developing at a pace no church hierarchy could fathom. Allen observed about the early church that "Christians who were scattered about the world could not possibly have been all ordained and commissioned by the apostles and they did not wait for any apostolic ordination to observe the rite which Christ ordained for them."[7]

Yet Allen was no ecclesial maverick. He "maintained that bishops were consecrated to oversee the planting of churches. And yet, it became evident to him that within many frontier regions where no ordained ministers existed (especially within African and Asian contexts) . . . the Holy Spirit sovereignly created new churches through the ministry of the laity."[8]

Furthermore, Allen's high view of the sacraments led him to advocate for more lay involvement:

> If it is admitted that Christ directed His servants, generally, to observe His sacraments, if that teaching which we commonly hear at home, that partaking of the Holy Communion as an act

---

4. Roland Allen, "Spontaneous Expansion: The Terror of Missionaries," *World Dominion*, no. 4 (1926): 218–24; quoted in J. D. Payne, "Roland Allen, Missiology and The Ministry of Expansion," in Allen, *Ministry of Expansion*, Kindle loc. 220.

5. The research literature on Allen is vast. For his pneumatological missiology, see Mark Oxbrow, "Pentecost and the World: Roland Allen, the Spirit and Remodeling Twenty-First-Century Mission," *International Bulletin of Mission Research* 44, no. 3 (July 2020): 215–32.

6. Payne, "Roland Allen," Kindle loc. 326.

7. Allen, *Ministry of Expansion*, Kindle loc. 1488.

8. Steven Rutt, "Background and Overview of The Ministry of Expansion," in Allen, *Ministry of Expansion*, Kindle loc. 745.

of obedience to Christ is true teaching, then anything whatsoever which prevents men from observing it is something which overthrows and annuls the command of Christ for them. I say that no custom or tradition can annul a command of Christ for Christians.[9]

By "custom or tradition" he is referring to episcopal ordination. In Allen's view, its absence is no reason to deprive of the sacraments Christians who are living in large dioceses infrequently visited by ordained personnel. Allen is adamant that "the grace of Christ is wider than the episcopate. The promise of Christ that He will be with two or three gathered together in His Name is prior to the ordained ministry."[10] Allen adds that "any theory of the ministry, then, which forgets that ministry of expansion, and attempts to compel the words of the New Testament to fit a hierarchy with defined functions, must necessarily find the task difficult, and its conclusions doubtful."[11]

Biblical theology shapes Allen's missiology, and especially his strong commitment to Pauline teachings.[12] For the argument of this work, Allen's reference to 1 Peter is of particular interest:

> We all agree that in the New Testament Christians are called to be a "royal priesthood" (1 Pet 2:9) and "priests" (Rev 1:6; 5:10; 20:6); and that as a priestly race and priests they offer to God sacrifices of praise and thanksgiving; and that their observance of the Lord's Supper is so markedly an offering of praise and thanksgiving that it very early received the title of Eucharist. We all agree that ministers of the Church in that Eucharistic service act, not vicariously for the congregation, but representatively, and that it is the whole body which offers using an ordained minister as its mouthpiece.[13]

Allen highlights the idea of representation – he notably does not use the word "mediation" – which he opposes to a vicarious act. There is also a somewhat loose yet real connection with IFES: for Allen, if clergy members represent believers before God, Allen presumes *real* faith in the congregants.

---

9. Allen, Kindle loc. 1134.

10. Allen, Kindle loc. 1589.

11. Allen, Kindle loc. 1914.

12. See his missiology classic: Roland Allen, *Missionary Methods: St Paul's or Ours?* (London: Scott, 1912).

13. Allen, *Ministry of Expansion*, Kindle loc. 1718.

Similarly, IFES leaders argue that students cannot rely on representatives – pastors, parents, and so on – but need to take charge of their faith – a view that assumes *immediacy* between students and God. Congruent with low sacramental theology, the only way IFES leaders or student leaders would *represent* others before God is through prayer. Furthermore, Allen explicitly attributes the priesthood privileges to every Christian, arguing against restraining sacramental practice to a specific group. Allen takes great pains to explain that this argument applies to "mission fields," but the form of the theological argument can be applied to other contexts as well. This was a far-sighted view that might prove fruitful in contexts marked by an increased dechristianization and shortage of clergy.

Relating to Clerical Traditions

Laypeople ministering had not been on the earlier radar of Allen, yet he found himself arguing against his former mentor, Bishop Gore,[14] and another Oxford luminary, Moberly. Allen contends that supporting lay ministry in far-off lands is not an act of ecclesial insubordination but an act of obedience to the Lord's commands and of service to fellow Christians. Allen submits that

> we are simply men, who being deprived of the assistance of the regular order, do the best that we can. We do not set up a theory of the superiority of the untrained, unqualified to the trained and qualified medical practitioner, because we help a man in distress to the best of our ability; neither do we set up a theory of the superiority of a charismatic ministry to the regularly ordained ministry because we do the best in our power in the absence of the regularly ordained ministry.[15]

These words read like the defence of a foreign envoy reporting to the "sending centre" of his church. While not challenging the doctrine of apostolic succession head-on, Allen nevertheless regularly challenged what he considered a legalistic and thus stifling interpretation of the doctrine, which in his view deprived members of the people of God of their rightful dues.

Allen's view is that if ordained clergy members were available in a foreign diocese, no questions would be asked about them being able to celebrate the sacraments or perform whatever clerical duties were necessary. In IFES circles,

---

14. His opposition to the early OICCU had been strong.
15. Allen, *Ministry of Expansion*, loc. 1617.

however, no such direct connection is granted between having a member of the clergy available and the celebration of the sacraments, primarily for historical reasons. Moreover, given the difficult relationship between early IFES leaders and church leaders – even though some of the early IFES founders were clergy members, ordained or not – there is in the IFES rhetoric an underlying suspicion that clergy members might be detrimental to the faith of students, for theological and sociological reasons.

The way Allen argued for the need for Christians to receive the sacraments, whatever their circumstances, is very close to the way those connected with IFES argue that students need to hear the Word. IFES leaders never explicitly adopted a sacramental view of Scripture. Nevertheless, functionally, the Bible assumed that role: Scripture is instrumental in uniting people to Christ and his mission. The importance that Bible expositors such as Stott have assumed in the organization's history supports this view. Like Calvin's view on the Scriptures "sincerely preached" being a mark of the true church, IFES leaders assume that a high view of Scripture and its diligent study are the marks of the "true IFES group/movement."[16] Incidentally, Allen supports his view of laypeople celebrating the sacraments by connecting the need for sacraments with the need for people to hear the Word: "what if we were depriving the world of the Word? Are churches possibly depriving the world of the Word of God out of a sheer lack of missionality?"[17] "Depriving people of the Word" was precisely what early IFES leaders would have accused WSCF circles of doing and hence justified their existence.

This idea of "deprivation" supposes that some people possess or understand something others do not: at the core, a missiological argument. On this logic, someone needs to bring something to somebody else.

Distant Lands? Allen's Reflections Applied to Student Ministry

Allen's concern was for Christians in foreign and vast lands where no episcopal ordination practices could provide enough clerical staffing. Remoteness was not a sufficient argument for restricting sacramental practice to ordained clergy. I would argue along the same lines for university campuses which, albeit not necessarily geographically, are often remote from ecclesial and theological

---

16. It could also be suggested that IFES leaders have exercised a sort of "episcopate by the book," ensuring a form of theological conformity throughout the fellowship by promoting many titles throughout the world.

17. Allen, *Ministry of Expansion*, Kindle loc. 1241.

centres.[18] Worldview perspectives, ideologies and scientific questioning are often far from the horizons of church leaders or "ordinary" congregants.

As Allen argued for contextual flexibility, IFES leaders argue for approaching university campuses on their own terms and understanding what preoccupies students. As Allen's contemporaries did not always understand the theological differences between their homeland and the mission field, so student ministry requires a good understanding of the academic world. For IFES, "remoteness" is sometimes geographical – as the insistence on "pioneering" in strategic plans shows – but, more often, "distance" is more conceptual. Indeed, remoteness does not need to be geographical. Bourdanné notes that

> the vast majority of non-Christian students cannot understand why someone without any previous knowledge of the university would address them. Having no respect for such a person, they will not even take the time to listen seriously to his message. Poorly prepared facilitators and pastors have been humiliated by students because of insufficient academic levels and knowledge of university culture.[19]

Politely questioning non-academic – that is, primarily church-based – student ministry, he further observes that

> student ministers need to have a good knowledge of the university culture. It is not enough to simply be a goodwill Christian to be successful in evangelising students. Some student evangelistic organisations and evangelical denominations rightly require that student leaders (university chaplains, facilitators, etc.) have a university background. This is not only because of their knowledge of the field, but also because it gives them a certain credibility with non-Christian students and the academic world in general (researchers, professors, etc.).[20]

If, then, campuses are in many ways "distant lands," they cannot be reached by a professional caste but need to be reached *from the inside*. This missiological conviction squares with the IFES principle that students are the

---

18. We take here a global view which does not apply to some of the oldest universities, especially in the West, where theology departments still enjoy some prestige even in elite universities.

19. Daniel Bourdanné, "Évangélisation des étudiants," in *Dictionnaire de théologie pratique*, ed. Christophe Paya (Cléon-d'Andran: Éditions Excelsis, 2011), 365.

20. Bourdanné, "Évangélisation des étudiants," 364.

primary ambassadors – akin to a *priestly* role – of the gospel wherever they are. This reflects a *missional ecclesiology*:

> Christian students are still being used by God to carry out his evangelistic mission in almost every country in the world. They take the Gospel with them to campuses, lecture halls, dormitories, laboratories, restaurants, social networks and the Internet beyond their national borders. Because of their great mobility in search of places to study, they travel all over the world, including to countries closed to the Gospel. They go where traditional missionaries cannot openly operate.[21]

Such a view challenges the idea that locations could be "closed to the gospel" and revisits student work missiology from the perspective of *missio Dei*, to which I turn below. From a missiological perspective, a campus cannot be "closed." There might then be an advantage to campus authorities "forcing" students to organize themselves if they aspire to assemble formally.

The historical section of this work has shown that the "internal impulse of the Spirit" has often been encouraged or fostered by IFES staff workers. The fact remains, however, that many accounts, especially from regions where the influence of Christianity has been the weakest, tell the stories of students who indeed felt an "inner commissioning" with the practical consequences envisaged by Allen: "They do their work spontaneously. No one sends them out to do it, no one appoints their place or time; they work outside all ecclesiastical organization, independent of all ecclesiastical organization, independent of all ecclesiastical authority and supervision – most of them unknown to any ecclesiastical authority."[22]

There are similarities with a very early account of student movements in Germany, the author of which was adamant that the Holy Spirit was

> not bound to any association organizations or church forms; under certain circumstances, both can act as inhibiting barriers. Therefore, we should not be surprised if new spiritual orientations often arise outside the official churches and organizations, and sometimes have to temporarily enter into direct opposition to them, because new life cannot be held in old forms (Mark 2:22). What happens in true obedience of faith, God can bless wonderfully.[23]

---

21. Bourdanné, 360.
22. Allen, *Ministry of Expansion*, Kindle loc. 1348.
23. Gruner, *Menschenwege und Gotteswege*, 379.

While not making a formal case for independence from episcopal oversight, Allen's arguments are a solidly biblical case for student leadership, especially in contexts where ecclesial authorities are remote, whatever form this remoteness may take. Moreover, the connection Allen draws between *priesthood* and *remoteness* illuminates the church-parachurch questions from an angle that could make the overall debate somewhat more straightforward:

> When the Christian is with the organized body, he is with the organized body and must recognize the fact. He is not the whole body but a part and can only exercise his priestly function as a part, with the other members and through the recognized mouthpiece of the whole. But when he is separated from the organized body, he, and any others who may be with him, are still priests because the Spirit is in them; and as Irenaeus said, "Where the Spirit of God is there is the Church and all grace"; and they must recognize that fact.[24]

Partial Synthesis: An Empowered Laity for Mission in Distant Lands

Although neither developed within the evangelical tradition nor originally applied to student ministry, Allen's missiological reflections shed a supporting light on the argument of this work. Essentially, Allen shows that theological logic and traditions need to be flexible when facing new missionary realities. Support structures are important to sustain the Christian faith: in the same way that Allen thought the sacraments to be indispensable, in IFES reading the Bible *individually* and *together* is held to be essential to a robust faith susceptible to being shared – *mediated* – on campus. Traditional ecclesial authority notwithstanding, *laypeople* can trust the Holy Spirit to guide them in life and ministry; clerical oversight is indispensable for neither Allen nor IFES. Consequently, even in lands that are distant – whether geographically or ideologically – Christian life can validly take place.

Underlying the thinking of both Allen and IFES is the notion that the mission of God is primary.

---

24. Allen, *Ministry of Expansion*, Kindle loc. 1833.

17

Participation in the *Missio Dei*

Though sometimes deemed controversial in evangelicalism, the notion of *missio Dei* has gained significant momentum in missiological circles since the 1960s.[1] IFES leaders have often argued that their organization was necessary because of the primacy of mission over ecclesial structures. To speak of *missio Dei* means that God is on a mission and calls his followers to *join in* this mission by virtue of their *participation* in his work.[2] Missiologist David Bosch defines *missio Dei* in the following words which I supplement slightly: "the *missio Dei* is God's activity, which embraces both the church and the world [including the university], and in which the church [also through the parachurch] may be privileged to participate."[3] This applies to students, whose witness and community on campuses form a kind of "outpost" of the church's engagement in the world. There is a close connection with the "priesthood of all believers": as *participants* in God's mission, Christians *mediate* God to their environment, and this takes the form of witness and service. However, this also means that the distinction between "world" and "church" is much more blurred than often assumed because God is at work in his whole creation and notably through Christ's priesthood, into which Christians are called. Hence, the *priestly* role of human beings instituted at the beginning of Genesis comes full circle. In Bevans and Schroeder's articulate summary,

---

1. For a short overview of the history of the concept, see Robert McIntosh, "Missio Dei," in *Evangelical Dictionary of World Missions*, ed. A. Scott Moreau (Grand Rapids: Baker, 2000), 631–33.

2. For a historical-analytical overview, see Stephen B. Bevans and Roger Schroeder, *Constants in Context: A Theology of Mission for Today*, AMS 30 (Maryknoll: Orbis, 2004), ch. 9.

3. David Bosch, *Transforming Mission: Paradigm Shifts in Theology of Mission* (Maryknoll: Orbis, 1991), 391.

the church community, participating in God's life, is God's special people, a people living God's life of communion in a covenant of relation and love, a people convinced of its fundamental equality through its common baptism in the name of the triune God. But as communion-in-mission, this image takes on a dynamic meaning as God's people on pilgrimage, God's people chosen not for themselves but for God's purposes, God's people respectful of the Spirit's workings outside their own boundaries but committed to sharing the full implications of God's covenant with all humanity.[4]

So if the *priesthood of all Christian students* is *participation in* and *modelled after* Christ's priesthood, then some promising implications can be drawn. The *priesthood of Christ* is efficacious because of his two natures. Christian students can also be understood as having – of course only derivatively – two natures: student and Christian. What Tomlin affirms about Christ could be adapted for any Christian: "He not only identifies and understands, he shares the very nature of both of the parties between which he *mediates*: God and humanity."[5]

The IFES group member indeed shares the very nature of both parties, thus *mediating* between God and the university.[6] This presupposes a broader understanding of the church as being "at work" not only within the walls of the gathered congregation but among its sent members. As Tomlin affirms, "the priestly role of the Church . . . exists not just at its centre, in worship, prayer and sacramental activity, but also at its edges. Perhaps even primarily at its edges."[7] These "edges" are similar to the "distant lands" of which Allen wrote. Similarly, even if he speaks about the church and not about a "parachurch" group, Greggs's point that the fringes of the community are the place where the priesthood of the church is best expressed remains fully valid:

> We might suggest . . . that the most intensive form of the priesthood of the church exists not at its centre or within its own communitarian structures, but at its fringes – in those areas in which its socio-poesis reaches out and attracts those around it in the world, drawing in and incorporating (in the strictest sense of the word) those outside the priestly community who are possessed

---

4. Bevans and Schroeder, *Constants in Context*, 299.

5. Graham Tomlin, *The Widening Circle: Priesthood as God's Way of Blessing the World* (London: SPCK, 2014), 23; emphasis added.

6. This work focuses on IFES but it is evident that these observations could apply to other Christian groups on campus.

7. Tomlin, *Widening Circle*, 109.

by the *cor incurvatus in se* into the community of priesthood in which the heart is opened by the Spirit to be simultaneously attracted (abducted) to both God and others.[8]

This context of encountering others "before they enter the ecclesial community" is precisely what happens when non-Christian students attend an IFES group meeting. Especially if the group meets on campus, the threshold is much lower than that of a church.

Seeing the priestly calling of church members as displayed *primarily outside* a context easily recognizable as *ecclesial* (like a church building, for example) has vast ecclesiological consequences. It implies recognizing the strategic aspect of *mediation* at the places where Christians spend most of their time: at work, at home, at university.[9] In the university, this *mediation* can also be a prophetic foreshadowing of a restored humanity. In Tomlin's words, "the priesthood of Christ concerns the perfecting of humanity, rescuing it from its damaged, broken and filthy state, bringing it to its proper, cleansed and complete fulfilment, enabling it to become what it was intended to be."[10] Albeit in limited and still sinful ways, many of the core activities of universities consist precisely in devising solutions to humanity's problems and furthering the common good.

So from within the university, Christian students seized by the "news" of Christ's work have a message to pass on to fellow students: *ad extra*, informing non-Christians of the Christian message, and convincing them to explore its relevance to the concerns of their personal lives and academic disciplines. Setting witness in opposition to regular preaching, which addresses believers who are supposed to obey their Lord already, Congar underlines the importance of this lay witness:

> Witness is addressed to people outside the Church before they enter the Church community and participate in the mysteries it celebrates. It is the personal communication of a conviction possessed, a shock received, an experience made. . . . The word of the laity finds its place more especially at the missionary stage

---

8. Greggs, "Priesthood of No Believer," 394.

9. "Christians often feel most 'priestly,' in other words, standing in a mediating position between God and the rest of humanity, when they are at work, rather than when they are in church. Being known as a Christian in the workplace, at the school gate [in the university auditorium], in local clubs or sports fields, is to represent God in a very tangible and conscious way." Tomlin, *Widening Circle*, 109–10.

10. Tomlin, 33.

of the Church, where it must take root and where, not yet having its institutional activities, it exists only in the living faith of the faithful and through the communication of that faith.[11]

What Congar calls the "missionary stage" is exactly how a Christian campus group can be understood. Nevertheless, the missiological relevance of a student group is not limited to non-Christians. *Ad intra*, discoveries made at university should prompt Christian students to study their faith's cultural and eschatological relevance to their studies and their future lives in the workplace. Ultimately, this is all about human vocation: human beings were assigned, from the beginning, a priestly vocation that draws upon the whole of God's history with creation. In Tomlin's words,

> if the human race is called to play a priestly role between God and Creation, mediating God's love to the rest of Creation, enabling it to be what it was meant to be, offering it back to God in worship, then the Church plays a priestly role specifically towards the whole of humanity, mediating God's love to the rest of the human race and enabling it to play precisely the priestly role assigned to it.[12]

Missiologically speaking, such a view leads to a high view of contextualization. This puts high demands on student ministry, for it requires intense engagement with the university context, for "priesthood requires not only relationality with God but also relationality with other humans; in a nation of priests, priesthood is the very form of sociality that creates the community as a community which ministers God to each other and each other to God."[13] As Shaw stresses, contextualization forces interactive reflection, and it is from the interplay between people's understanding of God's intention for all human beings as well as for their particular environment that transformation takes place – that is, a transformation that is both true to God's intent and also relevant within the context.[14]

Deep questions arise as to the interplay between contextualization and theological orthodoxy, for mission *at the edges* easily implies a certain degree of confrontation with what people think and how they behave. This can

---

11. Yves Congar, *Jalons pour une théologie du laïcat*, 2nd ed., Unam sanctam 23 (Paris: Éditions du Cerf, 1954), 422.

12. Tomlin, *Widening Circle*, 95–96.

13. Greggs, "Priesthood of No Believer," 392.

14. R. Daniel Shaw, "Beyond Contextualization: Toward a Twenty-First-Century Model for Enabling Mission," *International Bulletin of Missionary Research* 34, no. 4 (Oct. 2010): 212.

challenge deeply held doctrinal convictions and cause much soul-searching. Yet precisely the idea that God is already at work in the world can sustain a robust engagement with its intricacies. Hardy argues from the historical study of Christian missionary encounters that

> it is possible, for example, to combine strong assertions about the universality of Christ with a dialogical engagement with other forms of life and thought, where a strong standard and content for theological orthodoxy is held together with open searching for the implications for, and in, history. In such a case, the one is not merely the background to the other but functions as the reason for searching for the meaning in the other. Or the conviction that God deals with human beings in history serves as the framework for searching with others to find where and how God does so.[15]

In the same vein, Walls lists three conditions necessary to establish a commitment to missionary ministry outside the realm of a "crusade framework." He first notes that Christians need to be ready to commit to "live on someone else's terms, together with the mental equipment for coping with the implications."[16] This "someone else" can be the university, with its methodological requirements or cultural context. Moreover, as Christians cannot dispense with a supportive community, Walls defends the need "for a form of organization which could mobilize committed people, maintain and supply them, and forge a link between them and their work and the wider church."[17] This can be the role of an IFES group and, at best, how a "parachurch" can work. It is fascinating to expand this "connection to the wider church" by considering the church spread across the world. The last element highlighted by Walls is "sustained access to overseas locations, with the capacity to maintain communication over long periods."[18] The IFES history bears witness to the fact that many of its members, upon encountering the wider fellowship – notably through international events – got a much broader sense and appreciation of the universality of the gospel and were encouraged by such cultural diversity.

Walls's remarks are congruent with what we saw of God's project with the people of Israel as a holy nation for the specific purpose of blessing

---

15. Hardy, "Upholding Orthodoxy," 219.
16. Andrew F. Walls, "The Missionary Movement a Lay Fiefdom?," in *The Rise of the Laity in Evangelical Protestantism*, ed. Deryck W. Lovegrove (London: Routledge Chapman & Hall, 2002), 172.
17. Walls, "Lay Fiefdom," 172.
18. Walls, 172.

the surrounding nations. Summarizing Wright's appreciation that Jesus's message means the end of Israel's exile, Leithart notes that "this 'return' has an ironic twist, for the last word of the gospels is not 'gather' or 'wait' but 'go.' By eliminating the 'center,' baptism to priesthood reverses the direction of cultural force, which now leads centrifugally to the four corners of the earth."[19] However, even if "to be a royal priesthood involves working for peace, for the full shalom and blessing of God,"[20] it should be borne in mind that the priestly mission of the church is only secondary to the *missio Dei* and does not originate with itself. In Tomlin's words, "the Church is the agent through which Christ, through the Holy Spirit, recalls humanity to its proper place, and restores it into his own image, so that it is capable of playing its divinely ordained role within the world."[21] Such a wide vision frames a ministry like IFES in much broader terms than if it was considered a mere ecclesiological *aside*: the vocation of Christian students on campus is part of God's mission, not only the result of a group of like-minded individuals surviving university life. And this life on campus is sometimes a difficult pilgrimage.

Pilgrimage and Priesthood in Mission

Participating in the *missio Dei* is a powerful incentive for mission. Yet many Christians live in challenging contexts. In many countries, they are marginalized and cannot dream of anything like a "revival" as they engage in mission. If "being sent" is an essential vocation of Christians, their *priestly calling* is often to *mediate* something not yet accepted or known in a given environment. This environment is God's creation in which he continually acts and communicates himself. This also means that God sustains his people in whatever context they live, including exile. Far away from home, the community played a crucial role in sustaining the faith of the people of Israel. The church has the same calling and so do Christian students in their universities. As we have seen, the campus can sometimes be a "distant land" or feel somewhat *foreign*.

In his *Pilgrims and Priests*, missiologist and former IFES staff member Paas explores the ins and outs of missionary presence in the post-Christendom

---

19. Leithart, *Priesthood of the Plebs*, 211–12.
20. Greggs, "Priesthood of No Believer," 395.
21. Tomlin, *Widening Circle*, 96.

context.[22] Writing from the secularized context of the Netherlands, he develops a *missional ecclesiology* focusing on the role, essence and vocation of the church. This ecclesiology applies well to our study, as it describes the *exilic* situation of Christians, and the necessity for them to reflect on how they relate to their environment and try to *mediate* their environment, notably by *living out* a calling and *inviting* others. Moreover, since the university is a major channel of Western influence worldwide, missiological considerations brewed in the West can have promising potential for ministry in universities throughout the world, even if they all need to be reflected upon locally.

Priests in Exile

In the West, the steady disappearance of Christendom structures – often summarized under the vocable "secularization" – represents a seismic shift which, as Paas argues, most models of "revival" or "church growth" fail to appreciate.[23] In this context, Paas criticizes one of the IFES mottos which extends the invitation to "change the world, one student at a time" as being an example of an outdated "historical matrix of revivalism and moral restoration"[24] linked to the gradual loss of Christian influence on culture in the twentieth century.

For Paas, the metaphor that more accurately describes the situation of Christians in the post-Christendom context is that of *exile*, defined as "a time of confusion; . . . characterized by a loss of power; [which] requires looking after one's own identity; and . . . asks for a renewed spirituality."[25] Many Christians have experienced this exilic situation. Paas's biblical-theological analysis embraces the whole scriptural narrative to focus essentially on 1 Peter. Like the exiled Israelites and the early church, Christians in the West are in

---

22. Stefan Paas, *Pilgrims and Priests: Christian Mission in a Post-Christian Society* (London: SCM, 2019). As Paas has a background in IFES and has published his work recently, I chose to focus on his approach. Yet he is far from the only author to draw upon this notion of "pilgrimage" – notably *Ad gentes*, and, more broadly, of "resident aliens." See, for example, William Stringfellow, *An Ethic for Christians and Other Aliens in a Strange Land* (Waco: Word, 1973); Stanley Hauerwas and William Willimon, *Resident Aliens: Life in the Christian Colony* (Nashville: Abingdon, 1989).

23. This is obviously not the place to provide even a cursory sketch of this extraordinary change. Deep analyses can be read in Owen Chadwick, *The Secularization of the European Mind in the Nineteenth Century* (Cambridge: Cambridge University Press, 1975); Charles Taylor, *A Secular Age* (Cambridge: Harvard University Press, 2007); Mary Eberstadt, *How the West Really Lost God: A New Theory of Secularization* (West Conshohocken: Templeton Press, 2013); Peter Harrison, "Narratives of Secularization," *Intellectual History Review* 27, no. 1 (2 Jan. 2017): 1–6.

24. Paas, *Pilgrims and Priests*, 67.

25. Paas, 217.

a diaspora situation "where Christian beliefs or lifestyles have no plausibility whatsoever."[26] While this loss of plausibility does not necessarily imply that "you are ostracized, it does mean that the boundaries of your social space are usually prescribed by others."[27] This is disorienting and difficult, hence "the metaphor of pilgrimhood [which] highlights the rediscovery of the essential alien and marginalized nature of the Christian community in the world, [and] the priesthood image [which] helps us understand its missional calling."[28] An important dimension of this potential is that exile does not preclude *immediate access* to God. A sustained faith and a lively missionary engagement are possible because they do not rely solely on external supporting structures.

The core of the priestly dimension of the argument in 1 Peter refers to specific moments in Israel's history, the desert wanderings and the Babylonian exile, times "characterized by mobility and mission."[29] Yet exile does not hinder witness, and Paas sees this marginal position as congenial to the priestly logic: "Priests are a minority community by definition, who find their calling in seeking the peace of the city. There is nothing odd or imperfect about a minority church; on the contrary, it is its 'natural' position."[30] How then are such minority groups to relate to their environment? Paas's affirmation of the *priestly calling* of the people of God – the church – rests on the work of biblical scholars exploring the "priestly dimension" of biblical anthropology,[31] that is, "our mediating role between God and the rest of his creation . . . [which] is presented as a temple that is built for the glory of God, where humans are appointed as priests to lead creation into worship and extend God's blessing to creation."[32] Such a positive vision calls for a deliberate move for Christians to see a context where they are marginalized as a springboard for missional engagement.

Engaging with the Environment

If the church builds upon the priestly vocation of the people of Israel to be a channel of blessing for the nations, it can be seen "as the priest of humanity,

---

26. Paas, 247.
27. Paas, 243.
28. Paas, 250.
29. Paas, 250.
30. Paas, 297.
31. Notably John H. Walton, *The Lost World of Genesis One* (Downers Grove: InterVarsity Press, 2009).
32. Paas, *Pilgrims and Priests*, 249.

who offers praise to God on behalf of the world out of which she is chosen. Reversely, it is also true that she stands before the world as a priest, as God's servant."[33] Paas further contends that "the Church is a 'showcase', a sign of God's purposes with his creation. As a kingdom of priests, Israel was to be a model of dedication to God; it was to be transparent towards God for all peoples."[34]

If the church's vocation is to prolong Israel's calling, the traditional understanding of the doctrine of "the priesthood of all believers" can be widened towards missiological thinking. Voss credits Barth for this move, as his "emphasis on the missionary nature of the priesthood of all believers represents a paradigmatic shift."[35] The basic idea behind Barth's argument is that "the ontological union of believers with Christ has already made each member a sharer in Christ's priesthood."[36] Consequently, the sending of the disciples into their respective environments derives from Christ's sending into the world and applies to all Christians, without the need of any ordination other than baptism.[37] This ministry, as Voss summarizes Barth, "is first and foremost a ministry of proclamation, and the vocation of the royal priesthood is thus a vocation of witness."[38]

Following on from Barth, missional church theologians like Newbigin and Guder, to name only a few, have either implicitly or explicitly argued for a recovery of the priestly dimension of the Christian vocation to foster missional engagement with the world.[39] Similarly, the Lausanne Covenant emphatically affirms that "Christ sends his redeemed people into the world as the Father sent him, and . . . this calls for a similar deep and costly penetration of the world. We need to break out of our ecclesiastical ghettos and permeate non-Christian society."[40]

Being a "showcase" in the world implies thoughtfully engaging with the context in which Christians find themselves and not only focusing on what is

---

33. Paas, 255–56.

34. Paas, 258.

35. Henry J. Voss, "The Priesthood of All Believers and the *Missio Dei*: A Canonical, Catholic, and Contextual Perspective" (PhD thesis, Wheaton, 2013), 254.

36. Voss, "Priesthood of All Believers," 240.

37. Voss, 235.

38. Voss, 235.

39. Bevans and Schroeders argue that Newbigin had an indirect influence on the RCC, because his missiological thinking found its way into "*Ad Gentes*"; see Bevans and Schroeder, *Constants in Context*, 290–91.

40. Lausanne Movement, "Lausanne Covenant," para. 6.

sinful in the world. Commenting on Paul and Barnabas's speech in Lystra in Acts 14, Paas pointedly notes that it is

> quite contrary to the traditional revivalistic evangelism that many modern Christians are familiar with. Apparently, the Apostles do not find it necessary to point out to these Gentiles what they are lacking (and then present Jesus as the solution); rather they describe the abundance of blessing in their lives, and they invite them to give a proper liturgical response to such abundance.[41]

Such a positive vision has strong potential for how Christians consider the world they inhabit, and study, work or retire in. This also could mean "[overcoming] the pietist heritage that always wants to point the world towards its deficits, offering Jesus as the solution to fill the gaps."[42] Moreover, appreciation for what is done in the world is doxological if "doxology is all about the recognition of God as God; it is to acknowledge him as the creator and sustainer of all that is alive, the one who has saved us from sin and judgement."[43] This has vast missiological consequences:

> This "model" of the priestly church thus meets the requirements about doing mission in a culture that we no longer dominate morally or in any other way. What might have been a source of embarrassment and frustration (the goodness of so many non-Christians) now becomes a source of gratitude to a God of so much mercy.[44]

In a missionary context, and especially in the university, a "source of [potential] embarrassment" can refer not only to the character of non-Christians, but also, and maybe even more pressingly, to academic achievements. In an engagement with the university context and especially with students, staff and professors, it is crucial to keep in mind the importance of the personal encounter, especially given the growing diversity of university campuses. Paas stresses that "it is impossible to objectify or 'reify' someone's personality; you cannot study it from a distance. Precisely then the other's being-a-person will elude you. . . . What is necessary for scientific analysis, namely, disengagement and objectification, precludes a personal encounter."[45] This is why missionary

---

41. Paas, *Pilgrims and Priests*, 257.
42. Paas, 308.
43. Paas, 316.
44. Paas, 308.
45. Paas, 279.

training needs to be fuelled by embeddedness in the life of and love for the environment in which *mediation* occurs, an aspect to which we shall return in the last part of this work.[46] The crucial question to ask is,

> what is God doing in our neighbourhood? How does he want to involve us? How can we as a priesthood present the questions, the joy and the needs of this neighbourhood to God in worship, and how can we bless the lives of people on behalf of God and his story?[47]

Note the emphasis on the *communal* dimension. The church or student group "is not primarily a loose collection of individual 'priests,' but a priestly community . . . spiritually there is an 'us' that precedes 'me.' God is in a relation with 'us' and through this with 'me' – not the other way around."[48] Neither the personal life of a Christian, nor his or her witness, can be sustained in *exile* without the community, and the end of the Christendom era might be a providential moment fostering this reckoning.

A Missional Community

Crucial to Paas's understanding of priesthood as a *showcase* is its tangible character. Indeed, "there must be a community where salvation is real, even if provisionally and partially. This community is the Church."[49] Correspondingly, the church is not "an 'extra' or a useful addition to the real thing. She belongs essentially to what God does with humans."[50] The community's existence is evidence that the gospel has the redemptive power Christians pretend it has. To argue then that the "priesthood of all believers" means that Christians have *personal* and *immediate* access to God in no way diminishes the need for community involvement. As Paas adamantly affirms,

> insofar as believers participate in the Church they are members of the "priestly community" (*hierateuma*), and consequent on this they are also priests individually. But the order is crucial. God does not appoint individuals as priests in order to bring them

---

46. Greggs argues along similar lines, emphasizing that priestly mission is fundamentally an act of *love* towards others. Greggs, *Priestly Catholicity*, 418–20.
47. Paas, *Pilgrims and Priests*, 301–2.
48. Paas, 277.
49. Paas, 283.
50. Paas, 283.

subsequently together in a congregation. Precisely the opposite is true: by virtue of their baptism Christians are joined with Christ, embedded in the Church, and only thus they receive priestly status.[51]

Paas mostly comments on "Fresh Expressions" of the church and similar structures, which, however, he sees with a certain degree of scepticism. Yet he also concedes that

> under certain conditions such an extra-ecclesial group may surely develop into a community that is rooted within the Christian tradition, offers a safe and inspiring home for the soul, engages missionally with its neighbourhood, and maintains fruitful relations with other Christian communities. But if that happens, then in my view this group is no longer outside the Church.[52]

Applying Paas's argument to IFES then means questioning the ecclesial character of IFES groups. The logical consequence of such an argument is that, ultimately, an IFES group has indeed an ecclesial character. It is neither *outside the church* nor *beyond* or *beside* it. Yet essential to being part of the church are the relationships entertained with the rest of the body, which means that an IFES group is part of the church but cannot presume itself to *be* "the church." Here, the argument about the "priesthood of all believers" comes full circle: Christians can be fully *priests* if they are *members* of a community and not on their own. The same applies to an IFES group, which, though it has the same calling as a church, cannot be church "on its own." Community membership is inherent to missional existence.

Complete embeddedness in the Christian tradition is of utmost importance for the sustainability and breadth of the faith. As Newbigin emphasizes,

> if we are to be in truth a holy priesthood, we need a secret altar, a place in our innermost life where, day by day, we offer to God through Jesus Christ every bit of our lives, our most secret thoughts and our most public actions, and where we receive afresh through Christ God's ever-new gift of grace and mercy.[53]

Such insistence on personal commitment certainly fits the early (pietistic) IFES discourse and is coherent with Paas's insistence on the importance of

---

51. Paas, 272–73.
52. Paas, 271.
53. Lesslie Newbigin, "An X-Ray to Make God Visible in the World," *Reform* (1990): 7.

personal missionary spirituality. Furthermore, for Christians to withdraw from "formal" ecclesial membership would negate one of the essential aspects of their Christian identity: fruitful engagement with and mutual upbuilding within the broader body of Christians. Paas issues strong warnings against any aspiration to limit Christian existence to an individual "quiet time" which he deems akin to Gnosticism: "the individual bonds with an invisible, spiritual church or with an idealistic kingdom of God, without engaging with a concrete, human community of Christ in a local congregation that is connected with other congregations."[54] Muthiah similarly notes that "within the priesthood of all believers, an individual's identity and spiritual formation are rooted in a communal structure grounded in God's narrative. A person's identity is connected to a tradition. A person's identity is formed in relation to others. Christian identity formation in fact assumes a communal context."[55]

Consequently, arguing from the doctrine of the "priesthood of all believers" does not reinforce individualistic tendencies all-too-easily caught and developed in a competitive university context. Instead, it means helping students to see how they are part of a broader body, the church, for "salvation is ecclesiological; it means being incorporated into the people of God, the body of Christ. To belong to Christ is to belong to his Church; there is no other way."[56] Such missiological considerations should provide a helpful corrective to what Paas calls "hyper-Protestant views [in which] more often than not the Church is seen as the sum of (saved, sanctified) individuals who join together based on their own preferences."[57] Lutz argues along similar lines for a missional understanding of student ministry. In his view, missionally minded groups "come together in community *to preach the gospel to themselves and to help each other share it with others*. They come together for prayer, encouragement, and equipping. They come together to model the kind of community into which they're inviting others."[58]

A student group is, then, pneumatologically speaking, much more than an "affinity group." It is a context in which students might encounter Christian faith, for "God saves people by bringing them into a community with Christ and

---

54. Paas, *Pilgrims and Priests*, 272. It is safe to assume that the challenge of bodily Christian community will only become more pressing, as the long-term effects of the COVID pandemic remain to be seen.

55. Muthiah, *Priesthood of All Believers*, Kindle loc. 2820.

56. Paas, *Pilgrims and Priests*, 274.

57. Paas, 273.

58. Stephen Lutz, *College Ministry in a Post-Christian Culture* (Kansas City: House Studio, 2011), 609; emphasis added.

thus with others."⁵⁹ Qualifying such community as having "priestly character" aptly describes what happens when individuals encounter the lived gospel in a vibrant student group that is simultaneously the *mediator* and the place where the encounter takes place. Paas firmly insists that gathered Christian communities "proclaiming the mighty acts of God" are "the most visible, structured and public expression of the priesthood of the Church."⁶⁰ Even if he does not underline the role of Bible reading in his argument, the communal aspect of such groups can decisively be fostered by scriptural engagement. Lastly, if Paul in Romans 15:16 understands witness to be a service to God, there is an eminently prophetic anticipation of the eschatological gathering of the nations under the lordship of Christ:

> The future role of the faith community as priests has become reality in the present. The Christian Church praises God, also on behalf of those who do not (yet) praise him it welcomes converts as first signs of the harvest that is to come, and it goes out to invite the nations to the great wedding feast. And all this stands under the sign of God who works at the perfect restoration of his creation.⁶¹

Note the emphasis on the universality and essentially missional character of the church's vocation. If this holds true for the church, it can easily be transferred to a missionary student community. This missionary nature of the church co-occurs in two directions:

> The priest metaphor defines the missionary nature of the Church as a dual movement: the Church represents the world before God and she represents God before the world. She comes into the presence of God as a worshipping, praising, liturgical community and she engages with the world in a witnessing, inviting, friendly way.⁶²

Partial Synthesis

The post-Christendom situation of the West echoes many other contexts in the world where Christians are a small minority in society. This is what the Bible calls "exile." Yet, as the biblical story and the history of the church testify, God

---

59. Paas, *Pilgrims and Priests*, 287.
60. Paas, 256.
61. Paas, 322–23.
62. Paas, 260.

is faithful in exile and calls his people to be his witnesses wherever they are. This chapter has shown that the metaphors of "pilgrimage" and "priesthood" aptly describe the limitations and promises of challenging situations. Loving, listening to and caring for the context in which believers find themselves is what is called for, in line with their allegiance to their missionary God. Yet this witness is not the consequence of an individualistic notion of priesthood, but the outworking of a missionary faith sustained in the context of a supportive community.

"Priesthood" is a dual movement of *mediation*: an invitation to *participation* in God's community and the gathering to God of the first fruits of the nations. Most of what Paas argues for the church applies to student groups: students, members of the church qua Christians and supported by the church, are the scattered *pilgrim priests* of the church in the university, ministering in distinctive ways shaped by the missiological acumen necessary for faithful contextualization. Such faithful missionary presence means inviting others to experience God's presence. This represents a *mediation* of the gospel, as loving and serving one's neighbour are intrinsically priestly dimensions of service. Missionary engagement in the university is ultimately doxological, as priestly service to God and the nations, as the local student groups can be the *display-people* on campus of God's renewed humanity, a *missional community* inviting others to join in this eschatological foretaste.

In the next chapter, I explore how contextual engagement and mission are articulated in the notion of "apostolicity."

18

Apostolicity, Theology and Missionary Expansion

Having seen how Allen's thinking helps articulate leadership and church organization issues, how a "ministry at the edges" is elevated by considering its role in the *missio Dei*, and how even in challenging contexts Christian "exiles" can be courageous witnesses, another pressing missiological question is how theological and missional reflections are shaped by geographical expansion and contextualization.

The doctrine of the "priesthood of all believers" presumes locality and maturity. The logic of *immediacy*, which I have argued is integral to the doctrine, presupposes the possibility of relating to God wherever one finds oneself, geographical foreignness to supposed "theological centres" notwithstanding. It also presupposes maturity in spiritual and hermeneutical discernment: if God speaks to individuals, then these individuals' encounters with God and their world are an integral part of the experience of the body of Christ. As Christianity has spread across the world, the question of *mediation* has become more and more acute: not only is the gospel *mediated* by Christians, but they, in turn, *mediate* back their encounters with their environment – for students, cultural and academic – to their local churches and, in turn, theologically enrich the wider fellowship of which they are *members*.

In many quarters of evangelicalism, and certainly within IFES, "apostolicity" has been understood as relating to the "deposit of the teaching of the apostles." It can also be understood as the *missional character of the church*: to be "apostolic" means to be "sent." Such a view, which I examine in dialogue with Flett's recent *Apostolicity*,[1] does better justice to the priestly dimension of witness, which I argue throughout this work, and is congruent to the notions of *missio Dei* and priestly pilgrimage examined above.

Theology in World Christianity

The history of missions often underlines the connection between "empire" and "mission."[2] In the context of world Christianity, the notion of a "deposit of the faith," albeit unquestionably biblical in origin, often runs against the flow of the development of a genuinely indigenous faith underscored by the "priesthood of all believers." Power dynamics often mark relationships between theological "powerhouses" such as the United States and the United Kingdom, and the rest of the world, either directly or via the education of non-Westerners. As Walls astutely observes,

> like the old Jerusalem Christians, Western Christians [have] long grown used to the idea that they were guardians of a "standard" Christianity; also like them, they find themselves in the presence of new expressions of Christianity, and new Christian lifestyles that have developed or are developing under the guidance of the Holy Spirit to display Christ under the conditions of African, Indian, Chinese, Korean, and Latin American life.[3]

If this is true, the sheer diversity of the church should forbid any aspiration of one part of the body to dominate the narrative and the theologizing, or to decide for the rest which are the "essentials" of the faith. Flett observes that the idea of a "deposit of the faith" often "assumes the normativity of the 'European experience' and attempts to 'exercise control' over non-Western appropriations of the gospel through the insistence on the binding character of [the Western church's] formulation of the meaning of the Christian fact and Euro-American patterns of fellowship and worship."[4]

Stanley also observes the difficulty for certain quarters of evangelicalism – and this certainly applies to IFES – in acknowledging a degree of relativity to their own formulae:

---

1. Flett, *Apostolicity*.
2. Brian Stanley and Alaine Low, eds., *Missions, Nationalism, and the End of Empire* (Grand Rapids: Eerdmans, 2003); World Council of Churches, "Mission in the Context of Empire."
3. Andrew F. Walls, *The Cross-Cultural Process in Christian History: Studies in the Transmission and Appropriation of Faith* (Maryknoll: Orbis, 2002), 78.
4. Flett, *Apostolicity*, 27.

> Evangelical Christians, because of their proper concern to preserve the good deposit of the faith, have tended to be particularly hesitant about admitting the dynamically interactive and two-way nature of all true missionary encounters. They have sometimes been slow to realize that a primary focus on the substitutionary death of Christ for the penalty of human sin may not be a wholly intelligible or even theologically adequate interpretation of the gospel for some peoples from a primal religious background.[5]

Walls also astutely observes that

> the representation of Christ by any one group can at best be only partial. At best it reflects the conversion of one small segment of reality, and it needs to be complemented and perhaps corrected by others. The fullness of humanity lies in Christ; the aggregate of converted lifestyles points toward his full stature.[6]

As theological leaders emerge from the former "edges" of the church, the question of the local appropriation of the faith is becoming increasingly important. This geographical extension entails cross-cultural encounters that impact the way theology is conceived. As Flett insists, "we must acknowledge that no single theological tradition already possesses an 'international' culture, one justifiably so concerned with its purity to fear the integration of other appropriations of the gospel."[7] These appropriations are not marginal, but they have "sufficient theological merit to inform and challenge settled elements within the received Western tradition."[8]

This runs against the idea that the "apostolic deposit" would be sufficiently solid to protect the church against schismatic tendencies. Flett adamantly argues that a sole concentration on "cultivating" the deposit logically predisposes the church to self-maintenance over against *missional engagement*. In Flett's words,

> apostolicity, the historical continuity of the church, rests in the event of cross-cultural encounter and the processes of conversion

---

5. Brian Stanley, "Conversion to Christianity: The Colonization of the Mind?," *International Review of Mission* 92, no. 366 (1 July 2003): 322.

6. Andrew F. Walls, "Globalization and the Study of Christian History," in *Globalizing Theology: Belief and Practice in an Era of World Christianity*, eds. Craig Ott and Harold A. Netland (Grand Rapids: Baker, 2006), 74. Conversely, suspicion of "syncretism" in the theological formulations of "others" betrays a lack of awareness of the cultural embeddedness of one's own tradition; cf. Flett, *Apostolicity*, 247.

7. Flett, 185.

8. Flett, 158–59.

through the local appropriation of the gospel. This history is not the settled and measured development of a cultural entity but is marked by multiple instances of cross-cultural encounter and sometimes radical shifts in thinking. At base, world Christianity refuses the controlling duality of the cultivation of the faith over its proclamation. This liberates apostolicity to be construed in new ways.[9]

Hence "'safeguarding the deposit' refers not to the repetition of established forms but to their communication so that they are received by and shape the hearers."[10]

Mission and Apostolicity

The growing importance of world Christianity also evidences the universal dimension of a gospel responding to human beings' aspirations, dreams and needs.[11] This witnesses to the "translatability" of the gospel message better than the vindication of the idea of "spreading a fully defined message."[12] In pointed terms that resonate with Allen's arguments, Flett notes the positive potential of new openings:

> World Christianity is no emergency situation for which a range of accommodations might be made, a unique event detached from the continuum of Christian theology. Quite the opposite is true. World Christianity opens the theological field because it detaches that discourse from a singular concentration on a constricted history and its attendant range of questions.[13]

Similarly, student ministry is no emergency situation despite its constant fluctuations but rather represents trends of thought and action that will characterize the church of tomorrow. Thus, it can function as a model for how the church can relate to its environment. Another way of conceptualizing this "detachment" is to speak, although always in a derivative way, of the central

---

9. Flett, 288.

10. Flett, 285.

11. For a vivid narrative account, see Andrew F. Walls, "The Gospel as Prisoner and Liberator of Culture," in *The Missionary Movement in Christian History: Studies in the Transmission of Faith* (Maryknoll: Orbis, 1996), 3–15.

12. See Lamin O. Sanneh, *Translating the Message: The Missionary Impact on Culture* (Maryknoll: Orbis, 1989).

13. Flett, *Apostolicity*, 245.

Christian doctrine of the *incarnation*, implying that the Christian message commands "embodiment in the cultural specifics of a particular time and place. Generations may be utterly diverse, therefore, in their understanding and experience of the grace of God and yet belong together in the ultimate purpose of God."[14]

Richer than copy-and-pasting is the organic metaphor. A seed needs interaction with its environment, and plants will grow differently from one soil to another.[15] In his influential booklet, Idowu paints a vivid picture: the "deposit of the faith" can be understood as a flowing river,

> bringing from and depositing in each place something of the chemical wealth of the soils which it encounters on its way, at the same time adapting itself to the shape and features of each locality, taking its colouring from the native soil, while in spite of all these structural adaptations and diversifications its *esse* and its differentia are not *imperilled* but maintained in consequence of the living, ever-replenishing, ever-revitalizing spring which is its source.[16]

The image adequately reflects what has been happening throughout the history of the church. Almost inadvertently, in its "encounters," the deposit of the faith has been fertilized as it has flowed throughout the world. So Flett makes the argument that the observation of the development of Christianity across the world necessitates some serious rethinking of what apostolicity means. He contends that apostolicity consists first in the believer's grounding in Christ; second, and consequently, in his or her being "sent" as an apostle (understood in the broadest sense). Indeed, "Christian theology is expanding as it comes into contact with new areas of human experience, new accumulations

---

14. Walls, "Globalization," 76. For Blocher, the widely used notion of "incarnation" in missiological circles runs the risk of diminishing the unique character of Christ's incarnation, as human beings cannot but be incarnate; see Henri Blocher, "Permanent Validity and Contextual Relativity of Doctrinal Statements," in *The Task of Dogmatics*, ed. Fred Sanders (Grand Rapids: Zondervan, 2017), 117.

15. For a contemporary exploration of the topic by someone close to IFES circles, see Pauline Hoggarth, *The Seed and the Soil: Engaging with the Word of God* (Carlisle: Langham Global Library, 2011). See also Pope Paul VI, "*Ad Gentes*," sec. 22.

16. Emanuel Bolaji Idowu, *Towards an Indigenous Church* (Oxford: Oxford University Press, 1965), 19; quoted in Flett, *Apostolicity*, 177. Idowu's early approach is considered "broadly evangelical" by Demarest, former IFES Theological Secretary; see Bulus Galadima, "Evaluation of the Theology of Bolaji Idowu," *Africa Journal of Evangelical Theology* 20, no. 2 (2001): 112.

of knowledge, relationship, and activity. Themes are being recognized in the scriptures that the West had never noticed."[17]

Flett argues that if "apostolicity" essentially consists in keeping a supra-cultural content which should prevent the church from schism, it follows that "cultivation of the faith" will be privileged over "communication," thereby belying the otherwise alleged missionary nature of the church.

Therefore, Flett argues that as the church fulfils its missionary calling, it realizes, *in communicating the gospel* – I could say *mediating the gospel* – to the world, that integral to its "apostolicity" is its own "sent-ness." In other words, the church becomes more aware of itself in witnessing "others" appropriating the gospel's claims in their lives and becoming members of the church.

Such encounters occur on the (exilic) front line, but rather than threatening the "little flock" of witnessing Christians, dialogical engagement is constitutive of the community. Making Hoekendijk's argument his own, Flett even contends that the missionary encounter is integral to the formation of the witnessing community:

> The people of the new covenant are constituted in the fulfilment of the messianic promises, becoming a sociological reality only in the missionary encounter with the world. Because the people of God is a novum of the new creation, its structure depends on the "missionary situation." And, since mission is basic to the Christian gospel, no occasion or location exists that might be characterized as non-missionary.[18]

Such logic capitalizes on the relative opening to improvisation and flexibility which has historically been granted to missionary situations and harnesses it for the whole mission of the church. Ultimately, "what is admissible *extra muros*, for the sake of the salvation of the nations, will have to be legitimately possible *intra muros*."[19] Here lies a theologically much stronger rationale for the existence of "parachurch" organizations than merely pragmatic reasoning arguing for the importance of considering the independent character of young people enjoying new experiences. Instead of a (clerical) condescending attitude "granting" some degree of provisional freedom to students à la "students

---

17. Andrew F. Walls, "Christianity in the Non-Western World," in *The Cross-Cultural Process in Christian History: Studies in the Transmission and Appropriation of Faith* (Maryknoll: Orbis, 2002), 46.

18. Flett, *Apostolicity*, 215.

19. Johannes Christiaan Hoekendijk, *The Church Inside Out* (Philadelphia: Westminster, 1966), 159; quoted in Flett, 217.

will be students," a renewed understanding of the church's mission leads to acknowledging that the adaptability some church leaders have grudgingly granted to student organizations is what all church members need, even if their contextual realities are very different from those of intellectuals in training. This, in turn, highlights the necessity to have all the "front lines" enrich the church through their experiences and help to expand its understanding of God's work in the world. Muthiah also forcefully argues that offices do not suffice to assess the ecclesial character of Christian communities: "When office is extracted from the *esse* of the church, and when relationships are tied to the ecclesiality of the church, the priesthood of all believers becomes central because the gathering of any two or three Christians, even if none of them are office holders, constitutes the church."[20] This has not only ecclesial implications but also more fundamentally theological ones emerging from listening to "other" voices.

The challenge for the church universal is the same as that for IFES: "the *obligation* to listen to and learn from one another,"[21] as a missional community first and foremost formed and called by God. None of this precludes common ground, especially as biblical and theological anthropology presume a certain degree of commonality between human beings. Contrary to what common parlance often assumes,

> we do live in the same world as Abraham did! When traveling in the Middle-East, we cross the same valleys as he did, we drink from the same sources, we gaze upon the same stars, we breathe the same air as he did. The same physical laws ruled the world millennia ago – and they must have some effect on ways of thinking themselves.[22]

This commonality offers a ground for mutual understanding: "To claim apostolicity is to claim legitimacy and recognition for a lived experience of the gospel."[23] None of this imperils Christian heritage. Yet Stanley notes that "the process of translating the message into a new cultural medium will result in a message that carries accents and tones which it did not carry before, even though there must be sufficient continuity with previous formulations of the

---

20. Muthiah, *Priesthood of All Believers*, Kindle loc. 1460–63.
21. Craig Ott, "Conclusion," in *Globalizing Theology: Belief and Practice in an Era of World Christianity*, eds. Craig Ott and Harold A. Netland (Grand Rapids: Baker, 2006), 310.
22. Blocher, "Permanent Validity," 119.
23. Flett, *Apostolicity*, 241.

message for it to be recognizably the same message."²⁴ Muthiah suggests that the *membership* of all Christians in a "priesthood of all believers" makes exactly this act of spiritual discernment possible, as it welcomes and affirms in the world the unity in diversity that constitutes the Trinity:

> The type of unity that marks the priesthood of all believers and that marks good discernment allows for differences and distinctions – in fact, this type of unity assumes that differences will exist. As within the Trinity, unity amongst the people of God requires difference. If there is no difference, there is nothing to unite. This type of unity transcends differences without ignoring them. The Spirit indwells and unites believers who engage well in the practice of discernment even when they hold different views on a given issue.²⁵

From the encounter with others, Christians or not, fruitful reframing or reaffirming of core convictions can ensue. As Skreslet summarizes, "truly missionary encounters in history are intense moments, full of unpredictability but also of promise. Old certainties about what is essential to Christianity may be tested and found wanting in these engagements."²⁶ The navigation of the uncharted waters of post-Christendom might be powerful incentives for rethinking how the church can be a missional presence and contribute to the world's life. And because many Christians have already "been there" for a long time, fruitful mutual learning and enriching can take place within world Christianity.

Partial Synthesis

> Christian identity is not secured within the borders of a single historical narrative that follows the contours of a supposed center of Christian power and the controls of form and interpretation managed by such. The church finds its identity beyond itself, in the history of Jesus Christ. In this resides the possibility of conversion, the possibility of multiple Christian histories.²⁷

---

24. Stanley, "Conversion to Christianity," 321.
25. Muthiah, *Priesthood of All Believers*, Kindle loc. 3799.
26. Stanley Skreslet, "Thinking Missiologically about the History of Mission," *International Bulletin of Missionary Research* 31, no. 2 (1 Apr. 2007): 62.
27. Flett, *Apostolicity*, 320.

Co-opting Flett's ecclesial logic for the sake of this work, it is reasonable to affirm in the same way that ecclesial existence does not exhaust all of what Christian existence means. Consequently, the "narrative of the student parachurch" is a valid domain of Christian experience that cannot be dispensed with by appealing to its supposedly defective ecclesial character. If so understood, student ministry is a powerful tool of the *missio Dei*, a tool which the Lord uses not only to reach students on campus, but to shape young people who will be thoughtful and bold church members, ready to serve in their congregations, ready to support the mission of their local churches, and equipped to think missiologically about the challenges their fellow parishioners encounter where they are called to serve. Student ministry then works as a training ground for future missionaries understood in the broadest of senses – serving interculturally in foreign lands or in the context of their professions or neighbourhoods. That said, not all service and partnerships need to be postponed to the time after graduation. On the contrary, "mission societies link up with the local church in new concrete ways, and local churches see themselves as 'missional' in their own context. The missionary band remains an integral part of being Church, but must always find new expressions in new contexts."[28] The encounter with the "other," characteristic of university life, has a missiological potential that can be unleashed and celebrated. Ultimately, what is at stake is a vision of God and his mission in the world. Either God has done all he had to do in history – or there is room for current and future action. A creed-conforming insistence on the incarnation, death, resurrection and ascension of Christ does not preclude a necessary discernment as to what God is doing in a world that constantly changes, in the lives of new people with new interests, dreams, concerns, sufferings.

Highlighting the importance of individuals and communities brings us back full circle to the notion that laypeople cannot be dispensed with, for they are at the centre of God's mission in the world. It furthermore provides a theological rationale for the "rediscovery of the laity" to which WCC circles came in the 1960s, thereby to some degree catching up with evangelical missionary practice. That said, Kraemer, Newbigin and their colleagues theorized this rediscovery in a much more thorough fashion than evangelicalism itself explained.[29]

---

28. Daryl M. Balia and Kirsteen Kim, eds., *Witnessing to Christ Today*, vol. 2 of *Edinburgh 2010* (Oxford: Regnum, 2010), 121.

29. See Newbigin's thinking about the role of the laity, astutely summarized in Michael W. Goheen, "The Missional Calling of Believers in the World: Lesslie Newbigin's Contribution," in *A Scandalous Prophet: The Way of Mission after Newbigin*, eds. Thomas F. Foust et al. (Grand Rapids: Eerdmans, 2001), 37–56.

The "priesthood of all believers" is an adequate descriptor of what a student ministry like IFES is: it involves lay students examining Scripture together, exploring the joys and challenges of fellowship. It involves manifold expressions of mission. These expressions are constantly reshaped in the encounter with the diversity of cultures and theologies characteristic of world Christianity.

Part 5

Some Ways Ahead

19

Student Ministry in the Light of the Priesthood of All Believers

So far, I have shown how the history of IFES and its ecclesiology have worked on the premise that students have *immediate* access to God and can therefore legitimately *mediate* him to their environment by being *participants* in a community. Such vision presumes a *missional ecclesiology*: the church's community manifested on campus, notably in the IFES group. I have surveyed biblical and theological resources which outline the contours of how the "priesthood of all believers" can frame our understanding of the ministry of IFES and how this premise is congruent with archival evidence.

In this chapter, I bring together all the preceding threads and offer a constructive missiological proposal for the way forward, still taking IFES as a starting point. Ministering to students requires careful consideration of the *contextual specificities of the university* as well as of the distinctives of *students as agents of mission*, notably their *intellectual* character. Moreover, IFES has occupied a historical front seat in the spread of Christianity across the globe. This geographical diversity can serve as a unique springboard for a more thorough theological reflection on *indigeneity* and *contextualization* as cultures, life experiences and challenges come together.

Immediacy in Relationship to God

Mostly implicit in the way IFES has understood its ministry is the doctrine of the "priesthood of all believers," which presupposes that Christians can relate to God *directly*, most notably through the individual and communal reading of Scripture. This understanding applies to students. Students do not need clerical supervision to organize themselves and *mediate* God on campus. The existence of a support structure like IFES implies that encouragement and mentoring are necessary, yet this rests on a functional understanding of the role of staff workers and not on ontological distinctions. Woods does not mince his words when he charges that

> to suggest that only a person with a seminary training and ecclesiastical ordination, which too often is merely the placing of empty hands upon an empty head and heart, is the only person qualified to take Christian initiative and assume responsibility under God for heralding the gospel is to deny the doctrine of the priesthood of all true believers.[1]

This is possibly the most explicit reference to the doctrine of the "priesthood of all believers" found in the IFES written documents, but significantly it emanates from its first and influential GS.[2] This notion of immediacy is missiologically essential, for it implies that God can work in any context through his people who are already in place. Students do not primarily attend university for missionary purposes, but because they are on campus and maintain their relationship to God individually and in groups they in fact serve as God's ambassadors in the university. Nevertheless, as Greggs astutely notes, *immediacy* is a shortcut to speak about a relationship that does not presuppose the necessity of human interference. For an "unmediated" relationship to God is impossible for pneumatological reasons with far-reaching ecclesiological consequences:

> When we are possessed by and of the Spirit, we are so in our mediated creaturely way in its fallenness: there is no unmediated, direct experience of God; that has to wait until God is all in all in the eschaton (1 Cor. 15:28). But in space and time, we do experience God's Spirit mediating to us God's eternal work of salvation in the creaturely media of our present, contingent, and fallen (but being redeemed) spatiotemporality.[3]

To consider the university as a "fallen (but being redeemed) spatiotemporality" has far-reaching missiological consequences, on which I

---

1. Woods, *Growth of a Work of God*, 62.

2. More recently, Brown published a short book highlighting the "priesthood of all believers" as one of the gospel essentials rediscovered by the Reformation; see Lindsay Brown, *Into All the World: The Missionary Vision of Luther and Calvin* (Fearn: Christian Focus, 2021).

3. Greggs, *Priestly Catholicity*, 30.

comment below. In IFES, the privileged channel of the *immediate* encounter with God is the reading of Scripture. The idea of reading Scriptures with non-Christians was and sometimes still is often not taken as self-evident in many contexts and could well be counted as one of the distinctives of the IFES approach, one which allows for the empowerment of many lay students worldwide. The fundamental theological conviction that the Bible can be read in any context was, in any case, historically far-sighted and an essential reason for the sustenance of the ministry of IFES.

Students as Participants in God's Mission

The second essential aspect in IFES's understanding – which can easily apply to other university ministries or to other missionary organizations – is that all Christians, by virtue of their calling, are made *participants* in God's mission. Congruent with the idea of *immediacy* outlined above, laypeople and not only ordained personnel are called. Bosch outlines how this understanding connects the role of the laity and missional engagement:

> Laypersons are no longer just the scouts who, returning from the "outside world" with eyewitness accounts and perhaps some bunches of grapes, report to the "operational basis"; they *are* the operational basis from which the *missio Dei* proceeds. It is, in fact, not *they* who have to "accompany" those who hold "special offices" *in the latter's mission in the world*. Rather, it is the *office bearers* who have to accompany the laity, the people of God.[4]

To be a Christian means to *participate* in the *mission of God*. The previous chapters of this work have shown that this logic has shaped IFES's self-understanding as a community on mission, despite this not being expressed in such condensed words. This mission unfolds through witness, Bible reading, prayer and community. This fits squarely with Wright's summary of the church's mission as "our committed participation as God's people, at God's invitation and command, in God's own mission within the history of God's world for the redemption of God's creation."[5] This applies equally to the mission of a student group. The campus is where most of these activities occur, but they are not intrinsically different from what takes place in a regular church meeting.

---

4. Bosch, *Transforming Mission*, 472. Bosch summarizes Johannes Christiaan Hoekendijk, *Kirche und Volk in der deutschen Missionswissenschaft*, trans. Erich-Walter Pollmann (Munich: Chr. Kaiser, 1967), 350.

5. Wright, *Mission of God*, 22–23.

Presumed here is a *missional ecclesiology* that presupposes that church leaders will essentially *empower* the laity to carry out their mission faithfully. As Escobar highlights,

> laymen then penetrate society by a way of life that is new in family relations, business, citizenship, and every area of daily life. Consequently, to mobilize the laymen is not only to teach them short summaries of the Gospel, mini-sermons, and to send them to repeat these to their neighbors. It is also to teach them how to apply the teaching and example of Christ in their family life, in their business activities, in their social relationships, in their studies, etc.[6]

Students are called just as any other Christian is called, and this call lasts their whole lives, not only the few years spent at university. Calling happens where people are and as they are: "Gentiles do not need to become Jews. Gentiles remain Gentiles and are valued as such in Christ, meaning that they are to turn their own way of life to him."[7] In the same way, students remain students and are addressed by God as such, with all that that entails. Woods gives a clarion call for Christians to evangelize wherever God calls them to be involved:

> Quiet, steady, continuous evangelism involving intercessory prayer and the study and preaching of the Scriptures is not a task for a selected, gifted few. It is not limited to the minister of the church and his ordained assistants. Rather, it is the privilege and responsibility of every Christian. Regardless of special gifts, all are called and commissioned to this task. Every Christian is a missionary sent by God, a witness to Jesus Christ, in his or her way a herald of the gospel. God's supreme method is men – men and women indwelt and filled with the Holy Spirit.[8]

IFES operates on the premise that students can be God's witnesses by virtue of their Christian calling. This is important for sociological and missiological reasons.

---

6. Samuel Escobar, "Evangelism and Man's Search for Freedom, Justice and Fulfillment," in *Let the Earth Hear His Voice*, ed. J. D. Douglas (Minneapolis: World Wide Publications, 1975), 324.

7. Flett, *Apostolicity*, 327.

8. Woods, *Some Ways*, 106.

Students as a Specific Constituency

The unique time when young people study is characterized by a certain opening of mind and greater freedom to explore options and opinions. This creates a twofold opportunity: for Christian students to broaden their horizons, and for non-Christians to consider the Christian faith. This "freedom" has multiple variations globally: Chua notes that "each student is a 'man-in-community.' In terms of evangelism and discipleship we cannot ignore his family setting, cultural background and value system and religious world-view."[9] Hence the link between freedom and tradition can be complex. Having observed Latin American students in revolutionary times, Voelkel notes the specificities of the student constituency:

> The student's idealism carries him to a wholehearted enthusiasm for any cause deemed just, but his physical energy and impatience demand instant participation. He longs to see something get moving, and thus responds to protests, parades, rock throwing, and even violence. He wants to be involved, mind and body, in the activity of the moment. He wants to see it, talk it, write it, feel it, and cry it.[10]

If Voelkel is right, a ministry that leaves enough freedom for students to take responsibility and to have a say in how things are done has more potential for growth and persistence, including in times of unexpected crisis,[11] than would a ministry that is more directive. Moreover, Voelkel hints at one of the main reasons for some of the tensions between student life and church life: the possibility of being involved at every level in activism, which characterizes student-led groups, in contradistinction to church structures. Finally, the fact that most students involved in IFES groups are relatively young is important for wider mission training: "Because students are young and open to take risks, evangelical student movements have created models of sensitive multicultural mission teams. Participants in them have been able to look at their own culture from a critical distance."[12]

---

9. Chua Wee Hian, "Staff Letter 6" (May 1973), 6, BGC Box #5.

10. Voelkel, *Student Evangelism*, 47.

11. A significant part of this work was written during the COVID-19 pandemic, when it was astonishing to see the creativity and resilience of many student groups worldwide. They carried on meeting online, inviting their friends, organizing "outreaches" online, etc. This could not have happened if only staff-driven.

12. Escobar, "A New Time for Mission," 8.

This situation appears time and again in testimonies found in IFES archival documents or published stories. Contemporary sociologists tell a similar story: "In my interviews with them, these students often relished the chance for leadership, as one person affirmed, 'It's not so much like you're going to church, and you're listening to someone speak. It's like you're involved and you're making the whole thing happen.'"[13] Hence the necessity to carefully assess the context of missionary engagement with students, both for those who are already Christians and for those who are invited to become members of the Christian community.

Contextualization for the University

On university campuses, Christian students are often minorities. In biblical-theology terms, their situation resembles that of exile which I explored above. This has been the case since the foundation of IFES movements in many countries for ethnic and cultural reasons, and increasingly also in the West because of secularization. Still, even if students are *exiles* because they are Christians, they are nevertheless integral members of the campus culture. This is certainly an observable phenomenon for many Christian groups on campuses in the world. Like the first readers of 1 Peter, Christian students often "are part of their [university] culture all the way down, yet simultaneously they have become alienated from the [academic] world through their encounter with Christ."[14]

Volf contends that a view of culture – here easily transferred to the context of the campus – should be determined by the fact that students are already *insiders* of the campus on the one hand, but also that eschatology should shape the imagination:

> The question of how to live in a non-Christian environment . . . does not translate simply into the question of whether one adopts or rejects the social practices of the environment. This is the question outsiders ask, who have the luxury of observing a culture from a vantage point that is external to that culture. Christians do not have such a vantage point since they have experienced a new birth as inhabitants of a particular culture. Hence they are in an important sense insiders. As those who are a part of

---

13. Alyssa Bryant, "Evangelicals on Campus: An Exploration of Culture, Faith and College Life," *Religion & Education* 32, no. 2 (2005): 10.

14. Paas, *Pilgrims and Priests*, 246.

the environment from which they have diverted by having been born again and whose difference is therefore internal to that environment, Christians ask, "Which beliefs and practices of the culture that is ours must we reject now that our self has been reconstituted by new birth? Which can we retain? What must we reshape to reflect better the values of God's new creation?"[15]

As an evangelical movement stressing the importance of scriptural engagement for its mission, IFES always insists that Volf's complex exercise in cultural discernment is possible only if personal piety is primary. It usually focuses on devotional Bible reading, communally and individually. But the discernment exercise he calls for is not easy if one is indeed part of a given culture – "stepping back" from one's context is never easy – and this is where the help of brothers and sisters from world Christianity can help, being at the same time members of the people of God but with different cultural sensitivities.[16] This fits well with IFES's understanding of missionary engagement flowing out of the student's *personal relationship* to God – presented above as *immediate* and lived out in the community. But God's calling, in line with the priestly logic examined earlier, is always for Christians to be a blessing to others. This unfolds in a process I have called *mediation*.

Priestly Mediation

The biblical-theology part of this work has argued that this aspect of the Christian life can be adequately understood as "priestly," for it assumes the importance of mediating between God and the context. Bishop Neill's missiological observation applies well to our discussion about student leadership: "The Christian layman should be fired by imaginative sympathy with his world, wholly identified with it in its needs, though wholly independent of it in its mistaken desires. He must listen before he speaks, and make no hasty or over-confident judgments."[17] This last sentence stresses a core missiological assumption: being a missionary means listening to the people one wants to

---

15. Miroslav Volf, "Soft Difference: Theological Reflections on the Relation between Church and Culture in 1 Peter," *Ex Auditu* 10 (1994): 19, http://www.pas.rochester.edu/~tim/study/Miroslav%20Volf%201%20Peter.pdf.

16. For a distinctively evangelical approach, see Paul G. Hiebert, "Critical Contextualization," *Missiology* 12, no. 3 (July 1984): 287–96.

17. Stephen Neill, "Introduction," in *The Layman in Christian History: A Project of the Department of the Laity of the World Council of Churches*, by Hans Ruedi Weber and Stephen Neill (London: SCM, 1963), 26.

reach. The world is growing more complex and more diverse despite the unifying forces of globalization. Any ministry must be concerned about being truly respectful of its context to avoid exporting forms of belief which are the product of cultural blindfolds or political captivities. Since Christianity is the religion of translation, its universality and relevance for everyone on earth need not be doubted. Consequently, no "one size fits all" strategy will do justice to the diversity of God's creatures.[18]

Consequently, it is missiologically crucial to consider students as a specific public. University studies have traditionally implied broadening horizons by examining different perspectives, solutions and approaches for the future.[19] Divergent relationships to received knowledge characterize different university cultures, but most higher education institutions at least pay lip service to the importance of personal critical thinking in engaging with tradition. This socialization includes teaching and mentoring in the academic sense – notably the induction in the social practices that academic disciplines are[20] – and social relationships in a more general sense, either through common life on the university campus or through daily interaction with peers.

Christian student communities can showcase the relevance of the Christian faith – being a "display-people" on campus by being a community foreshadowing God's design for humanity. Similarly, student groups mediate God to the campus by inviting others to experience a relationship with God as individuals and within the community and in turn gather the first fruits of

---

18. On this, see among others Walls, *Missionary Movement in Christian History*; Sanneh, *Whose Religion Is Christianity?* More recently, Watkin has explored how the biblical narrative "diagonalizes" questions of universality and particularity. See Christopher Watkin, *Biblical Critical Theory: How the Bible's Unfolding Story Makes Sense of Modern Life and Culture* (Grand Rapids: Zondervan Academic, 2022).

19. As the literature on universities from a Christian perspective is vast, the reader might refer to John Henry Newman, *Idea of a University* (London: Longmans, Green & Co., 1852); Charles Habib Malik, *A Christian Critique of the University* (Waterloo: North Waterloo Academic Press, 1987); Douglas V. Henry and Michael D. Beaty, *Christianity and the Soul of the University: Faith as a Foundation for Intellectual Community* (Grand Rapids: Baker, 2006); Stanley Hauerwas, *The State of the University: Academic Knowledges and the Knowledge of God*, Illuminations – Theory and Religion (Malden: Blackwell, 2007); Gavin D'Costa, "The State of the University: Academic Knowledges and the Knowledge of God," *Pro Ecclesia* 20, no. 3 (2011): 312–16; Higton, *Theology of Higher Education*; Card. Pio Laghi, Card. Eduardo Pironi, and Card. Paul Poupard. "The Presence of the Church in the University and in University Culture", 1994. https://www.vatican.va/roman_curia/pontifical_councils/cultr/documents/rc_pc_cultr_doc_22051994_presence_fr.html.

20. Discussions of the fact that academic disciplines are "social practices" into which students are introduced abound. For a compelling overview, see Jerome Kagan, *Three Cultures: Natural Sciences, Social Sciences, and the Humanities in the 21st Century* (Cambridge: Cambridge University Press, 2009).

redemption and engage in doxological appreciation for what the university does: "Mission work is priestly work; it is about the gathering of the 'first fruits' and then offering these as a sacrifice to God."[21]

Hence, in line with the *priestly calling* of Israel and its prolongation in the church, students *mediate* between God and their environment in two main ways: intellectual and international.

Intellectual Mediation

One of the challenges encountered by IFES students throughout the history of the fellowship has been their dual membership: they are members of the people of God and at the same time members of the academic community. And as Van Aarde observes, this does not go without challenges:

> Every believer is called to practice *missional negotiation* between the culture of his church and local culture, whereas contextualisation belongs primarily to the field of missions. *The missional vocation is for every member of the church to engage his or her local context through missional negotiation in all areas of society, human life and creation.*[22]

This "missional negotiation" happens at the boundaries of the church, and the campus is such a boundary. As the university context increasingly secularizes its approaches, the gap can feel even more significant and, in any case, very different from the relative cultural homogeneity experienced by the ten founding IFES movements which, for the majority, operated in a Christianized context. Nowadays, large numbers of IFES movements operate in contexts with no such background. They have had to *mediate* between many cultural layers for many decades. Conversely, the West is relearning what it means for Christians to be "resident aliens."

In both cases, a double mediation occurs. First, as Christian students live, study, serve and witness on campus, they enrich, sanctify and bless the university. This necessitates thoughtful contextualization. Second, as Christian students go about their academic business, they discover more about the ins and outs of the creation which they know belongs to the God they worship. This means that academic life should enrich the lives of Christian students who

---

21. Paas, *Pilgrims and Priests*, 257.

22. Timothy A. Van Aarde, "The Missional Church Structure and the Priesthood of All Believers (Ephesians 4:7–16) in the Light of the Inward and Outward Function of the Church," *Verbum et Ecclesia* 38, no. 1 (31 Jan. 2017): 3; emphasis added.

will, in turn, be a blessing to their churches by bringing into them some of the good fruits of the academic land: new areas of knowledge, new insights, new ideas, new ways in which to love and serve the Creator and their neighbour.

Mediation to the Academic World

If the above considerations are true, a ministry to students needs to take their assumed intellectual character *very* seriously.[23] Attaching the label "intellectual" to such a diverse constituency as students associated with IFES movements serves as a methodological shortcut. Enormous differences in academic levels notwithstanding, students worldwide are supposed to acquire, process, refine and develop knowledge and skills which they will, in turn, put to use in their respective societies. Even if the percentage of the general population which attends university varies from country to country, students generally represent, at least in the Majority World, a fraction of their countries' demographics, with the added pressure and responsibilities attached to such privileges. This could be interpreted in overtly strategic terms and move missiologists to adopt approaches aiming at "capturing" the "power potential" of such a population to advance the gospel. As some scholars have argued, this could even be a "backdoor revenge" against the secularizing forces witnessed in the West.[24] This is at least the line of argument proposed by Neill, who sets the challenge in clear terms:

> If the Church is ever again to penetrate this alienated world and to claim it in the name of Christ, its only resources are in its convinced and converted laymen. There are vast areas, geographical and spiritual, which the ordained minister can hardly penetrate; the laymen are already there and are there every day. What happens to society in the future will largely depend on the use that they make of their opportunities, of their effectiveness as Christian witnesses in a new and as yet imperfectly charted ocean of being.[25]

---

23. "Assumed" in the sense that (1) not all students are equally expected to be critical of what is taught; and (2) not all students take this vocation seriously, whether because of intellectual abilities or other contingencies. The widely used concept in missiological circles of "people groups" could also be used here. Lutz argues that students might be one of the least "reached" people groups on earth. See Lutz, *College Ministry*.

24. See the summary of Wuthnow's thinking in Flett, *Apostolicity*, 160.

25. Neill, "Introduction," 22.

Similarly, very early in the history of IFES, Johnson highlighted the importance of letting students think by themselves, lest their intellectual capacities and their integrity as students be despised:

> However orthodox his church upbringing, and however faithful in doctrinal instruction his minister may be, there comes a time in the late adolescence of an intellectually active student when *he becomes aware of the urge to express his faith in ways appropriate to his age and training. He wants freely to discuss, to pray, and to enter into active evangelistic service in the company of others of his own age-group.* It is almost always for the good of his church, as well as himself, that he should do so. For only in this way can the faith take deep root in, and be transmitted in an influential form to, the next generation.[26]

Yet frequent warning calls were also issued against any attempts at "becoming powerful," namely that "the temptation within student groups can be to see Christianity solely as a set of intellectual propositions, rather than as a way of life based on the personal knowledge of God's love for us in Christ."[27] Commenting on recent field research in a group whose description squares closely with that of an IFES group, Bryant recounts the deliberate engagement with the content of the Christian faith students aspired to. They claimed to value intellectual rigor in the search for truth and answers. Clearly, the university culture, with the high premium it placed on intellectualism, pressed upon the Christian organization. To be taken seriously "in the marketplace of ideas," it was vital that they embrace academically valid means of truth-seeking, and many students were committed to such means in their search.[28]

Intellectually, the university's environment puts a premium on reflection and discovery, as well as on free enquiry. A robust doctrine of creation means first that God still loves the world and the humans who inhabit it; and consequently, that students are on safe ground when they study the world. They should enjoy the freedom to explore how their faith relates to their academic disciplines and to life on campus in the same way as all theology essentially needs contextualization. Christians can *mediate God to the university* by bringing a Christian perspective to the whole academic enterprise. This

---

26. Johnson, *Brief History*, 102–3; emphasis added.
27. Dransfield and Merritt, "'One-Another' Ministry," 37.
28. Bryant, "Evangelicals on Campus," 14.

perspective is that of loving participants rather than that of combatants.[29] As students, professors and other university staff, they can *mediate the world back to God* in prayer, and to the church, by bringing the questions asked by the university to the church for the missiological deepening of the latter's calling.[30] Framing the question within the discussion about the "priesthood of all believers" then opens new doors, for it considers the possibility for Christians to be individually and collectively responsible for their theological development *coram Deo*. This certainly fits the ethics of higher education. What happens within IFES is, ultimately, *student theologizing* rippling across the fellowship through writings, conferences and the increased weight of promising student leaders becoming voices within the fellowship and outside it, notably within the walls of academia. In other words, "to speak of Jesus Christ in another cultural milieu is to open that message to the range of questions, resources and idioms found in that culture."[31] Missiology, sociology and theology meet as the "campus priests," which students are, listen to the voices of the campus and feed them back to the church, which in turn needs to reflect theologically upon these new challenges.

The need for a connection between professed theological knowledge broadly conceived, on the one hand, and lived emotional piety, on the other hand, shows the breadth of concerns that a student group might need to address. Bryant and Astin's analysis postulates that

> students need reassurance that their struggles are justified and a legitimate part of their developmental process. So often these personal battles are waged alone, divorced from daily routines, classes, and work schedules. For fear of being misunderstood or stigmatized, students might attempt to conceal their troubled feelings – a practice that might overwhelm them even more. Regrettably, the pain of struggling might be amplified in environments that either refuse to acknowledge the existence of struggles or that call for premature and unsatisfactory resolutions

---

29. James K. A. Smith, "Loving the University: Engaging the Big Questions on Your Campus," *Emerging Scholars Blog*, 20 February 2023, https://blog.emergingscholars.org/2023/02/loving-the-university-engaging-the-big-questions-on-your-campus/.

30. Ward sees this process of renewal of practical theology as participation in the mission of God; see Pete Ward, *Participation and Mediation: A Practical Theology for the Liquid Church* (London: SCM, 2008), 102–3.

31. Flett, *Apostolicity*, 261.

to struggling for the sake of establishing commitment to one's faith tradition.[32]

Two conclusions can be derived from Bryant and Astin's analysis. First, IFES workers can and should have a deeply pastoral concern for the spiritual, physical and mental health of the students with whom they work, accompanying them in the challenging discovery of the university culture and practices. To be relevant, however, this pastoral care must be informed by an understanding of the university which is both valuing and lovingly critical. Second, if Bryant and Astin's suggestions are correct, it then means that there is great potential for student ministries to be creators of "space" where all people can explore matters of life and faith in a safe place – and this is notably a contribution that an IFES group can provide on campus.[33] It is indeed a firm conviction of IFES that equipping students for mission is relevant everywhere because the mission of God is universal, contextual difficulties notwithstanding.

Excursus: A Possible "Moratorium on Doctrine"? Students Exploring the Truth

The historical section of this work has highlighted the frequent question of the legitimacy for students to minister to their fellow students without being overseen by clergy members. Emblematic of the issue at stake is Woods's vivid narrative account of the tension as he experienced it in the 1940s, worth quoting at length:

> I had finished speaking at chapel at a great interdenominational theological seminary. The majority of that student body had come up during their undergraduate days with Inter-Varsity. The head of the department of biblical studies rushed up to me at the end of my message. "At last, I understand what you have been trying to tell me for the last ten years. You mean that you believe that students themselves can unite and have their own movement on campus and can witness to Christ. I don't believe it. I am no longer for you. Students know little or nothing. They cannot lead Bible studies; they cannot defend the faith. This is for the trained experts. Your approach will never work." The minister of one of the greatest independent churches in the eastern United States said, "I don't believe in your Inter-Varsity approach. I don't believe

---

32. Alyssa Bryant and Helen Astin, "The Correlates of Spiritual Struggle During the College Years," *The Journal of Higher Education* 79, no. 1 (2008): 23–24.

33. Luke Cawley, *The Myth of the Non-Christian: Engaging Atheists, Nominal Christians and the Spiritual but Not Religious* (Downers Grove: InterVarsity Press, 2016), especially ch. 9.

that untrained students can effectively present the gospel. I don't want my people in my church to try to point their friends to Christ. I am the ordained, qualified minister in this church. I have been to university and seminary, and I have my Ph.D. My people must bring their friends for whom they are praying. I will declare the gospel of God's grace. They will not be muddled up with immature, inadequate presentation. They will hear me and be converted according to God's sovereign grace. So, I do not endorse your point of view in terms of every student who is a Christian, a witness for Christ."[34]

Woods understood this reluctance to see the benefits of lay leadership as reflecting cultural captivity. In his words, "American Christianity has for too long been conditioned by American business ideology and practice. Only lip service is given to the biblical doctrine of fellowship and the priesthood of all believers. Clericalism in all its forms is all too rife."[35]

Yet the concern voiced by the American pastor that students would not be mature enough, and that the lack of clerical oversight would muddle theology and doctrine, is a missiological challenge for student ministry and is certainly not confined to the United States. So the question is sociological as well as doctrinal: could a possible *moratorium on doctrine* be presupposed for student ministry?

Such a "moratorium" would not be formalized but implicit in the way staff workers operate pastorally with students – and I would suggest that this is already the way staff members operate with students. Operating out of such a premise means essentially allowing students to suspend their judgment for the time they examine their faith as it is confronted with the (new) academic environment. From an organization's point of view, a moratorium does not mean abandoning any aspiration to doctrinal faithfulness because all office holders – including most student leaders – have signed the doctrinal basis and operate out of the convictions it articulates. It does, however, recognize that doctrinal convictions need time to be appropriated by a group of people whose daily occupation is the appraisal of ideas, of their respective benefits and potential shortcomings. Congar has astutely commented on the "frontier" aspect which characterizes the world of thinkers:

---

34. Woods, *Growth of a Work of God*, 61.
35. Woods, 61.

In the broad field situated, like the laity itself, at the seam of the Church and the world, lay thinkers, artists, researchers and scholars must be and feel freer than the clerics dedicated to theology properly speaking; they can develop there the partial but frank options into which the priest is much less able to venture, obliged as he is to remain the man of all; they can be more creative, not hesitating to open up new paths, whereas clerics, men of tradition, are sometimes tempted to transport the authoritative methods of dogmatics into other disciplines where they have no business.[36]

Congar's plea is not a case for doctrinal individualism but for the necessary acknowledgment that there are contexts in which people need a degree of freedom to examine what they often eventually receive as valid tradition.[37] This is the missiological price of intellectual integrity for a ministry that serves the student world. Stevens vividly notes that "this is theology being done 'from the bottom up.' Much of the theology being done is inadequate, but it is being done! Indigenous theology, on-the-spur-of-the-moment theology, while often reactionary, often reveals some unexplored dimension of Christian truth."[38]

The very possibility of discovering "unexplored dimensions of Christian truth" would not have seemed congenial to the founders of IFES, yet this is indeed what has happened throughout the history of the fellowship and is likely to continue happening as the organization is now present all over the globe. While they upheld the idea of having student leaders explore the truth together, the possibility of suspending doctrinal judgment was also a concern of the earlier leaders of IFES, and this issue was closely connected with the question of independence from established churches. As Woods astutely warned in 1957, "the history of the independent church is often a tragic one. Deprived of the scriptural means of united worship, instruction, and discipline,

---

36. Congar, *Théologie du laïcat*, 431.

37. Roberts argues in the opposite direction, affirming that (unquestioned) adhesion to the strict boundaries of the DB is necessary for students looking for certainty at a stage in life when so many other dimensions are already being questioned; see Vaughan Roberts, "Reframing the UCCF Doctrinal Basis," *Theology* 95, no. 768 (1 Nov. 1992): 432–46. This is already disputable for a society in which a large section of each generation goes on to higher studies, but it is probably even more questionable in the Majority World. In any case, the specificities of each individual's academic discipline's socialization must be accounted for in the relative need of doctrinal certainty for the appropriation of the faith, as well as one's personal inclinations, psychology and culture.

38. R. Paul Stevens, *The Abolition of the Laity: Vocation, Work and Ministry in a Biblical Perspective* (Cumbria: Paternoster, 1999), 18–19.

spiritual malformation almost inevitably is the consequence. Eccentricities and aberrations develop, and heresy frequently has been the end result."[39]

The connection with IFES groups is clear: mostly for sociological reasons, students should be able to explore, yet as student groups cannot replace church involvement, it is expected that the checks and balances in the exploration will be infused into the students in the context of church activities and teaching. What is important to note is that a "moratorium on doctrine" is less a question of structure than of practice: it is an attitude which consists in trusting the mysterious interplay of personal agency shaped in the community by the work of the Holy Spirit for the formation of belief and its contextual enlivening. This seems to be the necessary corollary to the frontier character of missional engagement, which calls for faithful improvisation.

Because students are encouraged to be members of local congregations, their exploration of doctrine is not done in a vacuum. It takes place on campus within the student group with all its dialogical practices and exploratory character, yet also in conversation with the greater ecclesial traditions, which embed the search in a system of checks and balances. To talk of a "moratorium on doctrine" means *naming* an exploratory phase through which many students go, not *abolishing* doctrine. It allows non-Christian students to ask tough questions of doctrinal elements without these questions being a threat to Christians; and Christians to ask the questions they might never have dared ask in a church context. In contemporary terms, it means that the local student group can be a "safe space" where doctrine can be explored and tested without the immediate risk of excommunication.

The idea – admittedly tentative – of a "moratorium on doctrine" takes into consideration Berger's argument that in a world where Christianity is no longer the evident worldview – and this is all the more so for locations where it has never been such – Christians are submitted to a "heretical imperative," that is, to "think by themselves."[40] At first sight, this runs against the grain of the very idea of orthodoxy, whereby "the Orthodox defines himself as living in a tradition; it is of the very nature of tradition to be taken for granted; this taken-for-grantedness, however, is continually falsified by the experience of living in a modern [academic] society."[41] Consequently, a ministry to students

---

39. Woods, "Evangelical Unions," 4.

40. Berger refers to the etymology of αἵρεσις, "the one who choses by him/herself." Peter L. Berger, *The Heretical Imperative: Contemporary Possibilities of Religious Affirmation* (Garden City: Anchor, 1979), 27.

41. Berger, *Heretical Imperative*, 30.

requires careful missiological consideration of the pluralist environment of the university where they are generally encouraged to think by themselves, even to "pick and choose." This pluralist socialization is the air students breathe. Believing in the validity of Christian beliefs allows ministers to trust that these beliefs will withstand the careful examination with which students are likely to confront them. The aim is, of course, to foster an honest and encouraging community within which students can make an informed choice to join in the Christian tradition. This community is the student group, which is, ultimately, part of the church.

Mediation to the Church

> The university is a continuing unevangelized field, a continuing Christian kindergarten.[42]

If students are, among other things, characterized by their intellectual engagement with the world, the university context presents specific challenges to some Christian students, especially within evangelicalism. Among the challenges are that university studies question preconceptions and long-held ideas about how the world functions, some disciplines challenge hermeneutical traditions, and so on. In the early days of IFES, this tension was essentially perceived as a threat. In the clear-cut categories characteristic of his style, Woods warned in 1970 that

> many Evangelicals, particularly graduates, in an effort to find acceptance in the current sociological-scientific society, *will continue to compromise* their biblical Christianity. This *erosion* of supernatural biblical foundations, particularly as applied to the reality of space-time events as recorded in Scripture, *will result in a loss of spiritual power and effectiveness*, and ultimately in *the loss of Christian faith itself*. On the other hand, God's consecrated minority, though small, will continue in unswerving loyalty to Christ and to His infallible Word.[43]

Woods's angst about a watering down of biblical convictions is presented with logic and clarity: in the beginning is "biblical Christianity," the tenets of which run against the academic grain, which entices those who want to succeed to give in to materialistic approaches, which in turn make faithful

---

42. Woods, "Student Work," 13.
43. Woods, "Perspectives and Priorities," 2; emphasis added.

witness impossible. Woods's understanding of IFES is that of a minority that needs to strengthen a minority in its own ranks. This minority was sometimes rather weak, as several accounts note,[44] but the idea close to Woods's heart, of a "consecrated minority" influencing its environment, is reminiscent of priestly language.

Woods and Williams were not alone in highlighting the tensions experienced by Christian students attending universities. But there is another dimension to the tension. Niringiye makes the plea that

> conversion cannot be assigned simply to the receptor cultures. Since authentic Christian mission originates in God's mission, Jesus's invitation to follow him to another culture bids us to re-examine our own perspectives, repent and believe the good news of the kingdom; it is an invitation to a journey of conversion, being transformed by God's grace and being drawn into fellowship with others whom he is drawing to himself through us.[45]

Suppose the above remarks by Niringiye are taken seriously. In that case, students need to consider scientific developments for their implications as to how the Christian faith is understood. Weary of watering down doctrine in the face of a "liberalism" that was more interested in science, IFES circles have not yet put significant energy into dialogue with scientific developments.[46] The idea that the university is at core a place that is potentially dangerous for the faith is a narrative plot often found in the testimonies of IFES students, who tell of significant conflicts of loyalty between their academic vocation and their ecclesial involvement.[47] That said, missiologically speaking, not only is "the university" in need of conversion, but the "messengers" also need to be reshaped by the encounter. Hence "campus ministry is an expression of the church's special desire to be present to all who are involved in higher

---

44. Williams, *Holy Spy*, 52–53.

45. Niringiye, *The Church*, 143.

46. Stackhouse notes in pointed terms for IFES movements that "many campus staff –and leaders on up the hierarchy of campus organizations – have only an undergraduate degree, and often in a field that prepares them badly for ideological contest and Christian disciple-making (e.g. engineering, natural sciences, commerce, medicine). More recently, more have a master's degree or better in a relevant field. But one wonders why such qualifications are not simply required, the way denominations and congregations require at least one theological degree to do the job. What is this job that requires so little theological training, so little philosophical awareness?" https://www.johnstackhouse.com/post/engaging-the-university.

47. This author has heard these kinds of feelings expressed by many students in many countries.

education and to further the dialogue between the church and the academic community."[48] This is not, however, how mission has traditionally been understood in evangelical circles. In the very specific case of the United States – from which we cannot extrapolate directly to the rest of the world but which is nevertheless influential, especially given its output in printed and other media formats – Bielo provides an astute, if not particularly charitable, critique of the relationship of evangelicals to the university:

> There is a dominant discourse among conservative Evangelicals that the academy is a territory where Christians must tread lightly. It is the breeding ground of "liberalism," "humanism," "secularism," and a variety of other unsightly "isms" that are antagonistic to Christians and to Christianity. The university is where human evolution, existential philosophies, and non-Western epistemologies are used to sweep the legs out from under Christian theology. It is where "tolerance" and "diversity" are "liberal"-speak for the evaporation of moral absolutes. This particular narrative plot includes the overly cerebral, smart-ass professor who intellectually abuses unsuspecting Christian students, forcing them to doubt their faith.[49]

This description applies more to the early years of IFES than to its subsequent years. Yet tensions at the intersection of academic life and Christian commitment remain. As Reimer postulates, "if some of the most religious students are intellectually engaged, pondering the implications of liberal education for their religious views, some softening of orthodoxy is likely."[50]

This "liberalizing effect" is not, however, in any way automatic, in Reimer's analysis. More intellectual engagement is required; that is, "the student must still engage these theories intellectually."[51] This represents a significant challenge for a ministry that encourages students to engage their studies with their minds. On the one hand, exposing one's faith to intellectual challenges means benefiting from a "stress test" of the faith and emerging with a more established, resilient faith. On the other hand, however, at the same time a more or less pronounced phenomenon of relativization seems to take place

---

48. Wonyoung Bong, "Toward Improving the Effectiveness of Campus Ministry at Universities," *Asia-Africa Journal of Mission and Ministry* 7 (2013): 28.

49. Bielo, *Words upon the Word*, 40.

50. S. Reimer, "Higher Education and Theological Liberalism: Revisiting the Old Issue," *Sociology of Religion* 71, no. 4 (3 June 2010): 396.

51. Reimer, "Higher Education," 394.

concerning certain dogmatic convictions, whether they are inherited from parents or from socialization within the IFES group itself. Yet such encounters do not automatically lead to less theological certainty, as Reimer further notes: "Active involvement in a campus Christian group preserved traditional beliefs and morals. . . . Higher education can expand and diversify social networks, which have been traditionally thought to undermine the religious orthodoxy that is best preserved through network closure."[52]

Within IFES, the value granted to books and education goes together with a warning that faith and doctrine need nourishment, out of a great concern for the sustainability of the student's commitment: "The Evangelical student who fails to be sufficiently tenacious of Evangelical belief and conduct in the University rarely succeeds in being so during the rest of his career."[53]

If this is true, the university represents a challenge to ecclesial leaders. The university can be seen either as a reservoir of people to be reached with contextual alertness, or as displaying characteristics that can be genuinely congenial to the flourishing of the Christian faith and of life together with people of shared and unshared convictions. "At its best, the learning that takes place in universities may therefore contribute, in however limited a way, to the task of learning to live together in the world as Christ's body, regardless of whether those involved in it understand their learning in these terms."[54] Similarly, Osei-Mensah draws upon theological imagination and history when he proposes that

> the Christian must rediscover for himself the original concept on which universities were first founded, namely the harmony between the supernatural and the natural. He must realize, moreover, that this harmony has reality only in the Lord who "upholds all things by the word of His power." This is the first step in the integration of study and devotion.[55]

Seriously valuing the life of the mind means appreciating the gift which reason is, and investing in its cultivation, which allows for a more thorough integration. Lutz, who in addition to his insistence on missional training is aware of the challenges the university represents to students, argues for

---

52. Reimer, 395.

53. Inter-Varsity Fellowship of Evangelical Unions, ed., *Principles of Co-operation* (London: IVF, n.d.), 16.

54. Mike Higton, "Education and the Virtues," in *The Universities We Need: Theological Perspectives*, ed. Stephen Heap (Milton: Taylor and Francis, 2016), 82.

55. Gottfried Osei-Mensah, "Integration Point: Against Dichotomy," *In Touch* 1 (1974).

unapologetically intellectual discipleship: "As people on mission to Higher Ed, we intentionally and rigorously develop the intellect. This means calling students to whole person transformation – mind, body, and spirit – through the gospel, a transformation that begins through the renewing of their minds (Romans 12:2)."[56]

In a similarly pressing tone, Malik urges his readers to take the university seriously out of theological conviction. It does not suffice to notice the growing student population; more care should be given to assessing the university from an institutional point of view, that is, from the lens of its impact on societies:

> If the university today dominates the world, if Jesus Christ is Who the church and the Bible proclaim him to be, and if we happen to believe that what the church and the Bible claim about Jesus Christ is the truth, then how can we fail not only to raise the question of what Jesus Christ thinks of the university, but to face the equally urgent demand: What can be done? We are dealing with the power that dominates the world; how can we then rest without seeking to ascertain where Jesus Christ stands with respect to this power? The university and Jesus Christ – these are the two inseparable foci of our thought.[57]

Malik's call cannot be answered by the sole encouragement a student ministry gives students to gather for prayer, fellowship and Bible reading, as well as witness in whatever form, without a *deliberate, consequential and sustainable* commitment to mentoring students in thinking hard about the issues at stake at university. Strikingly, Malik's claim that "to change the university is to change the world," which to this day features prominently on IFES public relations documents, has concretely been understood to mean that students *as individuals* are to be reached with the gospel and that they, in turn, will change the university and subsequently the world.[58] The theological premise is that conversion will eventually entice Christian students to change their universities. Yet the question remains: is there sufficient deliberate tackling of the bigger academic questions and issues – from both an institutional and an academic point of view – in the overall training of students that the "change vision" can reasonably be expected to be realized one

---

56. Lutz, *College Ministry*, 703.
57. Malik, *Christian Critique*, 21.
58. This view is criticized by Paas who says it is a leftover of Christendom restoration perspectives; see Paas, *Pilgrims and Priests*, 66.

day, even if Christian students remain a marginal community in the academy? Sommerville also draws upon biblical examples to encourage a positive attitude in the engagement of Christians with the university. Speaking primarily to a Western audience, he affirms that "Christians shouldn't need to dominate the secular before they feel safe around it. When St. Paul debated Athenians at Mars Hill, he didn't threaten them. When Jesus' public teaching was through questions, he was assuming he had an ally in the conscience and intelligence of his audience."[59] Bringing this reflection to bear upon IFES, in many countries there is no possibility of "dominating the public sphere" anyway, so Christian students have been used to being the minority for a long time. Yet, as the West disproportionately publishes and diffuses books on culture and Christian life questions, a recapturing of the potential for minorities to meaningfully engage their environment is essential, lest smaller movements think themselves to be limited to survival before they can contribute anything to the university.

So perhaps one of the first things that an IFES movement could consider is to make sure that in every Bible study, every teaching, every discussion with students, supporters and shareholders of the movement, questions are asked about the university context. Such questioning should not only occur from a purely "Christian" point of view, focusing on what is "bad" at university, but should also focus on what positive things are happening at the university and what the challenges are that people there (not just Christians) are encountering.[60] In the IFES training literature, no real such deliberate posture can be found, especially in the historical accounts. The logic of "personal spiritual growth which informs personal witness" is always primary, and the university context is mostly seen as providing a challenge to "remain faithful," more than as a place where discoveries are made, exchanges fostered and fascination nurtured. This alternative could be summarized by saying that "we do not 'take Christ' into the university; it is he who goes ahead of us and leads us there."[61] So, in the same way as public health specialists argue for a "health in all policies" approach to policy-making, those connected with IFES could adopt a "university in all endeavours" approach.

---

59. C. John Sommerville, *Religious Ideas for Secular Universities* (Grand Rapids: Eerdmans, 2009), 61.

60. Using a very traditional, Reformed framework could be a first step: looking at what reflects the goodness of creation, the badness of the fall, the changes occurring as consequences of redemption, and the fulfilment towards which history is heading in the restoration.

61. Vinoth Ramachandra, "Christian Witness in the University: Integrity, Incarnation, and Dialogue in Today's Universities," *Word and World* 4 (5 Dec. 2017), https://en.ifesjournal.org/christian-witness-in-the-university-6377e32e7bbf.

This intricate process of missionary mediation occurs on a theological level with the university and informs theology from an intellectual level. Yet what singles IFES out from many other organizations is how widespread it is, hence, though humbly, its foreshadowing the eschatological gathering of all nations and languages under the lordship of Christ.

International Mediation

The broad spectrum of peoples, cultures, denominational specificities, languages and many more represented in IFES showcases a unique foretaste of the multi-ethnic community of the people of God. They are a "display-people" to the campus – just as Israel and the church were called to be among the nations. As such, they are a channel for broadening perspectives (ecclesial, intellectual, doctrinal) of the church. IFES member movements serve each other by sharing in the community their contextual understandings of the Bible and, more broadly, of Christian life and doctrine.

However, yet another difficulty has often arisen, one closer to the heart of students' intellectual life: critical thinking, especially in cultures where such an academic tradition has not had a long history.[62] Rodica Cocar, at the time a student in Romania, remembers the following:

> After the 1989 revolution it was possible to publish Christian literature inside Romania, but it took time to establish a publishing house. The concept of these Bible studies [Kristensen and Lum's *Jesus – One of Us*][63] was so completely foreign to normal Romanian thinking because there were no definitive answers, right or wrong. It was said that in Romania you had to be a born-again Christian before you could think independently. The teaching tradition was authoritative and by rote throughout society including the Church. But student groups who saw the book were enthusiastic.[64]

---

62. The issue of the cultural embeddedness of the very idea of "critical thinking" cannot be discussed here. Suffice it to say that, despite being widespread in the globalized academic world, it cannot be assumed to be the only way of approaching research. Assuming the superiority of the (Western) critical thinking tradition would amount to an unethical diminishing of the achievements of the universities of Antiquity, for example.

63. Brede Kristensen and Ada Lum, *Jesus – One of Us: 52 Evangelistic Bible Studies Compiled into 8 Series*, International Fellowship of Evangelical Students (Nottingham: Inter-Varsity Press, 1976).

64. Quoted in Williams, *Holy Spy*, 154.

This demonstrates an interesting cultural mix: a university culture expecting students to think, but not necessarily out of the box – and this can apply both to the context of the lecture hall and to the church building. In this particular case, a book written by a Hawaiian lady, and published by an international body, encouraged Eastern European students to think for themselves, thereby challenging their church leaders and the culture of their own land. This global character of Christianity redraws ecclesial maps, and indeed, lay leadership may be a reason for Christianity's continuous appeal to large swathes of the population in the Majority World. Akinade astutely observes that

> *the anti-structural character of the non-Western phase of world Christianity* plays itself out in characteristics such as charismatic renewal, grassroots revival, massive exorcism, vibrant house churches, *robust indigenization efforts, and effective lay leadership.* Churches from the Third World are vigorously defining Christianity on their own terms.[65]

Kinoti similarly notes the importance of the global ministry of John Stott for the rise of indigenous Christian leaders in Africa:

> It was fashionable at the time for college students to dismiss Christianity either on intellectual grounds or as a white man's religion. John Stott's missions to African universities and his writings matched intellectual and spiritual needs of many. They helped to raise an educated class of African Christian leaders and professionals who in turn influenced, and continue to influence, younger people.[66]

Such testimonies run counter to other narratives of intellectual oppression by Western leaders. It is arguable that because of the growing globalization of universities, some of the challenges encountered by Western university students might correspond to issues raised by students in the Majority World. Similarly, in some situations, the participatory structure of groups like IFES appealed to students otherwise alienated from Christianity or who outrightly opposed it. Given that IFES operates within the context of an institution foreign to

---

65. Akintunde E. Akinade, "Introduction," in *A New Day: Essays on World Christianity in Honor of Lamin Sanneh*, ed. Akintunde E. Akinade, 1st printing ed. (New York: Peter Lang, 2010), 5; emphasis added.

66. George K. Kinoti, "Contribution towards Submission for the Templeton Prize" (University of Nairobi, 1996); quoted in Dudley-Smith, *John Stott*, 110.

most non-Western contexts – the university, which already propagates modes of thinking which are foreign to many cultures of the Majority World – it is arguable that the added export of Western methodologies for reaching students might still work, as the example of student-led Bible study tends to indicate. Conversely, an imported theology might still be detrimental to developing an integrated faith, whereby Christian doctrines are considered foreign to the Majority World, as are some academic methodologies – non-transcendental materialism being one example.

Moreover, the interdenominational character of IFES seems to have played a significant role in broadening ecclesial, theological and intellectual horizons, essentially through the encounter with other Christians and their other ways of conceiving faith, the world and life in general. Volf also argues that the importance of communal exploration of the Christian truth – what we have suggested in this work to be an aspect of mutual priesthood – amounts to an eschatological foretaste:

> By opening up to one another both diachronically and synchronically, local churches should enrich one another, thereby increasingly becoming catholic churches. In this way, they will also increasingly correspond to the catholicity of the triune God, who has already constituted them as catholic churches, because they are anticipations of the eschatological gathering of the entire people of God.[67]

Here, Christians mediate God to other Christians, a movement corresponding to another crucial aspect of the "priesthood of all believers." This *mediation* of God is derivative of Christ's unique priestly work into which Christians are drawn by being included in a group that is larger than themselves: the church.

---

67. Miroslav Volf, *After Our Likeness: The Church as the Image of the Trinity* (Grand Rapids: Eerdmans, 1998), 213. See also Pope Paul VI, "*Ad Gentes*," sec. 9.

20

General Conclusion

"Parachurch" organizations like IFES are mostly structurally *independent* from organized congregations, yet essentially *ecclesiological* for they are the outworking – in this case on university ground – of the *mission of the church* to bless its environment and to proclaim the gospel. Furthermore, students are *members* of the church universal as well as of local congregations. Their priestly work of mediation is done on the outskirts of the formally recognizable church. This presupposes a *missional ecclesiology*, which does not limit the church to what is immediately identified as such.

There are two levels to this *global community*: the limited community of IFES, and the broader community of the church universal and its local instantiations. The local church, of which students are encouraged to be members, nourishes students, staff and faculty associated with IFES and allows them to experience a wider expression of the body of Christ.

IFES's theologically motivated and regularly reaffirmed commitment to the necessary indigenous appropriation of the Christian faith – congruent with the idea of *immediacy* – undermines the idea that Christian mission was solely a colonization process that left no agency to local actors.[1] On the contrary, the very nature of the IFES public – students – implies agency on their part. This "local appropriation of the gospel" – notably not of Christian structures – is at the core of the IFES discourse, insisting that "workers serving in pioneer areas or with younger movements should do all they can to hand over full responsibility and leadership to national leaders."[2]

The above explorations have shown the connection between the way IFES has understood itself as a missionary organization and the notion of

---

1. Flett refutes such frequent accounts as too narrow; see Flett, *Apostolicity*, 182–83.
2. Chua Wee Hian, "Staff Letter 9," 1.

apostolicity. God's mission draws in individuals who organize themselves to witness to their immediate environment or to foreign lands. "Apostolicity" as "sent-ness" frames the whole pioneering enterprise characteristic of IFES, despite its structural ties to the logic of empire. "Apostolicity" thus understood relativizes ecclesial structures and is congruent with the *missional ecclesiology* outlined above. The spread of IFES also witnesses to the contextual adaptability of the Christian message, despite the tensions associated with the idea that a "deposit of the faith" needs to be passed on to whoever believes. Yet I have also highlighted the necessity for careful consideration of the conditions for the faith's local appropriation. This local appropriation is the consequence of the "priesthood of all believers" in that, because individuals, wherever they live, can *immediately* relate to God, they are called to *mediate* him to their environment. However, what was not originally foreseen by the IFES founders was that in the encounter with new realities, the way the gospel is understood would be broadened and would "nourish back" the *membership* of the fellowship, including its previous "sending centres." This does not occur without tension but lays the foundation for a better awareness of how Christians can relate to an environment in which they are a minority.

In the history part of this work I noticed how many church leaders have opposed IFES's ministry on the grounds that it was too dangerous for theologically untrained students to meet on their own, study the Bible, and encourage each other to share their faith without direct supervision from trained specialists. Allen counters by appealing to the metaphor of the *body*:

> If absence of tongues was used as an argument to forbid the body to express itself, if absence of hand was used as an argument to forbid the body to touch and feel, then we should get the position which those try to force upon us who use the absence of ordained ministry to forbid the priesthood of the body to express itself. When they do that, the specialized ministry does war against the universal common priesthood of Christians.[3]

Furthermore, I earlier advanced the argument that all the core activities students engage in can be linked to the different dimensions of priestly service inspired by the Old Testament priests and the calling of the people of Israel. Obviously, in some contexts, theological sidetracks can be taken by students left "on their own." However, the reality is that many students are left on their own anyway: either because no church leader takes an interest in them as

---

3. Allen, *Ministry of Expansion*, Kindle loc. 1797.

a specific public, or because the support or oversight provided is irrelevant insofar as none of the significant campus life issues is known to the ministers. Discipleship then runs the risk of being disconnected from Christian students and seekers' lives and spiritual struggles, thereby missing its target and possibly being reduced to promoting a form of moral conformism deprived of intrinsic motivation, soon to be cast aside. In this respect, any theology of student ministry needs to have an answer to the question of what Christian students are to do as they find themselves on the "foreign missionary front line" which university campuses often are today.

Student ministry is crucial. Yet it does not represent all of God's mission, and certainly not the entirety of the church's mission either. As Stackhouse notes,

> parachurch groups devoted to particular tasks and drawing on particular kinds of people can concentrate resources powerfully on important needs or difficult problems. But such groups can also foster a tunnel vision that sees the future of Christian morality, the fate of the country, or even the success of the gospel itself in terms of the success of their one particular cause.[4]

Therefore, it is helpful to remind students of the broader scope of the *missio Dei* and encourage them to avoid such "tunnel vision" which, if too strongly present, could undermine their full integration into the larger ministry of the local church upon completion of their studies. This is one of the areas where church leaders can sensitively walk alongside students who do not always have an "overarching framework to set things in order, to determine the relative importance of things, and to sort it all out."[5] It can be argued that there is a solid case to make for Christian students to necessarily join a student group on campus, be it IFES-linked or not. As IFES has argued throughout its history, students should be involved in local congregations as far as possible. Yet students often struggle to connect to local churches during their studies because of increased discrepancies between their new realities and their churches' horizons. This can lead to a tendency either to withdraw to a student group or, worse, to renounce any community involvement.

The intellectual status of students and their newly acquired skills and knowledge also represent a pastoral challenge: how are they to deal wisely with their newly acquired power? In many contexts, the addition of the opposite pairs *church-parachurch, academically trained-untrained, experienced-*

---

4. Stackhouse, *Evangelical Landscapes*, 34.
5. Stackhouse, 35.

inexperienced, ordained-lay and *young-old* makes cooperation and mutual understanding difficult, albeit not impossible, and many IFES leaders have gone to great lengths to encourage good communication between all parties. Pointing to a way forward, Debanné suggests that

> ideally, of course, church members should themselves become the channel of this communication. Such communication can be established by students in both directions: they will wisely bring the doctrinal and moral concern of their church to the inter-church work and, in return, they will bring back new issues which they have discerned as relevant to their own church life.[6]

This requires skilful communication and mutual understanding, yet if the logic of fear can be trumped by the logic of mutual trust between church leaders who see the importance and non-threatening nature of the parachurch for their own congregations, an immense potential for partnership in mission is opened up.

Hence church and student work can benefit from a positive dynamic of exchanges: just as

> pastoral work receives from theology and depends on it, in the order of the awakening of ideas, of the problems posed, of the shocks which lead to an enrichment of thought, [so] pastoral work can contribute much to theology. Most of the renewals that have taken place in the Church are due to the militants of the apostolic and missionary front shaking her up.[7]

Such examples illustrate how student experiences have been beneficial to the local church because students were allowed to operate on their own terms, thereby allowing God to bless others through their ministry as laypeople. What Van Aarde says of the missional church hence applies fully to IFES ministry: "The laity and their task of the priesthood of believers is to participate in God's *glocal* dimension of the *missio Dei* by participating and fulfilling the Great Commission by going next door."[8]

All the above supports a missiology of student ministry which values highly the ability of individual Christian students and communities of Christian students to faithfully discern what God is doing in the world and how his

---

6. Debanné, "L'étudiant chrétien," 43.
7. Congar and Varillon, *Sacerdoce et laïcat*, 9.
8. Van Aarde, "Missional Church," 5.

mission is unfolding in the university context. Taking seriously the calling to the life of the mind inherent to student life is the logical outworking of the belief that, because all Christians have direct, *immediate* access to God, they can discern how to act faithfully in the world. It also supports a high view of the contributions of all quarters of the church universal to the understanding of Christian doctrine, because God speaks to all of his children in an equally valid manner. It also supports a serious *missiology of the university* as a unique field of ministry requiring careful consideration of its culture and inhabitants. Lastly, talking of a *priesthood of all students* highlights the necessity of equipping and supporting *laypeople* for the mission of the church wherever they find themselves. This is also the foundation of a *missional ecclesiology*, thereby legitimizing a ministry on campus which is the contextual incarnation of the mission of the church and not anything *beside* it or potentially secondary to it. Missionality has a stronger creedal character than organizational aspects of a Christian community.[9] A missional Christian student group is closer to being a faithful church than a local church without a missionary orientation.

IFES has invented neither religious voluntarism nor mission to the university. However, the fellowship has contributed to channelling a specific strand of Christian convictions – evangelicalism – to a rising population of future influential leaders: students.

The work of IFES, despite being done mostly outside the walls of formal church structures, cannot be understood as either anti-ecclesial or a-ecclesial. Many of the marks of the church can be found in IFES groups. Many ecclesial concerns – notably the question of theological faithfulness – can be found in these groups which, although they have a sense of missionary urgency, do not give in to expediency to the detriment of thoughtful reasoning. By not being institutionally linked to ecclesial traditions, a parachurch organization can put safeguards in place to prevent theological atomization and heretical developments, notably by ensuring its theological core convictions are solidly rooted in theology and practice.

The best example of this intense ecclesial concern is the wealth of theological writings from IFES staff or people very closely connected to IFES and whose publications by IFES movements and speaking on stages at conferences attest to their recognized relevance to the work of student mission. These writings show a deep concern for the church but, in coherence with their

---

9. Flett agrees with Hoekendijk that "the church is the church of this apostolic God only when it lets itself be used in God's missionary movement. Its apostolicity (in its doctrine as in its church order) must prove itself in the apostolate." Flett, *Apostolicity*, 208.

involvement within the network of an international organization, focus more on the universal dimension of the *invisible* church than on issues of local church polity. This focus on the geographical and cultural diversity of the church was missiologically far-sighted. Theological premises, watered by a strong ethos of indigeneity, could grow on the soil of globalization and one of its far-reaching consequences: a lessening of the importance of denominational particularisms to the benefit of *glocal* thinking.

Sociologically respectful of students as "leaders-in-development," the priesthood of all believers hence provides an ecclesiastically respectful, though challenging, framework to understand the church's mission in context:

> The missional church movement makes a distinction in terms of function and office; it places the emphasis on the function of the ordained ministry instead of the office. The missional church specifically addresses lines of hierarchical distinction between the ordained ministry and laity in order to promote a dynamic functional church structure. It consciously and selectively chooses neutral and inclusive language which empowers the believers for their task and calling in the world.[10]

Therefore, it seems reasonable to propose that the "priesthood of all believers," as an "implicitly confessed" doctrine practised throughout the work of IFES, has paved the way to a missional understanding of the church. Such vision highlights the importance of valuing the contributions to world Christianity of parachurch organizations like IFES, and of leaving behind the obsolete idea that the parachurch and the church are competitors.

---

10. Van Aarde, "Missional Church," 6.

Appendixes

These appendices provide additional details on some aspects of the history and theology of IFES which for reasons of space I could not include in the main body of the text.

Appendix 1

Two Speeches That Changed Evangelicalism

This appendix provides an analysis of the addresses given by Escobar and Padilla during the 1974 Lausanne Congress. As these speeches represent a key moment during which people connected with IFES influenced the wider evangelical world, they are worth closer examination.

Given the fact that the drafts they had submitted to the delegates in advance generated no fewer than "something between 1500 and 2000 responses" each,[1] the final formats they delivered can be assessed as the result of a thorough dialogical experiment, since both speakers could already take some affirmations and reservations of their audience into consideration. Padilla's paper argued that the world was God's chosen sphere of action and that love for one's neighbours compels Christians to not only see the world as evil but also to love it. The paper also went further, denouncing an American captivity of evangelicalism in rather strong terms: "We have equated 'Americanism' with Christianity to the extent that we are tempted to believe that people in other cultures must adopt American institutional patterns when they are converted."[2] Further highlighting his insistence on contextualization was his other contention that "it is not surprising that at least in Latin America today the evangelist often has to face innumerable prejudices that reflect the identification of Americanism with the Gospel in the minds of his listeners."[3]

---

1. Chua Wee Hian, "Staff Letter 15," 1.
2. C. René Padilla, "Evangelism and the World," in *Let the Earth Hear His Voice*, ed. J. D. Douglas (Minneapolis: World Wide Publications, 1975), 125.
3. Padilla, "Evangelism and the World," 125.

In Stott's analysis, Escobar's paper caused even more of a stir, putting "the cat amongst the pigeons."[4] In Stanley's summary, Escobar

> argued that "the heart which has been made free with the freedom of Christ cannot be indifferent to the human longings for deliverance from economic, political, or social oppression," and [he] suggested that many of the countries which had succumbed to a violent revolution conducted on Marxist principles were those where Christianity had allowed itself to be identified with the interests of the ruling class.[5]

This was not only not "pulling [any] punches"[6] but also challenging a certain missionary pragmatism that favoured methods and urgency at the expense of missiology.[7] In Chapman's analysis,

> many Evangelicals bred on activism saw the sort of patience required to work through disagreements as a distraction from the life-and-death task at hand. For such, Padilla's and Escobar's calls for reflection and reorientation could seem a distraction at best, and much worse at worst. Activists wanted the practical professors from Fuller, not these theologians from the International Fellowship of Evangelical Students, to define the new field of evangelical missiology.[8]

The kind of theology proposed by Padilla and Escobar was the logical outworking of their ministry: the nature of student work is fertile ground for developing theological thinking about culture, trends and evolving worldviews, given the tendency for new forms of thinking and behaviour to develop first on university campuses before they reach wider society. Therefore, in the evangelical world, people involved with IFES were uniquely placed to develop the interdisciplinary approach characteristic of missiological endeavours. This was not seen as being without risks, however: exemplary of the relative unease with which the GS noted the newly acquired theological exposure of IFES people are Chua's next words of caution in the staff letter from which we have already quoted:

---

4. Stott, "Significance of Lausanne," 289.
5. Stanley, "Lausanne 1974," 542.
6. Dudley-Smith, *John Stott*, 211.
7. Chapman, "Evangelical International Relations," 360.
8. Chapman, 362.

Much as we are grateful for this exposure, it has inherent dangers. We must guard against pride and also the temptation to spread ourselves thinly because of the demands that others will be making on our staff and our literature departments to participate at conferences, seminars etc. . . . Now René and Samuel have presented two provocative papers on the social implications of the gospel. These gained the attention of many Christians. We must be careful that we match deeds with our words; otherwise we shall be labelled as empty talkers and theorists.[9]

Similarly, strong pushback was also expressed from within the ranks of IFES, with Barclay, IVF-UK GS and Chairman of the IFES board, "warning" Padilla of the "effects" of his paper.[10] It turns out that some of the congress's participants were not yet satisfied with its main product, the Lausanne Covenant,[11] and gathered to form an ad hoc group on "Radical Discipleship."[12] Strangely enough for a member of the planning committee, Chua notes with appreciation that these

> young and radical theologians . . . were exchanging information and sharing plans on how they could cooperate and serve side by side in fulfilling the missionary mandate. Had these people simply stuck to the regimented program they would have gained something, but not as much as they were able to gain by meeting with like-minded participants.[13]

Thus, the congress represents a turning point in the global history of evangelicalism and, arguably, IFES played a very significant role in it: because of prominent speakers, and also because of Stott's decisive influence. The rising star of conservative evangelicalism

> had taken up the concerns of those who spoke for Evangelicals in the majority world and interpreted them sympathetically to those, in the United States in particular, who were fearful that the new radical Evangelicalism was simply a reincarnation of the old

---

9. Chua Wee Hian, "Staff Letter 15," 1–2.
10. Kirkpatrick, *Gospel for the Poor*, 28.
11. Lausanne Movement, "Lausanne Covenant."
12. Their report is printed in J. D. Douglas, ed., "Theology and Implications of Radical Discipleship," in *Let the Earth Hear His Voice*, 1294–96.
13. Chua, *Getting through Customs*, 133–34.

"social gospel" which they believed had led inexorably to spiritual bankruptcy in the WCC.[14]

Another indirect influence from IFES was Michael Cassidy. He had become a Christian through the ministry of the CICCU and later founded African Enterprise. His plenary address entitled "Evangelism of College and University Students" was an extraordinary plea for a holistic engagement with the university context, tracing the contours of a missiological approach to campus ministry. As one quote eloquently shows, Cassidy had gone way beyond the common CICCU approach to evangelism[15] and was laying out missional ecclesiological views:

> The vision, I believe, which must be caught is that of the Total Body of believers (students and staff) reaching the total campus with comprehensive penetration at every level of the institution. Christians should not be a ghetto group, but a militant band of infiltrators, witnesses, and caring agents. Not only will they remind the campus of the true and full purpose of education as a search for truth, but they will seek both to evangelize individuals and to convert the structures of the university. The vision of full Christian involvement in sport, student politics, student government, residence life, the campus newspaper, the cultural activities of the university should be held high.[16]

---

14. Stanley, "Lausanne 1974," 547. The fact that the significant influence of Padilla and Escobar found its way into the Lausanne Covenant has also a lot to do with their personal friendship with John Stott, whom they had taken on a lecturing tour of their region a few weeks before the congress. "Their tour included a visit to 'hardline communist' political prisoners in southern Chile, who had been 'interrogated under torture' by the military regime." Kirkpatrick, "Origins of Integral Mission," 354. Information confirmed in Escobar, Interview.

15. This is confirmed by the trajectory of his ministry and advocacy for justice in South Africa. See David Goodhew, "Cassidy, Michael," in *Biographical Dictionary of Evangelicals*, eds. Timothy Larsen, David Bebbington and Mark A. Noll (Leicester: Inter-Varsity Press, 2003), 130–31.

16. Michael Cassidy, "Evangelization amongst College and University Students," in *Let the Earth Hear His Voice*, 756.

Appendix 2

The IFES Doctrinal Basis

The doctrinal basis of IFES shall be the fundamental truths of Christianity, including:
- The unity of the Father, Son and Holy Spirit in the Godhead.
- The sovereignty of God in creation, revelation, redemption and final judgement.
- The divine inspiration and entire trustworthiness of Holy Scripture, as originally given, and its supreme authority in all matters of faith and conduct.
- The universal sinfulness and guilt of all people since the fall, rendering them subject to God's wrath and condemnation.
- Redemption from the guilt, penalty, dominion and pollution of sin, solely through the sacrificial death (as our representative and substitute) of the Lord Jesus Christ, the incarnate Son of God.
- The bodily resurrection of the Lord Jesus Christ from the dead and his ascension to the right hand of God the Father.
- The presence and power of the Holy Spirit in the work of regeneration.
- The justification of the sinner by the grace of God through faith alone.
- The indwelling and work of the Holy Spirit in the believer.
- The one holy universal Church which is the body of Christ and to which all true believers belong.
- The expectation of the personal return of the Lord Jesus Christ.[1]

---

1. IFES. "What We Believe · IFES", 2 February 2023. https://ifesworld.org/en/beliefs/.

Appendix 3

Bibliology in the Doctrinal Basis

This appendix provides more details about the official IFES stance on the Bible. Given the important role Scripture plays in the activities of the fellowship, it offers the reader in-depth insights into bibliology and hermeneutics.

> C: The divine inspiration and entire trustworthiness of Holy Scripture, as originally given, and its supreme authority in all matters of faith and conduct.

Possibly no clause in the DB has been both more praised and more criticized for either providing a solid anchoring or narrowing people's minds, depending on the views expressed by the commentators. This clause is fundamental for understanding IFES, its doctrinal basis as a whole, and the underlying assumptions about the Bible held in IFES circles. More than being merely one of the tenets of the IFES identity, the IFES position on the Bible was held by its founders to be an existential matter. In the words of the first General Secretary,

> the heart of this doctrinal position of the I.F.E.S. and its member movements is their conviction with regard to the inspiration, authority and entire trustworthiness of the Bible. *Should our views concerning Holy Scripture ever change, then we should have lost an essential raison d'être for the existence of our national evangelical unions and their particular ministry.*[1]

When IFES was founded in 1947, no argument could have been made on the sole necessity of reaching students with means that churches would not have had, for in many countries the SCM was still alive and well. The consistent narrative of IFES, directly taken over from the British IVF's own story but consistent with the personal experience of most IFES founders, was that defence

---

1. C. Stacey Woods, "Biblical Principles for Unity and Separation," *IFES Journal* 20, no. 3 (1967): 4; emphasis added.

of an evangelical stand on Scripture had rendered the foundation of another movement necessary: what is more, it had made separation unavoidable. To quote Woods again, commenting on 2 John 7:7–11, "the command to separate specifically has to do with those who deny that Jesus Christ is the incarnate Son of God, but this principle also applies to those who hold other heretical views which affect essential Christian doctrine."[2]

Inspiration

Providing a full account of evangelical doctrines of inspiration would far outgrow the present work. In order to keep it within measure, we will focus on IFES's own understanding of inspiration to map out the terrain.

Right from the organization's foundation, the pioneers were aware that, while evangelicals could agree on inspiration, they would not agree on the exact terms of this doctrine. In the words of the first IFES president, "the I.F.E.S. proclaims the inspiration of the Scriptures, but no special theory of how this inspiration actually took place through the prophets and the apostles. Differences exist concerning this question amongst conservative evangelical Christians."[3]

The doctrine of inspiration derives from the idea that there is a direct link between the trustworthiness of the Bible and the nature of God: "If Scripture has its origin in God, then a true view of 'inspiration' of necessity includes a belief that what God has 'breathed out' partakes of His trustworthiness. It has the infallibility of God Himself speaking."[4]

Scholars disagree on the extent of the cultural captivity of the idea of plenary verbal inspiration to scientific visions and methodologies owing more to Enlightenment concepts than to Christian tradition. However, they usually agree that it was the American Princeton theologian B. B. Warfield whose "great legacy was the elevation of plenary verbal inspiration resulting in inerrancy to the primary position in the doctrine of Scripture."[5]

---

2. Woods, "Biblical Principles," 3.
3. Wisløff, "Doctrinal Position," 3.
4. Hammond, *Evangelical Belief*, 20.
5. Holmes, "Evangelical Doctrines," 42.

Dictation?

One of the commonly raised objections to evangelical views of biblical inspiration is the idea that they believe in some sort of "mechanical dictation," thereby forgetting the human dimensions of Scripture. Interestingly, IFES writers constantly emphasize that they do not believe in such a mechanical process. As Hammond adamantly specifies, "any theory which regards the process of inspiration as being one of mechanical dictation to a blank mind, i.e. in which it is suggested that the human writer was no more than the passive amanuensis, does violence to the internal evidence of the Bible as a whole."[6]

This concession to the humanity of Scripture best explains the specification in the DB that the Bible is inspired "as originally given."[7] This concession allows for a certain degree of textual criticism without committing the fellowship to any crucible of translations, but it is notable that this part of the clause does not play a primary role in the writings on hermeneutics in the IFES papers.

Yet consistent with the notion of a "given original" is the idea that the Bible is not merely a "religious" book but essentially the record of God's speaking in history, which must be passed on to future generations. In Woods's words,

> this is a message which is objective truth. God has spoken to us in His acts in history as well as propositionally. This word of God has been inscripturated in the Bible. It is this message unchanged, unadulterated, that we are to guard and to proclaim. We may neither alter it, add to it, nor subtract from it. We may not embellish it with our personal notions and reactions. We may only interpret it according to the normal rational canons of hermeneutics.[8]

Woods argues here that whatever the circumstances, whatever the translation, the Bible's essentials could not have been changed. This approach does not leave much room for cultural and historical circumstances, however. Hammond, for example, acknowledges that "the Bible has been subject to much the same contingencies as have confronted all literature coming down from ancient times."[9] Nevertheless, he goes on to provide a brief explanation

---

6. Hammond, *Evangelical Belief*, 19.
7. For an illuminating overview of the strengths and weaknesses of this recourse to autographs, see John J. Brogan, "Can I Have Your Autograph?," in *Evangelicals & Scripture: Tradition, Authority and Hermeneutics*, by Dennis L. Okholm, Laura C. Miguélez and Vincent Bacote (Downers Grove: InterVarsity Press, 2004), 93–111.
8. Woods, "Medium Is the Message," 8.
9. Hammond, *Evangelical Belief*, 27.

of how "linguistic scholarship"[10] establishes reliable editions. What Hammond wants to arrive at in his brief explanation, however, is a standard evangelical statement of the reliability of scriptural texts, which he explains as follows:

> A considerable amount of data has accumulated during the past hundred years from archaeological, linguistic and historical studies, which have compelled biblical scholars to become more conservative in their attitude to the text of the Bible and its historical value. It is a justifiable inference that the preservation and transmission of the documents have been such that we have today an accurate record of the original writings of the Old and New Testaments.[11]

So in contradistinction to ecumenical circles which were rather inclined to infer from their historicization of the biblical texts based on so-called historical-critical methodologies, Hammond sees IVF's tradition of direct recourse to biblical texts vindicated by the results of scientific enquiry.

Science

That an organization working essentially with members of the academic community would insist on the authority of its ancient text could not but raise some questions about tradition, enquiry and epistemology generally. What were students to do about the affirmations of the Bible relating especially to the natural world and its study carried out with the tools of academic disciplines?

The story of the 1910 CICCU has already shown that the idea of "free enquiry" was very important to SCM leaders and that IVF appeared to them to be submitting to a rule foreign to academia. However, in the context of the late 1960s, the questions arose again, this time from within IFES and not from the outside. Soon after the 1971 General Committee, outgoing General Secretary Woods summarized the conclusions of the ad hoc task force on the DB and reported that

> we were asked whether "entire trustworthiness" applies to chronology, history, geography, etc. This is a more complex question than it might seem to be and no comprehensive answer has been possible in the time available. We would, however, state that in the practice of interpretation, difficulties often arise from

---

10. Hammond, 27.
11. Hammond, 28.

the inappropriate imposition of modern scientific and scholarly conventions. On the other hand, we would stress that no a priori limitations should be set to the authority of the Bible.[12]

The tension is palpable here: the Executive had almost been cornered by the GC, and was in need of an opt-out. The appeal to time limitations seems to have been very convenient: in fact, it is rather surprising that such a "weak" response would be given since there was nothing new as such in the question. The organization's leadership could have dealt more thoroughly with this thorny issue much earlier and had done so to a certain degree. The IFES Theological Secretary had written a few months earlier that "we must recognize, for example, that the concept of Infallibility does not exclude allegory, parable, metaphor, or other literary devices, but that it does exclude deliberate misleading (e.g. the idea that Jesus accommodated Himself to His disciples' limited and erroneous knowledge in attributing the Law to Moses, etc.)."[13]

So while there was agreement on the necessity of tackling a certain type of kenotic theology, the IFES leadership preferred to consider the variety of opinions within the evangelical fold, and not unimportantly among the donors an attitude of prudence became here a matter of expediency. The subcommittee hence reported that the DB "states clearly and adequately what needs to be stated," that its interpretation allows for a certain freedom of personal conscience, and that "the words 'entire trustworthiness' have a broader and richer meaning than infallibility and inerrancy." The statement goes on to say that tensions between the entire trustworthiness and questions of chronology, science and so on "often arise from the inappropriate imposition of modern, scientific and scholarly conventions."[14] The report of this subcommittee was "acknowledged by acclamation."[15]

The question was treated in roughly the same somewhat superficial manner in the DB commentary issued after the 1971 GC:

The authority of Scripture applies to the whole of created reality including arts, science, politics. However Scripture does not set out to teach science, for example, yet it teaches how science or any

---

12. Woods, "IFES Doctrinal Basis," 11.
13. Harold O. J. Brown, "Inspiration and Authority of Scripture," 23. Note that there is no notion of "infallibility" in the IFES DB, contrary to that of the US and British movements.
14. "Minutes of the Meeting of the Eighth General Committee" (1971), 20.
15. "Minutes of the Meeting of the Eighth General Committee" (1971), 20.

human skill should be learned and applied ("faith and conduct") for the good of man and to the glory of God.[16]

Some years later, Bob Horn, General Secretary of UCCF, would, in his considerations on the DB – reviewed by many senior IFES people – answer the charge that a DB is not compatible with the freedom of academic enquiry by saying that "academic inquiry is not opposed to definite conclusions, provided that they are well grounded."[17] The recurring motive is that the Bible is sure and solid ground. Since academic knowledge is not only about freedom but about reaching conclusions about the nature of reality, the DB can be understood as nothing other than the result of a well-grounded enquiry.

Trustworthiness

Time and again, the question of what "trustworthiness" means recurs in the deliberations, articles, defences of the DB and controversies. As we have seen, the term was understood to allow for more room in understanding than the term "infallible." This difference between the IVF DB and the IFES DB is notable, because it stresses the relational aspect of the Bible's teachings and their adequacy for life, and not only the declaratory nature of its doctrines. Bürki underlines this in clear wording, stating that

> all Scripture is entirely trustworthy because God is trustworthy. "Trustworthiness" is a more comprehensive word than "infallibility"[18] and it emphasizes that biblical truth is not an abstract notion but a reality to be trusted in because God is truth. One cannot know, therefore, the truth of the word of God without trust, ie, without personal commitment to God and His divine will expressed in human words.[19]

This is a hermeneutic which is consistent with soteriology: the Bible cannot be properly apprehended *outside* of a personal relationship with God, hence the greater emphasis on trust – a more pietistic category – than on "infallibility,"

---

16. Bürki, *Essentials*, 29.

17. Horn, *Ultimate Realities*, 85.

18. Note that the current version of the UCCF DB, in contradistinction to Hammond's early commentary, develops the clause which now reads: "The Bible, as originally given, is the inspired and infallible Word of God. It is the supreme authority in all matters of belief and behaviour." UCCF, "Doctrinal Basis."

19. Bürki, *Essentials*, 28.

a more scientific-rationalist category.[20] This is, of course, somewhat at odds with the academic culture, which stresses the careful, distant and objective apprehension of "facts" over against subjective relation to what is studied. The theological rubber hits the academic road, but the difference in methodology can be explained pneumatologically: the natural scientist's object of study does not "speak" to the researcher in the same way as the Holy Spirit speaks to the reader of Scripture. This tension between a distant, ethically loose approach to the text and a pious, devotional reading is hence a possible explanation of some cognitive dissonance for students hard-pressed to conform to academic methodologies on the one side, and to ecclesiological habits and standards on the other side.

This tension between objectivity and subjectivity has been a recurring conundrum within writings emanating from people close to or working with IFES. Although neither infallibility nor inerrancy was officially hailed in IFES literature, the idea is present in the background. Hammond, commenting on the IVF DB which contains the word "infallible," insists that it is a marker between what could anachronistically be labelled an "existential" reading of the text, and a proper recognition of the *whole* authority of Scripture:

> The chief purpose for which the Bible has been given to man is to guide him "in all matters of faith and conduct." Therefore, some suggest, "the Bible is infallible only in what it is intended to teach." Such a view, however, is by no means so cogent as it might at first seem. First, it provides an uncertain and very subjective criterion. Who, for example, is to determine what, in fact, are the limits of what the Bible "intends" to teach?[21]

This work has postulated that the "priesthood of all believers" provides a helpful theological framework to understand IFES's relation to hermeneutics, leadership and mission, for it assumes the possibility of each believer's individual access to God, hence the insistence on "trustworthiness." What the quotation above shows, however, is the lurking tension in this respect: who decides, ultimately, what the Bible says? It has seemed better to affirm the *supreme authority* of the text without explaining how a specific tradition

---

20. Holmes's somewhat pointed summary is that "North American Evangelicalism, with a broad commitment to inerrancy, views the Bible primarily as a collection of facts to be believed; British Evangelicalism, stressing instead authority, views the Bible primarily as a collection of rules to be obeyed." Holmes, "Evangelical Doctrines," 53.

21. Hammond, *Evangelical Belief*, 55.

of interpretation – essentially the DB in this case – plays the role of a *norma normata* of biblical interpretation.

The debate was not limited to trustworthiness, as the previously quoted summary of the 1971 task force reported. Looming large was the possibility of the word "inerrancy" to better describe the status of the Bible. A strong point of contention, especially in the United States, "inerrancy at its most basic is merely the confession that the Bible is without factual errors in those things it affirms."[22] The question in the background is, of course, whether for an international organization of such ethnocultural diversity as IFES, real consensus can be reached on what the Bible affirms. While the word was never taken over into official IFES doctrine, the idea that trusting the biblical text was not a rationalistic epistemological faux pas but rather purely in line with historical practice within Christianity is well summarized by Holmes, who submits that

> there seems little doubt that it has been a generally held position within the Christian churches down the ages. It is not very difficult to find explicit affirmations that the Bible makes no errors from across the history of the church; even where no explicit affirmation can be found, however, there seems good reason to suppose that, if asked the question, the vast majority of Christian denominations and theologians prior to the rise of higher criticism would have affirmed inerrancy, as would conservatives of every stripe, not just Evangelical, more recently.[23]

Here again, the adoption of higher criticism by "liberal factions" is considered to be a kind of "hermeneutical original sin" of the late nineteenth century, with IFES taking on the role of the defender of the faith that others have abandoned.[24]

---

22. Holmes, "Evangelical Doctrines," 41. For more on the history, development and debates around inerrancy, see among others Okholm, Miguélez and Bacote, *Evangelicals & Scripture*.

23. Holmes, "Evangelical Doctrines," 41.

24. It is probably with these safeguarding intentions in mind that Woods's later words should be read. In his draft for an IFES history, he uses the term "infallible" as well as he comes back to the question of scientific knowledge: "the *raison d'être* of the IFES, both in its antecedents and present conviction, is that the Bible is and forever shall be, God's infallible Word, entirely trustworthy in all its parts. This is true not only in matters of faith, morals, ethics and conduct but also when properly understood in all its references to space/time-events, to persons, history and geography." Woods, "IFES History Draft," ch. 2, p. 13.

Authority

Very closely linked to the idea of trustworthiness is the notion of Scripture's authority, which emanates first from the concept of a dual nature to Scripture. In other words, in very similar fashion to how the Chalcedonian Creed affirms the dual nature of the incarnate Christ, the DB builds on the idea of the dual nature of the written word: "The Bible is both divine and human; this amazing confession of faith is analogous to the confession of Jesus Christ as the living word of God in human flesh!"[25]

Since Christians confess to following Christ, believing in him has the logical conclusion for the IFES writers that the believer has to submit to the Scriptures, because of Christ's direct involvement in their inspiration: "He has so inspired the Holy Scriptures that they are self-authenticating and they themselves give clear and explicit indications of their unique origin; and He enlightens the understanding of believers to understand the message and recognize the authority of the Bible, as being in truth the Word of God."[26]

The notion of "self-authentification" is very congenial to traditional evangelical hermeneutics and has evident missiological consequences. A local student group can assume the Bible's authority and invite others to read it, trusting that they do not necessarily need to make a strong theoretical case for scriptural authority: congruent with the doctrine of the priesthood of all believers is the free access to the supreme source of authority that anyone, eventually, would recognize.

The whole framework of the DB implies confidence in scriptural authority, but this is not solely a bibliological concept. It springs out of a clear theological conviction that the sovereign – and therefore authoritative – "God of Truth cannot and does not deceive."[27] If the Bible is his word, it must be authoritative. Brown concedes that this confession is not a matter of salvation, for "it is a fairly generally recognized principle that no Christian must confess a particular doctrine about the Scripture in order to be saved. Neither the Bible nor the Creeds presuppose this."[28] Brown nevertheless goes on to affirm the importance of a "proper" understanding of what the Bible is:

> But it is important that one have a firm confidence in the reliability of the Bible in order to understand the content of saving faith, and it is essential for one who wishes to teach the faith whether

---

25. Bürki, *Essentials*, 28.
26. Hammond, *Evangelical Belief*, 27.
27. Harold O. J. Brown, "Inspiration and Authority of Scripture," 23.
28. Brown, 21.

he be a theology professor, a pastor, a Sunday-school teacher, or any other Christian who accepts a responsibility for the spiritual welfare of others.[29]

Similarly, non-evangelicals might well ask *which* Bible is to be considered authoritative. In order to prevent deuterocanonical books from being considered authoritative, Hammond specifies that "the books known as the Apocrypha, which is incorporated in the Roman Catholic Canon, are excluded."[30]

That said, there is a certain degree of self-referentiality in the DB's appeal to Scripture as authority. Many other Christian traditions would agree with IFES that Scripture is authoritative; the question is rather *what kind* of authority is envisaged, or *how it functions* in a given context. In this case, it seems that the DB affirms the Bible's authority and *frames the way it should be read*. Collange somewhat ironically asks whether such an attitude does not come very close to that of "traditional Catholicism and its presentation of the truth of the letter of dogma and doctrine as 'papal infallibility.'"[31]

Similarly, what Willaime has observed in the case of French Reformed Churches applies well to the case of IFES, thus somehow blurring the boundaries between church and parachurch:

> The authority is in the Bible, but read and interpreted through the Church's Confession of Faith. . . . This text [the Confession of Faith] has a secondary authority to the Bible, but, since it defines what the centre of the biblical message is and how the Bible is to be read, it takes a central place in the regulation of the Church's faith.[32]

Willaime further concludes that a confession of faith functions like a tradition, for "alongside the Bible, there is a traditional legitimacy manifested in reference to the apostolic witness and the Confessions of Faith of the Reformation."[33] This is what Holmes also astutely observes:

---

29. Brown, 21.
30. Hammond, *Evangelical Belief*, 15.
31. Collange, "Les confessions de foi «évangéliques»," 74. It is striking to note that the French translation of Bürki's commentary also has the French original translation of the DB, which reads "son autorité *seul* est souveraine." Hans Bürki, *Fonder sa foi*, Points de repère (Lausanne: Presses Bibliques Universitaires, 1978), 25; emphasis added. It is in the context of a stronger Catholic presence that most French-speaking movements have for a long time used their own translation, in order to encourage Catholics aspiring to join their movements to step out of the RCC.
32. Willaime, "Formule d'adhésion," 292.
33. Willaime, 292.

"Supreme authority" sounds, rhetorically, like it is a strengthening, but in fact its logical status is potentially weaker than a simple claim to "authority," in that it implies the existence of other, real but subordinate, authorities. If the Bible is "the authority," then no other appeal is permissible; if it is "the supreme authority," then I may believe in the real, albeit subordinate, authority of other documents – the ecumenical creeds, perhaps.[34]

Bürki is also aware of this complex relationship to traditions. The concern of IFES seems to have been more properly a question of theological method than one of ecclesiastical policies:

The supreme authority of Scripture means that God's Word is not without tradition but above it.[35] It is not against reason but reason is not to be its arbitrator. It is not outside the church but over her, not without knowledge of transhuman manifestations but beyond their judgement.[36]

Proclaiming scriptural authority should go beyond theological affirmation to have ethical consequences. The idea of focusing on essentials led the early IFES leaders to concentrate on the premises of faithful Christian actions rather than on the practical outworking of such beliefs. Holmes, continuing his argument quoted above, notes that this does not go without dangers, however:

The same may be said of the addition concerning "faith and practice": the rhetorical effect is again strengthening, but the logical effect is to raise the possibility that there are matters not pertaining to "faith and practice" (or "faith and conduct") in which the Scriptures in fact have no authority – matters of science or history, perhaps. Such analysis makes the statements difficult to analyse, of course: did writers adding "supreme" to "authority" think they were strengthening, or grasp that they were weakening, the claim? What of those who agreed to accept the revised documents?[37]

---

34. Holmes, "Evangelical Doctrines," 51.

35. Bürki asks in the footnote: "What is the place of Scripture over and against the traditions of man? Mark 7:6–9, 13; Galatians 1:6–10." Bürki, *Essentials*, 30.

36. Bürki, 29.

37. Holmes, "Evangelical Doctrines," 51.

Pneumatological Prerequisites

Finally, the IFES hermeneutic has decisively pneumatological underpinnings. Congruent with Clause I of the DB and its affirmation that the Holy Spirit lives within the believer, the DB's assumption is that the Bible cannot be recognized as authoritative, nor be properly understood, without the Holy Spirit. What could appear to be a tautology is properly understood as a theological statement against the perceived rationalism of liberal theology. Those connected with IFES were constantly demarcating themselves from a theology that either would be done *etsi Deus non daretur* or would take pride in affirming only what could be rationally understood by modern people. Hence the insistence on the necessity of a transcendent active presence in the mind and heart of the believer who reads the biblical text. This is remarkable, for it also implies that reading the Bible does not presuppose a theological degree. In Hammond's words, the Bible "was designed to remain a book of universal acceptance and of equal value to all ages and all peoples in various stages of education. In the providence of God it is in a form in which its basic meaning may be grasped by all types of men."[38]

This elevates the Bible to another realm from that of any other text and hence entails some potential tensions in hermeneutical practice: it is easier to agree on common methodologies for studying classical historical texts, for example, in a university context and reach some scholarly consensus. However, what is remarkable is the insistence on the fact that the Bible is accessible to anyone who wants to read it.

As we have noted above, all the DB's official commentators insist that the clauses of the DB are derived inductively from the Bible, but not in unmediated fashion. In line with the traditional evangelical understanding of hermeneutics, the Bible cannot be appropriately understood apart from the internal illumination of the Holy Spirit. Thus, there is a complex interrelation between the believer's faith, his or her relationship to God, and Scripture. But the DB then mediates a shared understanding of what is understood to be the core of biblical truth:

> The conviction that the Bible is the written Word of God is wrought in the believer by the Holy Spirit. This inward testimony of the Holy Spirit is not something which acts independently of Scripture. It is given in order to witness to Scripture and to authenticate it as the medium of the divine revelation to man.

---

38. Hammond, *Evangelical Belief*, 56.

Concerning the actual process of inspiration, the Bible makes only one other general statement.[39]

We should note here that stressing the necessity of spiritual illumination presupposes a particular approach to human reasoning, namely one which is constantly marked by references to human limitations caused by sin: "we are made aware that unenlightened human reason and emotion alone cannot comprehend God's revelation. Every type of knowledge can easily lead to pride. He who thinks that he knows something, does not know how to know."[40]

Depending on the reader's perspective, this is either a dim view of what humans are capable of, or rather a way of highlighting the power of the Christian gospel. There is no doubt that in the IFES view, the latter is the case, and is rather an incentive for mission than a premise of despair.

---

39. Hammond, 18. Reference is made to 2 Pet 1:21.
40. Bürki, *Essentials*, 18.

Bibliography

ABUB. "No Que Cremos." Aliança Bíblica Universitária do Brasil. Accessed 22.02.2023. https://abub.org.br/quem-somos#!/cremos.
Achtemeier, Paul J. *1 Peter: A Commentary on First Peter*. Hermeneia. Minneapolis: Fortress, 1996.
Adeney, David H. *China: Christian Students Face the Revolution*. London: Inter-Varsity Press, 1973.
———. "Light to the Nations: 1987 IFES Presidential Address." *IFES Review* 23 (1987): 3–11.
———. "Student Work in Southeast Asia." *IFES Journal* 12, no. 1 (1959): 3–9.
Ahlstrom, Sydney E. "The Radical Turn in Theology and Ethics: Why It Occurred in the 1960s." *Annals of the American Academy of Political and Social Science* 387 (Jan. 1970): 1–13.
Akinade, Akintunde E. "Introduction." In *A New Day: Essays on World Christianity in Honor of Lamin Sanneh*, edited by Akintunde E. Akinade, 1–13. 1st printing ed. New York: Peter Lang, 2010.
Allen, Hubert. *Roland Allen: Pioneer, Priest and Prophet*. Grand Rapids: Eerdmans, 1995.
Allen, Roland. *The Ministry of Expansion: The Priesthood of the Laity*. Edited by J. D. Payne. Kindle. Pasadena: William Carey Library, 2017.
———. *Missionary Methods: St Paul's or Ours?* London: Scott, 1912.
———. "Spontaneous Expansion: The Terror of Missionaries." *World Dominion* 4 (1926): 218–24.
Anderson, Benedict. *Imagined Communities: Reflections on the Origin and Spread of Nationalism*. London: Verso, 1983.
Andria, Solomon. "Autonomy and Indigeneity." Hyundai Learning Center, Seoul, South Korea, June 1999. IFES e-archives. Old EC 1999 minutes, Appendix K.
———. "Pentecostal, Charismatic, Evangelical: Differences and Distinctives." Centre des métiers de l'électricité, Bingerville, Côte d'Ivoire, May 1994. IFES e-archives. EC 1994 minutes, Appendix L1.
Anizor, Uche, and Hank Voss. *Representing Christ: A Vision for the Priesthood of All Believers*. Downers Grove: InterVarsity Press, 2016.
Arana, Pedro. "Evangelization in the Latin American University." *International Review of Mission* 63, no. 252 (1974): 507–14.
———. "Towards a Biblical Public Theology." *Journal of Latin American Theology* 11, no. 2 (2016): 35–59.
Armitage, Carolyn. *Reaching for the Goal: The Life Story of David Adeney – Ordinary Man, Extraordinary Vision*. Wheaton: OMF Books, 1993.

Aulén, Gustaf. *Christus Victor: An Historical Study of the Three Main Types of the Idea of the Atonement.* [Den Kristna Försoningstanken.] Authorised Translation. Translated by A. G. Hebert. London: SPCK, 1931.

Australian Fellowship of Evangelical Students (AFES). "Doctrinal Basis." Accessed 21 May 2020. https://afes.org.au/about/doctrinal-basis.

Aw, Swee-Eng. "But When I Left College I Couldn't Fit into a Church." *In Touch* 1 (1984): 3.

Balia, Daryl M., and Kirsteen Kim, eds. *Witnessing to Christ Today.* Vol. 2 of *Edinburgh 2010.* Oxford: Regnum, 2010.

Barclay, Oliver R. *Developing a Christian Mind.* Leicester: Inter-Varsity Press, 1984.

———. "Guarding the Truth: The Place and Purpose of the Doctrinal Basis. Workshop at Formación 89." *IFES Review* 27 (1989): 29–40.

———. *Whatever Happened to the Jesus Lane Lot?* Leicester: Inter-Varsity Press, 1977.

Barclay, Oliver R., and Robert M. Horn. *From Cambridge to the World: 125 Years of Student Witness.* Leicester: Inter-Varsity Press, 2002.

Bebbington, David W. *Evangelicalism in Modern Britain: A History from the 1730s to the 1980s.* London: Unwin Hyman, 1989.

Bebbington, David W., and David Ceri Jones, eds. *Evangelicalism and Fundamentalism in the United Kingdom During the Twentieth Century.* Oxford: OUP, 2013.

Beckford, James A. "Explaining Religious Movements." *International Social Science Journal* 29, no. 2 (1977): 235.

———. *Social Theory and Religion.* Cambridge: CUP, 2003.

Becquet, Valérie. "Moment étudiant, moment d'engagement: regard sur les activités bénévoles des étudiants." In *Cent ans de mouvements étudiants*, by Jean-Philippe Legois, Alain Monchalbon and Robi Morder, 141–55. Edited by Groupe d'études et de recherches sur les mouvements étudiants (GERME). Paris: Syllepse, 2007.

Benoît, Pierre de, Gordon Scorer, Ferenc Kiss, Rev. E. L. Langston, René Pache and Gertrud Wasserzug-Traeder, eds. "Invitation to the 1936 International Conference in Beatenberg, Switzerland," 1936. BGC #193.

Benson, Hilda, Rev. Candy Douglas and Rev. Gerald Hutchison. "Extracts from a Report on the Conference for Missionary Advance, Toronto, 1946." Toronto: World Student Christian Federation, January 1947. WSCF Archive 213.16.39/2.

Bentley-Taylor, David. "Adventures of a Christian Envoy." Photocopied manuscript. London, 1992. IFES Archive, Oxford.

———. "African Diary, Part II." *IFES Journal* 20, no. 3 (1967): 23–32.

———. "The Seventh IFES General Committee: An Appraisal." *IFES Journal* 20, no. 3 (1967): 9–12.

Berger, Peter L. *The Heretical Imperative: Contemporary Possibilities of Religious Affirmation.* Garden City: Anchor, 1979.

Bevans, Stephen B., and Roger Schroeder. *Constants in Context: A Theology of Mission for Today.* AMS 30. Maryknoll: Orbis, 2004.

Bielo, James S. *Words upon the Word: An Ethnography of Evangelical Group Bible Study*. Qualitative Studies in Religion. New York: New York University Press, 2009.
Blackburn, W. Ross. *The God Who Makes Himself Known: The Missionary Heart of the Book of Exodus*. Downers Grove: Apollos, 2012.
Blanchard, Roger. "Concerns of Proposed Ecumenical Consultation." c.1955. WSCF Archive 213.16.39/2.
Blocher, Henri. "Lu et commenté: Dieu sans Dieu." *Chantiers*, 1965, 26–30.
———. "Permanent Validity and Contextual Relativity of Doctrinal Statements." In *The Task of Dogmatics*, edited by Fred Sanders, 107–31. Grand Rapids: Zondervan, 2017.
Bloesch, Donald G. *Life, Ministry, and Hope*. Vol. 2 of *Essentials of Evangelical Theology*. San Francisco: Harper & Row, 1979.
Bong, Wonyoung. "Toward Improving the Effectiveness of Campus Ministry at Universities." *Asia-Africa Journal of Mission and Ministry* 7 (2013): 27–45.
Bosch, David. *Transforming Mission: Paradigm Shifts in Theology of Mission*. Maryknoll: Orbis, 1991.
Bourdanné, Daniel. "Évangélisation des étudiants." In *Dictionnaire de théologie pratique*, edited by Christophe Paya, 359–66. Cléon-d'Andran: Éditions Excelsis, 2011.
———. "Foreword." In *Influence: The Impact of IFES on the Lives of Its Graduates*, 9. Oxford: International Fellowship of Evangelical Students, 2015.
Boyd, Robin H. S. *The Witness of the Student Christian Movement: Church Ahead of the Church*. London: SPCK, 2007.
Brackney, William H. *Christian Voluntarism: Theology and Praxis*. Faith's Horizons. Grand Rapids: Eerdmans, 1997.
Bramadat, Paul A. *Church on the World's Turf: An Evangelical Christian Group at a Secular University*. Oxford: Oxford University Press, 2000.
Briggs, John, Mercy Amba Oduyoye and Georges Tsetsis, eds. *A History of the Ecumenical Movement*. Vol. 3, *1968–2000*. 3 vols. Geneva: World Council of Churches, 1986.
Brogan, John J. "Can I Have Your Autograph?" In *Evangelicals & Scripture: Tradition, Authority and Hermeneutics*, by Dennis L. Okholm, Laura C. Miguélez and Vincent Bacote, 93–111. Downers Grove: InterVarsity Press, 2004.
Brown, Callum G. "What Was the Religious Crisis of the 1960s?" *Journal of Religious History* 34, no. 4 (2010): 468–79.
Brown, Harold O. J. "The Inspiration and Authority of Scripture." *IFES Journal* 23, no. 2 (1970): 19–24.
———. "Report of the Theological Secretary." 1971. IFES e-archives. GC 1971 minutes, Appendix H.
Brown, Lindsay. "Draft Global IFES Long Range Plan." Oak Hill College, London, England, 25–31.7 1993. IFES e-archives, EC 1993 minutes, Appendix H.
———. "The Growth of a Work of God: The Antioch Model; Address to World Assembly 1991." *IFES Review* 31 (1991): 3–10.

———. "IFES Jubilee." *Highlights*, December 1997, 1–2.

———. "IFES and the Orthodox Church." Hald Training Center, Mandal, Norway, 28.7–1.8 1992. IFES e-archives, EC 1992 minutes, Appendix I.

———. *Into All the World: The Missionary Vision of Luther and Calvin*. Fearn: Christian Focus, 2021.

———. "Report of the General Secretary to the General Committee of IFES." Kenya Commercial Bank Center, Nairobi, Kenya, 26 June 1995. IFES e-archives. GC 1995 minutes, Appendix D.

———. *Shining Like Stars: The Power of the Gospel in the World's Universities*. Nottingham: Inter-Varsity Press, 2006.

Brown, Dr. Sue. "The Future of Training in IFES." Oak Hill College, Southgate, London, England, May 1993. IFES e-archives. EC 1993 minutes, Appendix B1.

———. To Formación 1989 Contributors. 27 September 1989. BGC Box #5.

Bruce, Steve. "The Student Christian Movement and the Inter-Varsity Fellowship: A Sociological Study of Two Movements." Doctoral thesis, University of Stirling, 1980.

Bryant, Alyssa. "Evangelicals on Campus: An Exploration of Culture, Faith and College Life." *Religion & Education* 32, no. 2 (2005): 1–30.

Bryant, Alyssa, and Helen Astin. "The Correlates of Spiritual Struggle During the College Years." *The Journal of Higher Education* 79, no. 1 (2008): 1–27.

Bürki, Hans. "The Confrontation of Evangelism with Ideology." *IFES Journal* 1 (1967): 22–27.

———. *Essentials: A Brief Introduction for Bible Study Based on the Doctrinal Basis of the International Fellowship of Evangelical Students*. London: IFES, 1975.

———. *Fonder sa foi*. Points de repère. Lausanne: Presses Bibliques Universitaires, 1978.

———. "Student Unrest: Its Causes, Characteristics and Cures." Seminar paper, Schloss Mittersill, Austria, 1971. IFES e-archives, GC 1971 minutes, Appendix J.

Calvin, John. *Institutes of the Christian Religion*. Translated by Ford Lewis McNeill. The Library of Christian Classics. Philadelphia: Westminster John Knox, 2011.

Cambridge Inter-Collegiate Christian Union. *Old Paths in Perilous Times*. 1st ed. Cambridge, 1913.

———. *Old Paths in Perilous Times*. Edited by Basil F. C. Atkinson. 2nd ed. London: IVF, 1932.

Camp, Bruce K. "A Theological Examination of the Two-Structure Theory." *Missiology* 23, no. 2 (1995): 197–209.

Cassidy, Michael. "Evangelization amongst College and University Students." In *Let the Earth Hear His Voice*, edited by J. D. Douglas, 749–64. Minneapolis: World Wide Publications, 1975.

"Catechism of the Catholic Church". Accessed 23 February 2023. https://www.vatican.va/archive/ENG0015/__P4Y.HTM.

Caterson, Joe. "Proposals for Effective Partnership in Worldwide Student Evangelisation." Plenary Discussion Paper. Ashburnham Place, Battle, East Sussex, England, 27 July 1983. IFES e-archives. GC 1983 minutes, Appendix R.

Catherwood, Christopher. *Martyn Lloyd-Jones: His Life and Relevance for the 21st Century*. Nottingham: Inter-Varsity Press, 2015.

Cawley, Luke. *Campus Lights: Students Living and Speaking for Jesus around the World*. Edinburgh: Muddy Pearl, 2019.

———. *The Myth of the Non-Christian: Engaging Atheists, Nominal Christians and the Spiritual but Not Religious*. Downers Grove: InterVarsity Press, 2016.

Chadwick, Owen. *The Secularization of the European Mind in the Nineteenth Century*. Cambridge: Cambridge University Press, 1975.

Chapman, Alister. "Evangelical International Relations in the Post-Colonial World: The Lausanne Movement and the Challenge of Diversity, 1974–89." *Missiology* 37, no. 3 (2009): 355–68.

———. "Evangelical or Fundamentalist? The Case of John Stott." In *Evangelicalism and Fundamentalism in the United Kingdom During the Twentieth Century*, edited by David W. Bebbington and David Ceri Jones, 192–208. Oxford: OUP, 2013.

———. *Godly Ambition: John Stott and the Evangelical Movement*. New York: OUP, 2012.

Chua Wee Hian. "Breakthrough in the Seventies." *IFES Journal* 23, no. 2 (1970): 8–13.

———. "The CU and the Church." Audio tape. Formación 89, 1989. IFES Archive, Oxford.

———. "Foreword." In *Essentials: A Brief Introduction for Bible Study Based on the Doctrinal Basis of the International Fellowship of Evangelical Students*, by Hans Bürki, 7–9. London: IFES, 1975.

———. "The General Secretary's Perspective." Hurdal Verk, Norway, 27 July 1979. IFES e-archives. GC 1979 minutes, Appendix D.

———. "General Secretary's Report." El Hostel Duruelo, Boyaca, Colombia, 30.8–8.9 1987. IFES e-archives. GC 1987 minutes, Appendix B.

———. *Getting through Customs: The Global Jottings of Chua Wee Hian*. Leicester: Inter-Varsity Press, 1992.

———. "Graduate Ministry: A Postscript from the General Secretary." *IFES Review* 26 (1989): 45–48.

———. "IFES: The Big Picture." *In Touch* 3 (1987): 5.

———. "IFES General Secretary's Report 1991." Wheaton College, Wheaton, Illinois, USA, 27.7–4.8 1991. IFES e-archives. GC 1991 minutes, Appendix D.

———. "Major Trends and Developments in IFES." IFES Executive Committee, 5 May 1988. IFES e-archives.

———. "The Next Four Years." *IFES Journal* 25, no. 3 (1971): 7–9.

———. "Priorities 1." April 1988. BGC Box #5.

———. "Report of the General Secretary." Schloss Mittersill, Austria, 1974. IFES e-archives. EC 1974 minutes, Appendix A.

———. "Report of the General Secretary." Schloss Mittersill, Austria, 1975. IFES e-archives. GC 1975 minutes, Appendix.
———. "Staff Letter 6." May 1973. BGC Box #5.
———. "Staff Letter 8." July 1973. BGC Box #5.
———. "Staff Letter 9." September 1973. BGC Box #5.
———. "Staff Letter 15." October 1974. BGC Box #5.
———. "Staff Letter 31." November 1978. BGC Box #5.
———. "With Evangelical Students." In *Martyn Lloyd-Jones: Chosen by God*, edited by Christopher Catherwood, 110–24. Crowborough: Highland Books, 1988.
Chua Wee Hian and C. René Padilla. "God's Work in the World Today." In *Jesus Christ: Lord of the Universe, Hope of the World; Urbana 1973*, edited by David M. Howard, 167–78. Downers Grove: InterVarsity Press, 1974.
Clawson, Michael. "Misión Integral and Progressive Evangelicalism: The Latin American Influence on the North American Emerging Church." *Religions* 3, no. 3 (2012): 790–807.
Clowney, Edmund P. *The Church*. Downers Grove: InterVarsity Press, 1995.
———. *The Message of 1 Peter*. The Bible Speaks Today. Leicester: Inter-Varsity Press, 1988.
Coggan, Donald. *Christ and the Colleges: A History of the Inter-Varsity Fellowship of Evangelical Unions*. London: Inter-Varsity Press, 1934.
Collange, Jean-François. "Les confessions de foi «évangéliques»." *Autres Temps. Les cahiers du christianisme social* 3 (1984): 72–82.
Colon, David. "Face aux églises: un siècle d'organisations d'étudiants chrétiens." In *Cent ans de mouvements étudiants*, by Jean-Philippe Legois and Alain Monchalbon, 217–26. Edited by Groupe d'études et de recherches sur les mouvements étudiants (GERME). Paris: Syllepse, 2007.
Congar, Yves. *Jalons pour une théologie du laïcat*. 2nd ed. Unam sanctam 23. Paris: Éditions du Cerf, 1954.
Congar, Yves, and François Varillon. *Sacerdoce et laïcat dans l'église*. Paris: Vitrail, 1947.
"Constitution of the International Conference of Evangelical Students." 9 September 1935. BGC #193.
"Constitution of the International Fellowship of Evangelical Students." August 1947. BGC #193.
"Constitution of the International Fellowship of Evangelical Students." July 2015. IFES e-Archives.
Cox, Harvey Gallagher. *Fire from Heaven: Pentecostalism, Spirituality, and the Reshaping of Religion in the Twenty-First Century*. Reading: Addison-Wesley, 1994.
Cressey, Martin H. *The Conservative Evangelical in the Ecumenical Movement*. London: Student Christian Movement, 1960s.
Dahle, Lars, ed. *The Lausanne Movement: A Range of Perspectives*. Oxford: Wipf & Stock, 2014.

Davie, Grace. *Religion in Britain since 1945: Believing without Belonging*. Oxford: Blackwell, 1994.
———. *Religion in Modern Europe: A Memory Mutates*. European Societies. Oxford: OUP, 2000.
Davies, D. Eryl. "Lloyd-Jones, David Martyn." In *Biographical Dictionary of Evangelicals*, edited by Timothy Larsen, 370–74. Leicester: Inter-Varsity Press, 2003.
D'Costa, Gavin. "The State of the University: Academic Knowledges and the Knowledge of God." *Pro Ecclesia* 20, no. 3 (2011): 312–16.
Debanné, Marc. "L'étudiant chrétien, l'Église locale et les mouvements chrétiens étudiants: comment démystifier la place du «para-Église»?" *Théologie évangélique* 14, no. 1 (2015): 24–44.
Deschner, John. "Evangelism." Summary of address given at the 1956 WSCF Ecumenical Consultation. Céligny, 1956. WSCF Archive 213.16.39/2.
Dickson, Neil. "'The Church Itself Is God's Clergy.' The Principles and Practices of the Brethren." In *The Rise of the Laity in Evangelical Protestantism*, edited by Deryck Lovegrove, 217–35. London: Routledge Chapman & Hall, 2002.
Diétrich, Suzanne de. *Cinquante ans d'histoire: la Fédération universelle des associations chrétiennes d'étudiants (1895–1945)*. Paris: Ed. du Semeur, 1946.
Douglas, J. D., ed. "Theology and Implications of Radical Discipleship." In *Let the Earth Hear His Voice*, 1294–96. Minneapolis: World Wide Publications, 1975.
Dransfield, Julie, and Cindy Merritt. "The 'One-Another' Ministry of Students to Students." *IFES Review* 24 (1988): 37–42.
Dudley-Smith, Timothy. *John Stott: A Global Ministry*. Downers Grove: InterVarsity Press, 2001.
Dumbrell, W. J. *Covenant and Creation: A Theology of the Old Testament Covenants*. 1st ed. 1984. Biblical and Theological Classics. Carlisle: Paternoster, 1997.
Dunn, James D. G. *The Parting of the Ways: Between Christianity and Judaism and Their Significance for the Character of Christianity*. 1st ed. 1991. 2nd ed. London: SCM, 2006.
Durham, John I. *Exodus*. Word Biblical Commentary 3. Waco: Word, 1986.
Durnbaugh, Donald F. *The Believers' Church: The History and Character of Radical Protestantism*. New York: Macmillan, 1968.
Dutton, Edward. *Meeting Jesus at University: Rites of Passage and Student Evangelicals*. Burlington: Ashgate, 2008.
Eberstadt, Mary. *How the West Really Lost God: A New Theory of Secularization*. West Conshohocken: Templeton Press, 2013.
Edge, Findley B. "Priesthood of Believers." *Review & Expositor* 60, no. 1 (1963): 9–21.
Enns, Fernando. "Believers Church Ecclesiology: A Vital Alternative within the Ecumenical Family." In *New Perspectives in Believers Church Ecclesiology*, edited by Abe J. Dueck, Helmut Harder and Karl Koop, 107–24. Winnipeg: CMU, 2010.
Enoch, H. *Following the Master*. Mumbai: GLS, 1977.
Escobar, Samuel. *Diálogo entre Cristo y Marx y otros ensayos*. Lima: AGEUP, 1969.

———. "Evangelism and Man's Search for Freedom, Justice and Fulfillment." In *Let the Earth Hear His Voice*, edited by J. D. Douglas, 303–26. Minneapolis: World Wide Publications, 1975.

———. Interview. Coma-Ruga, Spain, 2018.

———. *La chispa y la llama: breve historia de la Comunidad Internacional de Estudiantes Evangélicos en América Latina.* Buenos Aires: Ediciones Certeza, 1978.

———. *La chispa y la llama: Volumen II.* Buenos Aires: Certeza Unida, 2022.

———. "A New Time for Mission: Plenary Address to IFES WA 1999." Hyundai Learning Center, Yong-In, South Korea, 23 July 1999. IFES e-archives.

———. "Our Evangelical Heritage: Major Paper Presented at the 1983 General Committee." *IFES Review* 14 (1983): 2–20.

———. "Report of the Associate General Secretary at Large." Raglan, New Zealand, 18 August 1978. IFES e-archives. EC 1978 minutes, Appendix E.

———. "Report of the IFES Associate General Secretary at Large." Oxon, England, 28.9–3.10 1977. IFES e-archives. EC 1977 minutes, Appendix E.

———. "Social Concern and World Evangelism." In *Christ the Liberator*, edited by John R. W. Stott, 103–12. Urbana 70. Downers Grove: InterVarsity Press, 1971.

———. "The Social Impact of the Gospel." In *Is Revolution Change?*, edited by Brian Griffiths, 84–105. IVP Pocketbook. London: Inter-Varsity Press, 1972.

———. *A Time for Mission: The Challenge for Global Christianity.* Leicester: Inter-Varsity Press, 2003.

Escobar, Samuel, C. René Padilla and Edwin Yamauchi, eds. *Quien es Cristo hoy?* Buenos Aires: Ediciones Certeza, 1971.

"Evangelical Declaration of Cochabamba: At the Founding Meeting of the Fraternidad Teológica Latinoamericana, December, 1970." *Journal of Latin American Theology* 11, no. 2 (2016): 185–88.

Fath, Sébastien. "Evangelical Protestantism in France: An Example of Denominational Recomposition?" *Sociology of Religion* 66, no. 4 (1 Dec. 2005): 399–418.

———. *Le protestantisme évangélique, un christianisme de conversion: entre ruptures et filiations.* Bibliothèque de l'Ecole des Hautes Etudes. Sciences religieuses. Turnhout: Brepols, 2004.

Fielder, Geraint. *Lord of the Years: Sixty Years of Student Witness – Story of the Inter-Varsity Fellowship/Universities and Colleges Christian Fellowship, 1928–88.* Leicester: Inter-Varsity Press, 1988.

Filiatreau, Mark. "Honouring Our Elders: Dr. James Houston, Founder of Regent College." BC Christian News, June 2001. https://web.archive.org/web/20090519095349/https://canadianchristianity.com/cgi-bin/bc.cgi?bc/bccn/0601/supelders.

Flemming, Dean E. *Contextualization in the New Testament: Patterns for Theology and Mission.* Westmont: InterVarsity Press, 2009.

Flett, John G. *Apostolicity: The Ecumenical Question in World Christian Perspective.* Missiological Engagements. Downers Grove: InterVarsity Press, 2016.

Ford, Barney. "A Shift of Strategy: From Expansion towards Greater Maturity." Bischofsheim, Germany, May 1998. IFES e-archives. EC 1998 minutes, Appendix E.

Foster Williams, David. "A Comparison of the Work of the Student Christian Movement and the Inter-Varsity Fellowship as Each Is Found in Latin America." Master's thesis, The Biblical Seminary in New York, 1959. WSCF Archive 213.16.39/1.

Fry, John R. "Anti-Intellectualism in the Church Today." *The Christian Scholar* 45, no. 1 (1962): 22–27.

"FTL: Fraternidad Teológica Latinoamericana." Accessed 27 July 2020. https://ftl-al.com/.

Fueter, Paul D. "New Christians for New Pagans." *IFES Journal* 21, no. 3 (1968): 1–9.

Galadima, Bulus. "Evaluation of the Theology of Bolaji Idowu." *Africa Journal of Evangelical Theology* 20, no. 2 (2001): 105–31.

Gebara, Ivone. "The Movement of May 1968 and Theology in Latin America." *The Ecumenical Review* 70, no. 2 (23 Sep. 2018): 264–71.

Gilliland, Dean. "Contextualization." In *Evangelical Dictionary of World Missions*, edited by A. Scott Moreau, Harold A. Netland and Charles Edward van Engen, 225–28. Grand Rapids: Baker, 2000.

Gloege, Timothy. "A Gilded Age Modernist: Reuben A. Torrey and the Roots of Contemporary Conservative Evangelicalism." In *American Evangelicalism: George Marsden and the State of American Religious History*, edited by Darren Dochuk and Thomas S. Kidd, 199–229. Notre Dame: University of Notre Dame Press, 2014.

Goheen, Michael W. "The Missional Calling of Believers in the World: Lesslie Newbigin's Contribution." In *A Scandalous Prophet: The Way of Mission after Newbigin*, edited by Thomas F. Foust, George R. Hunsberger, J. Andrew Kirk and Werner Ustorf, 37–56. Grand Rapids: Eerdmans, 2001.

Goodhew, David. "Cassidy, Michael." In *Biographical Dictionary of Evangelicals*, edited by Timothy Larsen, David Bebbington and Mark A. Noll, 130–31. Leicester: Inter-Varsity Press, 2003.

———. "The Rise of the Cambridge Inter-Collegiate Christian Union, 1910–1971." *The Journal of Ecclesiastical History* 54, no. 1 (2003): 62–88.

Green, Joel B. *1 Peter*. The Two Horizons New Testament Commentary. Grand Rapids: Eerdmans, 2007.

Greggs, Tom. *Dogmatic Ecclesiology*. Vol. 1, *The Priestly Catholicity of the Church*. Kindle. Grand Rapids: Baker Academic, 2019.

———. "The Priesthood of No Believer: On the Priesthood of Christ and His Church." *International Journal of Systematic Theology* 17, no. 4 (1 Oct. 2015): 374–98.

Grossi, Vittorino. "Priesthood of Believers." In *Encyclopedia of Ancient Christianity*, edited by Angelo Di Berardino, 3:302–4. Downers Grove: InterVarsity Press, 2014.

Gruner, Paul. *Menschenwege und Gotteswege im Studentenleben: Persönliche Erinnerungen aus der christlichen Studentenbewegung*. Bern: Buchhandlung der Evangelischen Gesellschaft, 1942.

"G. T. Manley to J. C. Pollock." J. C. Pollock, Papers on the history of CICCU. Cambridge University Library, n.d.

Guest, Mathew. *Christianity and the University Experience: Understanding Student Faith*. London: Bloomsbury, 2013.

Gutiérrez, Gustavo. *A Theology of Liberation*. Translated by Caridad Inda and John Eagleson. London: SCM, 1988.

Haight, Roger. *Comparative Ecclesiology*. Vol. 2 of *Christian Community in History*. London: Bloomsbury, 2014.

———. *Ecclesial Existence*. Vol. 3 of *Christian Community in History*. London: Bloomsbury, 2014.

Hall, Ronald Owen. "A Circular Letter from the Bishop to All Clergy to Be Discussed with Anyone Concerned with the FES." 1963. IFES e-archives. EC 1963 papers.

Hallesby, Ole. "The Distinctive Message of the Conservative Evangelical Movements: Address Given at the First International Conference of Evangelical Students, Oslo, September 1934." In *A Brief History of the International Fellowship of Evangelical Students*, by Douglas Johnson, 178–84. Lausanne: IFES, 1964.

Hammett, John S. "How Church and Parachurch Should Relate: Arguments for a Servant-Partnership Model." *Missiology* 28, no. 2 (1 Apr. 2000): 199–207.

Hammond, T. C. *Cómo comprender la doctrina cristiana: manual de teologia para laicos*. Buenos Aires: Ediciones Certeza, 1978.

———. *Evangelical Belief: A Short Introduction to Christian Doctrine in Explanation of the Doctrinal Basis of the Inter-Varsity Fellowship*. London: IVF, 1935.

———. *In Understanding Be Men: A Handbook on Christian Doctrine for Non-Theological Students*. 1st ed. London: IVF, 1936.

———. *In Understanding Be Men: A Handbook on Christian Doctrine for Non-Theological Students*. 5th ed. London: IVF, 1960.

Hanks, Tom. "Paternalistic – Me?" *IFES Journal* 21, no. 1 (1968): 1–7.

Hardy, Daniel W. "Upholding Orthodoxy in Missionary Encounters: A Theological Perspective." In *Christian Missions and the Enlightenment*, edited by Brian Stanley, 198–222. Grand Rapids: Eerdmans, 2001.

Harrison, Peter. "Narratives of Secularization." *Intellectual History Review* 27, no. 1 (2 Jan. 2017): 1–6.

Hatch, Nathan O. "Evangelicalism as a Democratic Movement." In *Evangelicalism and Modern America*, edited by George M. Marsden, 71–82. Grand Rapids: Eerdmans, 1984.

Hauerwas, Stanley. *The State of the University: Academic Knowledges and the Knowledge of God*. Illuminations – Theory and Religion. Malden: Blackwell, 2007.

Hauerwas, Stanley, and William Willimon. *Resident Aliens: Life in the Christian Colony*. Nashville: Abingdon, 1989.

Henry, Douglas V., and Michael D. Beaty. *Christianity and the Soul of the University: Faith as a Foundation for Intellectual Community*. Grand Rapids: Baker, 2006.

Hervieu-Léger, Danièle. "Le converti 'évangélique,' figure de description de la modernité religieuse." In *Le protestantisme évangélique, un christianisme de conversion: entre ruptures et filiations*, edited by Sébastien Fath, 207–13. Turnhout: Brepols, 2004.

Hiebert, Paul G. "Critical Contextualization." *International Bulletin of Missionary Research* 11, no. 3 (1987): 104–12.

———. "Critical Contextualization." *Missiology* 12, no. 3 (July 1984): 287–96.

Higton, Mike. "Education and the Virtues." In *The Universities We Need: Theological Perspectives*, edited by Stephen Heap, 77–90. Milton: Taylor and Francis, 2016.

———. *A Theology of Higher Education*. Oxford: OUP, 2012.

Hiraux, Françoise, ed. *Les engagements étudiants: des pratiques et des horizons dans un monde globalisé*. Louvain-la-Neuve: Academia-Bruylant, 2008.

Hiraux, Françoise, and Paul Servais. "Les figures de l'engagement étudiant." In *Les engagements étudiants: des pratiques et des horizons dans un monde globalisé*, edited by Françoise Hiraux, 31–58. Louvain-la-Neuve: Academia-Bruylant, 2008.

Hoekendijk, Johannes Christiaan. *The Church Inside Out*. Philadelphia: Westminster, 1966.

———. *Kirche und Volk in der deutschen Missionswissenschaft*. Translated by Erich-Walter Pollmann. Munich: Chr. Kaiser, 1967.

Hoggarth, Pauline. *The Seed and the Soil: Engaging with the Word of God*. Carlisle: Langham Global Library, 2011.

Holmes, Stephen R. "Evangelical Doctrines of Scripture in Transatlantic Perspective." *Evangelical Quarterly* 81, no. 1 (Jan. 2009): 38–63.

Hopkins, Charles Howard. *John R. Mott, 1865–1955: A Biography*. Grand Rapids: Eerdmans, 1979.

Horn, Gerd-Rainer. "Catholic Action: A Twentieth-Century Social Movement (1920s–1930s)." In *Western European Liberation Theology*, edited by Gerd-Rainer Horn, 5–43. Oxford: OUP, 2008.

Horn, Robert M. *Student Witness and Christian Truth*. London: Inter-Varsity Press, 1971.

———. *Ultimate Realities: Finding the Heart of Evangelical Belief*. Leicester: Inter-Varsity Press, 1999.

Horner, David A. *Mind Your Faith: A Student's Guide to Thinking and Living Well*. Downers Grove: InterVarsity Press, 2011.

Howard, David M. *Student Power in World Evangelism*. Downers Grove: InterVarsity Press, 1970.

Hunt, Keith, and Gladys Hunt. *For Christ and the University: The Story of InterVarsity Christian Fellowship of the USA 1940–1990*. Downers Grove: InterVarsity Press, 1991.

Huntston, George. "The Ancient Church, AD 30–313." In *The Layman in Christian History*, by Stephen Neill and Hans Ruedi Weber, 28–56. London: SCM, 1963.

Hutchinson, Mark, and John Wolffe. *A Short History of Global Evangelicalism*. New York: CUP, 2012.

Hylson-Smith, Kenneth. *The Laity in Christian History and Today.* London: SPCK, 2008.
Idowu, Emanuel Bolaji. *Towards an Indigenous Church.* Oxford: Oxford University Press, 1965.
"IFES and the Church: Notes Produced by the Task Force Group." Redcliffe College, Gloucester, England, 30 June 1996. IFES e-archives. EC 1996 minutes, Appendix F3.
IFES. "The International Fellowship of Evangelical Students: Who Are We? Why Do We Exist? How Do We Function?" Discipleship Training Center, Singapore, 17 August 1982. IFES e-archives. EC 1982 minutes, Appendix A.
———. "What We Believe." Accessed 2 February 2023. https://ifesworld.org/en/beliefs/.
"Instruction, Imitation, Initiation: A Composite Report (IFES Training Course, Mittersill, 1971)." *IFES Journal* 25, no. 3 (1971): 12–17.
International Fellowship of Evangelical Students, ed. "Living Stones: IFES Vision to 2020." 2008.
InterVarsity Christian Fellowship USA. "Our Ministry." Accessed 10 March 2016. https://intervarsity.org/our-ministry.
———. "What We Believe." 17 April 2017. https://intervarsity.org/about-us/what-we-believe.
Inter-Varsity Fellowship of Evangelical Unions, ed. *Principles of Co-operation.* London: IVF, n.d.
Jenson, Philip. *Graded Holiness: A Key to the Priestly Conception of the World.* JSOT. Sheffield: Bloomsbury, 1992.
Jochemsen, Henk. "Authentic Christian Witness Demands Authentic Christian Service; Lecture Given at the International Student Conference Held at Schloss Mittersill in August 1989." *IFES Review* 29 (1990): 35–41.
Johnson, Douglas. *A Brief History of the International Fellowship of Evangelical Students.* Lausanne: IFES, 1964.
———. "Christ Our Freedom: International Conference of Evangelical Students Cambridge; Advertisement Paper." 1939. BGC Box #193.
———. *Contending for the Faith: A History of the Evangelical Movement in the Universities and Colleges.* Leicester: Inter-Varsity Press, 1979.
———. Letter to Greer. 22 April 1943. WSCF Archive 213.13.94/7.
Johnston, James. "A Biblical Philosophy of Student Witness." *IFES Journal* 2 (1966): 7–10.
Joset, Timothée. "20 ans d'histoire des groupes bibliques universitaires de Suisse Romande: 1955–1975; L'histoire de la «Réformation» des étudiants en une période mouvementée ou comment concilier une foi séculaire dans un monde en mouvement." Master's thesis, Université de Neuchâtel, 2012.
Kagan, Jerome. *Three Cultures: Natural Sciences, Social Sciences, and the Humanities in the 21st Century.* Cambridge: Cambridge University Press, 2009.
Kärkkäinen, Veli-Matti. "The Calling of the Whole People of God into Ministry: The Spirit, Church and Laity." *Studia Theologica* 54, no. 2 (2000): 144–62.

Kinoti, George K. "Contribution towards Submission for the Templeton Prize." University of Nairobi, 1996.

Kirkpatrick, David C. "C. René Padilla and the Origins of Integral Mission in Post-War Latin America." *The Journal of Ecclesiastical History* 67, no. 2 (2016): 351–71.

———. "Died: C. René Padilla, Father of Integral Mission." Christianity Today, 27 April 2021. Accessed 22 July 2021. https://www.christianitytoday.com/news/2021/april/rene-padilla-died-integral-mission-latin-american-theology.html.

———. *A Gospel for the Poor: Global Social Christianity and the Latin American Evangelical Left*. Philadelphia: University of Pennsylvania Press, 2019.

Kraemer, Hendrik. *A Theology of the Laity*. Philadelphia: Westminster, 1958.

Kreyssig, Peter. "The Reality of the New Life in Terms of Conversion, Regeneration, and Sanctification." Summary of address given at the 1956 WSCF Ecumenical Consultation. Céligny, 1956. WSCF Archive 213.16.39/2.

Kristensen, Brede. "Report of the Assistant to the IFES General Secretary (Europe)." Raglan, New Zealand, 18 August 1978. IFES e-archives, EC 1978 minutes, Appendix F.

Kristensen, Brede, and Ada Lum. *Jesus – One of Us: 52 Evangelistic Bible Studies Compiled into 8 Series*. International Fellowship of Evangelical Students. Nottingham: Inter-Varsity Press, 1976.

Kuhn, Chase. "The Ecclesiological Influence of T. C. Hammond." *Churchman* 127, no. 4 (2013): 323–35.

Küng, Hans. *The Church*. New York: Sheed & Ward, 1967.

Laghi, Pio Card., Card. Eduardo Pironi, and Card. Paul Poupard. "The Presence of the Church in the University and in University Culture," 1994. https://www.vatican.va/roman_curia/pontifical_councils/cultr/documents/rc_pc_cultr_doc_22051994_presence_fr.html.

Lamb, Jonathan. "IFES Movements in Orthodox Countries." Confidential Memo to IFES Team Leaders only. Dimesse Sisteres Retreat Center, Nairobi, Kenya, 31 July 1993. IFES e-archives, EC 1995 minutes, Appendix A.

———. "Orthodox Progress Report." Centre des métiers de l'électricité, Bingerville, Côte d'Ivoire, 9 June 1994. IFES e-archives, EC 1994 minutes, Appendix K.

Lausanne Movement. "Cooperating in World Evangelization: A Handbook on Church/Para-Church Relationships." Lausanne Occasional Paper. 1983. http://www.lausanne.org/content/lop/lop-24.

———. "The Lausanne Covenant." 1 August 1974. http://www.lausanne.org/content/covenant/lausanne-covenant.

Legois, Jean-Philippe, Alain Monchablon and Robi Morder. *Cent ans de mouvements étudiants*. Edited by Groupe d'études et de recherches sur les mouvements étudiants (GERME). Paris: Editions Syllepse, 2007.

Lehtonen, Risto. *Story of a Storm: The Ecumenical Student Movement in the Turmoil of Revolution, 1968 to 1973*. Grand Rapids: Eerdmans, 1998.

Leithart, Peter. *The Priesthood of the Plebs: A Theology of Baptism*. Eugene: Wipf and Stock, 2003.
Lightfoot, Joseph Barber. *Saint Paul's Epistle to the Philippians; A Revised Text*. London: Macmillan, 1888.
Lineham, Peter J. "Students Reaching Students: A History of the International Fellowship of Evangelical Students." Unpublished manuscript, 1997.
Lloyd-Jones, D. Martyn. "Ecclesiola in Ecclesia." In *Approaches to Reformation for the Church*. Vol. 4. Puritan Papers. Hartshill: Tentmaker, 1965.
Lovegrove, Deryck W. *The Rise of the Laity in Evangelical Protestantism*. London: Routledge, 2002.
Lowman, Pete. *The Day of His Power: A History of the International Fellowship of Evangelical Students*. Leicester: Inter-Varsity Press, 1983.
———. "What Scripture Says, God Says." *In Touch* 3 (1982): 5.
Luther, Martin. *Selections from His Writings*. Edited by John Dillenberger. Garden City: Doubleday, 1961.
Lutz, Stephen. *College Ministry in a Post-Christian Culture*. Kansas City: House Studio, 2011.
Mackie, Robert C. "Draft Letter Enclosed in Confidential Memorandum on the Relationships of the WSCF and IVF Britain." Letter to Douglas Johnson. April 1943. WSCF Archive 213.16.94.
———. *Layman Extraordinary: John R. Mott, 1865–1955*. London: Hodder and Stoughton, 1965.
———. "The Relationships of National Student Christian Movements and the W.S.C.F. to the Inter-Varsity Fellowship of Evangelical Unions." Private document for use within the WSCF and not official pronouncement. Geneva: World Student Christian Federation, September 1946. WSCF Archive 213.16.39/2.
———. "The Relationships of National Student Christian Movements and the WSCF to the Inter-Varsity Fellowship of Evangelical Unions and the International Fellowship of Evangelical Students. Memorandum 2." Geneva: World Student Christian Federation, August 1947. WSCF Archive 213.16.39/2.
———. "Statement on the Relationship of the Federation with I.F.E.S." Official position paper. 1957 Symposium for the Use of Student Christian Movements and Their Leaders. Geneva: World Student Christian Federation, 1949. WSCF Archive 213.16.39/1.
MacLeod, A. Donald. *C. Stacey Woods and the Evangelical Rediscovery of the University*. Downers Grove: InterVarsity Press Academic, 2007.
Malik, Charles Habib. *A Christian Critique of the University*. Waterloo: North Waterloo Academic Press, 1987.
Malley, Brian. *How the Bible Works: An Anthropological Study of Evangelical Biblicism*. Walnut Creek: AltaMira, 2004.
Malone, Andrew S. *God's Mediators: A Biblical Theology of Priesthood*. NSBT 43. Downers Grove: InterVarsity Press, 2017.

Manley, G. T., G. C. Robinson and A. M. Stibbs. *New Bible Handbook*. London: InterVarsity Press, 1947.

Marsden, George M. *Fundamentalism and American Culture*. 2nd ed. New York: Oxford University Press, 2006.

Mathews, Basil. *John R. Mott, World Citizen*. New York: Harper, 1934.

Maury, Philippe. Letter to Rev. Sverre Magelssen. 14 February 1956. WSCF Archive 213.14.76/2.

———."Document IV and Additional Notes of the 1957 WSCF Symposium." Letter to South African Student Christian Association. December 1954. WSCF Archive 211.16.39/1.

———. "Memorandum on IFES. Report on a Meeting with Stacey Woods." Chicago, 21 December 1955. WSCF Archive 213.16.39.

McGrath, Alister E. *The Passionate Intellect: Christian Faith and the Discipleship of the Mind*. Downers Grove: InterVarsity Press Books, 2014.

McIntosh, Robert. "Missio Dei." In *Evangelical Dictionary of World Missions*, edited by A. Scott Moreau, 631–33. Grand Rapids: Baker, 2000.

McLeod, Hugh. "The Crisis of Christianity in the West: Entering a Post-Christian Era?" In *World Christianities c.1914–c.2000*. Vol. 9 of *The Cambridge History of Christianity*, edited by Hugh McLeod, 323–47. Cambridge: CUP, 2006.

———. "The Religious Crisis of the 1960s." *Journal of Modern European History* 3, no. 2 (2005): 205–29.

———. *The Religious Crisis of the 1960s*. Oxford: Oxford University Press, 2007.

Michaels, J. Ramsey. *1 Peter*. Word Biblical Commentary 49. Waco: Word, 2004.

"Minutes of a Meeting of the General Committee of the IFES." Library of Regent's Park College, Oxford, 28 March 1946. BGC Box #193.

"Minutes of Meetings of the Executive Committee of the IFES." Examination Hall, Cambridge, 27 June 1939. IFES e-archives.

"Minutes of the First Meeting of the General Committee of the Fully Constituted IFES." Phillips Brooks House, Harvard University, Cambridge, Massachusetts, 23 August 1947. BGC Box #193.

"Minutes of the First Meeting of the General Committee of the IFES." Phillips Brooks House, Harvard University, Cambridge, Massachusetts, 18 August 1947. BGC Box #193.

"Minutes of the Meetings of the Executive Committee of the IFES: Session I." Institut Emmaüs, Vennes-sur-Lausanne, Switzerland, 10 August 1948. BGC Box #193.

"Minutes of the Meeting of the Eighth General Committee of the IFES – 1971." Schloss Mittersill, Austria, 28 August 1971. IFES e-archives.

"Minutes of the Meeting of the Eleventh General Committee of the IFES." Ashburnham Place, Battle, England, 27 July 1983. IFES e-archives.

"Minutes of the Meeting of the Executive Committee of the IFES." De Witte Hei, Huis Ter Heide, The Netherlands, 19 April 1955. IFES e-archives.

"Minutes of the Meeting of the Executive Committee of the IFES." Branksome Hall, Toronto, Canada, 31.8–3.9 1956. IFES e-archives.

"Minutes of the Meeting of the Executive Committee of the IFES." Lunteren, The Netherlands; Wuppertal-Barmen, Germany, 27.8–1.9 1962. IFES e-archives.

"Minutes of the Meeting of the Executive Committee of the IFES." Uppigard, Norway, 30 September 1965. IFES e-archives.

"Minutes of the Meeting of the Executive Committee of the IFES." Casa Moscia, Ascona, Switzerland, 30.8–3.9 1968. IFES e-archives.

"Minutes of the Meeting of the Executive Committee of the IFES." Sanden Bjerggard, Denmark, September 1972. IFES e-archives.

"Minutes of the Meeting of the Executive Committee of the IFES." Schloss Mittersill, Austria, 30.8–3.9 1973. IFES e-archives.

"Minutes of the Meeting of the Executive Committee of the IFES." Oak Hill College, London, England, 20 September 1976. IFES e-archives.

"Minutes of the Meeting of the Executive Committee of the IFES." Charney Manor, Oxon, England, 28.9–3.10 1977. IFES e-archives.

"Minutes of the Meeting of the Executive Committee of the IFES." Raglan, New Zealand, 18 August 1978. IFES e-archives.

"Minutes of the Meeting of the Executive Committee of the IFES." London Bible College, Northwood, England, August 1988. IFES e-archives.

"Minutes of the Meeting of the Executive Committee of the IFES." Tao Fong Shan Christian Center, Hong Kong, 25 July 1989. IFES e-archives.

"Minutes of the Meeting of the Executive Committee of the IFES." Hald Training Center, Mandal, Norway, 28.7–1.8 1992. IFES e-archives.

"Minutes of the Meeting of the Executive Committee of the IFES." Oak Hill College, London, England, 25.7–31.7 1993. IFES e-archives.

"Minutes of the Meeting of the Executive Committee of the International Fellowship of Evangelical Students." Centre des métiers de l'électricité, Bingerville, Côte d'Ivoire, 29 July 1994. IFES e-archives. EC 1994 minutes.

"Minutes of the Meeting of the Executive Committee of the IFES." Urbana, Illinois, USA, 6 January 1997. IFES e-archives.

"Minutes of the Meeting of the Executive Committee of the IFES." Bischofsheim, Germany, 28.6–3.7 1998. IFES e-archives.

"Minutes of the Meeting of the Fourteenth General Committee of IFES." Kenya Commercial Bank Center, Nairobi, Kenya, 22.6–2.7 1995. IFES e-archives.

"Minutes of the Meeting of the Fifteenth General Committee of IFES." Hyundai Learning Center, Yong-In, South Korea, 23 July 1999. IFES e-archives.

"Minutes of the Meeting of the General Committee of IFES." Redeemer University College, Ancaster, Ontario, 18 July 2007. IFES e-archives.

"Minutes of the Meeting of the Incoming Executive Committee of the IFES." Kwang Lim, South Korea, 26 July 1999. IFES e-archives. New EC 1999 minutes.

"Minutes of the Meeting of the Out-Going Executive Committee of the IFES." Hyundai Learning Center, Seoul, South Korea, 14 July 1999. IFES e-archives. EC 1999 minutes.

"Minutes of the Meeting of the Retiring Executive Committee of the IFES." Phillips Brooks House, Harvard University, Cambridge, Massachusetts, 18 August 1947. BGC Box #193.

"Minutes of the Meeting of the Sixth General Committee of the IFES." Nyack, New York, 1963. IFES e-archives.

"Minutes of the Meeting of the Seventh General Committee of the IFES." Wuppertal-Barmen, Germany, 1967. IFES e-archives.

"Minutes of the Meeting of the Tenth General Committee of the IFES – 1979." Hurdal Verk, Norway, 27 July 1979. IFES e-archives.

"Minutes of the Meeting of the Twelfth General Committee of the IFES." El Hostel Duruelo, Boyaca, Colombia, 30.8–8.9 1987. IFES e-archives.

"Minutes of the Newly-Elected Executive Committee Meeting of the IFES." Ashburnham Place, Battle, England, 27 July 1983. IFES e-archives.

"Minutes of the North Atlantic Zone Committee of the IFES." Grundtvigs Höjskole, Frederiksborg, Hillerød, Denmark: EC 58 minutes, August 1958.

Moberg, David O. *The Great Reversal: Evangelism versus Social Concern*. London: Scripture Union, 1973.

"The Moratorium Debate." *International Review of Mission* 64, no. 254 (1975): 148–64.

Morder, Robi. "Années 1960: crise des jeunesses, mutations de la jeunesse." *Matériaux pour l'histoire de notre temps* 74 (2004): 62–69.

Morris, Jeremy. "Edinburgh 1910–2010: A Retrospective Assessment." *Ecclesiology*, September 2011.

Mott, John Raleigh. *Liberating the Lay Forces of Christianity*. New York: Macmillan, 1932.

———. *The World's Student Christian Federation: Origin, Achievements, Forecast; Achievements of the First Quarter-Century of the World's Student Christian Federation and Forecast of Unfinished Tasks*. [London?]: World's Student Christian Federation, 1920.

Muthiah, Robert A. *The Priesthood of All Believers in the Twenty-First Century: Living Faithfully as the Whole People of God in a Postmodern Context*. Kindle. Eugene: Wipf & Stock, 2009.

Napon, Moïse. "Holistic Ministry." Centre des métiers de l'électricité, Bingerville, Côte d'Ivoire, May 1994. IFES e-archives. EC 1994 minutes, Appendix LM.

———. "Ministry amongst Past Members of the GBU." London Bible College, Northwood, England, August 1988. IFES e-archives.

Neill, Stephen. "Introduction." In *The Layman in Christian History: A Project of the Department of the Laity of the World Council of Churches*, by Hans Ruedi Weber and Stephen Neill, 15–27. London: SCM, 1963.

Nelson, Warren. *T. C. Hammond: Irish Christian; His Life and Legacy in Ireland and Australia*. Edinburgh: Banner of Truth Trust, 1994.

Newbigin, Lesslie. "An X-Ray to Make God Visible in the World." *Reform*, 1990:7.
Newman, John Henry. *Idea of a University*. London: Longmans, Green & Co., 1852.
Niringiye, David Zac. "Beyond Pioneering." Discussion paper, May 1996. IFES Archive, Oxford.
———. *The Church: God's Pilgrim People*. Downers Grove: InterVarsity Press Academic, 2015.
———. "Parachurch Organizations and Student Movements." Presented at Christianity in Africa in the 1990s, Edinburgh University, May 1990.
———. "Towards an Understanding of Our Ethos: Some Reflections." Senior Staff Consultation, 2000. IFES Archive, Oxford.
Noll, Mark A. "Common Sense Traditions and American Evangelical Thought." *American Quarterly* 37, no. 2 (1985): 216–38.
———. *Jesus Christ and the Life of the Mind*. Grand Rapids: Eerdmans, 2011.
———. *The Scandal of the Evangelical Mind*. Grand Rapids: Eerdmans, 1994.
Okholm, Dennis L., Laura C. Miguélez and Vincent Bacote. *Evangelicals & Scripture: Tradition, Authority and Hermeneutics*. Downers Grove: InterVarsity Press, 2004.
Olofin, Samuel. "Pentecostals, Evangelicals and Charismatics." Centre des métiers de l'électricité, Bingerville, Côte d'Ivoire, May 1994. IFES e-archives. EC 1994 minutes, Appendix L2.
Osei-Mensah, Gottfried. "Integration Point: Against Dichotomy." *In Touch* 1 (1974).
Ott, Craig. "Conclusion." In *Globalizing Theology: Belief and Practice in an Era of World Christianity*, edited by Craig Ott and Harold A. Netland, 309–36. Grand Rapids: Baker, 2006.
Oxbrow, Mark. "Pentecost and the World: Roland Allen, the Spirit and Remodeling Twenty-First-Century Mission." *International Bulletin of Mission Research* 44, no. 3 (July 2020): 215–32.
Paas, Stefan. *Pilgrims and Priests: Christian Mission in a Post-Christian Society*. London: SCM, 2019.
Packer, J. I. *Keep Yourselves from Idols*. London: Church Book Room, 1963.
Padilla, C. René. "Evangelism and the World." In *Let the Earth Hear His Voice*, edited by J. D. Douglas, 116–133. Minneapolis: World Wide Publications, 1975.
———. "Introduction: An Ecclesiology for Integral Mission." In *The Local Church, Agent of Transformation: An Ecclesiology for Integral Mission*, edited by C. René Padilla and Tetsunao Yamamori, 19–49. Buenos Aires: Ediciones Kairós, 2004.
———. "My Theological Pilgrimage." In *Shaping a Global Theological Mind*, edited by Darren C. Marks, 127–37. Aldershot: Ashgate, 2008.
———. "The Roads to Freedom: Liberation Theology." *In Touch* 2 (1979): 7.
———. "Student Witness in Latin America Today." *IFES Journal* 2 (1966): 11–21.
Padilla, C. René, and Tetsunao Yamamori, eds. *La iglesia local como agente de transformación: una eclesiología para la misión integral*. Buenos Aires: Ediciones Kairós, 2003.

Payne, J. D. "Roland Allen, Missiology and The Ministry of Expansion." In *The Ministry of Expansion: The Priesthood of the Laity*, by Roland Allen, edited by J. D. Payne, 133–375. Kindle loc. Pasadena: William Carey Library, 2017.

Pelikan, Jaroslav Jan. *The Christian Tradition: A History of the Development of Doctrine*. 4 vols. Chicago: University of Chicago Press, 1987–94.

Pellowe, John. *The Church at Work: A Manual for Excellent Church-Agency Relations*. Elmira: Canadian Council of Christian Charities, 2012.

———. "Leading Ministries into Christian Community: A Practical Theology for Church-Agency Relations." Doctoral dissertation, Gordon-Conwell Seminary, 2008.

Perdomo, Lic Edgar Alan. "Una descripción histórica de la teología evangélica latinoamericana (Segunda de dos partes)." *Kairos* 3 (2003): 83–116.

Plantinga, Alvin C. "On Christian Scholarship." In *Christian Scholarship in the Twenty-First Century: Prospects and Perils*, edited by Thomas M. Crisp, Steven L. Porter and Gregg Ten Elshof, 18–33. Grand Rapids: Eerdmans, 2014.

Plantinga, Cornelius. *Engaging God's World: A Christian Vision of Faith, Learning, and Living*. Grand Rapids: Eerdmans, 2002.

Pollack, Detlef, and Gert Pickel. "Religious Individualization or Secularization." In *The Role of Religion in Modern Societies*, edited by Detlef Pollack and Daniel V. A. Olson, 191–220. New York: Routledge, 2008.

Pollock, John. *A Cambridge Movement*. London: John Murray, 1953.

Pope John Paul II. "*Christifideles Laici*." Post-Synodal Exhortation on the Vocation and the Mission of the Lay Faithful in the Church and in the World. Rome, 1988.

Pope Paul VI. "*Ad Gentes*." Decree on the Mission Activity of the Church. Rome, Vatican II, 1965.

———. "*Apostolicam Actuositatem*." Decree on the Apostolate of the Laity. Vatican II decree. Rome, 1965.

Potter, Philip, and Thomas Wieser. *Seeking and Serving the Truth: The First Hundred Years of the World Student Christian Federation*. Geneva: World Council of Churches, 1996.

Preston, Ronald. "The Collapse of the SCM." *Theology* 89, no. 732 (1986): 431–40.

"Procès-verbal de l'assemblée annuelle du Conseil des GBEU de Suisse romande; Discussion du soir." Vennes-sur-Lausanne, 24 February 1962. Conseil&Co. 1957–62, GBEU Switzerland Archives.

"Proposals Presented to the General Committee." Kenya Commercial Bank Center, Nairobi, Kenya, 22.6–2.7 1995. IFES e-archives.

Prudente, Adrienne. "Histoire des Groupes Bibliques Universitaires (GBU) en Suisse romande (de 1937 à 1953). Ou des stratégies pour une évangélisation efficace des étudiants." Master's thesis, Université de Lausanne, 2004.

Quebedeaux, Richard. *The Worldly Evangelicals*. San Francisco: Harper & Row, 1980.

Ramachandra, Vinoth. "Christian Witness in the University: Integrity, Incarnation, and Dialogue in Today's Universities." *Word and World* 4 (5 Dec. 2017). https://

ifesworld.org/wp-content/uploads/2020/08/WW4-Ramachandra-Christian-Witness.pdf.

———. "Some Reflections on 'Indigeneity' and 'Autonomy' in IFES." Hyundai Learning Center, Seoul, South Korea, June 1999. IFES e-archives. Old EC 1999 minutes, Appendix.

Regent College, Admissions & Finance. "Tuition Discounts." Accessed 14 July 2020. https://www.regent-college.edu/admissions-finance/costs/tuition-discounts.

Reimer, S. "Higher Education and Theological Liberalism: Revisiting the Old Issue." *Sociology of Religion* 71, no. 4 (3 June 2010): 393–408.

"Report of the Commission on Evangelism." Working groups of the 1956 WSCF Ecumenical Consultation. Céligny, 1956. WSCF Archive 213.16.39/2.

"Report of the Commission on the Student Christian Community in the University." Working groups of the 1956 WSCF Ecumenical Consultation. Céligny, 1956. WSCF Archive 213.16.39/2.

"Report of the Commission on Truth and Doctrine." Working groups of the 1956 WSCF Ecumenical Consultation. Céligny, 1956. WSCF Archive 213.16.39/2.

"Report on the Working Party Held on Suggestions for Our Behavior toward Communism." Nyack, New York: IFES General Committee 1963. IFES e-archives. GC 1963 minutes, Appendix H.

Richardson, Cyril Charles, ed. *Early Christian Fathers*. Philadelphia: Westminster, 1953.

Robert, Dana L. *Christian Mission: How Christianity Became a World Religion*. Hoboken: Wiley & Sons, 2009.

———. "The Origin of the Student Volunteer Watchword: 'The Evangelization of the World in This Generation.'" *International Bulletin of Missionary Research* 10, no. 4 (Oct. 1986): 146–49.

———. "Shifting Southward: Global Christianity since 1945." *International Bulletin of Missionary Research* 24, no. 2 (2000): 50–54.

Roberts, Vaughan. "Reframing the UCCF Doctrinal Basis." *Theology* 95, no. 768 (1 Nov. 1992): 432–46.

Robinson, John A. T. *Honest to God*. London: SCM, 1963.

———. *Layman's Church*. London: Lutterworth, 1963.

Root, Michael. "Freedom, Authority, and the Priesthood of All Believers." In *Critical Issues in Ecclesiology: Essays in Honor of Carl E. Braaten*, edited by Alberto L. García and Susan K. Wood, 88–104. Grand Rapids: Eerdmans, 2011.

Rouse, Ruth. *The World's Student Christian Federation: A History of the First Thirty Years*. London: SCM, 1948.

Rutt, Steven. "Background and Overview of The Ministry of Expansion." In *The Ministry of Expansion: The Priesthood of the Laity*, by Roland Allen, edited by J. D. Payne. Kindle. Pasadena: William Carey Library, 2017.

———. *Roland Allen: A Missionary Life*. Cambridge: Lutterworth, 2018.

———. *Roland Allen II: A Theology of Mission*. Cambridge: Lutterworth, 2018.

———. "Roland Allen's Apostolic Principles: An Analysis of His 'The Ministry of Expansion.'" *Transformation* 29, no. 3 (2012): 225–43.

Salinas, Daniel. *Latin American Evangelical Theology in the 1970's: The Golden Decade*. Religion in the Americas Series. Leiden: Brill, 2009.

Sanneh, Lamin O. *Translating the Message: The Missionary Impact on Culture*. Maryknoll: Orbis, 1989.

———. *Whose Religion Is Christianity? The Gospel beyond the West*. Grand Rapids: Eerdmans, 2003.

Scheitle, Christopher P. *Beyond the Congregation: The World of Christian Nonprofits*. New York: Oxford University Press, 2010.

Schreiter, Robert J. "From the Lausanne Covenant to the Cape Town Commitment: A Theological Assessment." *International Bulletin of Missionary Research* 35, no. 2 (2011): 88–90, 92.

Scruggs, Lane. "Evangelicalism and Ecumenism: The World Evangelical Alliance and Church Unity." *Fides et Historia* 49, no. 1 (2017): 85–103.

"Second Draft of Global IFES Plan July 1999 – July 2003." Bischofsheim, Germany, 28.6–3.7 1998. IFES e-archives. EC 1998 minutes, Appendix I.

Selles, Johanna M. *The World Student Christian Federation, 1895–1925: Motives, Methods, and Influential Women*. Eugene: Pickwick, 2011.

Sharma, Sonya. "Navigating Religion between University and Home: Christian Students' Experiences in English Universities." *Social & Cultural Geography* 14, no. 1 (2013): 59–79.

Shaw, R. Daniel. "Beyond Contextualization: Toward a Twenty-First-Century Model for Enabling Mission." *International Bulletin of Missionary Research* 34, no. 4 (Oct. 2010): 208–15.

Shedd, Clarence. *Two Centuries of Student Christian Movements: Their Origin and Inter-Collegiate Life*. New York: Association Press, 1934.

Shinn, Ruth E. "The International Fellowship of Evangelical Students (Inter-Varsity): Its Role in the Ecumenical Life of Christian Student Movements." Bachelor's thesis, Yale Divinity School, 1955. WSCF Archive 213.16.39/2.

Skaaheim, Anfin. "IFES and a Global Strategy for Mission Work among Students." Discussion paper. Yahara Center, Madison, USA, 21 April 1985. IFES e-archives. EC 1985 minutes, Appendix.

Skreslet, Stanley. "Thinking Missiologically about the History of Mission." *International Bulletin of Missionary Research* 31, no. 2 (1 Apr. 2007): 59–65.

SMD. *Rechenschaft geben von unserer Hoffnung: Festschrift zum 50jährigen Bestehen der Studentenmission in Deutschland*. Marburg: SMD, 1999.

Smith, Christian, and Patricia Snell. *Souls in Transition: The Religious and Spiritual Lives of Emerging Adults*. Oxford: OUP Premium, 2009.

Smith, James K. A. "Loving the University: Engaging the Big Questions on Your Campus." *Emerging Scholars Blog*, 20 February 2023. https://blog.emergingscholars.org/2023/02/loving-the-university-engaging-the-big-questions-on-your-campus/.

Sng, Bobby. "Unity and Diversity in IFES." Senior Staff Consultation, May 1998. IFES Archive, Oxford. SSC 98 papers.

Snyder, Howard A. "The Church as God's Agent in Evangelism: Conference Presentation." In *Let the Earth Hear His Voice: Official Reference Volume, Papers and Responses*, edited by International Congress on World Evangelization and J. D. Douglas, 352–60. Minneapolis: World Wide Publications, 1975.

———. "The Church as God's Agent in Evangelism: Working Paper." In *Let the Earth Hear His Voice: Official Reference Volume, Papers and Responses*, edited by International Congress on World Evangelization and J. D. Douglas, 327–51. Minneapolis: World Wide Publications, 1975.

———. *Liberating the Church: The Ecology of Church and Kingdom*. Downers Grove: InterVarsity Press, 1983.

Sommerville, C. John. *Religious Ideas for Secular Universities*. Grand Rapids: Eerdmans, 2009.

Spener, Philipp Jacob. *Pia desideria oder herzliches Verlangen nach gottgefälliger Besserung der wahren evangelischen Kirche, nebst einigen dahin abzweckenden christlichen Vorschlägen*. Original in 1675. Leipzig: Köhler, 1841.

Spies, Gernot, and Achim Schowalter. "Der Hochschul-SMD-Leitfaden zur Feier des Abendmahls in SMD-Gruppen." n.d. Internal training document.

Stacey, Vivienne, ed. *Mission Ventured: Dynamic Stories across a Challenging World*. Leicester: Inter-Varsity Press, 2001.

Stackhouse, John G. *Canadian Evangelicalism in the Twentieth Century: An Introduction to Its Character*. Toronto: University of Toronto Press, 1993.

———. "Engaging the University: The Vocation of Campus Ministry." *John G. Stackhouse, Jr.* (blog), 2007. https://www.johnstackhouse.com/post/engaging-the-university.

———. *Evangelical Landscapes: Facing Critical Issues of the Day*. Grand Rapids: Baker Academic, 2002.

Stallings, Robert A. "Patterns of Belief in Social Movements: Clarifications from an Analysis of Environmental Groups." *The Sociological Quarterly* 14, no. 4 (1973): 465–80.

Stamoolis, James. "An Evangelical Position on Ecclesiology and Mission." *International Review of Mission* 90, no. 358 (1 July 2001): 309–16.

Stanley, Brian. *Christianity in the Twentieth Century: A World History*. Princeton: Princeton University Press, 2018.

———. "Conversion to Christianity: The Colonization of the Mind?" *International Review of Mission* 92, no. 366 (1 July 2003): 315–31.

———. *The Global Diffusion of Evangelicalism: The Age of Billy Graham and John Stott*. Vol. 5 of *A History of Evangelicalism*. 5 vols. Downers Grove: InterVarsity Press, 2013.

———. "'Lausanne 1974': The Challenge from the Majority World to Northern-Hemisphere Evangelicalism." *Journal of Ecclesiastical History* 64, no. 3 (2013): 533–51.

Stanley, Brian, and Alaine Low, eds. *Missions, Nationalism, and the End of Empire*. Grand Rapids: Eerdmans, 2003.

Stark, Rodney. *The Rise of Christianity: A Sociologist Reconsiders History*. Princeton: Princeton University Press, 1996.

Steensland, Brian, and Philip Goff, eds. *The New Evangelical Social Engagement*. Oxford: OUP, 2013.

Stott, John. *Christ the Controversialist*. Downers Grove: InterVarsity Press, 1970.

———. "Evangelical Essentials: Plenary Address to IFES WA 1999." Hyundai Learning Center, Yong-In, South Korea, 23 July 1999. IFES e-archives. GC 1999 Papers.

———. *Evangelical Truth: A Personal Plea for Unity, Integrity and Faithfulness*. Downers Grove: InterVarsity Press, 2003.

———. *One People*. Downers Grove: InterVarsity Press, 1971.

———. "The Significance of Lausanne." *International Review of Mission* 64, no. 255 (July 1975): 288–94.

———. *Your Mind Matters: The Place of the Mind in the Christian Life*. Downers Grove: InterVarsity Press, 1973.

Stringfellow, William. *An Ethic for Christians and Other Aliens in a Strange Land*. Waco: Word, 1973.

Students' Christian Organisation (SCO) South Africa. "Statement of Faith." Accessed 21 May 2020. https://web.archive.org/web/20210621163925/https://www.sco.org.za/statement-of-faith/.

Sundkler, Bengt, and Christopher Steed. *A History of the Church in Africa*. Cambridge: CUP, 2001.

Swann, John T. "Priests." In *The Lexham Bible Dictionary*, edited by John D. Barry. Bellingham: Lexham, 2016.

"T2. Oral History Interview with René Padilla." Transcript of audio tape. Vol. 2. 4 vols. "Collection 361 Oral History Interviews with C. René Padilla." Wheaton College, 1987. https://archives.wheaton.edu/repositories/4/archival_objects/238467.

Tatlow, Tissington. *The Story of the Student Christian Movement of Great Britain and Ireland*. London: SCM, 1933.

Taylor, Charles. *A Secular Age*. Cambridge: Harvard University Press, 2007.

Tertullian, *On Exhortation to Chastity*. The Ante Nicene Fathers. Edited by Alexander Roberts and James Donaldson. 1885–1887. 10 vols.

Thacker, Justin, and Susannah Clark. "A Historical and Theological Exploration of the 1910 Disaffiliation of the Cambridge Inter-Collegiate Christian Union from the Student Christian Movement. Unpublished Conference Paper." Evangelicalism and Fundamentalism in Britain, Oxford, 2008.

Tomlin, Graham. *The Widening Circle: Priesthood as God's Way of Blessing the World*. London: SPCK, 2014.

Torrey, Reuben Archer. *What the Bible Teaches: A Thorough and Comprehensive Study of What the Bible Has to Say Concerning the Great Doctrines of Which It Treats.* New York: Fleming H. Revell, 1898.

Treloar, Geoffrey. *The Disruption of Evangelicalism: The Age of Torrey, Mott, McPherson and Hammond.* 5 vols. London: Inter-Varsity Press, 2016.

———. "Hammond, Thomas Chatterton." In *Biographical Dictionary of Evangelicals*, edited by Timothy Larsen, 286–87. Leicester: Inter-Varsity Press, 2003.

———. "T. C. Hammond the Controversialist." *Anglican Historical Society Diocese of Sydney Journal* 51, no. 1 (2006): 20–35.

Trueman, Carl R. *The Real Scandal of the Evangelical Mind.* Chicago: Moody, 2011.

Turner, John G. *Bill Bright and Campus Crusade for Christ: The Renewal of Evangelicalism in Postwar America.* Chapel Hill: University of North Carolina Press, 2008.

UCCF. "Doctrinal Basis." Accessed 9 May 2020. https://www.uccf.org.uk/about/doctrinal-basis.htm.

Van Aarde, Timothy A. "The Missional Church Structure and the Priesthood of All Believers (Ephesians 4:7–16) in the Light of the Inward and Outward Function of the Church." *Verbum et Ecclesia* 38, no. 1 (31 Jan. 2017).

Van den Toren, Benno. "Can We See the Naked Theological Truth?" In *Local Theology for the Global Church: Principles for an Evangelical Approach to Contextualization*, edited by Matthew Cook, Rob Haskell, Ruth Julian and Natee Tanchanpongs, 91–108. Pasadena: William Carey Library, 2010.

Vaux, Roland de. *Ancient Israel: Its Life and Institutions.* London: Darton, 1961.

VBG. "Geistliche Leitlinien: Leitlinien der VBG." 25 March 2017. https://wp.vbg.net/spirituelle-traditionen/.

Village, Andrew. *The Bible and Lay People: An Empirical Approach to Ordinary Hermeneutics.* Explorations in Practical, Pastoral, and Empirical Theology. Aldershot: Ashgate, 2007.

Voelkel, Jack. *Student Evangelism in a World of Revolution.* Contemporary Evangelical Perspectives. Grand Rapids: Zondervan, 1974.

Volf, Miroslav. *After Our Likeness: The Church as the Image of the Trinity.* Grand Rapids: Eerdmans, 1998.

———. "Soft Difference: Theological Reflections on the Relation between Church and Culture in 1 Peter." *Ex Auditu* 10 (1994). http://www.pas.rochester.edu/~tim/study/Miroslav%20Volf%201%20Peter.pdf.

Volz, Verna Claire. "The InterVarsity Christian Fellowship and the Lacks in the Student Christian Movement Program Which Its Rise Reveals." Master's essay commissioned by the Program Commission of the National Intercollegiate Christian Council (YMCA), Union Theological Seminary, 1945. WSCF Archive 213.14.66/1.

Voss, Henry J. "The Priesthood of All Believers and the *Missio Dei*: A Canonical, Catholic, and Contextual Perspective." PhD thesis, Wheaton, 2013.

Walls, Andrew F. "Christianity in the Non-Western World." In *The Cross-Cultural Process in Christian History: Studies in the Transmission and Appropriation of Faith*, 27–48. Maryknoll: Orbis, 2002.

———. *The Cross-Cultural Process in Christian History: Studies in the Transmission and Appropriation of Faith*. Maryknoll: Orbis, 2002.

———. "Globalization and the Study of Christian History." In *Globalizing Theology: Belief and Practice in an Era of World Christianity*, edited by Craig Ott and Harold A. Netland, 70–82. Grand Rapids: Baker, 2006.

———. "The Gospel as Prisoner and Liberator of Culture." In *The Missionary Movement in Christian History: Studies in the Transmission of Faith*, 3–15. Maryknoll: Orbis, 1996.

———. "The Missionary Movement a Lay Fiefdom?" In *The Rise of the Laity in Evangelical Protestantism*, edited by Deryck W. Lovegrove, 167–86. London: Routledge Chapman & Hall, 2002.

———. *The Missionary Movement in Christian History: Studies in the Transmission of Faith*. Maryknoll: Orbis, 1996.

Walsh, Michael. "The Religious Ferment of the Sixties." In *World Christianities c.1914–c.2000*. Vol. 9 of *The Cambridge History of Christianity*, edited by Hugh McLeod, 304–22. Cambridge: Cambridge University Press, 2006.

Walton, John H. *Ancient Near Eastern Thought and the Old Testament: Introducing the Conceptual World of the Hebrew Bible*. Grand Rapids: Baker, 2006.

———. *The Lost World of Genesis One*. Downers Grove: InterVarsity Press, 2009.

Ward, Pete. *Participation and Mediation: A Practical Theology for the Liquid Church*. London: SCM, 2008.

Warner, Rob. "Evangelical Bases of Faith and Fundamentalizing Tendencies." In *Evangelicalism and Fundamentalism in the United Kingdom During the Twentieth Century*, edited by David Bebbington and David Ceri Jones, 328–47. Oxford: OUP, 2013.

Watkin, Christopher. *Biblical Critical Theory: How the Bible's Unfolding Story Makes Sense of Modern Life and Culture*. Grand Rapids: Zondervan Academic, 2022.

Webster, Warren W. "The Messenger and Mission Societies." In *Perspectives on the World Christian Movement: A Reader*, edited by Ralph D. Winter, 763–69. Pasadena: William Carey Library, 1981.

Wellings, Martin. *Evangelicals Embattled: Responses of Evangelicals in the Church of England to Ritualism, Darwinism and Theological Liberalism 1890–1930*. Carlisle: Paternoster, 2003.

Wells, Robin. "A Work amongst Graduates for a Student Movement?" London Bible College, Northwood, Middlesex, England, August 1988. IFES e-archives.

White, Jerry E. *The Church and the Parachurch: An Uneasy Marriage*. Portland: Multnomah, 1983.

Willaime, Jean-Paul. "La formule d'adhésion, la déclaration de foi et le problème ecclésiologique du protestantisme: un point de vue sociologique." In *Vers l'unité pour quel témoignage? La restauration de l'unité Réformée (1933–1938)*, edited by Jean Baubérot, 288–304. Paris: Les Bergers et les Mages, 1982.

———. *La précarité protestante: sociologie du protestantisme contemporain.* Histoire et Société 25. Geneva: Labor et Fides, 1992.

Williams, Alex. *Holy Spy.* Budapest: Harmat, 2003.

Williams, Clifford. *The Life of the Mind: A Christian Perspective.* Grand Rapids: Baker Academic, 2002.

Willmer, Wesley Kenneth, J. David Schmidt and Martyn Smith. *The Prospering Parachurch: Enlarging the Boundaries of God's Kingdom.* San Francisco: Jossey-Bass, 1998.

Winter, Ralph D. "The Two Structures of God's Redemptive Mission." *Missiology: An International Review* 2, no. 1 (1 Jan. 1974): 121–39.

Wisløff, Carl F. "The Doctrinal Position of the IFES." *IFES Journal* 3 (1963): 1–6.

———. *I Know in Whom I Believe: Studies in Bible Doctrine.* Norwegian original 1946. Minneapolis: AFLC Seminary Press, 1983.

Woods, C. Stacey. "Biblical Principles for Unity and Separation." *IFES Journal* 20, no. 3 (1967): 2–5.

———. "Evangelical Unions and the Church." *IFES Journal* 10, no. 3 (1957): 3–5.

———. "God's Initiative and Ours." *IFES Journal* 1 (1966): 2–4.

———. *The Growth of a Work of God: The Story of the Early Days of the Inter-Varsity Christian Fellowship of the United States of America as Told by Its First General Secretary.* Downers Grove: InterVarsity Press, 1978.

———. "The IFES Doctrinal Basis." *IFES Journal* 25, no. 3 (1971): 10–11.

———. "IFES History Draft." Unpublished manuscript. Lausanne, 1977.

———. "The Inner-Directed Christian." *IFES Journal* 1 (1966): 17–19.

———. "The Medium Is the Message." *IFES Journal* 21, no. 1 (1968): 8–10.

———. "Memorandum on Charismatic Gifts." September 1970. IFES e-archives.

———. "Perspectives and Priorities in the 1970's." *IFES Journal* 23, no. 2 (1970): 1–4.

———. "Report of the General Secretary." Schloss Mittersill, Austria, 1971. IFES e-archives. GC 1971 minutes, Appendix A.

———. "Report of the General Secretary to the Seventh General Committee of the IFES." Wuppertal-Barmen, Germany, 1967. IFES e-archives. EC 1967 minutes, Appendix B.

———. *Some Ways of God.* Downers Grove: InterVarsity Press, 1975.

———. "Student Work: Strategy and Tactics." *IFES Journal* 1 (1966): 13–16.

———. "Take Heed unto Doctrine." *IFES Journal* 1 (1955): 14–16.

World Council of Churches. "Baptism, Eucharist and Ministry." Faith and Order Paper no. 111. Geneva, 1982. https://www.oikoumene.org/resources/documents/baptism-eucharist-and-ministry-faith-and-order-paper-no-111-the-lima-text.

World Council of Churches. Commission on World Mission and Evangelism. "Mission in the Context of Empire: Putting Justice at the Heart of Faith." *International Review of Mission* 101, no. 1 (Apr. 2012): 195–211.

World's Student Christian Federation. "The Relationships of the World's Student Federation and Student Christian Movements with the International Fellowship of Evangelical Students and Inter-Varsity Fellowships." Symposium for the use of Student Christian Movements and Their Leaders. Geneva: World Student Christian Federation, 1957. WSCF Archive 211.16.39/1.

Wright, Christopher J. H. *Knowing Jesus through the Old Testament*. Downers Grove: InterVarsity Press, 2014.

———. *The Mission of God: Unlocking the Bible's Grand Narrative*. Downers Grove: InterVarsity Press Academic, 2006.

Yamamori, Tetsunao. *God's New Envoys: A Bold Strategy for Penetrating Closed Countries*. Portland: Multnomah Pub, 1987.

Yri, N. "Wisløff Carl Fredrik." In *New Dictionary of Theology*, edited by Sinclair B. Ferguson, David F. Wright and J. I. Packer, 726. Downers Grove: InterVarsity Press, 1988.

Zald, Mayer N. "Theological Crucibles: Social Movements in and of Religion." *Review of Religious Research* 23, no. 4 (1982): 317–36.

Langham Literature and its imprints are a ministry of Langham Partnership.

Langham Partnership is a global fellowship working in pursuit of the vision God entrusted to its founder John Stott –

> *to facilitate the growth of the church in maturity and Christ-likeness through raising the standards of biblical preaching and teaching.*

Our vision is to see churches in the Majority World equipped for mission and growing to maturity in Christ through the ministry of pastors and leaders who believe, teach and live by the word of God.

Our mission is to strengthen the ministry of the word of God through:
- nurturing national movements for biblical preaching
- fostering the creation and distribution of evangelical literature
- enhancing evangelical theological education

especially in countries where churches are under-resourced.

Our ministry

Langham Preaching partners with national leaders to nurture indigenous biblical preaching movements for pastors and lay preachers all around the world. With the support of a team of trainers from many countries, a multi-level programme of seminars provides practical training, and is followed by a programme for training local facilitators. Local preachers' groups and national and regional networks ensure continuity and ongoing development, seeking to build vigorous movements committed to Bible exposition.

Langham Literature provides Majority World preachers, scholars and seminary libraries with evangelical books and electronic resources through publishing and distribution, grants and discounts. The programme also fosters the creation of indigenous evangelical books in many languages, through writer's grants, strengthening local evangelical publishing houses, and investment in major regional literature projects, such as one volume Bible commentaries like *The Africa Bible Commentary* and *The South Asia Bible Commentary*.

Langham Scholars provides financial support for evangelical doctoral students from the Majority World so that, when they return home, they may train pastors and other Christian leaders with sound, biblical and theological teaching. This programme equips those who equip others. Langham Scholars also works in partnership with Majority World seminaries in strengthening evangelical theological education. A growing number of Langham Scholars study in high quality doctoral programmes in the Majority World itself. As well as teaching the next generation of pastors, graduated Langham Scholars exercise significant influence through their writing and leadership.

To learn more about Langham Partnership and the work we do visit **langham.org**

www.ingramcontent.com/pod-product-compliance
Lightning Source LLC
Chambersburg PA
CBHW070231240426
43673CB00044B/1757